The Complete Lectures of Sir Syed

Volume III

COMPILED BY ATA KHURSHEED, PhD

TRANSLATED FROM URDU
BY ARIF ANSARI

ISBN
Paperback 979-8-89363-893-6
Hardcase 979-8-89446-626-2

Contents

Volume III
(★ Newly Discovered Lectures)

131. Sir Syed's Speech in Meerut ★ 693

132. Related to Charitable Endowments of Muslims 707

133. Mohammedan Educational Committee 711

134. Sir Syed's Views on Women's Education 713

135. Speech in Reply to an Arabic *Qasida* 717

136. Thanks to Ahmed Ali Shauq ★ 719

137. Thanks to Mian Nizamuddin, *Raïs* Baghbanpura ★ 720

138. Address Presented by the Muslim Students of Lahore 722

139. Sir Syed's Act at the Penny Reading Theater 730

140. A Speech Regarding the History of the *Madrasatul Uloom Musalmanan* . . . 733

141. Gratitude for the Gift from *Huzoor* Nizam 772

142. Speech Regarding Writing Articles for Awards 775

143. Speech Regarding a Blasphemous Book 778

144. Annual Report of the Fourth Session of the Muhammadan Educational Congress ★ 781

145. How to Facilitate Ease in Holding the Sessions of the Muhammadan Educational Conference ★ 791

146. Speech on Changing the Name of the Educational Association 796

147. Opinion Regarding Exclusion of Persian From the Curriculum 798

148. Speech Regarding Industrial Education 807

149. Preservation of Antique Books and Old Coins 817

150. Speech on the Excellent Achievements of *"Anjuman al-Farz"* 819

151. Reply Address 821

152. Annual Report of the Muhammadan Educational Conference at the
Fifth Session 1890 ★ 823

153. Expression of Condolence 839

154. First Meeting: Election of the President of the Session ★ 841

155. Speech Related to Women....................................... 843

156. Regarding Amendment of Rules ★................................ 845

157. Sir Syed's Apology ★ 847

158. Introduction of Dr. Muhammad Akbar ★ 848

159. Speech Related to Maulana Hali 849

160. On the Lecture Given by Hafiz Maulvi Nazir Ahmed *Saheb* ★......... 851

161. The Harmful Effects of Bad Customs ★........................... 852

162. The Practice of Arabic Education ★.............................. 853

163. *Shams-ul-'Ulama* Maulvi Syed Ali Bilgrami ★ 854

164. Speech on Sending Muslim Students to England for Education 855

165. Motion to Increase Grant-in-Aid ★ 859

166. Annual Report of the Muhammadan Educational Conference: Sixth
Session, 1891 ★ 864

167. Arts and Academic Interests ★ 871

168. Religious Education of Muslims 872

169. Thoughts on Students Going to Europe and Getting Married 874

170. Motion for the Development of Greek Medicine 876

171. In Support of Mr. Beck's Proposal Regarding Progress of the
Education of Muslims 879

172. Syllabus Textbooks of the *Anjuman Himayat-e-Islam* ★ 882

173. The Objective of the Muhammadan Educational Conference ★ 883

174. Address to Muslims as a Plea from Syed Ahmed Khan 885

175. Report of the Seventh Session of the Muhammadan Educational
Conference ★ 893

176. Religious Education of Muslim Students 902

177. Deciding the Fate of Muslims 903

178. Speech on the Occasion of Syed Ross Masood's *Bismillah* Ceremony 925

179. Deputation of the *Madrasatul Uloom* Aligarh in Jalandhar and
Presentation of an Address 931

180. Lecture Given by Sir Syed on December 7, 1894 to the Students of the
Madrasatul Uloom 937

181. Annual Report of the Eighth Session of the Muhammadan
Educational Conference, 1893 ★ 945

182. Lecture on Avoiding the Ill-Effects of English Education 955

183. Sir Syed's Speech on the Occasion of Foundation Dinner ★ 967

184. New Scholarships for College Class Students from Syed Families ★ 969

185. Regarding the Need to Construct a Bungalow ★ 971

186. Annual Report of the Ninth Session of the Muhammadan
Educational Conference, 1894 ★ 972

187. The Need for Educating and Nurturing Muslim Children 979

188. Aligarh College: The Centre for English Education of the Muslims ★ . . . 989

189. Management of English Schools for Muslims ★ 990

190. Publication of an Urdu Newspaper from Punjab 991

191. A Meeting of the Students at the Conference ★ 992

192. Annual Report of the Tenth Session of the Muhammadan
Educational Conference, 1895 ★ 993

193. Establishment of Local Committees ★ 1002

194. Welfare of the Community Depends on Education 1003

195. A Memorial to Her Gracious Majesty Queen Victoria Monarch of India . . 1015

196. Speech ★ 1017

197. Address on the Occasion of Reception ★ 1027

198. Speech by Sir Syed Ahmed Khan Bahadur ★ 1030

199. Sir Syed's Shortest and Most Poignant Speech 1037

200. A Meeting to Congratulate Her Majesty Empress of India on Her
     Diamond Jubilee, June 22, 1897 ★ 1038

201. The Policy for Appointing Trustees of the Muhammadan
     Anglo-Oriental College ★ 1040

202. Increase in the Monthly Salary of Prof. Arnold ★ 1043

131

Sir Syed's Speech in Meerut ★

Related to Education of Muslims in Reply to an Address
(Aligarh Institute Gazette, May 22, 1888)

O my Muslim brothers!

First of all, I have to thank you for the kindness and courtesy you have shown yesterday and today to an insignificant person such as me. I am but an insignificant man and the worth you have given me is much more than it truly is. Although I have not been able to thank the Muslims of Meerut for the kindness shown to me yesterday and today, I do want to state that this is not the first time that my friends in Meerut have done so. Meerut is a city that I have been familiar with since a young age, whose elders have shown brotherly love toward my elders, and which has always been my benefactor. I can never forget the support and favor of the elders of Meerut at the time when, during the days of the Mutiny and after victory over Delhi, I went to Delhi and saw that our home had been looted, the homes of our family deserted and desolate, and we were surrounded by all kinds of trouble. I brought them all to Meerut. It was Meerut that sheltered us and our kinsfolk. The elders of noble descent of this city were very kind to us at that time and have shown me all kinds of favors since. And so, the kindness that you gentlemen have shown me yesterday and today is nothing new. I have another special connection to Meerut, which is that my beloved mother is buried here, the memory of which has never left my heart. Well, that was a personal connection that has passed, but the kindness shown by the elders on such occasions is forever remembered.

Now, the matter at hand is that you gentlemen have kindly presented an address and stated that I have done something for our community. O friends, we should see what has become of our community. All the Muslim families of India are being ruined and devastated day by day. Go to Delhi, which was once a famous place, and see how nothing is left there except some crumbling walls and a few decaying skeletons. In fact, this couplet, which refers to a difficult and heartbreaking event, is now exactly appropriate for Muslims.

> Misfortunes have befallen me
> Just as day falls into night

Anyone who has seen the condition of Muslims in recent times would confirm this couplet as a testimony to their present state and would wonder how they live their lives and are even alive. In such a state, it was essential that some person worry about it and make all possible efforts to improve the condition of his brothers, who were once accorded much respect and were well known throughout the world for their wealth, fortunes, and rulership.

O gentlemen! To worry about the condition of the Muslims and make efforts to improve it is related to two things. The first is their state in the hereafter and the second is their worldly condition. There is no concern about the state in the hereafter for those who proclaim '*La ilaha illa Allah Muhammedur Rasul Allah*,' there is no god but God, and Muhammad is the messenger of God. As our beloved Prophet, the Messenger of God, may God bless him and grant him peace, said, as long as this faith is in our heart, "even if Abu Dharr's nose was put in the dust," these words will be the basis of our salvation. It is the belief in these worlds that will make us win over the hereafter and give us everything that the hereafter holds. If we need to be concerned about anything, it is whether our faith in these words will always remain in our hearts. But whatever trouble is upon us and worries us is in this wretched world. Although we have to live on this earth for only a few days, we have to keep things right and that is what everyone is concerned about, that is what is needed, and that is what we are involved in night and day. O gentlemen! The world is a strange two-faced statue. One of its faces is very scary and the other very attractive. You look at the other side of it, do you think that Islam is a statue whose face is visible to everyone? No, it is not such a statue, rather its face is seen in those people who are Muslims, those who call themselves Muslims, and who have been raised in a relationship with Islam. I believe that if the worldly condition of Muslims deteriorates and they are mostly humiliated among all the nations, then Islam will also be humiliated along with them. So, you must look at the other face of this world, whose beauty reflects the beauty of Islam. Embrace this world, not for the sake of the world but for the sake of your faith, even though thanks be to God there are very few Muslims who have converted from Islam. But the real reason for those Muslims who converted to Christianity was poverty and need. Therefore, is improving the worldly condition of Muslims not correcting the condition of Islam? If you look at the jails of India, you will find that the proportion of Muslim in them is much larger than their proportion in the population. The reason for that is the same poverty and need that forces human beings to commit heinous crimes. Therefore, is it not better for religion and the world to improve their worldly condition? If the world is wronged for the sake of the world, then there is nothing worse than that. And if the world acts for the sake of God for the betterment of the community, then there is nothing more reconciling with God. Suppose that this fine cloth of red baize that you have laid out for this occasion is with an eye toward boasting, arrogance, and self-glorification, then this cloth will take you to hell. If it has been laid out to maintain the honor of Islam and the community, then the same red cloth will take you to paradise in the hereafter. The most concern you should truly have is to keep the honor of Islam established and maintained in this world. I have been thinking about the welfare of the community and worrying about it night and day for 35 long years.

O my friends, deliberate the fact that each age that has passed has been of a different shade. Unless we follow the ways of this age, we can never find success. Think about your past history; there was a time when Akbar reigned. During his reign, the scholars and historians and the learned and the poets were valued. During his reign, people developed knowledge and the arts that were a source of their pride and honor. Now think about those bad times that passed during the reign of Muhammad Shah and the inappropriate and improper reign of the kings of Lucknow in very recent times. In those times, smut and vulgarity were the only things popular and nothing was done that would gain respect for the royal court. That was the only focus of the people. Those times have passed. This is the age of the British government. We should think about how we can maintain our honor and reputation in this era. I think that in this age, other than acquiring a high grade education there is no other means to gain self-respect. The word 'education' is such a hard one that it is very difficult to convey its meaning and understand its purpose. When the Umayyad and Abbasid Caliphates were determined to spread education among the Muslims, they spent enormous sums of money to build schools, to assemble Jewish and Christian scholars, and to enable them to translate books from the Greek language. Those days have been left far behind; they have left our minds and are hidden from our eyes. There are so many people assembled here at this time; if they are asked how knowledge came and spread among us, there will be only a few who will be familiar with the answer to that. We came to India as foreigners, conquered it with the force of our swords, but in fact we did not establish any system of education here. To the extent that it happened, the remnants of which are still visible to our eyes, it was through students reading in mosques and shrines, getting by on bread handed out by people, looking at books sitting in the light of a lamp or walking by the light hanging from the ride of a nobleman, or being taught by those kind scholars who taught without being remunerated. And that is the method that is still popular among us and that we desire in our hearts. But it should be understood that those days have passed and the knowledge that is customary in this era [*moth damaged manuscript…*]. In this era, our community should follow [*moth damaged manuscript…*] it is futile to expect success by following the method. In this age, unless our community gathers its strength together, provides the education that is needed for this age, and convinces itself that in this age, acquiring education is impossible without spending money, it is unlikely that a high grade of education can be given to its people.

The method of education in this age is also not beneficial for our community of this era. We want to create honor, respect, courage, and empathy for our people, which is the root of progress for the community. But if we eat the bread of charity and live in a humiliated state, it is unlikely that attributes conducive to getting education can be created for our community. Can you point to any person who got his education by eating the bread of charity in mosques, and who has retained honor, respect, courage, and empathy for our community in spite of becoming a very learned scholar? Hence, our foremost task is to think about what method we should adopt for the education of our community by which they acquire the knowledge which is necessary for this age, their nurturing is also of a high moral and cultural value, and a feeling of honor, which is called '*self-respect*' in English, is also present in them.

The government, out of its generosity, has established schools in many places but Muslims have taken very little benefit from them. I will accept that the objection presented by the Muslims is no less relevant to the community, that there is no religious education in the government schools and it is very essential that Muslim children get some religious education from the beginning. But I cannot blame the government for not having religious education in their schools. I am strongly opposed to those people who desire religious education in government schools. It is incumbent upon the government not to interfere in any way in our religious education. The policy that the government has adopted to not provide religious education in its schools to Muslims, Hindus, or Christians is a very fine policy and it is based on a very rational idea. I do not want to get into the details at this time, but I want to say this much that we ourselves cannot allow the government to interfere with our religious education.

The real reason behind Muslims lagging in education is being unfamiliar with modern knowledge. They did not appreciate its worth and considered it insignificant and shallow compared to their own knowledge that they had acquired from the Greeks. Absurd religious prejudices joined in and the result of it all was that they paid no attention to acquiring this knowledge. Other communities paid attention to it and they advanced a lot, and now it has become difficult for our community to keep up with them. A student can experience that if he studies with a group of students from his own community, who are similar in educational aptitude, his heart's desire, joy, and passion for education will be significantly enhanced. In contrast, if he is included in a group of students of other communities with whom he is not at par in aptitude, his heart will be saddened and he will not score as high as his fellow students in the exams, his enthusiasm will wane, and he can neither get help from his fellow students nor will his desire for education remain fresh. There is a school in an alley in Calcutta whose name is the "Calcutta Madrasa" in which English is not taught in higher grades. Near it, in another alley, is another school in which English is taught in higher grades. But in this school there are nearly 100% Bengali students with just a few Muslim students enrolled. The big group of Bengali students in this school derive a lot of benefit from it while those few Muslims in the school do not.

Besides that, I have an idea which I will present before you whether it is right or wrong. My desire is not only to spread education among the Muslims but also to create two things in them. One of them is the right nurturing. In the past, the boys of our families used to be taught by a *Mian-ji*, a traditional teacher, and would be nurtured by their parents and the elders of the family, who were steeped in a high level of a special traditional culture. Even though that nurturing was of a different kind than that of recent times, it had a very lofty nature. It is still remembered, and it should be remembered, but now the difficulty is that our elders, whose virtues we remember and whose traits guided us to develop our own nature, have all passed away. There is no one among us whose morals and nurturing we should follow. What used to be our nurturing system is completely broken. It is like a bunch of twigs tied together with a twine. If the twine breaks, all the twigs will scatter. Now if they are collected and tied with another twine, they cannot be held together. The times keep on changing, and all the things that are with the times also change, and that is the reason why nurturing that was appropriate for those times is no longer appropriate in these times. So, unless we give proper nurturing to the children of our community with education appropriate for these times, the benefit that we seek cannot be achieved.

The second thing that I want to create in Muslims is enthusiasm and pride for the community, and that cannot be created unless groups and groups of our children come together to be educated. At this time, with all of us Muslims assembled here, this gathering affects our hearts in and of itself, and our voices are raised crying "our community, our community." And if all of us are scattered, that effect is scattered and ineffective. This is not just what my views are and I hope that all of you will accept that. If you think on religious principles, you will know the reason why our beloved Prophet the Messenger ordered all Muslims to pray together five times a day in the neighborhood mosque, for all the Muslims of the town to pray together in the town-mosque, and for all the Muslims of the city and its surrounding area to offer the Eid prayers in the district mosque. The reason was the same, that a gathering of people would affect everyone, give rise to a feeling of community in their hearts, and the crowd would exhibit the glory of the community. These external things have a lot of effect on the internal being. They create unity among the individuals. These thoughts do not arise in man unless they are created. Hence, it is necessary that Muslims gather in one place for education and nurturing, so that they live and eat together and develop affection and compassion among each other. I believe some students of our college are present in this gathering. Although I do not like to praise them to their face, I will say that if you look all over India, you will find that nowhere else is there so much compassion for the community, mutual affection, and fraternal feelings among the students as you will find in our college. Although these feelings in them have not arisen to the level that one would wish, it is expected that these attributes will be perfected and give them more respect.

There are many difficulties in the education of Muslims. To end that, there is another challenge, and that is to unite the people behind a common goal. To understand the meaning of the word unite to mean that people agree on everything is to misconstrue its meaning. It is naive to think that all the people will agree on every detail of any work to be done anywhere in the world. The meaning of agreement is that there is consensus that the principle and objective of the work to be done is to provide benefit to the people. If that is true, then that work should be supported. If there is disagreement in the details, then it is essential that efforts be made to correct and resolve these differences. If, due to difference of opinion, those disagreements cannot be resolved, then to be united is to give credence to the real purpose, to support it, and ignore those differences in the details. If someone is hungry, you should give him bread. But to not give him bread because he is one-eyed and therefore flawed is not an act of the wise. Man's plans are never without defect; that power is only with God that all His work is perfect. If people, out of their misconceptions, ignore the good qualities of the work and think only about its flaws, and don't support this work of community welfare because of these perceived flaws, then you can imagine yourself what will become of your community. Why should we think that everything should be done in a way that there is no disagreement in its every detail. A long time has passed till today. Prophets have passed, saints have passed, those who worked for the welfare of the community have passed. Can anyone tell if all the work they did was such that everybody agreed with them. Difference of opinion is in man's disposition and when anything is done which is contrary to someone's opinion, he considers it bad. Empathy for the community is not to separate yourself from the work due to these perceived shortcomings and disagreements, but to recognize the good things in it and its attributes from which the community will benefit in some way and to support it. So, the shortcoming that our community needs to eliminate the most is this, and if we can successfully eliminate it, then if we act on the principle of compassion for the community that I just described, the community will benefit a lot.

We need peace in the country. The progress of the country to the extent we would like needs English education. Who can deny that we have both of these things under the British government [*Cheers*], and that is why it is essential that the British Government remain firmly established in India forever. [*Cheers*] Do not think that in saying this I favor the government. No, rather I consider it necessary for the welfare of our community and our country. [*Cheers*]

We cannot gain respect from the British government without acquiring higher education in English, just as in our empire when it was established in India, no one could earn respect without acquiring knowledge and the arts that prevailed in the kingdom. My friends the late Maulvi Muhammad Qasim *Saheb* and the late Maulvi Muhammad Yaqub *Saheb* had established a seminary in

Deoband that taught Arabic. You must have heard in the speeches that I made at the Educational Congress that I am very much in favor of learning the ancient religious and Oriental knowledge which was very popular among our elders. And I consider the survival of this knowledge among our people necessary for the survival of our community. But this type of education is needed for one reason and higher education in English is needed for another reason. A relative of my friend *Pir-ji* Muhammad Arif used to study in the Deoband seminary. He completed his course and went through the *Dastar-e-Fazilat* ceremony, the turban of honor tied at the convocation of the seminary. He wrote a letter to *Pir-ji* Muhammad Arif. He brought that letter to me and asked me what kind of employment his relative could get. I answered that *Pir-ji* should tell him to sit in the mosque, say "God, God," repeatedly, and to give the call for prayers five times a day. Because he has not prepared himself for the business of this world, but that of the other world. How many men in this gathering are engaged in the business of leaving this world and finding the other world? Many men say in so many words that they consider this world to be shallow and superficial and seek the other world. But this outward confession seems to have little effect on the heart. We should talk about what we ourselves can do, not give advice to people to do what we cannot do ourselves. We need worldly progress and for that we need higher education in the English language and knowledge to a level that others have achieved. If we don't do that, we cannot gain respect.

Now I will look from all sides at the need for English studies and present before you every facet that proves the need to acquire English knowledge. Acquiring knowledge is per se one of the great virtues of man. So, if a person wants to know how far knowledge has progressed, and he has a desire in his heart to acquire this knowledge, he would not be able to acquire even an iota of that knowledge or have the slightest idea of the progress that has been made without learning a European language, be it French, or German, or English. I have appropriated the English language to make my point for the reason that extremely easy means are available in India to learn it, otherwise, to my understanding, French and German are better languages for this particular purpose. Even a holy cleric, if he wants, can collect enough material for requital in the hereafter through the English language and English knowledge. You see how many missionaries are spread throughout India and how they make such false allegations against the religion of Islam and how they deceive people. So, if you want to support Islam, you cannot counter them without knowing English and without learning the knowledge that is in

European languages. And from this point of view, the learning of English language reaches the level of becoming a *farz-e-kifaya* for the Muslims, a divine obligation that when fulfilled by an adequate number of individuals of a community absolves all other members. You are very familiar with Maulvi Rahmatullah *Saheb*. He countered the missionaries and voiced his support for Islam, but he felt the need to know English and he appointed a Muslim well versed in English as his assistant. If Maulvi Rahmatullah or his aide were fluent in the European languages, you would have found much more information in their writings because the books they studied don't even have an iota of information on Islam compared to that found in the European books. And the opposition to the Christian religion that is contained in books written by European scholars is much more than in what they wrote. If you want to see the magnificent blessings that the religion of Islam has spread in the communities of the world, then too it is essential that you study English knowledge. In Europe, there have been many kindhearted authors who have described the qualities and blessings of Islam with such excellence that you can hardly find in your own books. In any case, to acquire European knowledge and literature is very necessary for both faith and worldly matters, whichever of the two is one's purpose. Hence, the opposition that you have assumed toward European knowledge and literature should be dropped. I acknowledge that the expectations we had from those in our community who have studied English have not been fulfilled to the extent we had hoped, but it should be understood that all the vessels that a potter bakes in his kiln do not come out hardened or even in one piece. Some get broken and some not baked well and only a few come out hardened and unbroken. In the same way, it is one in a thousand persons that is the reason for the honor of a community. We should not be disheartened if all those in our community who study English do not achieve success.

Many people have the idea that by studying English, the religious beliefs become infirm. To that I will give a definite answer that after getting higher education in English, it is out of the realm of possibility [*moth damaged manuscript...*] and would have affirmation for any other religion in his heart. It is not that the outwardly deeds of all those who have not studied English are correct that you would blame those who study English. If, as a result, they develop any doubts in their heart about Islam, your scholars do not dispel these doubts. It is their duty to dispel these doubts rather than consider a ban on studying English as the remedy for that. The lamp does not go out just because you shut your eyes, rather man goes blind. When Greek philosophy spread among Muslims, there were thousands of men whose beliefs were disturbed. The scholars of that age paid attention to that and cleared these doubts. If the scholars of this age are capable and accept supporting Islam, why are they sitting at home and making small-talk? Why don't they remove those objections and clear those doubts? The fact is that in the previous age, doubts were raised in Greek philosophy and the scholars of those days were themselves scholars of Greek philosophy, and that is why they had the power to clear those doubts. But scholars of our time are simply ignorant of these modern philosophies from which the contemporary doubts have arisen. They know neither literature nor science and that is why they are fit for nothing except to sit in the mosque, climb on their pulpit, and declare that studying English is infidelity and the one who studies English is an infidel. This kind of talk is nothing more than raw superstition. I would expect Muslims who have studied English at a very high level to be the ones who support Islam. So, we must try to make higher education in English a practice in our community.

It was on this basis that the Aligarh *Madrasatul Uloom* was established for the education of Muslims and its main purpose is to bring Muslim boys together for their education and nurturing and to create a feeling of compassion for the community. And that is the reason for building a very grand boarding house in this school. Yes, it was also necessary that along with giving the boys an English education, they should be taught religious principles and beliefs. Consequently, arrangements were made for that as well. A Shia cleric was employed for the Shia boys and a Sunni cleric for the Sunni boys, who teach them based on the same traditional principles as their ancestors did. I hear that due to some matters that I disagree with, people talk a lot about religious education at the *Madrasatul Uloom*. Any faults in my beliefs and principles are due to me. You should not have any issues with my being; rather what you should see is under what doctrines education is given at the *Madrasatul Uloom*. If they are educated according to the beliefs of your forefathers and are taught from the same books that your forefathers have read, then I should be left to my own devices and it should be considered that a low-caste *Chamar* laborer is building a mosque for you. The benefits of the mosque should not be overlooked just because the person building it is a *Chamar*, and focus should be on the benefits of the mosque and not the *Chamar*. And if you find the religious education there to be contrary to the religious education of your forefathers and find flaws with it, then come and reform it. To slander from the heart and say false things – has Islam permitted these things now? All the accusations that have been made against the *Madrasatul*

Uloom are completely false. The religious education journals on the table here are the ones that are taught at the *Madrasatul Uloom*. Those who want to see what religious education is given at the *Madrasatul Uloom* should take a look at these journals. And if any one has any objection, then raise it. To adopt such unscrupulous ways as I mentioned earlier is a sign of the Almighty's fury that keeps people from doing good work. These are signs of divine wrath and satanic temptations that the slanderers and the gossipers have assumed. It has been 15 years since I left my employment to serve the community. I left my hometown and settled in Aligarh, where I have no kith or kin nor do I own even a patch of land. If our community did not face these satanic temptations, would it not be attracted toward this work? And would this work not have been completed soon to a great degree. And it would have become a source of pride for the community. This honor would have made the community proud, not only in India but across Europe. All the world would have said that although India's Muslims have become fatigued, they have an enthusiasm for their community and they have done such noble work for their community that has not been seen in Asia till date. It is the same satanic deception and the displeasure of the Almighty that is upon them due to which the work has not been completed till now. There is nothing else to cure that but to pray to God and be humble before Him. He is the only one who will remove all these difficulties. I have hope that the day will come when all these difficulties will be removed and the truth will shine like the sun.

In this address you have mentioned the boarding house and asked for the reason why the second and third tiers of the boarding house were demolished. You will pardon me when I point out that there is a slight mistake in this, because the second and third tiers of the boarding house have not been demolished but the first and third tiers. When the school was established, there were the first, second, and third tiers of the boarding house. The students of all these three tiers used to sit and eat separately with the students of their respective classes. But after this practice was observed, it was found that it had a bad effect on the disposition of the students that was opposite to creating the communal unity that we want. The first-tier boarders thought they were the kings of the boarding house and the second-tier boarders were inferior to them. In the same way, the second-tier boarders considered themselves superior to the third-tier boarders. For a long time, those members who had more of a hand in the management of the boarding house were of the opinion that this division should be abolished. Over time, incidents occurred which convinced us that the boarders were not on good terms with each other and instead of communal unity there was separation and hostility between them. This hostility reached the extent that on one occasion, the first- and second-tier boarders refused to have a joint-dinner with each other. One time, a first-tier boarder was admonished because he insulted a second-tier boarder. When such ill-effects of the tiered system were observed among the boarders, it became necessary to abolish this division. It became clear that by abolishing this division, the number of boarders would go down, but it was determined that it would be better for the number of boarders to be reduced than there be bad feelings between them.

Extreme moderation has been shown in taking down these tiered boarding houses and the middle tier has been adopted for all of them. There are different types of buildings that make up the boarding houses and different boarding fees have been assessed for these buildings. The students have the freedom to choose whichever building they want to live in and pay the required fee. A joint meal for all the boarders at midday and one in the evening has been proposed, the fee for which was fixed at what was being charged for the second-tier meals previously. It has been ordered that all boarders sit together in one place and have the two meals. It has been proposed that students can also have the morning breakfast and afternoon refreshments, but the fee for it has been assessed separately which the students will have to pay to avail of the facility. So, with this plan, we have adopted a mid-tier policy by which the students who were in the higher tier would be able to reduce their fees and the students who were in the lower tier would see a very small increase in their fees. In a community college, which was set up to promote harmony and a community feeling, was it appropriate to maintain such a bad policy which created a bad feeling among the students and contempt and humiliation for each other? In India, decency and courtesy are two things that keep everyone on an equal footing even if wealth gives someone a brighter shine and raises his stature. With the arrangement we have made, we see that there is more compassion for each other. A wealthy boy does not see a noble but poor boy with contempt. This boy [*pointing toward Aftab Ahmed Khan*] is a student and a boarder in our college. He comes from a very rich family and is the son of a Nawab, but he happily has meals, plays, and studies with a poor boy of nobility. In games, even if wealthy boys are on the losing side, all the boys regardless of being wealthy or poor yell together, "we won, we won."

In England, even though everyone has the freedom to enter the university colleges, there are some colleges that are so expensive that other than the sons of the wealthy and the '*gentlemen*,' no one is able to get into them. But if a person of lesser means is able to get in, he would consider himself equal to the son of a duke who was also admitted. And that is why it was necessary that every boy that we admitted as a boarder was on an equal footing. We are also concerned about the poverty and lack of means in our community and we have kept our expenses as low as humanly possible. Only Rs. 8 per month are collected for the two meals daily, which pays for the salary of the boarding house employees, food related expenses, and the cost of electricity used in the boarding house rooms. How can there be any further reduction in the fees for the meals? Can anyone say that if the student lives somewhere else, he can get by with less expense? Certainly not.

Now, for those students who cannot spend even that much and want to study only by getting bread as charity, I must clearly say that the boarding house is not a home for the needy where the poor are fed. It is for the sake of the students on whom we pin our hopes for the upliftment of the community. Those who rely on the bread of alms and depend on it to study do not shed the effect it has on them. They never develop self-respect and no sense of respect and honor is found in them. We certainly cannot admit such students to the boarding house, nor can we cook pilaf and lentils in the same pot, and nor can we allow students from whom we expect compassion and pride for the community to get lost among these fakirs.

That notwithstanding, we have not neglected to, as much as we can and as much as our funds allow, provide assistance and aid to the noble and talented poor students. We did not make our students beg, rather we begged on their behalf. We gave out a considerable number of scholarships and stipends to those who proved to be hardworking and meritorious in their studies. They regarded this as a reward for their hard work and they didn't feel the effects of our begging for them. There are also a few students who are from nobility and appear talented but do not have the ability to spend even a paisa. We have admitted them into the boarding house as well and everything is provided to them. But no person other than the Almighty, me, and '*nature*' knows who these students are. They are absolutely equal to the rest of the boarders, all their fees, which is equal to the fees of other boarders, is deposited on their behalf, and they live with the same respect as the other boarders. And that ill-effect of living on charity never even enters their mind. If our community became such that it had no respect or honor,

I would pray to the Almighty that the earth may open up and swallow my entire community.

Our community should pay utmost attention to respect and honor and should nurture their children in such a way that a sense of self-respect and honor remains in them. The task that we have undertaken for our community is one that we surely expect our community to be diligent in, although hundreds of times these expectations have changed to disappointments. But we do not cease our efforts. Suppose that all expectations of success in our endeavors fade away. Even then, I will never cease my efforts until my death. I do not want my reward for these efforts either from the community or in this world or in the hereafter. If, on Judgement Day, the Almighty were to say that He will take me to paradise as a reward for my endeavors, I would tell Him, *Huzoor*, let me be. I do not make these efforts for the Almighty, but for the community. Yes, I do plead with the Almighty, Lord of the Worlds, and pray that there may be compassion for the community, and the community helps to finish this magnificent work that is for the betterment of the community. I request all you gentlemen to join me in this prayer. [*Very loud chants of 'Amen!' and 'Cheers!'*]

132

Related to Charitable Endowments of Muslims

(Third Annual Session of the Muhammadan Educational Congress, December 27, 1888)

The third annual session of the Muhammadan Educational Congress was held in Lahore from December 27 - 30, 1888. In this session, Khan Bahadur Muhammad Barkat Ali Khan presented a resolution (Resolution No. 3) in connection with the implementation and action according to the resolution passed by the Government of India in July 1985 regarding Muslim endowments that had given Muslims reassurance. Sir Syed seconded this resolution with the following speech.

Mr. President of the session! I support the resolution moved by my honorable friend Khan Bahadur Muhammad Barkat Ali Khan and with your permission would like to say something briefly. In February 1882, the Central National Muhammadan Association of Calcutta, in one of its petitions addressed to the government, made many requests regarding the current state of Muslims in general. It also wrote that such endowments exist in various places that, besides having a religious purpose, can also be useful for the education of Muslims. It requested the government to appoint a commission to investigate whether these endowments could be invested in the education of Muslims. Based on this petition, the Government of India issued a resolution on July 15, 1885 in which it stated that it was an impossible task for the government to interfere with a religious endowment. The people who are associated with these kinds of endowments have been granted broad rights under Act No. 20 of 1863 to manage these endowments. Nevertheless, in this resolution the government, by way of assurance to the Muslim people, made it clear to the governments of Madras, Bombay, Bengal, North-Western Provinces, Awadh, and Punjab to form small committees to consider and report on this matter.

The rule that was established for forming the committees was that each committee would have an experienced revenue officer, one or two prominent Mohammedan *'gentlemen,'* at least one competent Muslim jurist, and one or more government related legal advisors. The Bengal government appointed a committee as per this resolution, whose report is in my hands. But, as far as I know, no such committees have been appointed in the North-Western provinces or Awadh, and I believe it hasn't been appointed in Punjab either. So, the motion that is being made right now is merely that the Government of India's resolution must be implemented in these provinces as well to the satisfaction of the Muslims.

Mr. President! By presenting this resolution, we do not intend to encroach on these endowments, or cause any disturbance in the possession and rights of the people who are donors or trustees of these endowments, or alter or change the purpose for which the endowment was established. Rather, our aim is to do the required research to find out the actual number of Muslim charitable endowments present in India, for what purpose they have been established, and who are their donors and trustees.

Mr. President! I understand that at this time there is no such list available in any district from which the above mentioned details can be determined and the government itself is not very familiar with the details of the endowments. If such a situation is created in which detailed information about the local endowments of every district or every state is known, then these details would not be entirely useless for the government to know and groups of Muslims would also become familiar with all the endowments that are there in the country. Undoubtedly, the government has granted a lot of powers to the Muslims regarding the endowments by way of Act No. 20 of 1863, but if the state of the endowments is concealed and secret, then the Muslims cannot do anything toward reforming, amending, or developing them. If their real condition is known, it is possible that Muslims will try to reform them.

Those people who currently control and are trustees of the endowments should be reassured that we have no intention of interfering with their purpose, nor do we have any undue right to, rather our aim is to protect and advance the endowments. And it is our desire that these endowments are utilized for the purpose that they were endowed, and we are confident that if the donors and the trustees understand this intent of ours, they will consider this work of ours to be of great help in their efforts and happily give us support in our work.

I know the state of some endowments, that due to some random events they went into debt. If we know its state properly, Muslims can try to take this endowment out of its debt so that the purpose for which it was set up can be fulfilled.

I would like to narrate an incident that I became aware of, that a few shops of a mosque went into the possession of a person, and so much time passed that statute of limitations applied. When this happened, Muslims collected money among themselves, bought the shops from the person, and returned them to the possession of the mosque. In the same way, if we know the state of an endowment fully, then the Muslims will, I hope, be there to try in every way to save their endowments. By the creation of such a circumstance, for which this resolution has been proposed, there is no doubt that the Muslims will find a great opportunity to protect the endowments.

The endowments of the Muslims, as far as I know, are of two kinds: those which are endowed entirely for religious matters and those which have a fixed portion endowed for religious matters and a fixed portion for educational purposes.

Mr. President! While mentioning the education of Muslims through endowments, I must mention that in the commission that sat in Bengal, there was unfortunate difference of opinion among the members, i.e. some members were of the opinion that English education should be given through endowments and some members were of the opinion that income from those endowments cannot be spent on English education. But I hope there will be no such difference of opinion in our congress since a resolution was passed in the session of the congress last year that the custodians of the endowments should focus on the education of Arabic knowledge, which includes hadith, jurisprudence and exegesis of Quran, according to ancient traditional methods, and spending money from these endowments on English education is not according to the intent and desire of the donors to the endowment.

Mr. President! The stated objectives of our Educational Congress, which are detailed in its constitution, include an important goal of bringing into practice appropriate schemes for the sustained education of Oriental knowledge and theology using traditional methods that have been passed down among our scholars. So, if endowments that have a portion dedicated to the education of Muslims are used for the purpose of continued education according to the same ancient methods, one of the objectives of our congress will get a big boost.

The address that was presented by the Mohammedan Anglo-Oriental College to His Excellency the Marquess of Dufferin and Earl of Ava included a thanks to the Government of India for this resolution. In his reply, His Excellency stated, "Given the attention that you Muslims pay to education, it is incumbent on you to be concerned that the organization of educational endowments be done in a way that you achieve the good purposes from it that you hold in your hearts. You are aware that local governments have been utilized in the matter of their organization and, with full confidence, I leave their decision in these districts on the opinion of such a Lieutenant Governor who is as aware of your needs and as empathetic of your desires as Sir Auckland Colvin[1]."

I acknowledge from the heart what His Excellency said with regards to *Janab* Sir Auckland Colvin but I am very certain that *Janab* Sir James Lyall, Lieutenant Governor of the province of Punjab, is also desirous in the same way of the advancement of the education of Muslims. I have no doubt that as far as the laws and regulations allow, the Honorable *Huzoor* will also pay sincere attention to it. Therefore, for these reasons, I consider it necessary that in accordance with the resolution of the Government of India, a request should be made to the government for the complete and proper organization of the endowments to the satisfaction of the Muslims.

---

[1] Sir Auckland Colvin KCSI KCMG CIE (1838 - 1908) was a colonial administrator in India and Egypt, born into the Anglo-Indian Colvin family. From 1883 - 1892 he was in India, first as financial member of council and then as Lieutenant-Governor of the North-Western Provinces and Awadh. He founded Colvin Taluqdars' College in Lucknow.

133

Mohammedan Educational Committee

(Third Annual Session of the Muhammadan Educational Congress, December 28, 1888)

In the December 28 session, a resolution was presented to establish a Mohammedan Educational Committee in each district headquarter. This standing committee would be under the general educational committee of the province and together they would be under the central standing committee, which would be headquartered in Aligarh and whose secretary would be the secretary of Muhammadan Educational Congress. In support of this resolution, Sir Syed stood up and presented his thoughts as follows.

Mr. President of the session and other dignitaries! I wholeheartedly support the resolution that has been proposed by our honorable President. If we think about it, there are so many associations and societies in all of India which have been established by Muslims under various names and for various purposes that perhaps cannot be found even in an advanced and highly developed country. Hearing their great names and lofty goals leaves a person perplexed, but when we see what they have done, it is with much regret that we say absolutely nothing. All these associations, in which I will include Muhammadan Educational Congress at the top as well, have done nothing more than meaningless talk. As much as we say with our tongues and as much empathy and compassion for the community we express with words, if we brought even one-fiftieth of that into action, the community would get unfailing benefits.

Other than Anjuman-e-Himayat-e-Islam of Lahore, I have not heard of any association that has actually done any practical work for the welfare of Muslims, although I am not fully aware to what extent even they have done any practical work. In any case, what we need is practical action. The resolution that has been presented is the basis for practical work, i.e. if the people really want to work for the good of the community, the way to do it would be to establish standing committees to execute this work in various places and for them to be a part of one network in a way that they stand separately as well as together. The first drawback of our efforts is that every person wants to take their brick and a half from the resources and build their own mosque separately and, due to this, everyone's work remains incomplete, deficient, and useless. But if we incorporate these individual efforts into a network, we will be able to do a lot. Without a doubt, this resolution is such that if it is acted upon, it will bring enormous benefits to the community. I hope that all the well-wishers who are gathered here will pass this valuable resolution with sincere agreement. But our happiness is not limited to just passing this resolution, rather its passing would give rise to an apprehension in our hearts of whether there will be any practical action on it. We should not despair of God's grace and we should hope that just as this resolution will be passed by consensus, efforts will be made to come together in agreement and put it into practical action.

134

Sir Syed's Views on Women's Education

*(Third Annual Session of the Muhammadan Educational Congress held in Lahore,
December 28 - 30, 1888)*

In the third annual session of the Mohammedan Educational Congress held in Lahore, on December 29, 1888 a resolution was presented for approval which read, "The Mohammedan Educational Congress agrees that Muslim women's schools should be established for the education of Muslim girls that are in accordance with the religion of Islam and agreeable to the ways of the honorable people of Islam." When this resolution was presented, loud and noisy debates ensued among those in favor and those opposed to it. In the end, Sir Syed stood up and presented his views on the resolution in the following words.

Mr. President of the session!

I regret that this resolution, which was a very simple one, was unnecessarily debated. I do not want to say much about the education of women because whatever my opinions are on this topic I have already expressed them in this very Punjab a few years ago. Even at that time, people were surprised, and may be surprised again that although new ideas are attributed to me in many matters, regarding the education of women I have the same ideas that our ancient forefathers had.

I cannot approve of the modern arrangements that are made these days for the education of women, be they by the government or a Muslim individual or an Islamic association. To establish schools for the education of women and to imitate the girls' schools of Europe is no way appropriate under the current conditions in India and I am strongly opposed to it. People have only heard that there are schools in England for the education of girls, and they assemble in them and study together in the same way that boys assemble in schools and study and live together. Due to the favor of some friends, I have actually seen, particularly in London, girls' schools where girls from noble families study and live. I can assure you that the level of fineness, composure, education, and nurturing that can be found in those schools, it will require hundreds of years for India to get there. If I imagine that such schools can be established in India, I would tell the noble families to certainly send their girls there, but O friends! I assure you that for that to happen in India right now is inconceivable.

I do not approve of the kinds of subjects that are being proposed to be taught to women either because they are neither suitable for our condition nor will our women need that kind of knowledge for a hundred years. To read the Holy Quran without being told its meaning, which is looked down upon with disdain, is, in my mind, a means of spiritual nurturing, spiritual kindness, and attention to the Supreme Being like no other.

At this time, I do not want to talk about this at length; let me just say that there is no mention of starting girls' schools in this resolution but mentions 'maktab,' an academy where children are given primary education, with the stipulation that it is in accordance with and appropriate for the religion of Islam and the ways of the honorable people of Islam. Hence, when these stipulations are stated in the resolution, there can be no objection to approving it.

I am not fully aware of what kinds of girls' *maktabs* have been started by Anjuman-e Himayat-e Islam, but I think it is appropriate that I explain to you the method of educating girls among the nobles so that you gentlemen can consider it and form an informed opinion regarding this resolution. It would be better if I described the method that was carried out in my own family, with which I am well acquainted and much of which I have seen with my own eyes. I have seen three types of women in my family. One type was those who were companions of my mother and her sisters. I observed that they all knew how to read and there were some who could read Persian books. I myself studied some lessons of *Gulistan* from my mother and often read lessons from beginner's Persian books to her.

The second group was that of my sisters who were in my age group and who were educated at home. I observed the method for their education was that a respectable and accommodating household would be selected for their education and all the girls of the family would assemble there to study. An elder woman of the household, who would be a mother or a grandmother or an aunt to one of the girls, would supervise them, a number of *ustanis*, or schoolmistresses, would be employed to nurture the girls, and the elder women of the household who were well read would themselves educate the girls along with the *ustanis*.

A portion of that house, which would be the customary large chamber of a house in the district, would be designated as the *maktab*. Platform beds covered with clean sheets would be laid out in this chamber and girls would sit on them and study and be taught by the *ustanis*. The elderly women of the house would go to this chamber from time to time, observe the girls being taught, and supervise their instruction. Sometimes a male relative, a brother, father, uncle, or grandfather would listen in on the lessons and would sometimes teach some of the girls. Up until now, there are some among those women who are somewhat familiar with the Arabic language and can ably read books such as *Mishkat Shareef*, a collection of Hadith by Sunni Islamic scholars, *Hasan-Husain*, a centuries-old Islamic play recounting the story of Prophet Muhammad's grandsons, and *Chahal Hadees*, the 40 Hadith of Prophet Muhammad, memorizing which is considered a blessing.

The third type is those girls who were babies for me and have now grown up. Their nurturing has also been in the same tradition in front of my eyes. The Arabic letters they would write would be corrected by my own sister's husband. From morning till lunch would be study time. The girls would have lunch with the mistress of the house. After lunch till the time for *Zuhr* prayers would be spent learning sewing, embroidery, and other household skills. At *Zuhr* time all the girls would offer prayers and would be immersed in their studies till *Asr* time in the late afternoon. After *Asr* prayers, they would get into their palanquins and return home.

Friday used to be a very interesting day. All the girls would come to the house early in the morning and cook different kinds of food which in our vernacular were called *hand-kuliyan*. One of these girls would be chosen as the host and all the girls ate what she cooked.

Sometimes the girls would also bring their brothers of similar ages and serve them food. In short, in this way the women were taught those things that were necessary for them to learn. Their education did not include those subjects that people want to insert at this time in imitation of Europe. It is perhaps necessary to include these subjects in the education of girls in Europe and America given the state of the society there, since it is possible that women there can become postmasters or telegraph masters, or members of parliament, but it is neither that time in India nor would it be time in hundreds of years. So, the knowledge that was useful for the women of India at that time is still the knowledge that is useful for women at this time, and that knowledge is only in theology and ethics. The women in those days used to read the Holy Quran, read its translation, and read about the matters of prayer and fasting. Those who advanced in education and learned Persian were taught stories of the prophets, narratives of the saints, similar books of ethics, and poetry of Maulana Rumi, may God bless him and grant him peace. At the time when *Mishkat Shareef* had not been translated into Urdu, and girls had expressed their desire to read the Hadith, they were taught Sheikh Abdul Haq Dehlavi's commentary on *Mishkat Shareef*. In recent times, the Urdu translation of *Mishkat Shareef* and Zafar Jaleel's translation of *Hasan-Husain* have been included in most of the syllabi. Out of their own interest, some girls had read *Malfuzat* of Hazrat Khwaja Nizamuddin Auliya, may God have mercy on him, i.e. *Favaid al-Fuaad*. I am aware of only one girl who had read Tuzuk-i-Jahangiri, the Persian autobiography of the Mughal Emperor Jahangir, taught by her father, but her playmates would say to her, "*Bua*! What is the use of that? Read some books about God and His Messenger."

These were some of the methods of education that instilled a sense of kindness, fear of God, mercy, affection, and morality in the hearts of girls and this was the education that was sufficient for both their faith and secular needs. It is still the same education that is sufficient for them. I do not see what is the need to teach women the geography of Africa and America, or the rules of algebra and trigonometry, or the narratives of Ahmad Shah and Muhammad Shah and the battles between the kingdoms of Delhi and Marathas.

O gentlemen! To me, the phrase 'girls' *maktab*' in this resolution means such a school that I just described, and the description in the resolution that the schools should be in accordance with the religion of Islam and agreeable to the ways of the honorable people of Islam means exactly the kinds of *maktabs* that I have detailed. Hence, I ask you to consider this resolution again and attribute those meanings to its words that I have elaborated, and make the decision whether it is necessary and appropriate to make such arrangements for the education of girls or not. And after that, pass or reject this resolution as you see fit.

★

135

Speech in Reply to an Arabic *Qasida*[2]

*(Third Annual Session of the Muhammadan Educational Congress held in Lahore,
December 28 - 30, 1888)*

On the last day of the third annual session of the Mohammedan Educational Congress held in Lahore, i.e. on December 30, the end of all the proceedings of the session was announced. Some of the elders asked the president of the session, Sardar Muhammad Hayat Khan *Saheb*, for permission to read their compositions and say a few words. With the permission of the president, a gentleman, Maulvi Abdul Majeed, Pleader, presented a written *qasida* to Sir Syed in elegant and eloquent Arabic. Following that, Sir Syed stood up and expressed his thanks with these brief words.

Janab Maulana!

I am not capable of appreciating your excellent Arabic poetry. I am afraid of the article of anonymous appreciation proving to be true. I am amazed that esteemed gentlemen such as yourself hold an insignificant person like me in such high regard. I wonder if all of this is happening in unconsciousness or in a dream. In any case, it is my duty to thank you for your favor but I am afraid that I do not have words to express it.

You will forgive me if I state something regarding your verse:

'And I will curse you, foolish people'

Janab Maulana! Those whom you have described as fools, the truth is that I love them sincerely and consider their slander as a necessary means to achieving my goals. When you hear the reason for that, I am hopeful you will agree with me.

[2.] A '*qasida*' is a genre of poetry in poem or ballad form eulogizing a person.

I assure you that as much as I strive for a high level of progress in European knowledge and literature in our community, I strive more for them to truly understand Islam and remain steadfast on '*La ilaha illa Allah Muhammedur Rasul Allah.*' For this purpose I have written some things, said some things, and authored some books. Those people whom you have called fools consider my faith or my words to be opposed to Islam. Suppose that this idea of theirs is wrong, but the fact that they called me bad with the thought that my faith is opposed to Islam is proof enough of the fact that they remain firm on Islam and love Islam, which is my exact goal. Hence, their slander lets me achieve my goals and that is the reason why I am happy with their slander and thank the Almighty for it:

I said bad things and I said them to God
The bitter reply is sweet on the lips

136

Thanks to Ahmed Ali Shauq ★

*(Third Annual Session of the Muhammadan Educational Congress held in Lahore,
December 28 - 30, 1888)*

On the last day of the third annual session of the Mohammedan Educational Congress held in Lahore, i.e. on December 30, after all the proceedings of the session had ended, Munshi Ahmed Ali Shauq, editor of the newspaper *Azad* published from Lucknow, recited seven *rubaiyat* or quatrains, stanzas of four lines, that he had written extemporaneously. The last stanza was as follows:

> May only his hands have a hold in the world
> May the faces of the wretched envious be black
> As long as God remains in this universe
> May He maintain old Syed's fame and success

Following that, Sir Syed stood up and expressed his thanks for the *rubaiyat* with these brief words.

Janab Maulana Shauq! I did not know that your last *'fire'* would be on me. I thank you for the love and kindness that comes from your heart. Without a doubt I take pride in the fact that among all the many elders who are assembled here, which includes such an eloquent and sweet-spoken person as yourself, you have such love and kindness for the person you have called old, although he considers himself a handsome young man. So, I thank you with heartfelt humility and humbleness.

137

Thanks to Mian Nizamuddin, *Raïs* Baghbanpura ★

(Third Annual Session of the Muhammadan Educational Congress held in Lahore, December 28 - 30, 1888)

On the last day of the third annual session of the Mohammedan Educational Congress held in Lahore, i.e. on December 30, after all the proceedings of the session had ended, among the few people who stood up and spoke was Mian Nizamuddin *Saheb, Raïs* Baghbanpura, who particularly thanked Sir Syed, Syed Mahmud, and Sardar Muhammad Hayat Khan. In reply, Sir Syed stood up and said the following words.

Mr. President of the session! I am sincerely grateful for the kind and compassionate words that my friend and benefactor Mian Nizamuddin *Saheb* has spoken about me. But, along with that, I cannot refrain from saying that I am truly not worthy of the pedestal on which my gracious friend has placed me. We all want to come together and work for the welfare of our community. May the Almighty bless these efforts and bring benefits to the community.

Mr. President! Your session is about to come to a close. It would be very ungrateful of me if I, as secretary of the congress and on behalf of all its members, do not express my thanks to Anjuman Islamia Lahore and its courageous secretary who is a lover of the community, Khan Bahadur Mohammed Barkat Ali Khan *Saheb*.

The generosity and compassion with which Anjuman Islamia Lahore invited the congress to Lahore and the hospitality it extended is worthy of gratitude not only from the members of the congress but from the entire community.

The hard work of serving the guests done by the secretary of Anjuman Islamia, Khan Bahadur Mohammed Barkat Ali Khan *Saheb*, and the trouble he took night and day has far exceeded the extent of garnering gratitude and has reached the level of amazement. There was no duty or service that Barkat Ali Khan himself was not present to perform. It is not out of place that Anjuman Islamia would be proud of such a secretary and for us to collect all the gratitude for the Anjuman and present them to the secretary. All the thanks we can give is little.

The session in Lahore cannot be more proud of selecting such a worthy, illustrious, compassionate, and noble president. The excellence and competence with which you, *Janab* President *Saheb*, presided over the meetings of the congress is worthy of great praise and immense gratitude. For that, I thank you on behalf of the congress with the hope that you will accept this thanks from an insignificant person such as me.

138

Address Presented by the Muslim Students of Lahore

(Supplement Report Third Annual Session of the Muhammadan Educational Congress held in Lahore, December 28 - 30, 1888)

On December 30, 1888, in the session of the congress held in Lahore, with the permission of its president Sardar Muhammad Hayat Khan Bahadur, all the Muslim students of the schools and colleges of Lahore presented an address to Sir Syed Ahmed Khan. Many other organizations and associations sought permission to present addresses but Sir Syed did not approve. Sir Syed gave a reply to the address presented by the students, which was included in the supplement to the report for that year.

Mr. President of the session!

Before I reply to the address presented by my dear students, please allow me to apologize to those elders and friends who have extended their love and kindness to me on this occasion by desiring to present an address to me on behalf of various organizations and associations, for which I was truly not worthy, and for that reason, with much courtesy and humility, I requested to be excused. And despite that, I did not refuse the address of the students.

But those elders would understand that I could not have refused to receive the address from the dear students. All students, and particularly Muslims students, be they fair skinned or dark complexioned, be they from Punjab, Bengal, Madras, or Bombay, are all very dear and darling to me. They are the saplings of the garden of my ideas and the fruits of my hopes. Then, who can be more dear to me? The wonderful thing is as much as I consider them dear to me, I also look at them with respect and courtesy. Then, in my heart, I hesitate with my choice of words to address them. But whatever they may be and whatever I am, I am still older than them in age and I feel a lot of love for them. So, due to my age and my love for them, it would not be inappropriate if I were to address them as 'beloved son,' or 'piece of my heart,' or 'my dearest.' And so, if I have such a relationship with the students, the other gentlemen will pardon me for asking to be excused from their address presentation while accepting the address presented by the students.

O dear students! The love with which you presented this address to me, thanking you for it is another matter; I want to assure you that any honor that can be bestowed in this world from kings and emperors would be insignificant compared to the honor you have kindly given me today. If you think about it, the honor bestowed upon someone by a king or an emperor is in the form of a physical display and the honor you have given me today is spiritual and unconventional. Whatever you have stated in your address, if I have truly done what you think I have, then it gives joy to my heart and a spiritual honor to my soul.

O my dear ones! It is my wish to see the children of my community soar higher than the stars and shine brighter than the sun. May their light spread inside those blue domes such that the light of the sun, the moon, and the stars appears dim in their comparison. I hope to God that it happens. O Almighty! Do so! O God! Do so! Amen!

O my dear ones! When you just heard me say here that the children of our community should be like this and the children of our community should be like that, what do you think I mean 'my community'? Perhaps you don't assume I am referring only to Syeds, rather you must have understood that I am talking about all the Muslims. Hence, you must understand that if you become a star in the sky and not remain a member of our community, then the connection or relationship I have formed with you gets completely detached. There is nobody in this world who is not a sinner. Everyone is a sinner before the Lord, He who is alone and has no equal. But there is a means to our salvation, and that means is a rope with which if we are all tied together, we will remain one community. What is that rope? To have faith in the Almighty and His Messenger, Muhammad, the Prophet of God, may God bless him and grant him peace, and to fulfill our duties toward them. All I want is that all my children who are students in colleges, and for whom I wish that they would attain proficiency in European knowledge and literature and be included among the most learned in the world, not forget the words '*La ilaha illa Allah Muhammedur Rasul Allah.*'

O my friends! There is some external sign or another of whatever is internal. The entry of a soldier in an army is an internal matter but the uniform he wears, which proves that he is a soldier in that army is an external sign. In the same way, being a Muslim and sincerely believing in God and His Messenger (peace and blessings of God be upon him), which only God knows, is an internal matter, but its external uniform is to attend to the worship of God five times a day. O my friends! If you neglect praying, I am sorry to say that you would be taking off the uniform and throwing it away, and would no longer be in the army of God or included in our community. Every regiment and every platoon has some insignia, on the hands, the arms, or the shoulders. The sign of our regiment or divine platoon is on our forehead when it rests on the ground in front of God's majesty. [*At this point, with much heartfelt passion, Sir Syed rested his forehead on the desk in front of him, then raised it and resumed speaking*] O friends! I assure you that I am from among the '*Ahl al-Sunnah wa'l-Jamāʿah*' who offer five prayers at five instances during the day. But if, due to human nature, you are sluggish and lazy or have trouble finding the time to pray five times, I will be extremely happy even if you offered the five prayers over three times during the day. All I want to say is that in any case and in any situation, you must somehow retain the insignia of your platoon, which is a very significant insignia, otherwise you will be separated from your platoon. It is essential that you respect the collection of all human morals and characteristics and the quintessence of all of God's creation, and make yourself a proof of His existence. It grieves and saddens me a lot when I see or hear that some boys of our community (you will excuse me, I am not talking about anyone in particular), who start studying English do not fully retain this respect. The social and moral characteristics of Europeans are of a high stature. If we try for centuries, maybe we can get there. But it is sad that our youth do not even pay any attention to these superior characteristics while fully embracing their faults. And if they do adopt any of their good characteristics, they do it in such a bad way that even these good characteristics turn into faults.

Consequently, they have learned the word freedom. They have heard the word but not understood its merits and for that reason have used it in the wrong sense. They have started being careless when dealing with their elders and do not show their parents as much respect as they should. They have abandoned the reverence they should have for those that are older than them and for the friends of their elders. All these things are very sad and retard and destroy the progress of the community that I so desire. So, I plead with the children of our community that as much as they advance in European knowledge and literature, they must also progress in developing their morals and having respect for their elders.

Those who have gone to England, I have heard complaints about the conduct of some of them, although I have not seen any of this behavior myself. But if there is any such person, it is a matter that gives them a bad name and it proves that they did not get the opportunity to mingle in sophisticated society in England. Just as there are low-level uncultured societies in our country like those of *chamars* and *qulis*, and their social norms and morals are different from ours, there are also low-level people in England and their social norms and morals are as different from those of the *'gentlemen'* class as night and day. Hence, to go there and not acquire the high morals is grounds for much disgrace, because everyone who is familiar with the state of Europe would say that they did not imbibe in the high social norms and morals of the cultured class and stayed among the very low-class and unworthy people.

Let this go also, and distinguish that even if they did not have the opportunity to live among the high social norms and morals of the English society, why did they forget about the morals of their forefathers. Did you not grow up hearing of the fables of your families and the traditions of your religion which stress reverence for your parents and respect for those who are older than you? The ways of your forefathers were so excellent and worthy of following. There are fables in our culture of such respect for our teachers that are perhaps not found in any other culture. Similarly there are unparalleled examples of how to act with true friendship toward friends. I do not know English and do not understand what is written in small letters in English books, but look at your books from your own heritage. Read books like *Kitab al-Sadaqa* and *Kitab al-'Adab* and see what excellent morals they teach. Despite the fact that I deeply respect and honor European civilization, when you read and act upon the books of your forefathers, you will become even more civilized than the Europeans.

You have mentioned in your address that Muslims were prejudiced against learning European knowledge and literature. I also speak your language but the use of the word 'prejudiced' hurts my heart. It would be better if you called it stupidity. I am from one of those people who, without any prejudice or absurd ideas, acquired Greek knowledge, which was quite advanced at that time. We were not prejudiced against learning from the Greeks, who believed in three gods instead of one and worshiped the cross instead of God. We learned from and were not prejudiced against the Jews who, like us, believed in one God and in those elders whom we call prophets, but who did not believe in our Prophet, the Messenger, may God bless him and grant him peace, and many other prophets that we believe in. We spread our hands in front of the enemies of our prophets and asked them too to give us whatever they had to give. This proves that our leaders had no religious bias to learn and acquire knowledge from men of other faiths. We took very little from them and advanced it so much and spread it around that from a seed it became a magnificent and shady tree.

Then we did not keep the benefits to ourselves. Instead, in the same way that we acquired it with an open mind and large-heartedness, we gave it away without prejudice and with graciousness to whomever asked for it, and made a big part of the world beholden to us. Which people of Europe were storied for their knowledge? The same people who had acquired knowledge from the Muslims who are now sinking. To which people did the schools belong to in which the European students were proud to be admitted, and when they returned to their home countries, those countries would be proud of them? To the same Muslims whose people are now sinking. Suffice it to say, we did not show prejudice in acquiring knowledge, nor in disseminating it. Now the tide has changed. God has made the English our rulers and the keys of the treasures of knowledge have gone around and landed in their hands. Hence, we must now acquire that knowledge and the arts from them with much gratitude. If you do not want to show gratitude, then at least recover the debt owed to your forefathers. If we haven't done it so far, it is stupidity, not prejudice.

But I want to mitigate this stupidity as well to some extent. Think about how much the Muslims had advanced in their knowledge. They thought they had reached such heights and such high levels that no one else had reached. They thought they had reached beyond the heavens, and the truth at that time was not far from that. The same hereditary idea has reached us. We did not look at our incompetence, but we did not abandon this thought, and we looked down with contempt at the nations that had made modern progress in this knowledge without examining it. We did not even look up at the tree that bloomed from the seed we had planted and which the people of other nations trimmed and made beautiful with all kinds of fruits and flowers. It is very natural that a person who considers himself big has trouble seeing someone else as big. This was the main reason for this negligence. It wasn't all stupidity but human nature that came into play. But thanks to God that curtain is being raised now and things are beginning to change. Time itself has good advice. It has flogged us a lot. It says you must walk now, there is no place to sit. Perhaps a few more flogs are needed. When they strike, we shall surely walk. May God make it so.

You have given me the honor that I have made some improvements to the Urdu language. Perhaps this notion is correct, but at a time when such an eloquent and elegant writer as Maulvi Nazir Ahmed is in front of my eyes, when Maulvi Mohammad Husain Azad is here in Lahore, when Maulana Hali is sitting here next to me, when my friend whose pistol-shots you just heard [*Munshi Ahmed Ali Shauq*] is present here, and when we have heard of the fame of Munshi Amir Ahmed *Saheb*, although I have not seen him, then when I hear that I have served Urdu in some way, it gives me pause. Only a day has passed since you heard the Urdu lecture of the pride of our Delhi, Maulvi Nazir Ahmed *Saheb*. Perhaps there is no other person who could give such an eloquent lecture in which both the eloquence of Urdu and scholarly wisdom are present. He is a fixture of Delhi and a poet, and the few Urdu couplets he recited that you heard were so elegant. All of you gentlemen must have heard of Maulana Hali's "*Musaddas.*" It is a lamentation for the community that is spoken by the tongue and descends into the heart. All these people are the suns that have paid attention to reforming Urdu. I am only feeding on their leftovers and a gleaner of their benefaction, nothing more than that.

O my friends! You have mentioned the Muhammadan Educational Congress in your address. Your mention of it is very timely. I am very happy that this third annual session of the congress is taking place with such excellence in Lahore. Undoubtedly it is a matter of great joy. I join in the hope that has been expressed and the prayers that have been said for its usefulness and ask God that your community be blessed with much more blessings from this gathering than you have expressed the desire for. But I don't want to hide the truth. This is the third annual session. I think about two things regarding these sessions. The first thing is trivial, or perhaps it is not but it is first and foremost, that every year this gathering of Muslims takes place in which there is neither any dancing, nor any color or spectacle. There are just discussions about education for which so many Muslims gather to listen with a lot of interest and talk about nothing but education. If these sessions continue to be held like this, then I acknowledge one benefit to surely come from it and accept that it will certainly happen.

But, my friends! To only make talk is in my opinion not worth more than expressing quixotic ideas. Speeches are given with heartfelt passion seemingly giving rise to a movement, but there is no outcome except a lot of academic discussions. Someone reads a poem, some others say 'bravo, bravo,' and yet others scold and rebuke. Everyone is out to please their hearts, and then nothing happens. The matter pleased everyone in the congress, on which everyone agreed, on which they gave impassioned speeches, expressed their heart's discontent, and then everyone dispersed and went away, flying away like sparrows. Then there is no thought given to it, none of that heartache is expressed, none of those plaints are heard, let alone any action on it. Now this is the third session that is being held in Lahore. Our friends in Lahore are brave, their hearts are on fire, they are flag bearers of elite families, they have influence over our community as well; I am hopeful that the people of Lahore will not be like that and disappoint the congress with the lack of real results. The real purpose of the congress is to implement the resolutions that have been passed and make every effort to bring them into action. When this happens there can be expectations and we can expect God to help, otherwise they are only prayers.

You have written something very accurate in your address. In my opinion, not only the people of Punjab but also those from the North-Western Provinces and Awadh should be sincerely grateful to Corniel Halride *Saheb*. As much as I could, I looked at the books from Calcutta, Madras, and Bombay universities prescribed by him in schools, but the books that were translated in connection with education in Punjab or were written in Urdu are so excellent in terms of their contents and so cultured in terms of their language that there are none like them and are unmatched for the purpose of general education. Thanks to him and his efforts, there are these useful books now present in the country, but I will say with pride that this work was done by the same people of Delhi that are around him.

In any case, whoever they may be, a sword does not work in the hands of those who are not skillful. But the sword was in the hands of Corniel Halride; the sword was excellent as well and he showed very good skills with it. I value and appreciate all the books that came out in connection with education in Punjab.

Dear ones! All that I have stated is a story of heartache or gratitude for your kindness, and both these things are so lengthy that they even dwarf out the poet's definition of long, which is the lover's tresses. But a lot remains to be done by us, so I will stop here, because if you cut the long tresses of the lover and let them fall only up to her ears, they too appear strangely beautiful. With gratitude for the address, I give two pieces of counsel: as much as possible, don't abandon the respect for your elders and the medal of God (five prayer offerings).

Another thought is churning in my heart. Do not think that I am presumptuously speaking ill of someone, but I want to say something that is in my heart. I regret to say that the consumption of alcohol is increasing among people. What our God and His Messenger called '*Umm al-Khaba'ith*,' or "mother of all vices," is becoming customary among Muslims as well. O my dearest ones! People think that this is the effect of English education. You must beware of this and not become an example of this suggestion that English education and consumption of alcohol go hand in hand. Along with other vices that can be born from *Umm al-Khaba'ith*, this vice could be a huge stumbling block for the education of our community, in which we all are putting our efforts. All you Muslim students should form a strong association and make an effort to ensure that no one in your circle is falling into this habit. There is good in that for this world as well as the hereafter.

I thank you again for your kindness and pray to God to give you blessings for both the worlds. May God accept my prayer. Amen.

139

Sir Syed's Act at the Penny Reading Theater

(Collection of Lectures Including a Brief Biography, compiled by Munshi Muhammad Sirajuddin, Lahore, 1890)

Sir Syed also performed theater to collect donations for the *Madrasatul Uloom* and came on stage to playact as well. On February 6, 1889, at the annually occurring *Numaish* [*Exhibition/Fair*], a play was arranged. On this occasion, the speech that he gave to the community while playing a role is entered below.

Ladies and Gentlemen!

Who among you is surprised to see me on stage today? Only those who don't feel the pain of their community, those who are filled with false bravado and false pride. Woe unto them who consider those things that bring shame, indignation, and dishonor to the community to be the reason for their pride and honor. Woe unto the community that considers those things that are done for the welfare of mankind, which are done in good faith for good intentions and kindness, to be dishonorable. Woe unto that community which deceives God by covering their face with a veil of sanctity made of the black thread of conceit and arrogance but doesn't seek any redress for its ugliness and the evil in their hearts. Woe unto those who sees their community drown in a sea of humiliation and misery and sits there laughing. With open treasures in their homes, they act with such shamelessness and immodesty that it would put shamelessness and immodesty to shame, but they consider working for the welfare of the community to be shameful and a curse.

O *Raïses*! And the wealthy! Don't be proud of your riches and wealth and think that no matter how bad the state of the community is, your children have more than enough. That was also the thought of those people who came before you and now their children are in that condition for which we stand here on this stage.

O gentlemen! Everyone admits that without education the condition of the community deteriorates day by day. The community has become poor and without their ability to meet the expenses for the education of their children, they are being further humiliated and debased. I did not leave any stone unturned to find financial support for the expenses of the education of the poor children of our community, but it is a pity that I did not find success. I begged people myself but found scant support. I tried to recruit volunteers but found very few and those who did volunteer could not do much. So, I have come on this stage today for the same purpose, to do something for the education of the children of our community.

Ladies and European gentlemen! I know very well all that you have done for the poor children of your nation. Many a grand duke and duchess have come on stage and have found honor in helping poor children. Here too, at this time, Europeans have proved their large-heartedness that they are with us despite the fact that they are not from our community. In a short while, our European friend and district collector, Mr. Kennedy - no, no, my friend Mr. Kennedy - will appear on this stage. But Indians do not have that thought, that desire or that kind-heartedness that is the basis of such work. This is the first time in India that I stand on a stage for this community work. I will do as much as I can for the welfare of my community and I will do it with determination, and I will let the people rant and rave as they want. What is it that people have not said about me, and I will be happy if they will say whatever else remains and be done with it. At this time I will read a [*Persian*] poem by Hafiz *Saheb*, may God bless him and grant him peace, which is appropriate to my feelings and to which I have added two couplets[3].

Up, *Saqi*! Let us pay the wine's wage;

And strew with dust the sorrow of our age;

Give me the wine cup; that when filled with glee,

From this blue-hued cloak, I may set myself free.

---

[3]. Translation of the poem "Silvern Cypress Tree" excerpted from "The Selected Poems of Hafiz," translated by Ali Salami, Mehrandish Books, Tehran, 2016, except the two couplets in italics added by Sir Syed.

Wise men may think me bare to shame;
But I do not care for name or fame.

Bring me wine! How many a man lost,
With wind of pride the honor for dust?

My heart fumes, my sighs so loud,
Scorched yon rough cruel crowd.
The secret of my mad heart, none can know,
Even the people of both high and low.

Even by that sweetheart charmed am I,
Who once from my heart magic sweetness flew.

The one who once saw my Silvern tree,
Can he see the cypress that in the turf can be?

Whose head is it that's head and shoulders above all
I find faith and heart and peace in
Our people, O our people, it is because of you
I have given name and fame to the wind

Hafiz! Be patient in adversity night and day,
Till you will see a bed of roses on your way.

After Sir Syed had recited this poem, six more poems were sung. Some dignified gentlemen also sang some verses of poems. Some roles were played and some Arabic couplets were recited in a melodious voice. After that, this one of a kind theater ended. It is worth mentioning that some professors of the college participated with Sir Syed in the theater as actors.

★

140

A Speech Regarding the History of the
Madrasatul Uloom Musalmanan

(December 27, 1889 in Aligarh)

On December 27, 1889 the fourth annual session of the Muhammadan Educational Congress commenced in Aligarh and lasted till December 30, 1889. In the first meeting of the session, Sir Syed gave a lengthy lecture on the topic "An Historical Perspective of the *Madrasatul Uloom* Aligarh and Recent Events," which was published as a supplement to the report of the fourth annual session of the Muhammadan Educational Congress as well as a stand-alone publication.

Mr. President of the session!

There is no doubt that the *Madrasatul Uloom* Aligarh, in whose biggest (but sadly unfinished) hall you are enjoying your meetings, is a very big institution which has been established for the education of the community, and for that reason it is closely associated with our Muhammadan Educational Congress. Hence, it is very appropriate that to inform the many elders of the community gathered in this hall, I discuss this from a historical perspective of the institution and in light of the recent events. My lecture will not be for the purpose of inciting passion in the hearts of the listeners for any action nor for the purpose of claiming that I am a great speaker and eliciting praise for the eloquence and elegance of my speech. Rather my purpose is to inform the community of the state of the college in clear words. I cannot forget in my heart the lesson learned from an incident that turned a person away from both religion and worldly affairs and immersed him in love and compassion for the community, and in fact it is that incident which is the first stone in the foundation of this college. Although I never wanted to reveal this incident, now I cannot remain without revealing it.

The wretched era of the 1857 Mutiny has not faded from the minds of the people. I was in Bijnor at that time and saw the disaster that befell the then English and Christian administrators, men, women, and children. Just based on the idea that it would be remote from humanity not to stand with them in their time of trouble, I stood with them. It is heart-wrenching to hear even the mention of the events of what the Englishmen, women, and children had to endure in the Mutiny and the effect it had on the renowned families of our community getting ruined and devastated. After the Mutiny, the sadness I feel is not for my house getting looted nor for the destruction of my property and belongings; the sadness I feel is for the ruining of my community and what the English suffered at the hands of Indians. When my friend, the late Mr. Shakespeare[4], in whose miseries I participated and who participated in mine, in return for the said loyalty, wanted to bestow upon me the Taluq (subdivision) of Jahanabad, which belonged to an eminent Syed family and had an annual income from it exceeding Rs. 100,000, I was shocked. I said to myself that there is probably no one whose actions would be more unworthy than mine that my community is in ruins and here I am taking their property and becoming a Taluqdar. I refused to take it from him [*Mr. Shakespeare*] and told him that I do not intend to stay in India, and in fact it was absolutely true. At that time I did not think at all that the community would thrive again and would gain any respect, and I could not bear to see the state that the community was in. I stayed in those thoughts and with that sadness for a few days. Believe me, this sadness made me old and turned my hair gray. And when I came to Moradabad, which was a sorrowful location due to the devastation of many of the *Raïses* of our community, this sadness deepened somewhat. But at that time the thought arose that it would be a matter of great failure and disregard if I left my community in such a state of devastation to retreat into a corner of comfort. No, one should stay with it in its time of distress and should have the courage to make efforts to remove whatever is causing it distress; it is one's duty toward his community. I suspended the idea of emigration and embraced the idea of empathy for the community.

I did not embrace it, but I don't know who embraced it and who was inclined toward it. The politically charged days of the Mutiny were still ongoing when I

[4.] Sir Syed was a Sadr-e-Amin, deputy to the chief justice, in Bijnor when the 1857 Mutiny began. Sir Syed saved the life of Mr. Shakespeare, Collector of Bijnior, his family and many other Englishmen by personally staying awake to guard their house. The gift of the estate was in return for this act.

wrote a book on the innocence of the community which is titled "Causes of the Indian Revolt." I do not wish to describe those times and what my friends believed would become of me as a result of this passionate empathy for the community, which I myself can call madness, that was about to engulf me. My first sentiment was compassion for the community, my sympathizers were an impediment, and my heart would say to them:

O hermit, you are not a rival of his bloodthirsty explorations
First acquire a jugular, then watch the spectacle of the lancet

During the same time, I wrote a few articles and published them, which are well known under the title "Loyal Mohammedans of India," but I thought about them and realized that they are not of primary importance. We should think about the real reason why the community is in such distress and how it can be relieved. The answer I got was that the community lacked education and nurturing, it had no harmony and unity with the English, whom God had appointed to rule over us, and there was mutual dislike between the two based on religious and traditional differences, a hostility based on the proverbial water beneath the grass delusions. I believed that if these two things weren't there, the events of the Mutiny would not have occurred, and if they had, they would not have produced such a disaster for the government, the country, and our community.

Then I asked my heart if the education of the community according to the needs of the time and the dissemination of European knowledge among them was actually against Islam. The answer I got was no. Then I wondered if true friendship with the English, who were our rulers, and with Christians in general, and guileless unity, heartfelt friendly harmony, amicable socializing, and mutual compassion with them was against Islam. The answer I got was no. Hence, I adopted the same two principles and girded my loins to act for the welfare of the community based on those principles, which I will never abandon. When I had firmly established those two principles for the betterment of the community, one being education and the other true unity and friendship with the English, I established a school in Moradabad in early 1858 when no such school existed there. But, with the favors of Sir John Strachey, a combined Urdu-English school was established there.

Then I went to Ghazipur where I laid the foundation for a school where Urdu, English, Arabic, and Persian would be taught. Its foundation stone was laid by the hands of my friend the late Sardev Narayan Singh and *Janab* Maulana Muhammad Fasih, may God bless him. That school has been running quite successfully and is known by the name Victoria School.

My thought at that time was that I would provide the benefit of high level European knowledge and the arts to our community by means of translations into Urdu. I put my efforts into it and in 1864 the Scientific Society was established whose magnificent building you see right here in Aligarh. Many books were translated into Urdu and one of its newspapers is still published under my supervision. I do not deny the fact that translating books into Urdu is without a doubt useful for the country, but I am now certain that the high level of education and nurturing that the community needs, the advancement of its social conditions, and harmony between the ruler and the ruled, which are the objectives of my creed, cannot be achieved without studying English and achieving an advanced level in European knowledge and literature. I would think about all these things and not know what to do.

At that time, the government of the North-Western Provinces selected Syed Mahmood to go to London for his education. For that I am much obliged, first of all, to Sir John Strachey, and after that to Sir William Muir and the late Lord Lawrence. I also got the opportunity to go to London and become familiar with those methods of education and nurturing by which the English nation has achieved such a high degree of progress. I went there, I stayed there, and I saw what I saw and thought what I thought, but what I did realize was that our community had fallen in such a deep and dark pit with regards to both religious and secular awareness that it seemed impossible to climb out, and if you will excuse me, still seems near impossible in certain parts of the provinces. But I did not lose courage and will not lose it for as long as I live.

In London itself, I decided to establish this school and completed all the proposals for it. In fact, the design plans of the buildings that you see coming up around here were finalized in London. Unfortunately I am not familiar with English. I am very grateful to Syed Mahmood for the help he rendered in all my assimilation of familiarity and information. I am very happy to admit that had it not been for his help, the purpose for which I had gone to London would have remained unaccomplished.

It would be unjust to say that the concept of the boarding house and the method by which the school is run and will continue to run were devised and established by me. In fact, it should be clearly stated that a large part of it was proposed by Syed Mahmood from his own familiarities and after discussions and consultations with his capable friends.

Syed Mahmood was of the opinion that the college should be of such a high grade that all the European knowledge and the arts along with the Asian knowledge that was the pride of our elders be taught there at a high level, and the college be known as the Mohammedan University. He is of the opinion that Arabic and Persian literature is an emblem of the Muslim community that we should never abandon. He is very sorry for the closure of the Oriental department, which was established in the school solely on his proposal. He always puts the blame on me for not patronizing it, but that thought of his is wrong. The state of the country is such that it could not continue. He has a firm intention of establishing it himself at some point. May God grant him success in that. Suffice it to say, when the proposals were finalized, I decided to return from London, after establishing three ways in London itself to start this important work:

- First, such a plan should be adopted which would dispel the general prejudices held by Muslims and the idea that studying European knowledge and literature amounts to infidelity and is against the religion of Islam.

- Second, Muslims themselves should be asked why they do not study European sciences and literature and what they are worried about in doing so.

- Third, donations for the college should be started and to establish the college in Aligarh when the opportunity arises. In London itself, the location had been determined to be Aligarh.

After returning to India, as per the first proposal, I launched *Tehzeeb-ul-Akhlaq*. Do you know that the tape that gets printed on it which contains its name and has the border of a beautiful vine was designed and typeset in London itself and I brought it with me? Although there was a lot of opposition to *Tehzeeb-ul-Akhlaq*, and many newspapers and pamphlets were launched to oppose it, it met with a lot of success. But if the people's opinion is true that *Tehzeeb-ul-Akhlaq* shook up all of India and persuaded the people toward empathy for the community, then perhaps it will be enough for my salvation as well.

According to the second proposal, a committee was established and the name given to it was "Committee for the Development of Education of Indian Muslims." Through the use of replies to articles, the opinions of the general Muslims were solicited. You may not be surprised to learn that an announcement related to this was printed in London itself, and the articles to which responses were solicited were written and proposed by Syed Mahmood. The committee had a lot of successes and its work ended with a big success.

The intention of the third proposal was nothing but the establishment of the college. In 1872, a committee was established in Banaras to collect donations which was named "Mohammedan Anglo-Oriental College Fund Committee," and its work started with a lot of successes. In its June 30, 1872 meeting, the committee established sub-committees in various locations for the purpose of collecting donations. One of these sub-committees was established in Aligarh and Maulvi Muhammad Samiullah Khan *Saheb*, Raja Syed Baqar Ali Khan *Saheb*, the late Muhammad Inayatullah Khan, Kunwar Muhammad Lutf Ali Khan *Saheb*, and Munshi Muhammad Mushtaq Husain *Saheb* were appointed as its members.

In the same year, a proposal was presented in the committee meeting in Banaras regarding where the school should be established. After inquiries, suggestions, and opinions, in the November 27, 1872 meeting, it was decided that the school would be established in Aligarh.

In the February 10, 1873 meeting, Syed Mahmood presented a comprehensive proposal for general education which he had prepared in London after consultation with competent professors and scholars there. If the school reaches the level of that type of education, the fortunes of the community will brighten, but it will take a long time to get to that level.

In the April 14, 1873 meeting, there was a debate about establishing small schools in various locations which would come under the *Madrasatul Uloom* and become branches of it. After soliciting the opinions of the members and discussions on this topic, in the May 3, 1873 meeting, many rules and regulations were laid down for the establishment of subordinate schools in locations other than Aligarh. For the Aligarh location, Maulvi Samiullah Khan Bahadur CMG was requested to plan for the opening of the primary school and to make efforts to solicit donations from the *Raïses* there. As a result he endeavored and for that we should be grateful to him.

In the January 10, 1874 meeting the committee accepted several proposals:

1. The government should be asked for the land that is lying unutilized in the old cantonment area of Aligarh.
2. The secretary was given the permission to start work on the construction of the school if the land is made available. But cash and capital of the school

should not be spent on it and only interest or income from it and funds donated specifically for construction should be used.

In the March 19, 1874 meeting, the secretary reported that the government had promised to grant the land where the *Madrasatul Uloom* had been proposed to be established. Adjacent to the land that the government had agreed to grant were four bungalows owned by individuals that needed to be purchased. Maulvi Samiullah Khan *Saheb* announced the purchase of three of these bungalows for the sum of Rs. 15,000 and requested that if the committee could grant Rs. 8000, he would arrange for the remaining Rs. 7000 from the donations received in the fund raising drive that he had recently started. He also requested that the Rs. 2000 that Raja Syed Baqar Ali Khan had given to the Sadar committee in Banaras should be included in the fund he had opened in Aligarh. Consequently, the name of Raja *Saheb* was removed by the Sadar committee from its list.

On October 4, 1874 all the three bungalows were bought but Maulvi Samiullah Khan *Saheb* asked for an additional Rs. 2000 for the cost of the bungalows. These additional funds were sent from Banaras and the committee approved the transfer of these funds in its October 17, 1873 meeting. The fourth bungalow, in which the union club is currently housed, was purchased by the committee from its owner who was in Lucknow.

In the January 25, 1875 meeting, the Banaras committee proposed to open an elementary school in Aligarh and the following resolution was passed.

Resolution No. 3: All the members except the secretary agreed that an elementary school should be started and Maulvi Samiullah Khan *Saheb* should be requested to present a proposal for how many teachers should be appointed, what their salaries should be, and what subjects and languages should be taught. It would be better if he would consult and seek advice on this matter from his sub-committee as well as his friends and submit a report to the committee. The expenses required should include rent for the building in which the school would be opened.

I was completely in favor of this proposal and to remove my name from the resolution was not for the purpose of opposition to it, because everyone knows that if my opinion and consent was not in favor of starting this education, then no other member of the committee would have given a contrary opinion. Maulvi Muhammad Samiullah Khan *Saheb* sent his report and proposed an expenditure of Rs. Rs. 857 per month for salaries of the teachers and Rs. 132 per month for establishing scholarships, for a total expenditure of Rs. 989 per month. The Banaras committee approved this expenditure in its April 18, 1875 meeting and wrote to Maulvi Samiullah Khan *Saheb* to open the school starting June 1, 1875 and to advertise this in the newspapers.

Later, in its May 20, 1875 meeting, the committee in Banaras changed the starting date of the school and decided for it to be on May 24, 1875, that day being the birthday of Her Majesty the Queen, and wrote to Maulvi Samiullah Khan *Saheb* that the opening ceremony of the school should be held on that day. Consequently, I myself and a few members came to Aligarh on that date and the school was opened.

At the time it was decided to open a school in Aligarh, I decided to take pension and informed the High Court through Judge *Saheb* that I intend to take pension, asked the Accountant General for the retirement plan, and requested that my tenure and pension entitlement be confirmed. It took however long it did for the completion of this process and in mid-1876 I came to Aligarh. This is also the intent of Syed Mahmood, that for his patronage of the college he will take up residence in Aligarh, the time for which is not far away. He advised me that the house I had in Aligarh, which had been mortgaged to pay for the expenses of the trip to London, is small, and to sell it and pay off the mortgage from the proceeds. He suggested that he will buy another house that will be big enough for both of us to live in. Consequently, Syed Mahmood bought the house in which I currently live. I sold my house to Maulvi Samiullah Khan *Saheb*, in which God-willing he will come and live and put his efforts into the development and completion of the school.

After that the elementary school was opened. All the expenses were paid in installments by the College Fund Committee. In the early months of 1875, Rs. 5766, 7 *ana*, and 9 *pai* were sent by the committee from Banaras and in the same way, till the headquarters of the fund was moved to Aligarh, all the expense money was regularly sent to Maulvi Samiullah Khan Bahadur.

At that time, the number of students was small and there was no boarding house. The students were packed into small classrooms but gradually there was progress and improvement all around. The construction work that I had started also progressed. It was our intent that the foundation-stone laying ceremony would be performed by the hands of the Viceroy, Earl Northbrook, but that intention could not be fulfilled due to his sudden departure. In the time of Lord Lytton, after the establishment of the court of Qaisar-i-Hind, it was decided that the foundation-stone laying ceremony would be performed by the hands of Lord Lytton. On January 8, 1877 the honorable *Huzoor* came to Aligarh and in an extremely formal ceremony, the foundation stone was laid.

The grand *Raïs* of our province, Haji Harmain-Sharifain Nawab Kalb Ali Khan Bahadur, *Khuld-e-Ashiyan*[5], Wali Rampur, who was a patron and a mentor of the school, stated that the expenses for the foundation ceremony and dinner for Lord Lytton would be borne by him, but the generous *Raïs* of our district, Kunwar Muhammad Lutf Ali Khan *Saheb*, who was the president of the committee, desired that the ceremony and the dinner be given on his behalf and be sponsored by him, and our courageous Raja Syed Baqar Ali Khan *Saheb*, vice-president of the committee, desired that it be on his behalf and sponsored by him. Maulvi Muhammad Samiullah Khan found it expedient for the ceremony to be jointly sponsored by the two *Raïses*. Following that, I corresponded with His Excellency Lord Lytton through his private secretary, and through the efforts and with the recommendation of Sir John Strachey, Lord Lytton accepted the invitation. I thanked His Highness Nawab of Rampur for his generosity and the foundation ceremony was conducted on behalf of the two *Raïses*, for which we thank them and are grateful for their kindness. After the foundation ceremony, when His Excellency Lord Lytton reached Simla by way of Calcutta, he honored the president of the committee, Kunwar Muhammad Lutf Ali Khan, by awarding him the Qaisar-i-Hind medal. We had a tribute to his beneficence inscribed in pleasing letters on beautiful pieces of stone and had it installed in two rooms of the college and had a plaque honoring *Janab* Maulvi Muhammad Samiullah Khan installed in another room.

The school, which was opened in 1875 for education up to the entrance level, advanced to the FA level in 1878, and to the BA and MA levels in 1889. The elders of all environs and all those who wished for the welfare of the community, in fact all those who wanted to do good for humanity, in particular the braveheart elders of Punjab, the *Walis* of estates and its various nobles and *Raïses*, and especially the Islamic State of Hyderabad were very generous with their assistance. It is obligatory on me to personally express my extreme gratitude particularly to these elders for trusting an insignificant person such as me and entrusting me with hundreds of thousands of rupees in donations. They never asked the

---

[5] 'The late, with his abode in Heaven'

committee nor any member for an accounting of where and how the money that they gave was spent.

I cannot be so proud of any work I have done in my life as I am of the trust and reassurance that the elders of our community and from outside have bestowed upon me.

Initially, when the College Fund Committee was formed, which was actually going to establish the college, it laid down some brief by-laws that suited its needs at the time. Then it amended and modified these by-laws as per the needs that arose as the college grew. In 1883, modern by-laws were adopted that were appropriate at the time. For the management of the college and to provide proper education, the College Fund Committee proposed to establish under its authority and supervision four more committees in which many of the College Fund Committee members were included.

One of the committees included thought leaders for the teaching of different languages and secular knowledge. This committee included our European friends with whom it was necessary to consult and from whom it was necessary to take advice on educational matters.

One committee included thought leaders for the teaching of '*Ahl al-Sunnah wa'l-Jamā'ah*' and a parallel committee for the teaching of Shia '*Imamia Asna Asharia*'. Another committee was for the administration of the school's boarding house.

These committees made many regulations and guidelines at different times and as needed based on which the administration and operation of the school was carried out.

But the college and its properties had developed so much and people had so much confidence in it that people deposited thousands of rupees in the committee for the education of their sons, which is still in the accounts of the committee. Besides that, many other reasons arose for why it was becoming untenable for the committee to be in charge of the general operation of the college and it became necessary to appoint trustees as per the prevalent government laws at the time. It also became necessary to draft new regulations for this purpose which would apply to all the requirements and components of the college, and to include in it the process that was being implemented then so that no activity would be outside the laws and rules. This would also ensure, as much as possible, that the future stability and survival of the college was maintained according to the scale and objectives that I had envisioned.

Our European friends, who care about the welfare and progress of our college, and especially Mr. Waite, the Director of Public Instruction, would give us friendly advice that the state of the college was now such that it had become extremely necessary to formally appoint trustees and to create a school code for all its activities. In view of all these circumstances, in the members' meeting held on March 11, 1888, I presented this matter and took permission to appoint trustees and establish a code of laws and regulations. I also took permission to appoint Mr. Strachey, barrister-at-law, to compile the code. The committee approved this motion and I, with the participation of Syed Mahmood and Mr. Strachey, prepared the compendium of laws and regulations which is under discussion currently. Since many of the articles to be included were with reference to European staff, Principal *Saheb* was included in the compilation of those portions so that there would be no objections later.

Although there were 82 members in our College Fund Committee, according to the existing rules it was not required to solicit their opinions on any matter or to inform them about proposals and arrangements. Only five men could come together and do whatever they wanted. This was actually quite a harmful and inappropriate way of doing things. I think that all the elders never objected to those inappropriate ways because they had full faith in me. But with this modern law of trustees, this defect has been removed.

In its sections 22-23, a rule has been made that three days prior to each meeting, the trustees should be notified of the date of the meeting in writing via registered mail and the status of each matter to be presented in the meeting should also be made available to them. Then, in section 30, a rule has been made that if a trustee cannot attend a meeting, he can send his vote in writing to the secretary. In this manner, all trustees will be able to participate in future proceedings, they will be more interested in and familiar with all the operations of the college, and no longer will the secretary or any member have the authority to get five men together and do whatever they want.

The rule for the election of trustees has been made in such a way that elders of each province are included among the trustees. The number of trustees has been distributed across all provinces. For example, so many from Punjab, so many from the North-Western Provinces, so many from the Hindustani provinces, so many from Hyderabad, etc., etc. The trustees have been empowered to increase or change this distribution. Through this arrangement, the people of every province will be able to have a say in the operation of the college and have an interest in it.

In order for proceedings to commence, as is customary in the laws governing trustees, a group of people had to be named as trustees. I selected a few elders from each province who were members of the College Fund Committee and nominated them as trustees. I also included the list of members that I had not selected to be trustees so that any of them could be nominated as trustees. From among the noble families of Aligarh and Bulandshahr districts, a trustee was chosen from each family regardless of whether they were against or in favor. I believe that I have performed this function with great sincerity and good intention, but unfortunately my action was perceived as mala fide and a provocation intended to rouse those who had not been nominated as trustees. In the latter they were somewhat successful, to the extent that an elder who had not been nominated as a trustee wrote that "if all of the 82 members had been appointed trustees, this storm tide of opposition would not have arisen. And a windstorm of objections would not have blown." Apart from this, there are also objections to the remaining members not being given the right to vote along with the trustees.

O gentlemen! In the draft law concerning the trust, the total number of trustees has been set at 70. Out of them, only 49 have been appointed. At that time, it was not necessary for me to appoint all the trustees; in fact it was necessary to leave some room for the appointed trustees to be able to name other trustees if they wanted to.

The statement that all the members of the College Fund Committee were life members and that all of them, without any exception, had the right to become trustees is not correct. With the appointment of the trustees, the College Fund Committee stands *abolished*, i.e. it is dismissed. Its members had the right to be life members of that committee as long as it existed. When the committee has been *abolished*, then no member remains nor will there be any member in the future. What is the logic in not dismissing that committee during the life of its members and not bringing modern practices into operation?

As much as possible, I have tried to accommodate them in the draft law, but how can they be able to vote along with the trustees? According to the existing rules, the members of the College Fund Committee have only the authority to vote for approval or disapproval of the expenses of the college. This authority was also not necessarily given to all members. Now the trustees have been entrusted with a wide range of authorities and to make the final decision on all matters related to the college. Hence, they [*members of the committee*] have no right to vote in all those matters.

According to the existing rules, convening a meeting of the members depended only on the opinion and wish of the secretary. The members did not have the absolute authority to insist on convening a meeting for any purpose based on any rule. In the recent draft law, four ways to convene a meeting have been established: 1) when the secretary deems it necessary for any purpose, 2) when a third of the trustees deem it necessary, 3) the annual meeting at the end of the calendar year in which matters related to the reform of rules and regulations and other necessities and operations are considered and discussed, and 4) at the end of the financial year in which the general accounts related to the college are examined, and considering the income and expenditure of the college, the budget for the following year is approved.

This method of operation is very good and stable, and perhaps satisfactory to all the trustees. But one big problem that it faced was that if all the components were made to depend on this process, especially those matters that must be executed or managed immediately and are required to be completed sooner rather than later in the interest of the college, then the performance of work, administration of the college, and in many situations the education and convenience of the students would suffer. Therefore, to solve this problem, a few other rules were inserted in the draft law.

Among all the issues, one matter is related to the budget. The budget of the college's income and expenditure that is prepared contains two types of incomes. One is that which comes from government or municipal grants, landed estates, stipends established by the nobles of the country, capital gains, rents from buildings, tuition and fees collected from students, etc. These incomes are spent on the salaries of the officers and other employees of the college and all other expenses related to education, and a part of this income, as much as possible, is earmarked for students' scholarships and stipends.

The second type of income is that which comes from grants given by the well-wishers of the community for students' scholarships and stipends or money that is acquired through other means for this purpose. This type of income is not spent on anything but scholarships and stipends. If money from one of these types of income is leftover at the end of the year after expenses, it is not spent for any other purpose but is instead reserved for this type of expense in the following year.

One attribute of the compilation of the budget is that income and expenses are entered in it as estimates. The result is that in some years the income is equal to the estimate and in some years it is more or less than the estimate. The same is the case with the expenses. In some years, such necessary expenses are incurred that the expenditure exceeds the estimate or exceeds the estimate of that category of expenses.

The money is only for the expenses of the college. Therefore, if there is a surplus in any category and the need arises in another category, and to use the money from one category for another requires the process outlined above for the trustees to approve, there will be so much delay in its completion that no work will get done and all the objectives will suffer. That is why the secretary has been given permission to transfer money from one category of expense into another as necessary. In fact, it is not that the money belongs to just two categories, it is part of the total sum for expenses. It has also been stipulated that if the secretary has, as per his discretion, reallocated Rs. 500 or more in the existing financial year, he will need to present a reason to the trustees in their meetings for approval of any further reallocation of funds in that financial year.

O gentlemen! Our hard work is only for the welfare of our community. It is now acknowledged in all of India that the condition of the Muslims is such that those who are actually destined to get educated and through whom the honor of the community will remain established cannot continue their education to a higher level without assistance. Sometimes, as a matter of fact, often, it happens that the amount allocated to scholarships and stipends in the budget has been exhausted and then a few competent, intelligent, and worthy students from noble families are admitted who cannot continue their education without assistance. To my mind, it is the foremost duty of the college to help them immediately if it can. For that reason, section 130 permits the secretary to grant scholarships in excess of the allocation for it if the budget allows. Sometimes it happens that the number of students in a classroom increases and the students have to be split up into two classes. Sometimes it happens that to increase the proficiency of the class, separate arrangements have to be made. There are other reasons of this sort and these are the type of arrangements that should be made immediately. Therefore, the secretary has been permitted, after consultation with the principal, to hire additional teachers if the need arises.

My elders! All these issues are not new. I have been working on them for 15 years. Now, in the draft law that has been compiled, these implementations have been organized as provisions of the law. But now there is opposition to the powers given to the secretary and there are suggestions that these powers should be withdrawn. I will be happy if these powers are withdrawn, but tell me how the work will continue.

In the same way, there is the matter of construction. As I mentioned, the College Fund Committee in its March 18, 1874 meeting gave me permission for construction of buildings without any conditions. From that time until today, I have been looking after the construction work according to my opinions and the proposed design plans. The old houses that were within the college compound and which were deemed unworthy to maintain or were irreparable were demolished. Those that were repairable were repaired. Neither the committee nor any of its members interfered, nor is there anyone among the members who is familiar with construction work, and nor is construction work such that it could be put into practice based on the various opinions of those unfamiliar with the practice of construction. Now that a complete draft law has been prepared, I have organized the process for construction under a single section. So, now the objection is that the secretary has been given too much authority, although this authority has been given to me personally and the secretary after me will not have the same authority. Along with that, I am accused of moving money from one fund to another and from being spent on one building to another building. Hence it is necessary that I describe to you the funds that exist in the college. Three separate funds have been established in the college. One is the '*Capital Fund*,' i.e. it holds a fixed capital. The principal amount in this fund cannot be spent, only interest and income from it may be spent.

The second is the '*College Expenses Fund*,' i.e. money for the operational expenses of the college. Money from this fund can be spent on all the expenses with monthly accounting and on scholarships and stipends, and, if there is money left over, on the construction of buildings. It can also happen that if there is a need for money in this fund, the amount that has been spent from it for construction purposes can be replenished from the construction fund. But the money that is earmarked specifically for scholarships and stipends cannot be used for any other purpose.

The third is the '*Building Fund*,' i.e. money for the construction of buildings. Money that comes from any source and under any name for the purpose of construction is held in this fund. Those who say that money that is for the purpose of one building is applied to another building are unfamiliar with the construction process. Construction material is not purchased separately for each room and each wall. Thousands of bricks are requisitioned or purchased together. Thousands of maunds of crushed stone for concrete is purchased in bulk. Thousands of maunds of wood, coal, and limestone are bought in one purchase. Iron beams cannot be brought from England separately for each room, rather they are bought together in counts of 50 or 100. Teak wood from Calcutta and stones from the quarries of Roopbaas or Dholpur are bought in large volumes and are paid for from the *Building Fund*, which holds the money for the construction of all the buildings, whether they are common ones or special ones. In this way, all the material is collected and buildings are gradually built. The buildings that appear necessary to be built sooner are finished quicker and the buildings that seem like they can wait are finished later. With as much construction as has been finished to date, there is no building for which particular donations were started and sufficient money collected that have not been completed, except for the boarding house of the late Muhammad Inayatullah Khan *Saheb*, given that they have allocated a place for its construction and until the construction process reaches that particular location, its construction is impossible. If the construction work is not undertaken in this way, not a brick could be overlaid on a brick.

O gentlemen! I am humbled to say that it was my own hard work and determination that you are seeing such magnificent buildings of the college and the boarding house that have been built. These are buildings that not only the people of India but tourists from Europe and America are amazed at the hard work and toil that I had to put into them through summers, winters, and monsoons. I have worked as a coolie, I have done the work of an *'overseer,'* and I have worked as an engineer. I did not hesitate to spend my own money. The reward for this has been given by our friends in this pamphlet that was printed and distributed in Aligarh, which said that the construction work is under the control of the secretary so that he can profit from it. May God reward them with more and more goodness. But my friends! I am not offended by these things. My people have called me worse things than that. If the community was not in such a dire state, why would we all be so concerned about its welfare? Sometimes I emphasize that *"our reward is only with God."* If what I have actually done for the community is truly for their benefit, I do not expect its reward from the community nor hope for a reward from God:

I say frankly that I am happy with what I have said
I am the servant of my love and free from both worlds

My elders! You will certainly acknowledge that every work that is done can reach two stages. One is that the work has been completed and all its objectives accomplished. All the means for it have been procured and nothing remains to be acquired that is essential for its success. The other stage is that it has not been completed, every aspect of it remains unfinished, and the greatest need is that of a person or persons who will take it to completion. The methods of work for these two stages are entirely different. In the first instance, you have the right to make whatever rules or regulations you want, take away the powers of whomever you wish, and bestow powers on whomever you wish. You do not have to create anything; all you have to do is just preserve and protect what has already been created and is in your hands.

But the second case is completely different from this. First something has to be created, only then you can preserve and protect it.

The state of our college has progressed only a little bit beyond a preliminary stage. Much remains to be done for it. Then, if you wish to say things that are more befitting to say once the work is completed, then you are not doing justice to the effort but doing harm to it.

People have gotten the impression that the college has accumulated a lot of money and that it has a lot of capital which can enable it to function without any difficulty. Up till now, the sources of income for the college, with a few exceptions, are as unreliable as those of the schools we scorn. And even those incomes are not sufficient to meet the expenses of the college. The first of every month is a time of calamity and hours have to be spent distressing and worrying about how and from where to distribute the salaries of the employees. In this year's budget, the expenses of the college have been estimated to be Rs. 2000 in excess of the projected income. On top of that, the situation is further exacerbated by the projection that the income could be Rs. 4000 less than expected. While we are mired in the worry about what will happen and how things will work, and place our trust in God to save us, our friends sit unconcerned giving us advice that we should come to agreements with the European staff, form a committee in London, and through it hire European staff. On what basis are these opinions expressed? What do we have that would enable us to do that? We should refrain from such advice, no matter how good they seem. Tell us those methods that would work in the current situation.

During this monsoon season, our friend Dr. Moriarty, civil surgeon, who has been entrusted with the medical care of the students, ordered that for the health of the students water drainage should be immediately facilitated from the boarding houses and the surrounding areas. An order was sent for procuring medicines from England to stock the medicine cabinets of the boarding house. Neither does the committee have the Rs. 1000 – Rs. 1200 to make a water drainage system nor does the hospital fund have the capacity to pay for the medicines. So, either you get by the way you know best or risk exposing the boarders – who are separated from the laps of affection and whose parents have sent a piece of their heart with their beloved sons in our care – to potentially deadly illnesses. Our friends sit and find faults with the wretched secretary being given so much authority and how he does things without permission from the committee. Sir! The present condition of the college is such that work cannot be done except for this way. First you have to let the college become stable and self-sufficient, then you can make rules for anything your heart desires.

There is not a single paisa in the college's *Building Fund.* The need to build some houses and to annually repair those that require it is so great that there is no way forward without it. The wretched secretary collects money by begging for it, spends his own money, and borrows money on documents prepared with his personal guarantees in order to complete these necessary tasks. While there is not a single paisa in the construction fund of the college's coffers, our friends propose rules that the secretary should not have the authority to spend on construction. Well sir! You first have to deposit money in the treasury, then you can make rules as well, remove the secretary, and do as you wish. The biggest need right now for the welfare of the community is to provide financial assistance to the students for their education in the form of scholarships and stipends. There is very little expectation from the sons of the wealthy that they will be the pride of the community. If there is any hope, it is from the sons of the noble families. But sadly it has to be acknowledged that they cannot complete their education without financial assistance. Except for a small amount, or rather a very small amount of capital, the college does not have any funds for scholarships or stipends. Every year the secretary has to beg. Friends are asked so many questions that they get tired of being asked thousands of questions every day. One has to scrounge up some money for scholarship by selling books, opening a bookstore, singing and dancing in a theater, and playing different roles. And then one starts worrying for the following year. Here, our friends ask if it happens anywhere in the world that the secretary grants more scholarships or stipends than sanctioned by the committee, no matter how great the need is. Well sir! You first have to put money in the treasury for scholarships and stipends, then you can stop anyone from spending it.

Instead of trying to solve these problems and putting efforts into procuring these means, our friends only blame me for these problems. Some say that expenditure on European staff has increased too much. Educated Bengalis can be hired for much less salary and can get the students to obtain university degrees – what else do you need? They point to colleges where only Bengalis and no Englishmen are employed, and many students there pass the FA and BA exams every year.

Some friends say no, it is necessary to have European staff. They say that they are not opposed to that, but the incompetent secretary has increased the salaries of the European staff too much. European professors can be hired at much lower salaries. O gentlemen! Do you believe that and can you work for the welfare and betterment of your community without hiring European staff who are complete '*gentlemen*'? I say that if we do not hope to achieve an outcome consistent with the scale on which we have established the college and the results that we seek from it, or if there are indications contrary to those expectations, then it is absolutely futile that we continue to keep the college established and put such a great deal of strenuous effort into it. It is not possible that we create *gentlemen* in our community without hiring fine '*gentlemen staff.*'

There is another matter which does not have an easy solution, and that is the appointment of staff in the college. All matters related to academics are the responsibility of the principal. Suppose that a master or a teacher in the school or the college is hired by the trustees but the principal does not consider him competent and is dissatisfied with his work. Also suppose that the principal's opinion is wrong and the teacher is very competent. But if the principal has lost confidence in him, then either appoint another person in place of that master or teacher, and if the same thing happens to that person as well then appoint a third person in his place, or absolve the principal of all conceivable academic responsibilities.

These issues do not arise only in our college and sometimes arise in government colleges as well, but the government has a big education machinery and it can easily replace one teacher with another, be they Indians or Europeans. What are we to do in such a situation? All we have is meagerness of resources and lack of money.

To eliminate this problem, a rule has been established that if the need arises for an Indian professor or teacher, the secretary and the principal can agree on a person and appoint him, and the appointment is approved by the trustees in their meeting. If a European professor is needed, then the principal, Syed Mahmood, through whom and by whose advice all European professors are appointed, and the secretary agree on a selection and he is appointed after the approval of the trustees.

But there is a problem related to European professors that are brought from England. When a person who resides in England is selected to be a professor at the college, a telegram is sent to inform him of his appointment and inviting him to come so that he can arrive at the college as soon as possible and assume his duties. The professor wishes to be confident without a doubt or reservation that he has been appointed to the position. So, if the confirmation of his appointment and his coming to the college is dependent on the satisfaction and the approval of the trustees in their meeting, the academics of the college suffer and the students are left unattended without the presence of a needed professor. Their studies are hampered and their preparations for the university exams are affected. If we, as per the rules, wait for the meeting of the trustees to happen and inform them of the agenda one month prior to the meeting, nothing gets done. To solve this problem, a rule has been made that if a European residing in England is needed to be at the college quickly for the purpose of teaching, then the appointment made by three persons, namely the principal, Syed Mahmood, and the secretary, will be deemed as if it has been approved by the trustees. Till date, many appointments have been made in this way. Now I have entered this process in the draft law. Objections have been made to this proposed rule and it is argued that all the authority should be vested in the trustees. Well sir! Authority should be vested in the trustees alone, but tell me how the trustees will appoint teachers, masters, and professors? And how will these problems that the college faces be eliminated and how will the work of the college go on?

The most difficult task that the college faces right now is to bring European staff from England and keep them in the college. Now we must focus on those issues that we face in bringing respectable and competent European professors from England.

The college cannot pay them the same salaries as officers of the same rank are paid by the government or professors and teachers of the same caliber are paid by the financially-aided colleges. In the employment of our college, they are neither hopeful of advancement nor of getting a pension.

Our college operates under a committee of Indians that exercises despotic authority over all its employees. Although it is sad to say, when it is true there is no shame in saying it, that there is not much confidence and reassurances that a European gentleman can have in an Indian committee.

Our college does not have the means to enter into a contract with a European officer for any length of time. For the fulfillment of the contract, a bank guarantee would be required, and no bank would guarantee a contract unless the amount of money that would be required in case of breach of contract is deposited with it in cash or promissory notes worth that much value that have been endorsed to it. Our college cannot afford to guarantee such a contract.

Furthermore, it is simply useless for our college to have professors who enter into such contracts. In our college, there is a need for such European officers who are passionate about education and have a passion in their hearts to take a distressed community, which was once famous for knowledge and grace, out of its state of backwardness and into an advanced level of knowledge and education. Without a doubt, such people are hard to find, but I say with much happiness and pride that all of our current European staff have this feeling provided we treat them with the same friendliness as they treat us and give them more honor and respect than they expect from us.

For such work as ours, there could be nothing worse than an agreement, for they will consider their duty only to the extent of the terms of the contract being fulfilled. You will always be looking over your shoulder to see if every term of the contract is being fulfilled. Education cannot be given by being on such guard and watching-out. We need a heart that imparts education to our community. Such a heart comes hand-in-hand with affection and friendship, not with agreements and contracts.

When the school started, it was difficult for us to find not just a European but a *gentleman headmaster*. Even though we did not need to get one from Europe but to find one from within India, we would never have succeeded had it not been for our friend and a friend of the college, Mr. K. Dayton. Giving attention to the matter, he brought to the college first Mr. Siddons and then Mr. Nesbit, who happened to be in India. These gentlemen had full confidence in Mr. Dayton, who was the president of one of our college system's committees, the 'Committee for the Education of Secular Knowledge and Different Languages.' Mr. Dayton, who is a very old friend of mine, personally trusted me and had a lot of confidence in me. It was our good fortune that we got a hold of Mr. Host as a result of certain fateful events, otherwise it would not have been possible for him to come to our college.

After that, the college became so advanced that it would have been in vain to search for a principal or a professor in India. To make it work, there was no other way but to get people from England who were graduates of English universities. To fulfill our purpose, it was not enough to be a graduate, but it was also necessary to be from a respectable family and have a gentlemanly disposition that would be worthy of a friendly or fraternal behavior toward us and full of paternal love for the children of our community. I assure you that if Syed Mahmood had not taken responsibility for this task and completed it, we would not have been able to acquire a single person from England. People came from England relying only on their friendship with Syed Mahmood, and through him having confidence in me. Trusting that they would have to deal with only these two persons, they came to our college without any conditions or agreements. One European gentleman, who intended to come to our college, asked Sir John Strachey in England on what terms it would be proper for him to go there. Sir John replied that the college was in the hands of Syed Ahmed and that the best condition would be if he had confidence in Syed Ahmed. O gentlemen! Everyone can claim to do everything but I too have some connection to this college and I too have some or a lot of empathy for the college. I too should understand how one can do a job that he claims to know how to do. It is my sincere belief that if in the future we have to get another European professor from England, Syed Mahmood's connections are unavailable, and the current European officers are not able to satisfy this person with regards to our disposition toward the European staff, it would be impossible to get any person to come. Everyone has the right to say that these thoughts of mine are wrong and superstitious. Hundreds of graduates of English universities wander aimlessly and all it would take is a telegram to get them here, but I cannot have confidence in that process nor can I, to be honest, leave the college in a situation that I am sure will lead to a bad and disorganized future.

When the European officers came to our college, they saw that a committee consisting of people of various temperaments, dispositions, and cultures governed it. Five men who knew neither the English language nor the needs and requirements of the Englishmen made each and every decision. Naturally, they were concerned about who would become the secretary after the current one and whether they would be able to work with him satisfactorily to carry out their functions in the college. In all fairness, their concerns are not unjustified. Unfortunately, along with this, other things happened that not only firmed up their feelings of uncertainty but convinced them of it without a doubt. Anyone just saying that they are imagining things cannot be reassuring to them. There was no desire on their part to interfere with the process of choosing the next secretary but, undoubtedly, they wished that it would be known and settled who would be the secretary after the current one. After that they would make their own decision regarding their situation. If they feel they can do the work of the college with satisfaction, they will continue, otherwise they will bid us in God's care and be on their way. Indeed, they feel that if Syed Mahmood becomes the secretary in the future, they can continue to do the work of the college satisfactorily as long as God wills.

They did not keep these thoughts hidden. They expressed these views to their European friends in the district and to those European friends who are ardent supporters of the college and well-wishers for its all-around progress.

All my European friends advised me that it would be extremely essential for the improvement of the college to keep and have sufficient confidence in the European staff, and that keeping in mind the welfare of the college, it was incumbent upon me to put it to rest very soon that Syed Mahmood will be the secretary for life after me.

In this particular matter, I regard the opinion and expedient ideas of my European friends to be more valuable than those of my Indian friends and certainly consider their expedient ideas to be more beneficial for the college, but given that Syed Mahmood is my son, I was hesitant to act on it.

Besides that, it was my duty to worry about what will happen to the college after me. To say that I leave it up to God is the thinking of pious and virtuous people. I am just a man of this world and to work the problems of this world within the confines of it is the natural desire of every person. This college is no longer a school whose administration can be done willy-nilly. By God's grace, it has advanced to a high level. Classes at the MA level are taught in it. Allahabad University, recognizing it as an advanced level college, has included its principal as an ex-officio member of the syndicate of principals. To run such a college, it is necessary to have a secretary who is himself well-versed in English knowledge and European knowledge and literature, understands English education, and can work with the principal in an advisory and consulting role in matters related to education. He should understand the state of education in the college. If there are any shortcomings, he should be able to recognize and rectify them, and as a designated representative of the college in the university, he should be capable of making proposals for their reform. He should be capable of corresponding on college matters with the director of public instruction and the Government of India on matters related to education and especially related to the education of Muslims. I myself confess that I do not have the ability to perform all these tasks. They are accomplished only with the help of Syed Mahmood. The use of the word help is improper here; in fact it should be said that Syed Mahmood carries out these tasks. Principal *Saheb* consults Syed Mahmood on matters related to academics and administration of the university. If you look into our office, you will find that all the important letters related to the college have been written or formulated by him.

There is another matter which I consider of great importance even though people consider it to be insignificant. The purpose and policy with which I established this college and the outcome of the advancement of the community for which I have endeavored should be maintained in the college after me. Syed Mahmood has been the dominant partner in these efforts in his advisory role and I am fully convinced that no one can run the college in this way except him. You can say that this idea of mine is wrong but I am compelled to say it because I have the utmost confidence in it. But yes, after a period of time, when the college is well established, any one will be able to run it. All these events, current affairs, and emotional circumstances have persuaded me to appoint Syed Mahmood as the joint-secretary for life in the proposed draft, which is actually the task he has been performing since the beginning, and as life honorary secretary after I am gone. I think that in doing so, I will receive all kinds of taunts from people and there will be no mistrust or accusation that I will not face. I say that if I consider and believe that the betterment of the community is in doing so and do not do it only for fear of reproach, then there is no bigger fraud, traitor, and enemy of the community than me. So I did what I had to do and did not fear blame and accusations. My intentions will not be judged by my friends with their nonsense, but by another ruler, for it is the Ruler of all rulers who will judge whether my intentions are good or not.

Around the same time, our friend Mr. Dayton, who is a member of the college's committee of directors and, when he was in India, was president of one of the committees, wrote a letter to me from England regarding this matter, which I would like to read to you. It goes as follows:

"My dear Syed Ahmed!
I am sorry, but not surprised, to hear that Maulvi Samiullah Khan wants to stop your efforts to give the college a strong constitution. I can easily understand your desire to appoint Mahmood as your successor and that you are afraid to insist lest it comes across as self-serving. But all those who have the welfare of the college at heart and are capable of understanding the situation will agree with you in this important decision that Mahmood should be your successor. Although I know that it will take many years for him to take charge of his duties there, I hope you will forgive me when I say that it is your duty that starting tomorrow you put aside the kinship between you and Syed Mahmood and emphasize this very diligently....This is a very dangerous time for the college and its future state depends on your actions....I urge you to be strong and push for the promulgation of the constitution. I will be very sorry if you refrain from the actions that you have started.

Place: Deptford, London   I remain, your old and dear friend,
[August 8, 1889]   K. Dayton"

O gentlemen! The winds of opposition to this proposal blew from the most unexpected direction. All those people who participate in the labors of the college when I am secretary could participate in them and assist the college even when Syed Mahmood is secretary. But unfortunately there was opposition and in such a strong way that it not only defamed those who were in opposition but the whole community. The opposition did not end with opinions but reached the level of hostility and personal malice. Magazines were printed, articles were written in newspapers, and pamphlets in English were distributed everywhere. No level of opposition was spared and in the words of Pioneer, it was proved that Muslims do not have the ability to get any major work done by consensus.

Not content with these written forms of opposition, a group of opponents was formed which held meetings and involved people in legitimate and illegitimate ways. The proceedings of the meetings of this illegitimate committee were printed and disseminated. A few resolutions were passed which noted that they passed unanimously.

You will be surprised to hear that among those who unanimously passed these resolutions was Mohammad Abdul Shakur Khan *Saheb*, *Raïs* Bhikampur, who is a serious-minded and respectable elder. The Sherwani Afghans of the district are proud of him. He wrote to me that "the purpose of holding the meeting was only to consider and consult on the draft regulations for the trustees, not to pass or approve any regulation." But in its proceedings, the passing of many resolutions are noted, many of which were to reject certain sections of the draft.

As for Syed Mahmood's appointment as joint-secretary and later becoming secretary for life, he wrote, "I had expressed the opinion that the sections that mention this provision should be amended in such a way that would allow the secretary, if he so wishes, to appoint without remuneration any trustee of his choice to be an assistant joint-secretary. There is no reason why the honorary secretary should be refused an assistant or joint-secretary from among the trustees of the college to support him if needed. I have learned through credible sources that for some years now, official written correspondence in English and reports etc. related to the *Madrasatul Uloom* are formulated from the opinions and writings of Honorable Justice Syed Mahmood. Also, the selection and appointment of European staff is done on the recommendation and planning of the Honorable Syed Mahmood. Therefore, first, the joint-secretary Honorable Syed Mahmood should, as per the desire, be the honorary secretary, but there is no privilege or necessity for him to be joint-secretary for life. After the position of honorary secretary becomes vacant, the first right to be appointed to this position would be of the joint-secretary by reason of privilege and equitable justice, for a term of three years as stipulated in the regulations for the appointment of the secretary. But there should be no honorary secretary for life, nor has any privilege been expressed to be a secretary for life. So, the points that have been made regarding the administrative capabilities of Honorable Syed Mahmud or the proof of the high level of his capabilities of all kinds that has been presented to establish that he is deserving of the honorary secretary for life position can both be practically verified in either case of the honorable gentleman being appointed to the position of joint-secretary for the first time or to the position of honorary secretary for the specified term. It would be amazing if Honorable Mr. Syed Mahmood, during his tenure as the honorary secretary, would prove himself deserving of honorary secretary for life, and the gentlemen who opposed him earlier for that position would see justice in supporting him. In such a situation, it would also be necessary that for the satisfaction of the future European staff, their special terms be agreed upon between them and the trustees of the committee so that at no time there is an appearance of mismanagement resulting from the ill-will of the European staff. This arrangement of a formal satisfaction will be established on a much more firm basis than the satisfaction of a single individual.

Per the restrictions placed by section 46, the secretary should have the authority to appoint a registrar, but from among the trustees and for a period not exceeding three months. If a longer term appointment is required or a person other than the trustees is deemed necessary to be appointed, first the approval of the trustees needs to be obtained.

Regarding sections 5 and 11 related to the number of trustees, in the meeting held on August 27, 1889, I had expressed my opinion that it is not necessary to appoint all the members as trustees due to the fact that at the time the college was established, due to a lot of opposition to it and an abundance of core supporters, the college needed to increase the number of members by any means possible and not delve into the merit and status of the members. Now that the condition of the college has progressed to the present level and all the opposition to English education and the establishment of the college has receded, it is necessary to exercise care in the selection of the members. However, at the time of writing this opinion, I looked at the list of the current members and found that some worthy and very trusted members have not been selected as trustees, such as Maulvi Muhammad Ismail Khan *Saheb*, *Raïs* Koil, Syed Akbar Husain *Saheb*, *Raïs* Allahabad and the erstwhile *Munsif Havali* Koil, etc."

But, it is a pity that the opinions of Mohammad Abdul Shakur Khan *Saheb* are not mentioned in the proceedings at all and they are contrary to the many resolutions that were said to have been passed unanimously. O gentlemen! Perhaps the Almighty sees some good in this opposition. "*And perhaps you hate a thing and it is good for you; and perhaps you love a thing and it is bad for you. And God Knows, while you know not.*" Now only one night remains in the middle and tomorrow everyone will know what the majority of the members will decide.

Regarding how information related to the European staff that was presented to the committee was dealt with, the matter had been settled in the meeting of the committee held on March 12, 1887 and relevant regulations had been established. The same rules have been included in the draft laws for trustees but no rule had been established regarding the departure of European staff. Modern regulations had to be established regarding this which have been included in the draft.

Respected gentlemen! Our college has a special status. The rules that are prescribed in the government for the departure of education related employees are not applicable to our college. When a government officer departs from his position, a replacement is appointed immediately and there is no gap in the service of education. In our college, when a European staff departs, it is impossible for us to find a replacement before that staff leaves his position. That is why the rules governing the departure of an employee have been established in a way that the service of education is not disrupted.

The making of these regulations would have been simply futile if the European staff did not consider them suitable for their needs. Hence, it was necessary to involve the principal of the college in making them and in determining which regulations were harmful and which would facilitate ease. It is very easy to criticize them but I think these regulations have been very well constructed, which do not harm education nor do we have to find a substitute at the time of the employee's departure. And the European staff is also agreeable with it. To say that the agreement of the European staff is not necessary and the committee can make whatever regulations it wishes is not a notion that can work in our college.

After a thorough consideration of all these requirements, I drafted these laws. Of course, Syed Mahmood, who is also a member of the College Fund Committee and has the right to frame the rules of the committee and present them to the rest of the members, was the dominant participant in the drafting of these laws, and Mr. Strachey was involved as a legal advisor. When the draft was completed, it was sent to all the members for feedback. Now it is said of me that I have been irregular in compiling and distributing the draft of the law to the trustees, but I think I have exercised more care than was necessary. Under section 45 of the current regulations, the College Fund Committee has been given the authority to amend the existing regulations but there is no provision in it for any member who wants to amend any regulation to first seek permission from the committee and then present it to the committee, and to distribute the proposed amendment after the committee has given permission. Rather, every member of the College Fund Committee had the authority at all times to present a memorandum regarding a change or modification to any regulation without notice to or approval and permission of the committee. It was required that the memorandum be circulated among all members and their opinions solicited, and was subject to majority vote for its approval. The word 'committee' in this section does not refer to the three or four members of the College Fund Committee who hold meetings for general purposes, but to the full committee of members. Therefore, according to this provision, as a member I had the full authority to propose a draft law without permission of the committee, and as secretary to distribute it to the members to solicit their opinions. Yes, of course, the draft could have been approved or rejected by majority opinion.

But I took precautions and in a meeting of the committee in which 11 members participated, I explained the state of the college and presented the need for appointing trustees for it. Everyone agreed with the need for appointing trustees and the necessity of prescribing regulations for it. The need to present this matter in the meeting was that, in my opinion, there was a need for a legal advisor who would be remunerated for his services in drafting the law. The remuneration could not be given without an approval from a quorum of members of the College Fund Committee. Its approval had to be obtained, but I, as a member, did not have to seek permission to draft the law, and, as the secretary, to distribute it for soliciting opinion.

There is no requirement in this section to appoint a select committee with respect to any proposal for amendment of the regulations presented by me or any member. A select committee may be appointed but it can consist of only a few members and those members cannot have the absolute authority to change or modify the written record or the compiled draft, because according to this section any change or modification or any approval or rejection can be carried out only through the majority opinion of all the members of the College Fund Committee. A few members along with some appointed members of this committee, totaling 15 members, organized a big meeting on their own to consider the proposed laws. They discussed and debated the draft laws and the consensus they reached amounts to no more than some proposals to change and amend a few sections. So, if it is my sin that I did not appoint a select committee, it has been fully atoned for.

There could not have been a better legal advisor for this work than Mr. Strachey, barrister-at-law. Mr. Strachey is my and Syed Mahmood's sincere friend without any formalities between us. He is a friend and well-wisher of our college which was actually established with the gracious support of his renowned father, Sir John Strachey. Among our European staff, he is good friends with Mr. Beck, the principal, who is a representative of all the staff members. His legal acumen is so renowned that it doesn't need my commentary.

The draft law, which had been approved for compilation, needed to have many provisions related to the European staff, such as their dismissal, suspension, salary structure, and departure, etc. The huge difficulty was that the rights available to the European staff of the government's education department could neither be given to our college's staff, since the committee did not have the requisite powers, nor were these rights appropriate for our college. So, it was most appropriate that the legal advisor be a good friend of both parties. On the one hand he could take care of the condition of the college and on the other, understand the rights and needs of the European staff, and convince both of them, or rather exercise a friendly force on them, to agree to a moderate solution. So, my friends! If I have wronged you as well by my complicity in the selection of Mr. Strachey for this work, as is generally attributed to me, I have no hesitation in confessing my mistake and seeking forgiveness for it.

But I am very happy to state that this scheme has given us great success. Granted that in most cases the rights of the European staff have been greatly reduced in the proposed draft from those enjoyed by the European staff of the government's education department, although in some cases we have given considerably more rights, our European staff is fully satisfied and convinced that even though some of their rights may have been curtailed, it was unlikely that the committee in its current state could have done more. We gave thought to these needs and they considered the state of the committee and its compulsions. Both parties trusted Mr. Strachey. These issues were resolved with such great satisfaction and assurance that if any other method had been adopted, it would have been impossible to resolve them.

I am also guilty of the sin that on my own I appointed the deadline for receiving the opinions on the draft without the approval of the committee. But you should know that since the time this committee was established until now, the fixing of dates for meetings and deadlines for tasks has been the special privilege of the secretary and not the prerogative of the committee. In all the institutions and universities that currently exist the world over, it is the secretary's job to fix the dates for meetings and deadlines, otherwise no work will get done. If the committee has to be convened to fix dates for every task, who will have the task to fix the date to convene this meeting? In any case, I as the secretary, in accordance with the standing rules, fixed a date. The members who did not send their replies by this date and wanted more time could have been given an extension at the discretion accorded to me as secretary, but I was careful, presented the matter to the committee, and a long, in fact a prolonged extension was given. So, despite everything, if I am the sinner, then I cannot say anything except this:

How will it be measured on the day of our eternal destiny?

I am surprised at the charge that the secretary did not send a memorandum requesting amendments, even though it is a draft law amending existing rules. The memorandum sent did request amendments. I do not understand what other memorandum was required. Besides, I had sent a letter accompanying it in which I had explained to the extent necessary the need for formulating regulations related to the trustees and requested the help of all the members to ensure the future stability of the college and support the tasks that remain to be finished. In addition to that, more information was sent to the members who wanted it and other documents and the old regulations were sent to those members who asked for them. The extension given for receiving opinions was so prolonged that no member could complain that he had not had an opportunity to explore the facts sufficiently.

My elders! A matter related to the boarding house is worth more consideration too. In the draft law, a committee for the boarding house by the name of '*managing committee*' has been set up. Since Hindus are also boarders, Hindus are also included as members of this committee. In this draft, the principal and the civil surgeon of the district, who is responsible for the medical treatment of the boarders and for keeping the boarding house in a clean and sanitary condition, have also been included as members.

When several members interfere in the administration of the boarding house, a lot of disruption takes place. One member gives an order for a certain task to be done in a certain way. Another member comes and orders it to be done a different way. If one member chastises a student for his misdeeds or expels him from the boarding house, another member absolves him of it and readmits him to the boarding house. As a result of this, the students become extremely daring and disobedient and they are no longer afraid or respectful of anyone. They know that if a certain member expels them from the boarding house, they can ask another member to readmit them. This has happened numerous times. This was the real reason for the rebellion that took place in the boarding house in February of 1887.

To remedy these defects, a proposal has been made for the trustees to authorize one member of the managing committee to be in charge of the general supervision of the boarding house, and if such a charge has not been given, then the secretary shall be in charge of the general supervision. By secretary I mean either Maulvi Samiullah Khan *Saheb*, who is honorary secretary for life of the managing committee, or Syed Ahmed, who is honorary secretary for life of the college.

Members of the managing committee have been empowered to call for a meeting of the members if they find any damage to the general condition of the boarding house and to notify the trustees of any rectification they deem appropriate.

The principal, in his capacity as the head of the boarding house, has been given the authority to maintain discipline and to mete out chastisements that have been established for the misdeeds of the students.

Those who have decided to oppose us in every matter disagree on even the clearest of issues and are of the opinion that the task of supervision of the boarding house should be given only to a Muslim member. They dislike the fact that the responsibility for the supervision of the boarding house at this time has been graciously accepted by the principal, for which I am extremely grateful to him. It is not mandatory for the principal to take charge of the boarding house; he has taken the trouble to do this only as a favor. Maulvi Samiullah Khan *Saheb* writes: "There should be no interference from the principal in the boarding house."

O gentlemen! I ask you if there is any college in Europe, Asia, India, or America with a boarding house attached to it where the principal does not have the same authority over the boarding house as he does over the college. To think of the boarding house as separate from the college is the same as thinking of a human being as separate from his soul.

Besides that, there is a union club attached to the boarding house where students are taught elocution and debating. They are taught English literature in various ways and have to show progress in their study of this literature. If the principal does not supervise them, who will?

The cricket club is in the boarding house. Students practice playing cricket there. Officers of the college's union play with them. They play matches against European civilian and military teams and when they travel to other cities to play against European teams, a European officer of the college travels with them. If they do not play a role in the supervision of the boarding, how will anything get done?

In the boarding house, the students are given '*imposition*,' i.e. chastisement to sit in one place for a fixed period of time and read or write. For this purpose and for the morning school, a place has been designated in the boarding house which is in the charge of the principal. Therefore, if he does not have a say in the boarding house, who will do this work? And if the principal does not have the authority to maintain discipline in the boarding house and chastise the wrongdoers, then why has this arrangement been made and how will it continue to work?

Reports on the behavior and conduct of all the boarders in the boarding house is requisitioned by the collector *Saheb* from the principal and, according to the formal regulations too, the principal should be the one writing these reports. If the principal is not aware of what goes on in the boarding house, who will write these requisitioned reports?

It has been my intention for a long time to have the boarders work hard to learn the rules as it would be very beneficial to their health and strength. Lethargy and laziness will be removed and diligence will develop in their character. Our principal has started something along those lines and there are many reasons why it would be appropriate that this effort should remain in the hands of a European officer and they themselves take part in it.

Apart from this, my main aim in establishing the college is to develop friendly customs and traditions between the Muslims and the English and remove the prejudice and hatred between them. I think there has been a great success in this and the real reason for it is the presence of European officers in our college who have a paternal love and friendly affection for the boarders When an officer of another district comes to Aligarh and sees how genuine and friendly all the ladies and European officers are toward the students of the college and the students toward them, how they participate with them in sports, have dinner together, attend the boarding house dinners, the ladies of our district serve the students lunch on the day of a match, all the ladies, European officers, and students sit and eat at the same table, and how they mix together in a friendly but respectful way, he is amazed and sees a new world in Aligarh.

It hasn't been a long time since Sir John Strachey, Chief Justice of Allahabad, came to Aligarh and had dinner with the boarders in the boarding house. Recently, Earl Dufferin, Viceroy and Governor-General of India, came to our college, sat with the boarders in the same dining hall of the boarding house, and had tea and refreshments with the boarders. All the leaders and

European gentlemen have appreciated and respected our rule of not serving alcohol at the table while happily participating in the boarding house lunches and dinners. All this is the result of the friendly and genuine relationship between the boarders and the European officers of our college, which has been a good influence on our boarders and has garnered respect for our boarding house. My aim in establishing this college has been achieved to some extent. So, those who oppose us in this matter do not concern me even an iota, nor do I want to keep the boarding house in a state that they like. If I cannot achieve this purpose of mine, it would be a thousand times better to abandon this effort than to maintain this college. Through this college and boarding house, we want to create friendship and affection between the Muslims and the English, not malice and hostility.

Hence, it is my opinion that the European officers of our college, be they the principal, professors, or the headmaster, should be involved in the boarding house as much as they please and take upon themselves to provide favors and administrative duties in the boarding house, and with humility and gratitude we should leave it in their hands. If the college garners sufficient means, I fully intend to appoint a European officer as a full time '*governor*' of the boarding house. At that time, I will feel that the entire arrangement of the boarding house has been completed.

O gentlemen! I can assure you that ever since my friend, in fact a friend of the Muslim community, Mr. Beck, the principal, was gracious enough to take the responsibility of the supervision of the boarding house, it has been so well managed as never seen before. Discipline has been established in every workstream and as a result the students have become very regular with their prayers, which was never the case before.

So, all the efforts of the Principal *Saheb* toward the boarding house deserve our extreme gratitude.

I would like to take this opportunity to congratulate Mr. Beck, that although some members have opposed the authority of the principal, some very religious members have appreciated his services very much. Nawab Intisar Jung Maulvi Mushtaq Husain *Saheb* writes, "Mr. Theodore Beck is the principal of our college. I am as satisfied with and confident in entrusting the boarding house to him as I would be with it being in the hands of a Muslim officer of the same ability, cultured manners, and feelings. In addition to providing other very valuable services, the sincerity with which he supervises the prayers, fasting, and recitation of the Holy Quran by the Muslim boarders, the respect he has for these things, and the affection he has for the boarders stemming from his highly cultured values deserves more gratitude than we can express. And if he willingly takes the trouble of managing the boarding house out of his own desire, it is also a favor to the Muslims. These are the people who leave their memories in golden letters in the history of other nations and who are remembered by nations and countries for ages."

This notion is not that of Nawab Intisar Jung alone. Our patron Khan Bahadur Munshi Qadir Bakhsh *Saheb* has appreciated the boarding house being in the hands of our college's principal Mr. Beck with sincere enthusiasm. Maulvi Muhammad Yusuf *Saheb* and Syed Zahoor Husain Amrohvi also appreciated it. Most of all, we are happy that all the brave-hearted Islamic associations of Punjab, namely Anjuman Islamia Punjab Lahore, Anjuman Islamia Gurudaspur, Anjuman Islamia Jalandhar, Anjuman Islamia Multan, Anjuman Islamia Wazirabad, Anjuman Islamia Amritsar, and many elders who desire progress for the community have preferred their children and the boarding house to be under the supervision of Mr. Beck. So, what more can our college be proud of than to have so many Muslim organizations have full faith in its principal, Mr. Beck.

Distinguished gentlemen! Now there is only one more thing for me to say, that you should pay attention to the past history and observe that there have been many generous elders who have shown great generosity in community and religious affairs. They have given money, houses, shops, hamlets, estates, mosques and shrines to charity. But now they are in such a depleted state and their properties have perished in such a way that even the souls of the benefactors must be feeling sorry. Our community has not yet developed the faculties to carry out any great work or sustain any effort in good measure without the patronage of the government. This is especially true for establishing educational institutions, and that too for teaching European knowledge and literature, for which we need the help of the government from time to time due to financial issues and other reasons. Therefore, I thought it appropriate that in this draft law, the government should be empowered to exercise general supervision of the college and to correct its course when it deviates. In view of this, I have inserted the following provisions in the draft:

- First, it has been proposed that the Director of Public Instruction be designated as the present Visitor. He has been empowered to inquire into the educational status of the college and examine all accounts of revenues and expenditures whenever he wants so that he may report to the government whatever his opinions may be and the government may correspond with the trustees in this matter.

- Second, the government has been authorized to examine the college's accounts and books whenever and in whatever way it wants.

- Third, if the government has the knowledge that any of the trustees are not doing their job properly, it is empowered to compel them to correct their actions.

- Fourth, it is desired that if the trustees wish to keep the collateral for a government secured promissory note in a property in some department of the government, the government should accept that arrangement.

- Fifth, the charge of the college dispensary should be given to the district's civil surgeon, remuneration for which will be paid by the college.

All these five provisions, which are included in the draft, have been approved by the government. This gave our college a lot of reassurance.

In addition, there were three other matters in which I considered the intervention of the government to be appropriate, or rather necessary:

- First, it was proposed in section 18 of the draft law that if it was necessary to remove a trustee for a specific reason, two conditions would have to be met: two-thirds of the trustees agree that the trustee should be removed and the government approves the trustee's removal. The government did not consider it appropriate to intervene in this matter.

- Second, it was proposed in section 117 that when the trustees wanted to change or modify the regulations, they should get approval from the government. The government did not consider it appropriate to intervene in this matter as well. In fact, it was necessary to have two conditions for this section as well as they are in section 18, i.e. two-thirds of the trustees agree to this change or modification and the government approves it. The phrase "two-thirds of the trustees" is there in my draft but was accidentally omitted from the printed version. This is a mistake that cannot be rectified. If the draft as compiled, which includes this section, gets approved by a majority vote, then in a meeting of the trustees and after getting the opinions of all the trustees, this section can be validated and expanded to include that when two-thirds of the trustees agree, the amendment and repeal of the regulation may come into effect.

But at this time, the purpose of explaining this to all of you, who are mentors of the community and are attentive to its reform and welfare, is that if the aforementioned sections are passed by a majority, the status of which will be known tomorrow, then the government would have refused to intervene in them. But all these supporters of the community will continue to maintain these conditions and will try to get the government to accept these conditions, because the condition that has been established in section 117 as the basis for amendment and repeal of regulations is the life of the college's establishment and its continued existence. If it is removed, the existence of the college in a decorous manner will be greatly endangered.

His Honor the Lieutenant-Governor did not consider these provisions out of place and unnecessary and wrote that these matters are our great responsibility. He said that as long as he remained the Lieutenant-Governor, he would help in this, but he cannot defer this responsibility to his successor. So, our effort should be to have a special constitution that governs our college be passed by the government's council so that every Lieutenant-Governor has the basis to act accordingly and the college's establishment, continuity, and high-quality constancy are fully assured.

When the trustees have removed the error that has been made in section 117, i.e. giving the trustees the authority to repeal and amend regulations with the agreement of two-thirds of them, there will be no harm to the functioning of the college, because the conditions for the approval by the government are subject to its acceptance of them. Hence, until these conditions are accepted by the government, they will be deemed null and void and the authority of the trustees to act will remain unrestricted by these conditions. I have an all-around hope that the well-wishers of the community who desire the continuity and constancy of the college will help me in every way in this chapter of the college being successful in getting a special constitution for the college passed by the legal council.

The third matter, which was related to the settlement of traveling allowance etc. for the European staff and in which the settlement of the traveling allowance was approved by the accountant general, who also expressed his approval for other settlements, is not a major issue for which I need to trouble you with details.

O gentlemen! In hearing these explicit details of the situations, you must have learned that this college is still in need of sincere help from you gentlemen. But there is also no doubt that until now there is no precedent of such a big institution being established with the support of and for the good of a community. So, it is hoped that all of the community and the country will wholeheartedly support its completion. If, God forbid, this effort is not successful, you can be certain that our courage to make an effort in the future for the welfare of the community will be extremely weakened and there will be no expectation of any such attempts for hundreds of years.

O friends! At a time when every individual in the community needed to make a concerted effort to complete the establishment of the college, it is very regrettable that there are so many disagreements and these efforts have been prolonged so much only because of one thing, even if you suppose that is my own fault, my own bad faith, or my own selfishness. But there is also the wisdom of God in it. The community trusted me, gave me hundreds of thousands of rupees for this community work, and then never asked what happened to that money. I wondered what sins against the community I was guilty of. Hence, I am very happy that my friends, who consider themselves to have insider knowledge of everything, and in fact do, opposed me so much, found out all my sins, and exposed them and presented them to the public. Even though I am surprised that these sins turned out to be so few, whatever my friends unearthed are now in front of the public. So, now the community has the right to forgive those sins or not as it wishes.

O gentlemen! I do not have any personal interest in the college other than that I have established it for the welfare, betterment, and progress of the community. Suppose there is no success in it; so what? Thousands of prophets and reformers lie buried in the ground whose endless efforts for their communities were wasted, then how significant is it if my efforts fail as well? Noah tried for a hundred years, though he said in anger, "*And Noah said, 'My Lord, do not leave on earth an abode of the disbelievers.'*" But he would look at his nation sinking in the ark under the waves that would rise higher than the Himalayas and say, "God, it is Your will." Socrates would end up drinking a cup of poison rather than be able to reform the traditions of his nation and counsel them. So, if these incidents occur in my efforts as well, it would be nothing new. However, understand that those who wish for the welfare of their community die and their efforts are wasted but the curse of God remains on the community. O Almighty! O Almighty! Don't do this to my community. Forgive me.

O gentlemen! I hope that when the matter in which there is disagreement is resolved, then everyone will agree with each other and work together for the betterment of the college and say to each other:

"Our Lord, do not impose on us what we cannot bear and excuse us and forgive us and have mercy on us."

141

Gratitude for the Gift from *Huzoor* Nizam

(Excerpted from the fourth annual session of the Muhammadan Educational Congress held in Aligarh, December 27-30, 1889)

The fourth annual session of the Muhammadan Educational Congress was held in Aligarh on December 27-30, 1889. In 1889, *Huzoor* Nizam Hyderabad had compassionately donated the sum of Rs. 5000 per annum to provide scholarships to the Muslim students from the provinces of Bombay, UP, and Punjab. Sir Syed presented a resolution thanking *Huzoor* Nizam and gave the following speech. Presented on December 27, 1889, this was the first resolution and its initiator was Sir Syed himself.

Mr. President of the session and other elders!

It has been recognized by all people, people of different views, that Muslim students attending college classes cannot attain a higher level of education if they are not provided financial assistance. Everyone is certain about the fact that the times compel people toward those expenses which are needed for living, for the well-being of humanity, and for honor and respect. In these times, the personal expenses of every person and of every kind have increased tremendously and keep increasing day by day. A laborer who could live his life on two *ana* cannot afford to feed himself with two *ana* now. Everyone's personal expenses have increased. A *khidmatgar*, household-assistant, who could be employed for two rupees, is not available now for even six or seven rupees. The day-to-day household expenses also keep going up in the same way. So, when all kinds of expenses keep on increasing over time, there is no reason why educational expenses should not increase as well. Due to this, the expenditure on education has also increased and you can be certain that it will keep increasing day by day.

But it is a pity that what has not progressed is the condition of the Muslims. If there was progress, that progress has been reversed, for which the simple and straightforward word 'declining' is applicable. Now we have reached the other side of the same coin. On one side is the decline of the Muslims and on the other the rising cost of education. Therefore, if there is no strategy to bring Muslims out of their decline, they must despair of higher education. It may be said that Muslims have made as much effort as possible, but with that it is regrettable and without a doubt that those efforts failed.

To say that the Muslims are not in a position to do anything is simply wrong and counterintuitive. If the Muslims are determined, understand that their community must be saved from drowning, and believe that their survival depends only on taking their children toward higher education, then let alone the 50 million Muslims of India, even if there are the likes of another 50 million, we can take them all to appropriate levels of education.

Here, there are just two things lacking in the community: first, in all of the community, in fact in all the communities of Muslims and in all their dwellings, there is little attention to the education of children, and especially to the education that is needed in this day and age.

Another major disaster is that the people who want to do something have different ideas and different methods that they want to adopt. I don't know what has become of people. Instead of lighting a lamp with a thick wick, they separate every strand of it and light it and think that they spread light in many parts of the world. But this light doesn't last even the blink of an eye, then there is the same darkness all around.

Now let us look at the rich and powerful people of our country. We cannot tell if any of the rich, the *Raïses*, and the wealthy think for even a minute about the education of the best, the brightest, the children of the community. It is a pity that in their dream-filled repose, they dream a thousand dreams but they have neither dreamt of the welfare of the community nor thought about the education of its children. They don't even know about the state of the community.

In such a situation, a Muslim head of a sovereign, whose empire should be a source of pride for the Muslims, thankfully thought about the education of the community. He did not limit his empathy and patronage to just his dominion, but very generously paid attention to the development and education of all Muslims, be they in his empire or in other parts of the country. Who is that? *Huzoor* Nizam of Deccan, who has established scholarships for the advancement of the education of Muslims of all of India in addition to the subjects of his empire.

It is a law of nature that even the tallest tree comes from a seed that someone planted. I am very happy to say that the one who planted the seed of this tree of goodness is a source of pride for all the Muslims of India and a pioneer of both traditional and modern education, Syed Hussain Bilgrami, Imdad-ul-Mulk Bahadur.

O gentlemen! We regret that there is no education in our community and there are no such persons as in other communities, but we are as proud of Syed Hussain Bilgrami as the sky is to have the sun in this universe. He has no equal in the knowledge of English language and literature, as well as in the knowledge of the Arabic and Persian languages and literatures, his goodheartedness, his morals, his honesty and true friendship, and his open disposition. He had the idea that the Muslims in the provinces of India other than the dominion of Hyderabad Deccan who cannot afford higher education should be helped. He made this request in a report to the office of the prime minister of the Nizam, which was approved. The documents and the order that were issued by the government of His Highness the Nizam in this regard are in my hands, which I will present before this gathering and read them for you, and they are as follows.

[After that, Sir Syed read the order]

142

Speech Regarding Writing Articles for Awards

(Excerpted from the fourth annual session of the Muhammadan Educational Congress held in Aligarh, December 27-30, 1889)

The fourth annual session of the Muhammadan Educational Congress was held in Aligarh on December 27-30, 1889. One of the resolutions presented in it was that to develop the interest of Muslims in education, they should be invited to write articles that would be eligible for awards and to have many of them published. This was the third resolution and was presented by Allama Shibli. Sir Syed seconded it with the following speech.

Mr. President of the session and other elders!

I second the resolution that has been presented at this time. You must have observed that the purpose of this resolution is not to debate any topic at this time or to make any decisions on it. A topic has been presented to the congress not for it to be debated but to have essays written on it by the press and to have awards given for them subject to certain conditions. So, at this time, only this matter is to be decided and no other matter needs discussion. The situation is that these types of topics or very similar ones have been presented a few times in the past three sessions, and one gentleman instantly started to discuss it without giving it much or sufficient consideration. The discussions that ensued among the people were varied, the arguments of the proponents not comprehensive of all the aspects or the benefits, and neither were the opposing discussions enough to negate the arguments of the proponents and the benefits of their proposal. That is why it is not necessary that people form their opinions through their own considerations and reflections and every gentleman ponder over its each benefit and harm, rather this purpose can be fully achieved by having the press write several articles on the topic, a proposition that is included in the resolution.

Gentlemen! Our country and our community is in a curious situation. Take the name of anything practical, of a low or high level, and then ask if the community needs it. The answer you will get for everything is yes. We need schools that teach the Quran. We need schools that teach Arabic and Persian. We need seminaries that teach Hadith and Islamic jurisprudence. We need schools that teach in English at the lower primary, primary, middle, entrance, FA, BA, and MA levels. In trade, we need everything from small shops to large warehouses. We need industries that manufacture everything from needles and matches to fine pocket-watches, strange thermometers, and the most delicate instruments. To make yarn, paper, cloth, suffice it to say there is nothing that we don't need which is necessary for our present lives. So, with respect to education related actions, one person may say that there is a great need to spread education at the elementary level in the community. Another person may say that without higher education, the community will decline day by day. Both of them are correct in terms of the state of the community and their arguments are not refutable, but the question is what method should those who want to raise this fallen community, which is in need of everything from the basic to the highest of levels, adopt? Is it appropriate for us to take on everything at the same time, which is impracticable and, with the community getting fragmented, would make it impossible to achieve even one thing? Or is it essential for us to take on the one thing that is the root of all ills?

Suppose a person is sick and is suffering from many diseases. Is it appropriate for the physician who is treating him to immediately give a single treatment for all his illnesses or to first treat the one that may be fatal? The community as a whole is like a single person and he truly is suffering from a lot of diseases. The only debatable question is which illness is the most severe and the most fatal, on whose treatment we should therefore all agree and for which we should make efforts first.

I am confident that no one will disagree with this principle, which has been recognized by great rulers. Where there can be some difference of opinion is in the diagnosis of the illness that should be declared the most severe and fatal.

For a long period of time, our community was under the shadow of death, but now there is some movement and it is turning on its side, and its movements are determined and restless. Or, it is an example of stagnant water that has remained in one place for a long period of time; without a doubt there is movement in it and it has started to flow in different ways. Its physical effect is that it starts flowing in different places and many branches of it are formed. Its end result cannot be anything but that they dry up after flowing for a little bit. It is the task of the people who are taking charge of the community to suggest good opportunities for it to flow and to direct all those branches into a pathway so that they can all join and flow into a river and gradually make their way into an ocean.

I had great pity for the condition of the community but I am very happy that the dam of stagnant water has broken and started to flow in different directions. I hope to God that all those streams turn into one and join together to become a river. So, you must ponder how these streams can become one and how they can join together to become a river. This is also the purpose of the topic that has been presented. Without a doubt, this is a topic on which every person would write according to his own opinion. But thinking about it, to the best of my knowledge, there is one English word that cannot be translated into Urdu. Maybe Maulvi Nazir Ahmad *Saheb* can translate it: that word is '*utility*.' I do not know the equivalent word in Urdu, but I will interpret it to the best of my ability. There is nothing in the world that does not have both benefit and harm. Having said that, the meaning of *utility* is that if you list all the benefits on one side and all the harms on the other, give each of them a '*value*,' (unfortunately, I do not know the Urdu word for that either; whoever is interested can ask Maulvi Nazir Ahmad *Saheb*), then use the rules of algebra and comparison to determine whether there is more benefit or more harm in it and adopt those things that have more benefit. We should have no trouble doing the algebra and the comparison, given that *Shams-ul-'Ulama* Maulvi Muhammad Zakaullah is present. He can do the calculations in a minute and tell us which has a higher number and we should adopt that function.

In any case, in my mind this topic deserves to be carefully examined and pondered in its every aspect by all persons who write on it. When those articles come and are submitted to the committee, I hope that the *utility* will be evaluated and some of the submitted articles will be appreciated. At this time, it is only necessary to approve the writing of such articles, and I hope that no one will disagree with it. If there is someone who disagrees somewhat and has some concern, it is me, and that concern is that the award that will be designated for it cannot be given from this year's membership dues since it has been decided that the dues collected this year, less the miscellaneous expenses of printing etc., will be given to the scholarship fund or will be presented in the meeting later this year. The award can be given out of the income from next year's dues. Besides that, a single award of Rs. 100 is too little. At least three awards should be established, one for Rs. 100 and two for Rs. 50 each, so that more people have the opportunity to win an award.

★

143

Speech Regarding a Blasphemous Book

(Excerpted from the fourth annual session of the Muhammadan Educational Congress held in Aligarh, December 27-30, 1889)

In the fourth annual session of the Muhammadan Educational Congress held in Aligarh on December 27-30, 1889, Maulvi Bashiruddin (Editor, *Bashirat*, Etawah) presented a resolution against Mr. Cox's history book[6], which was prescribed as a textbook for the students and included blasphemous text against Islam, asking it to be removed from the syllabus. After this fourth resolution was presented, Sir Syed delivered the following speech.

The resolution presented by our respected Maulvi Bashiruddin *Saheb*, which was seconded by Munshi Ahmed Ali *Saheb*, is a resolution that all the members of the Muhammadan Educational Congress will not only agree with but will consider it a matter of honor for the educational congress. Our educational congress has been in existence for four years. There have been many debates in it and many resolutions have been presented and passed, but today it has done something that was necessary for it to do.

It is our misfortune that the Muslim community has remained separated from English education for a long time and considered it against our religion. After much difficulty, discussion, and effort, there is some inclination toward English education. But if such books and such inappropriate and repugnant articles, which are in fact patently false and inappropriate, enter into this education, then surely the Muslims will hate English education and our community will be harmed.

---

[6] George William Cox's "History of the Establishment of the British Rule in India," first published in 1881, was an in-depth analysis of the events and actions that led to the British colonization of India.

It is without a doubt that literature of any language is not devoid of the religious ideas of the people to whom it belongs. But it is one thing for religious ideas, which tend toward the good in every religion, to be found in literature, and another to condemn other religions, especially in a history book. When writing history, the merits and demerits of human actions can be discussed but not those of religious issues, nor can one's actions, however abominable, be argued as religious defects. Unfortunately, there are very few history books in English that are free of prejudice and in which the history of Muslims has been written dispassionately.

It is a pity that no one has been born in our community so far who is accomplished in English literature and can write such history books in English that are worthy of being included in the syllabi of schools and colleges as excellent literature and text. That is why we are compelled to study those books which have been written by the English, whose authors are of both biased and unbiased kind, and there is no other source from which we can acquire English language and knowledge. I myself am a member of the senate of universities. I absolutely cannot perceive that the government or the universities intend to include such books that attack any religion, Hindu or Muslim, in the syllabi of colleges and schools. The members of the senate and the faculty of arts select books based on their excellence in literature, elegance of style, and simplicity of text, and as much as possible avoid books with a religious hue. Nevertheless, some pages or paragraphs do turn up that the Muslims consider an attack on the religion of Islam or an insult to it. The same is true of Cox's history book. I have come to know that the able headmaster of our college has removed from instruction those sections that our respected Maulvi Bashirddin *Saheb* has indicated. The masters and teachers of every school should do the same.

A few days back, I had heard complaints about Cox's history book. I immediately wrote a letter regarding it to the Director of Public Instruction and sent him a few newspapers in which these complaints had been published. In response to this, the honorable gentlemen paid a lot of attention to the matter. There is no doubt that such a book entered the syllabus only by mistake or by chance; it should never be thought of as done on purpose.

Every word from the beginning to the end of the books that are included in the syllabi is not read by those who select them. They look at them on the whole and select them on the basis of their overall goodness or include famous or noted books in the syllabus. So, if there is a stance in these books that is against a religion, in my view the blame for it is on those who select them and the best recourse is not to include them in the syllabi.

O gentlemen! These are trivial things. If some book has been removed from the syllabus or some good master has removed a page or pages from its instruction, how does it matter? Our students who study the English language and English knowledge read on their own many books of literature and history other than the prescribed books. In them, they come across stronger text that is more harsh and disgusting than the material in Cox's history book, and wrong from top to bottom regarding Islam. So, what we need most is that our history and our religious views be written in the English language with great excellence and in the form of good literature that is worthy of reading and deriving benefit. The kind of books against which there have been complaints should be reviewed by us with great care and clarity, but unfortunately there are neither the people in our community who can do this nor has our community turned its attention toward it. But we should not despair of the Almighty. The day will come when we will be able to fulfill all those intentions.

It is without a doubt the duty of the Muhammadan Educational Congress to also turn its attention to the kinds of issues that our respected Maulvi Bashiruddin *Saheb* has raised. The task that the Muhammadan Educational Congress was supposed to do in this matter has been completed today by Maulvi Bashiruddin *Saheb*. So, for this motion, we should be grateful to the honorable Maulvi *Saheb*.

144

Annual Report of the Fourth Session of the Muhammadan Educational Congress ★

(Fifth annual session of the Muhammadan Educational Conference held in Allahabad, December 28-30, 1890)

In your service,
Janab Sardar Muhammad Hayat Khan Bahadur, CSI
President of the fifth session of the Muhammadan Educational Congress in Allahabad

My dear sirs!
It has been declared my duty that every year at the beginning of the session of this educational conference, I present the statuses of actions taken on the resolutions of the past year. Therefore, I fulfill this obligation, but with regret. I present before you the following status.

In the last year's session, the resolution No. 4 was passed to the effect that Cox's history book, which contained some words that insulted Islam and that were taught to the entrance class, be expunged from the syllabus, and in this regard I was instructed to correspond on behalf of the conference with the University of Allahabad and the officers in the department of education. Accordingly, I wrote a letter dated October 6, 1890 to the Director of Public Instruction and a letter addressed to the registrar of the University of Allahabad and sent the English translation of the resolution along with them. I am happy to report that the book has been removed from the syllabus.

The Director of Public Instruction forwarded my letter to the registrar of Allahabad University with the intention of presenting it in the meeting of the syndicate of the university, but the registrar wrote to me that the book had already been removed from the future exams for the course. I have no doubt that the book was included in the syllabus by mistake and without considering the fact that it has a few instances of out of place, inappropriate, and downright false references to our pure religion of Islam. If the officers of the university had noticed these instances, they would never have included it. The headmaster of our Mohammedan Anglo-Oriental College Aligarh had directed the students not to read those sections and they were not included in the instruction.

But the difficulty that arose was that the academic year was about to end and the students had already read the book. If the book had been immediately replaced by another for the exam, it would have hurt the students very much. As you know, some of the instances that were objected to were removed from the exam and the students were not required to include them in their preparations. Consequently, the registrar wrote to me that another book has been proposed for the syllabus starting in 1891, since replacing the current book with another one for the exam would have hurt the students. He asked me that given this, did I still want my letter to be presented in the syndicate.

As for our purpose to remove Cox's history book from the syllabus for the future academic sessions, it was achieved. Hence, I thanked him and wrote to him that now there was no need to present it in the syndicate. The letter from the registrar is included here.

No. 717, 1890
From:
Registrar,
Allahabad University,
Allahabad

To:
Honorable Sir Syed Ahmed Khan Bahadur, KCSI, LLD
Secretary, Muhammadan Educational Congress, Aligarh
Dated: October 9, 1890

Dear Sir!
With reference to your letter dated October 6, 1890, I inform you that instead of Cox's "History of the Establishment of the British Rule in India," it has been decided that the exam for the Indian history course at the entrance level in 1892 will be based on Talboys Wheeler's "Tales from Indian History."

If, in place of Cox *Saheb*'s book, another book is used for the 1890 entrance level exam, it will deprive the students of the benefit of 15 months of instruction. Hence, in such a situation, I ask if you still want your letter to be presented in the syndicate.

I regret that any part of any book in the syllabus has caused the students to be aggrieved.

Yours truly,
Archibald E. Gough, MA
Registrar

This resolution was well complied with and its objective was fully achieved, but I regret that I cannot present a report regarding the success of other resolutions. In the Lahore session, a resolution was passed regarding adoption of fund-raising schemes to establish scholarships for poor students in the college classes and another resolution was passed for the purpose of establishing standing committees at a central location of every district to promote the aims of the Muhammadan Educational Congress. When compliance with both these resolutions could not be achieved, a resolution (No. 2) was passed in the Aligarh session for the purpose of stressing that attention must be paid to the Lahore resolution and the Anjuman Islamia, the Islamic associations, of all these places were requested to try to fulfill these objectives.

After that, Mr. Theodore Beck, principal of the Mohammedan Anglo-Oriental College and member of the Muhammadan Educational Congress, tried to establish a standing committee in Aligarh as per this resolution. A committee was established and held its meeting on February 16, 1890, and all the members were requested to pay attention to this matter, but it did not meet with any success.

But in the Jhang district in Punjab, a standing committee was established whose secretary is Qadir Bakhsh *Saheb*, third clerk of the district office. He has started efforts for this aim of the resolution and the dues of all the members that have been signed up for membership of the Muhammadan Educational Congress have been collected on the condition that all of it will be deposited in a fund whose income will go toward stipends and scholarships.

Even though the collection of the membership dues on this particular condition was debatable with respect to the Muhammadan Educational Congress' rules, since the congress had always given some amount of money for the stipend and scholarship fund, I accepted this condition and hope that none of the members will have any objection.

Recently, in Balia, with your particular attention, a standing committee has been appointed in accordance with the Lahore resolution (No. 3) that was confirmed in Aligarh. So far, it has recruited 13 members for this educational session; let us see what happens next in this process. It is a pity that the Muslims of Multan, I think, are in a constrained situation; other than that I have not received information of standing committees being appointed from any district, which I regret.

It is also important to find out which Islamic associations have given assistance to students who are studying in college level classes in various institutions and need assistance. I only know that Anjuman Islamia of Jalandhar has fixed a stipend of seven rupees a month for a student of our college, but no information from any other Islamic association has come to me so far. If I get information by the time the report is sent for printing, I will include it.

At the *Madrasatul Uloom*, the friends who have always assisted by giving private scholarships have given similar generous help this year, details of which along with all their names have been entered in our annual budget.

A most important resolution was passed on which, in my opinion, the welfare of the community depends. A community does great injury to itself by dispersing its strengths. Unless these strengths are not collected in one place, no beneficial and tangible result can be achieved. The resolution I am referring to asked "whether, in the present circumstances, it is more useful for the progress of the community to concentrate its efforts on higher education and to collect the means for it, or to concentrate on elementary education."

At that time, it was proposed in the session that essays be solicited on this topic, and three awards were established for that; one of Rs. 100 and two of Rs. 50 each. For these awards, Khan Bahadur Sheikh Ahmed Husain Khan *Saheb*, Taluqdar of Paryawan area of Awadh, had promised a donation. But it is our misfortune that he fell ill and the money was not received, and it was not considered appropriate to trouble him given his health. For that reason, an advertisement soliciting these essays and announcing the awards was not put out. Now, by divine grace, the respected gentleman has regained his health, and the advertisement will be put out once the money is received.

Although the resolutions related to stipends and scholarships for students were not complied with, we are happy that our honorable friend Munshi Syed

Jafar Hussain *Saheb*, a Ziladar in Naharganj, has taken up this work as a volunteer. He took leave from his job for a few months and started traveling as a community volunteer at his own expense, collecting money for stipends and scholarships. He has already traveled to a few places and till now has sent me Rs. 346 and 4 *ana*. It is his desire and that of those who have donated that this money not be spent on anything but put into a capital fund, the income from which should be used to give stipends. Therefore, I have deposited this money in the Allahabad Bank Ltd. I am sincerely grateful to Syed Jafar Hussain *Saheb* and I am sure that the entire community is grateful to him.

Surely, it is very gratifying that this year the community elders of these parts have paid great attention to the Muhammadan Educational Congress. Sheikh Naseeruddin *Saheb*, who is a Talukdar from the town of Mau and a great *Raïs* of that district, took it upon himself to provide hospitality to the members of the congress and arrange for their ease and comfort in every way. It was due to the assurance and confidence he gave us that Allahabad was chosen as the venue for the conference sessions.

Our revered and venerable Khan Bahadur Maulvi Syed Fariduddin Ahmad Khan has given sincere attention to supporting the objectives of the conference. He has visited many locations, taking the trouble to travel to these places and establish committees to further the aims of the conference, for which the entire community should be thankful to him.

The first meeting was held in Roohi, pargana Chapal, district Allahabad, which was presided by Sheikh Muhammad Hadi *Saheb*, attorney, landlord, and member of the local board, and the secretary was Sheikh Shamsuddin *Saheb*, lawyer.

The second meeting was held in Mandara in the subdivision of Soraon in district Allahabad, which was presided by Ahmad Ali Khan *Saheb*, Taluqdar of Bareilly and *Raïs* of Mansurabad, and the secretary was Syed Ali Jawwad *Saheb*, Taluqdar of Mandara.

The third meeting was held in Katra in district Allahabad, which is the main place of residence of Khan Bahadur Maulvi Syed Fariduddin Ahmad Khan. It was presided by Sheikh Kamaluddin Ahmad *Saheb*, and the secretary was Shah Ruknuddin *Saheb*, *Sajjada-Nashin* of the shrine of Maulana Khwajagi.

The fourth meeting was held in Bamrauli, pargana Chapal, district Allahabad, which was organized by Chaudhary Kamaluddin *Saheb*, Chaudhary Jamaluddin *Saheb*, and Chaudhary Muhammad Musa *Saheb*, Taluqdars of Bamrauli.

The fifth meeting was held in Niwan, pargana Chapal, district Allahabad, which was presided by Sheikh Abdul Samad *Saheb*, Taluqdar.

The sixth meeting was held in Kathgaon, pargana Chapal, district Allahabad, which was presided by Sheikh Abdul Samad *Saheb* Qadri, who is a complete dervish and people are attracted to his blessed soul.

The seventh meeting was held in Hamirpur through the efforts of Maulvi Muhammad Shakir *Saheb* and people became members from there as well. I am very happy that Mr. Denniston *Saheb*, who was the collector and magistrate of the district at the time, agreed to become a member.

The eight session was held in the town of Mandiahun of district Jaunpur, which was presided by Maulvi Muhammad Shibli *Saheb*, the noble son of *Janab* Maulana Maulvi Sakhawat Ali Khan, may God bless him and grant him peace, and the secretary was Munshi Muhammad Yahya *Saheb*.

After that, Khan Bahadur Maulana Maulvi Syed Fariduddin Ahmad Khan Bahadur reached the town of Sandila in district Lucknow and a meeting organized by Khan Bahadur Chaudhary Nusrat Ali *Saheb* and Chaudhary Azim Khan *Saheb* was held there.

Our kind friend Munshi Nawal Kishore[7] *Saheb*, owner of the press that publishes *Avadh Akhbar*, also held a meeting in his residence and enrolled members, and became a member of the Muhammadan Educational Congress himself.

In the same way, in Faizabad, Basti, and Gorakhpur as well, meetings were held due to the attention of Khan Bahadur Maulana Maulvi Syed Fariduddin Ahmad Khan Bahadur.

Janab Khan Bahadur Qazi Syed Raza Hussain *Saheb* in Patna, Munshi Syed Akbar Hussain Khan Bahadur, Munshi Muhammad Rahmatullah *Saheb* Raad, and Munshi Nazir Ali *Saheb*, members of *Ikhwan al-Safa* of Kanpur, Anjuman Islamia of Jabalpur, respected Syed Hussain *Saheb* in district Fatehpur, Maulvi Ali Ahmad Khan *Saheb* in Fatehabad in district Agra, and friends in many other places put their efforts into publicizing the aims of the Muhammadan Educational Conference and gathering members for it.

---

7. Munshi Nawal Kishore (3 January 1836 – 19 February 1895) was a book publisher from India. He has been called the Caxton of India. In 1858, at the age of 22, he founded the Nawal Kishore Press at Lucknow. This institution today is the oldest printing and publishing concern in Asia. Mirza Ghalib was one of his admirers.

The effort deserving the most appreciation is the one that was made in Saharanpur. On October 19, 1890 the elders there held a meeting and formed a deputation in which Maulvi Abdullah Khan *Saheb*, advocate of the court, Maulvi Fariduddin Ahmad Khan *Saheb*, head clerk of administration, Maulvi Sakhawat Hussain *Saheb*, second master in the government school, Munshi Mohammad Ali *Saheb*, *Raïs* of Saharanpur and son of Khan Bahadur Mohammad Hameed Ali *Saheb*, retired District Judge, Munshi Nazir Ahmad *Saheb*, *Raïs* of Saharanpur, and Maulvi Abdul Ghani *Saheb*, son of the late Maulana Maulvi Ahmad Ali *Saheb*, *Muhaddis*, were included. This deputation went around lamenting to the people the disastrous situation that the community was in and telling people about the aims of the Muhammadan Educational Conference. These efforts produced excellent benefits and results. If Maulvi Abdul Ghani *Saheb* were to give me a detailed report of these proceedings, I will publish it in the appendix.

Suffice it to say, those who want the good of the community tried in every way, and the foremost result of those efforts is that you see so many names from this sleepy community in our list of members that we did not expect to participate. Undoubtedly, the general enthusiasm and passion that our people have shown toward this community forum is unparalleled. For a person like me, who is more disappointed with the community than anyone else, this is amazing and goes toward mending those broken expectations. May God give the community the same kind of passion to fulfill the great pending tasks for its welfare. Amen.

In Allahabad proper as well, all the elders are very interested in this educational conference. Our bravehearts from Punjab have shown the same interest in the welfare of the community as they always do, despite the fact that this year the session was held at a great distance from Punjab. In this year's session, their participation has been as lively and enthusiastic as it has always been. I am very happy that this year as well, the president of the session is a braveheart from Punjab, and the greatest source of pride and blessings is *Janab* Maulana Hafiz Muhammad Hussain *Saheb*'s spiritual grace that touches people in the same way as the bounty of his education. Our humble Muhammadan Educational Conference is blessed to have him as a member.

Another happiness, which is no less than this happiness, is that the *Raïses* of Daryabad, who are members and are well known, are all helping us in this work in every way. A very regrettable division that exists between the two Muslim sects, which should not be there, is non-existent in Allahabad in our Muhammadan

Educational Conference, just as it is in our *Madrasatul Uloom*. Shias and Sunnis, in other words all Muslims, are heartily helping.

It is also a matter of happiness that in the list of members you will also see the names of Hindus of our nation. No person can be happier than me that these countrymen Hindu brothers and Muslims live in harmony with each other. Our educational congress, which I hope will be called a conference in the future, is an educational gathering, and has nothing to do with any political or religious discussions. So, it is essential that all inhabitants of India, whether they are Hindus, Muslims, Christians, Jews, Parsis, or any other should help it.

But, O Mr. President, the success, in the hope of which we have established this annual educational gathering, is still many miles away. Nobody needs to pick faults with our community gathering; we ourselves talk about our deficiencies and are not hopeful of its success. But, *"you never know, maybe God wills something good to come out of this."* We ourselves regard the activities as futile debates, impractical ideas and absurd actions. We ourselves say that till now we have been spending money on this every year without any returns. What else remains to be said by anyone? But what else can we do? We cannot bear to see our community dying. Everyone knows that it is useless to give medicine to this dying soul, yet we continue to push medicine down its throat. That is all we can do; it is in God's hands to give salvation or not.

Mr. President and O my dear friends! Although the state of our community is one of despair, I will tell you an amazing thing which can replace that despair with some amount of hope. I was not aware of this development in Aligarh and was informed about it just a few days ago after coming to Allahabad. There can be no doubt that the boarding system method that we have adopted in our college, in which all the Muslim students have gathered in one place, living, studying, and eating together, has seen friendships, mutual affection, and compassion for the community increase day by day. By the grace of God, the number of boarders at this time is 172.

Some days ago, a few of the students of our college agreed among themselves to form a society which they named '*Duty Society*,' meaning that it is a duty to do something for the welfare of the community. Those who are its members are called '*servants*,' i.e. they serve the community. It is the duty of every member, i.e. *servant*, to fulfill his *duty*, i.e. serve the community.

Now it has been absolutely proved that if Muslims are not assisted with stipends and scholarships, it will be impossible for them to get an education, which is the first step toward progress in the community. Hence, every member or *servant* of this society considers it his duty to collect money for stipends and scholarships for Muslim students.

The second duty that they have sworn to is that they will support their college, which is a community college in which they have studied throughout their lives, and will always love it like a child loves their mother. I was very surprised to hear of this sentiment and that Indian students can have such feelings too.

Now they have adopted the method of collecting money when they are away on school holidays to award stipends to college students, whom they consider their intellectual brothers. Even if they get an *ana* or a *pai*, they accept it with joy and honor and add it to their collection. Shamsul Hasan, a student from a very honorable family, collected Rs. 50 in this manner.

They feel no humiliation in, if the opportunity arises, to set up a shop in a marketplace and sell wares like an ordinary shopkeeper. Recently, the annual athletic meet was held in our college in Aligarh, which was presided by the collector and magistrate of Aligarh. Our European friends and ladies and Indian fraternity came together for this event. On this occasion, these students set up a tea shop and earned Rs. 16.

When the prizes were being distributed in the athletic meet, they set up a table on which there was a banner that read *"Duty."* Their fellow students, who won cash prizes, chose to donate a portion to their brothers, and Rs. 18 were collected. In this way, they have so far collected more than Rs. 100. The honorable and respectable professor of our college, Mr. Arnold is its treasurer. All this money and any that is collected in the future will go toward stipends for the students.

You know that this sentiment was born among the students of England and it brought great benefit to the nation. Their work greatly increased the feeling of compassion for the nation. May God make it happen in India as well.

Since our college is on a holiday break during this session of the Muhammadan Educational Conference, these servants of the community had requested that provisions for tea not be included in the arrangements for the guests so that they could come and set up a tea shop here. Those who wanted to drink tea could buy it from this shop.

Given that making such a request was a matter of pride for the community, and also to develop their courage and sentiments was a cause for the prosperity of the community, I very humbly appealed to Sheikh Nasiruddin *Saheb* and other elders who were involved in the arrangement of hospitality for the guests to accede to their request. I am happy to say that it was decided to proceed according to the wishes of these students, i.e. the hosts will not serve tea to the guests and any guest who wishes to have tea would be able to buy it from this shop that promotes respect for the community.

This is the reason why you see a tea stall on the premises with a board on which the word "*Duty*" is written in bold letters.

The members of this society are boys from honorable and respectable families of our community. Muhammad Mustafa Khan, Mazharul Haq, Tufail Ahmed, Mumtaz Hasan, and Inayatullah have set up a tea stall here. It is possible that the hard-hearted, whose hearts are harder than stone, will mock them, but even for them, God says, "*And verily, some rocks gush rivers; others split, spilling water; while others are humbled in awe of God. And God is never unaware of what you do.*" So, even those hearts that are made of this kind of stone will consider these boys to be a source of pride and honor and will consider them a magnificent sign of progress in the community.

Place: Allahabad
Dated: December 28, 1890

Signed by Syed Ahmed Khan
Honorary Secretary, Muhammadan
Educational Congress

145

How to Facilitate Ease in Holding the Sessions of the Muhammadan Educational Conference ★

(Report of the fifth annual session of the Muhammadan Educational Conference held in Allahabad, December 28-30, 1890)

In this session that was held in Allahabad, section 9, "Rules for conducting the conference," was amended. Prior to the amendment, this section directed that the conference meeting should be held where the people desire to hold it, provided that the people of that location accept the responsibility of arranging and organizing the meeting there.

After the amendment, the secretary has been empowered to determine the location of the meeting as he sees fit.

One objective of this amendment seems to be that the venue for the meeting should not be determined by the wishes of the people but by where it benefits the community the most.

The second objective seems to be that the arrangements for the meeting also should not depend on the desire of the people, and rather that appropriate arrangements should be made wherever it is decided to hold the meeting.

So, if the objectives of this amendment are the ones that have been stated, it will indeed make it easier to organize the meetings.

The most difficult part of organizing the meeting is making the catering arrangements. These arrangements need the involvement of a lot of organizers. The food items that are procured are subject to loss and damage in various ways. It takes a lot of time for food to be prepared. People don't get their meals in a proper and timely manner, though the expense is large and in vain. People are inconvenienced as well. If some decent arrangements can be made for this, it will ease the arrangements for the conference meetings to a great extent.

The first mistake is to regard the elders, who are well-wishers of the community and come to the meetings, as guests, since they come for the benefit of the community in which they themselves are included. So, they are their own guests and their own hosts.

There are hundreds of such meetings in Europe. First, we must see what happens there. What happens there is all the members that come make their own arrangements to stay with a friend, at a club, or in a hotel. No special accommodation or food arrangements are required and every person makes their own arrangement at their own expense.

Hotels are not available everywhere in India nor are hotels in sufficient numbers to accommodate all the people who come to these meetings. So, we must see what happens in India on the occasions of such large gatherings.

The largest gathering was in Agra at the time when His Highness the Prince of Wales visited and the royal court was held in Agra. For this occasion, the government had appointed an officer and a camp was set up for people to stay. In this camp, a tent served as the mess and food arrangements were made as in a hotel. The price of each meal was fixed and those who stayed there had their meals in the mess and paid for it as they would in a hotel. The government officer was there only to see to it that the food was good.

Recently, His Excellency Lord Lansdowne held court in Agra, which had the same kind of arrangement. Meals were served at fixed rates and managed by qualified cooks under contract. Meals were prepared as they would be in a hotel and people would go there to eat at their own expense.

We should adopt the same arrangement. Wherever the conference decides to hold its meeting, it should make arrangements for attending delegates to stay and for a hotel-like facility where all kinds of meals are prepared under the supervision of an organizer or a contractor.

A bakery shop should be set up where the servers and workers can have the meals of their choice.

In this way, the members attending the meeting will be very comfortable. The organizer or contractor of the mess can prepare whatever meals the delegates prefer, which they can have at any time they wish and pay for it.

There is no doubt that the expenses of the delegates who come to the meeting will increase somewhat, but I hope that no member will find that expense objectionable. The conference meeting lasts three or four days. If the daily expense for meals is one rupee per person, it amounts to no more than a total of three or four rupees for each member. These members, who come from faraway places and bear such large expenses, will not find this small increase unbearable for the cause of perseverance of the congress and welfare of their community.

I look forward to hearing the opinion of friends in this regard.

This year's expenses for the hospitality of guests were borne by Sheikh Naseeruddin *Saheb*, Taluqdar of Mau in district Allahabad, who also paid for two dinners held for the members and visiting delegates. All expenses other than meals were paid from this year's membership dues and donations and, as per the decision taken by the congress, the money that remains after all these expenses and other expenses such as printing of the proceedings will be deposited in the scholarship fund. So, thanks should be given to Sheikh Naseeruddin *Saheb* for this hospitality.

Even though the meeting of the conference comes to a positive and upbeat close and all the friends are happily and cheerfully returning to their homes, you gentlemen know that there is nothing in this world that does not have some sadness mingled with happiness. There is no rose that does not come with thorns. I present two matters which will be of sorrow to this gathering and to all the people. Ever since our conference was established, Nawab Sir Nawazish Ali Khan Bahadur, CSI, the great *Raïs* of Lahore, has been a steadfast supporter and proponent, a well-wisher of the community, and a promoter of education in every way. In fact, he has been a great patron of the Muslims and a pillar of strength for them.

In the same way, our friend Munshi Qadir Bakhsh Khan *Saheb*, *Raïs* of Kasur, was a great friend of our conference and always put his efforts into its development and progress. Both these elders passed away this year. Our community service has suffered a great loss with the passing of these two friends. Even though we will never lay eyes on them again, our hearts will never forget their compassion for the community. But we want to establish a memento to preserve their memory for future generations, and therefore I move that a vote of sorrow and mourning be passed in memory of these two most noble members.

Now I have one thing left to say clearly about the originators of the idea that the meeting be held in Allahabad, and they are: Khan Bahadur Maulvi

Syed Fariduddin Ahmad Khan, our respected *Janab* Syed Mir Zahoor Hussain, High Court lawyer, our venerable Munshi Mohammad Inayatullah *Saheb*, head clerk in the Allahabad collectorate, Maulvi Muhammad Abdul Majid Esq., barrister-at-law, Maulvi Abdul Lateef *Saheb*, clerk in the High Court, Munshi Muhammad Hanif *Saheb*, bailiff of civil court, Mir Hadi Ali *Saheb*, honorary magistrate and member of municipal committee, our respected Maulvi Raza Hussain *Saheb*, MA, head clerk of the government department in Allahabad, Maulvi Muhammad Azimuddin *Saheb*, interpreter in the High Court, Maulvi Ghulam Mujtaba *Saheb*, lawyer in the High Court, Sheikh Abdu Ghani *Saheb*, Sheik Abdul Samad *Saheb*, Sheik Dost Muhammad *Saheb*, and Sheikh Gulzar Ali *Saheb*. These are the people who were the originators and executors of the idea that the meeting should be held in Allahabad and the arrangers, organizers, and implementers of the meetings. All that happened here was due to these elders. The hard work and devotion shown in this work by Mir Zahoor Hussain *Saheb* and Munshi Mohammad Inayatullah *Saheb* cannot be described. One or two days prior to the start of the meeting, Syed Hussain *Saheb*, collector of Khaga, also arrived and helped us in our work with such diligence that he cannot be thanked enough. No prayer is more fitting for them than the wish that God gives these gentlemen guidance to have even more compassion for the community. It is obvious that there is no need for us to thank them because what they have done is for themselves and their community.

Mohamad Tafazzul Hussain *Saheb* has made a lot of effort in getting this house ready for the meeting. All the elders that I have named earlier and all those who were involved in organizing and arranging the meeting are of the opinion that Mohamad Tafazzul Hussain *Saheb* be presented with a certificate for his services bearing the signatures of the president and secretary of the session. Mir Syed Zahoor Hussain *Saheb* wishes to present him with a beautiful and special shawl as a personal gift. It is our desire that all these things be presented to him by the president.

The certificate was signed by the president and the secretary and the president presented it along with the shawl to Mohamad Tafazzul Hussain. The words on the certificate were as follows:

Mohamad Tafazzul Hussain Saheb, resident of Allahabad:

This conference is very appreciative of your around the clock efforts in the preparation of this beautiful and magnificent house for the meeting in such a short time that we did not expect it to be ready, and for your hard work and industrious efforts in getting this beautiful hall ready. This certificate is presented to you as a memento of your hard work along with a shawl presented by Syed Mir Zahoor Hussain, honorable member of our conference and lawyer of the High Court.

Dated: December 30, 1890   *Signed*
Place: Allahabad   *Sardar Muhammad Hayat Khan Bahadur, CSI*
                                                                   President

146

Speech on Changing the Name of the Educational Association

(Report of the fifth annual session of the Muhammadan Educational Conference held in Allahabad, December 28-30, 1890)

On the first day of the fifth annual session of the Muhammadan Educational Congress (held during December 28-30, 1890 in Allahabad). Maulvi Raza Hussain presented the resolution that the name of this association should be "Muhammadan Educational Conference" instead of "Muhammadan Educational Congress." Sir Syed's speech seconding this proposal is reproduced below.

Mr. President of the session!

I second the motion that my honorable friend Maulvi Raza Hussain *Saheb* has made to replace the word "congress" that is there in the name of our educational association with the word "conference." For a long time I have thought that the word "congress" is not suitable to be the name of our association. The word "congress" is more appropriate for the political assembly of the ambassadors and deputies of two monarchs to settle or decide the mutual affairs of their countries. Our educational association has no connection to such matters or to any political issues. That is why that name was undoubtedly unsuitable for it.

The word "conference" is more commonly used for gatherings that meet to discuss or debate with each other in good faith and friendship and with the purpose of exchanging opinions and providing advice and guidance in certain matters. Forcing someone to follow this advice or guidance is not in its tenor. Rather, following the advice and guidance is only up to the will of the people. That is the task of our educational association, to find a way for the advancement of Muslims by consulting among ourselves and to inform people that if they follow this path and adopt this method, they will reach their destination. There is nothing more in our power or our purpose.

It is said about this association of ours that till now it has not been of any use. I also accept that although Maulana Shibli considers this opinion wrong. But I may be excused when I say that certainly no one till now has claimed to have followed the advice and guidance of this educational association fully and found no benefit. Our community is like that person who gets a prescription from a doctor but does not fill the prescription and get the medicine, and expects to get well just by having the doctor write the prescription.

Well, that is a parenthetical remark, but there is no doubt that replacing the word "congress" with the word "conference" is extremely appropriate and I hope that all the members will agree.

> Consequently, all the members who were present unanimously agreed with this proposal and the name of this association was changed from "Muhammadan Educational Congress" to "Muhammadan Educational Conference."

147

Opinion Regarding Exclusion of Persian From the Curriculum

(Report of the fifth annual session of the Muhammadan Educational Conference held in Allahabad, December 28-30, 1890)

In 1890, the government wanted Persian education to be excluded from the curriculum. In the fifth session of the Muhammadan Educational Congress, a resolution was presented on this topic, appealing to the government that excluding the Persian language from the university curriculum, or to include Persian in the Arabic course, or to combine the conjugation and syntax of the two languages is absolutely not right, and in fact is harmful. Presenting this resolution, which was the third of the session, Sir Syed delivered the following speech.

Mr. President of the session!

Perhaps the people gathered in this big hall are wondering why this resolution, which is such that no one can even think of going against and is so clear and obvious as to be a proof of its own argument much like "the light of the sun is proof that the sun exists," has come up for debate. But they will be even more surprised and astonished when they hear that at the time when our Allahabad University was established, the first heart-breaking proposal that could destroy India's culture and its assembly of knowledge was that Persian should be excluded from the university curriculum. Every person to whom God has given wisdom will decide for himself what the real reason for this is, but the false argument that has apparently been presented is that Persian is not a classical language. Why is it not? Because, unlike Sanskrit, it is not a dead language, i.e. a language that is not spoken anywhere in the world, since it is still spoken in Iran. Hence, it is a living language, and therefore not a classical language.

This is an astonishing new interpretation of the world "classical." That is, the word "classic" with its meaning is joined with "-al" to produce a meaning that invokes death, and hence the meaning of classical language is a dead language.

It is a pity that Johnson is not alive, otherwise he would have considered this interpretation as a great help in his unequaled work of making a dictionary,[8] and would have proudly entered these meanings into his dictionary. But alas, his life was not faithful and he was deprived of this unique help. Webster[9] came afterwards, but unfortunately he too was destined to be deprived of it.

I am not familiar with English or English words, not even with its alphabets. To describe my knowledge of English, two nonsensical words of our language are very suitable, "*katar-matar*," i.e. a mishmash of words taken from here and there. But English scholars have written something about the word "classical." They write that the word "classics" is derived from the Latin word "classicus," from which the word "classical" is derived. This was related to the status of the people of Rome, particularly those of the highest status. Therefore, the adjective 'classical' was applied to authentic writers, particularly Greek and Roman, as well as to modern writers and their writings.

Now we have to see if Persian has the status of a classical language. Is there a tongue that could muster a no? Which is the sweetest language of all languages of the world? Persian. This is such an incontrovertible fact that every rational person has recognized it. Its poetry has acquired such a status in poetic literature that it has risen even above the status of the great Latin and Greek poets. Omar Khayyam's *Rubaiyat*, Firdausi's *Masnavi*[10] (*Shahnama*), the *ghazals* of Hafiz – can there be more piquant and sophisticated verses? Can a more authentic authority be found than Saadi, Nizami, Jami, Khusro, Anwari, Khaqani, and many others on a list that is very long? I will also add the names of Abul Fazl and Faizi, who were born in India, Ghalib, who lived during the same era, and Qaani, the Iranian

---

[8] "A Dictionary of the English Language, sometimes published as "Johnson's Dictionary," was published on April 15, 1755 and written by Samuel Johnson, an English writer who made lasting contributions as a poet, playwright, essayist, moralist, literary critic, sermonist, biographer, editor, and lexicographer. It is among the most influential dictionaries in the history of the English language.

[9] Noah Webster (1758–1843), the author of the readers and spelling books that dominated the American market at the time, spent decades of research in compiling his dictionaries. His first dictionary, "A Compendious Dictionary of the English Language," appeared in 1806. In it, he popularized features which would become a hallmark of American English spelling (*center* rather than *centre, honor* rather than *honour, program* rather than *programme*, etc.)

[10] The *Masnavi* is a poetic collection of anecdotes and stories derived from the Quran, Hadith sources, and everyday tales. Stories are told to illustrate a point and each moral is discussed in detail.

poet of more recent times, to the ranks of the great legends that I just mentioned with pride.

If you look at Persian as an academic language, you will find books on philosophy, ethics, politics, astronomy, astrology, mathematics, history, medicine, etc. available in Persian. Suffice it to say, there are books in the Persian language on all knowledge and in such numbers that if one copy of each work is collected, they would probably not fit in the hall of our university. Persian is such a powerful and eloquent language that it can express all the issues of any knowledge or subject without borrowing words from another language. The modes and exemplars of the writings of Sasan the Fifth are reflected in the conventions and terminologies of philosophy and not a word has been borrowed from another language.

The Persian language in India has, in general, advanced culture, civil discourse, academic associations, and all activity related to the minds and thoughts of mankind. Incontrovertible proof of this can be found by comparing those who have learned Persian to those who have not, no matter how proficient they are in another language.

The system of a second language in universities has been established with the concept of 'Aryan stock' and 'Semitic stock' in mind. Since these stocks have multiple languages in their heritage, those that have achieved the status of 'classical' have been included in the university curriculum. Altogether, the Persian language from the Aryan stock and Arabic and Hebrew from the Semitic stock have been recognized by the faculties of all Indian universities and even of other countries. Then what is the reason why our university will not recognize it?

I believe that all the members and visitors who are gathered in this hall, where 1000 chairs were laid out and most if not all of them are occupied, have an academic bent of mind. Therefore, by virtue of this position, this gathering has the right to claim that it is the representative of 50 million Muslims. I am certain that they, and all the other Muslims, consider the proposal to exclude Persian from the university curriculum to be the first attack on the education of Muslims. But we are certain that our universities will always look after the education of Muslims and will be our mother, not our destroyer.

It was not long after we had repelled this severe attack that we faced a similar attack, this time assuming another form, i.e. recurrence of an illness even more severe than its first occurrence. This time it was argued that since the university course included Sanskrit as a second language for Hindus, and the counterpart for Muslims would be either Arabic or Persian, Arabic was undoubtedly the right counterpart to Sanskrit since Persian was a simple language. Persian could not be compared to Sanskrit. So, it will be an injustice to those who study Persian relative to those who study Sanskrit. Therefore, only Sanskrit and Arabic should be included as second languages and Persian should be removed from the university curriculum.

I will certainly admit that the advanced grammar of the Sanskrit language, which is not even understood by many scholarly pundits, is mostly more difficult than Persian grammar. But is the higher level of Sanskrit grammar, which is known to be difficult, included in the university curriculum or taught in the universities? Absolutely not. Teaching of Sanskrit in universities includes elementary grammar such as review of phrases and understanding of passive verbs and nothing more. This level of Sanskrit grammar is certainly not more difficult than Persian grammar. Yes, an eloquent man can bring his eloquence to bear regarding this, but remember that eloquence is not necessary to prove the truth. Rather, it is an art of deception with which an eloquent man takes even something false and explains it to people in a way that they think it is true. So, presenting this argument that in terms of the curriculum implementation and the level of teaching in our universities, Sanskrit is a more difficult language than Persian is only a sham of the art of eloquence.

Another thing worth considering is that it is not enough to say that one language is more difficult than the other in order to include it in the curriculum, because even in the language that is considered more difficult, there are books available that are actually easy and simple in terms of the subject matter and style of writing. Similarly, in the language that is considered easy, there are books that are in fact difficult and time consuming. So, in order to compare courses in two languages as they are implemented and taught, it should be evaluated how they compare in the subject matter and style of composition. It is possible that the more difficult course will turn out to be easy in this regard and the easier course more difficult. Therefore, to only consider which language is more difficult than the other, to fill the halls of the universities with the echoes of this idea, and to leave aside the actual fact and instill faith in people's heart for something that is not a fact is the same sham of the art of eloquence.

Now let me take a look at Allahabad University's Persian course to see what level they are in terms of subject matter and style of composition. I see that the syllabus includes works by Firdausi, Khaqani, Zaheer Faryabi, Amir Khusro, Hafiz Shirazi, Zuhuri, Abul Fazl, Faizi, Qaani, Yaghma, and Ghalib, as well as

Akhlaq-e Jalali, a book on ethics and civics. All these books are from among the best books in terms of subject matter and some of the sections that have been selected are very difficult in this regard. I regret that I do not know the Sanskrit language. My esteemed Muslims friends on the other hand are great scholars of the Sanskrit language as well and I have been assured that the Sanskrit course is simpler compared to the Persian course. And when I came to know of the subject matter of the Sanskrit course, I certainly agreed that the Persian course is more difficult in this regard.

We do not want to interfere at all in the Sanskrit course. If the course is difficult, make it as easy as you want and facilitate the learning of this great and ancient language as much as you want. We accept it with great pleasure, but we can never accept anything that harms the education of 50 million of us Muslim subjects of Her Majesty the Empress of India.

O my friends! Do not think that these attacks on the education of Muslims are over. No, the attacks of the '*Reserved*' forces still remain. They have taken this wrong idea that this language is difficult and that language is easy, and ignoring the fact that it is a course which is easy or difficult as I have just described, they have attacked from the other side that Arabic and Persian should be combined into one course so that the course becomes difficult and on a par with the Sanskrit course. And every student, i.e. Muslim students should be required to pass this course, and whoever fails to do so should not be allowed to pursue education. That is, no university degree, which has become a prerequisite for day-to-day government jobs, private jobs, and any job on which the business of life depends, should be given to them unless they pass this course.

Although this attack was very severe, for the reason that it was against an academic principle, it did not include any communal aspect. Wouldn't you be surprised that the Persian language is from the *Aryan stock* and the Arabic language is from the '*Semitic stock*,' their conjugation and syntax, etymology, and composition style are so different from each other that they cannot be combined into one at all, and yet they tried to combine them. Indeed, underneath this magnificent building of the university, the Ganges and Yamuna rivers have come together. But is it in its power or in the power of any human being to combine two languages, which God created as two separate languages, and to merge them into one stream like the Ganges and Yamuna. Heaven forbid! It is out of the question. Regrets, hundred regrets! But this regret gets even more exacerbated when the encroachment is from those people who do not know how to swim in either the Ganges or the Yamuna, i.e. they are neither familiar with Arabic nor with Persian. Then, what can the purpose of such statements be except to destroy the education of Muslims, which we have somewhat set on course after 20 years of hard work? If our university does that, I will not call it mother but a destroyer. But I have faith that it will not do such a thing.

O my esteemed friends and O supporters of the community! And O people! You who are gathered in this hall for the sake of your educational purposes know full well that university education till the entrance level is only elementary education, and even less than elementary in terms of a second language. The students in this class, in terms of their education level, are like those children whose breath still hasn't lost the whiff of milk. In such a situation, other than the English language, do they have the ability to grasp the conjugation and syntax of either the Arabic or the Persian language and to pass the exam of this bi-colored *chap* course in which Arabic and Persian have been combined?[11]

Then there was another attack by the '*Reserved*' forces; it was that the Persian language cannot be learned without learning the conjugation and syntax of Arabic, and so books on Arabic conjugation and syntax, from *Mizan* to *Sharh al-Kafiyah ash-Sahfiyah* should be included in the syllabus along with Persian. This will allow a better learning of Persian since Arabic words have been included in Persian, making it necessary to know Arabic conjugation and syntax. Do you know what kind of book *Sharh al-Kafiyah ash-Sahfiyah* is? It is that difficult text which has been removed even from the Arabic language syllabus.

An attack that is laden with empathy is undoubtedly harsher, but it actually has its foundation laid on sand. That is why it would be appropriate if I narrated some of the history related to the mixing of Arabic words in Persian.

The country of Persia, which is the home of the Persian language, was ruled for a long time by people belonging to that country itself, whose greatness and dignity will always be remembered in history. The honor of their flag "*Derafsh Kaviani*"[12] will never be forgotten by the world. But it was God's will that a Bedouin people from a sandy and gravelly country - who do I mean? Arabs! Arabs who? Our forefathers! – would conquer it with the power of their swords.

---

11. *Chap* (چپ) is a bicolored pigeon or a bicolored paper kite.

12. Derafsh Kaviani (Persian: درفش کاویانی) was the legendary royal standard Derafsh (in Latin: vexilloid) of Iran (Persia), a flag-like object used as a military standard since ancient times until the fall of the Sasanian Empire. The banner was also sometimes called the "Standard of Jamshid", the "Standard of Fereydun" and the "Royal Standard"

And so our forefathers conquered it. Firdausi, who had descended from the fire-worshiping Zoroastrians and had become a Muslim, was carrying in his heart the national grief from being conquered when he said this:

> After drinking camel milk and eating lizard
> The matter reached the level to which those Arabs
> Aspired to possess the crown of a King
> Damn, oh time; damn, oh time

We consider these verses, which he said with derision, to be the pride of our forefathers. Yes, we camel milk drinkers and lizard eaters conquered the throne of the Kyan, the ancient kings of Persia, and God placed the camel-herding nation on the throne of the empires of Dara, Jamshid, Cyrus, et al. Hence it was certain that three types of words would enter the Persian language in the same way that our Urdu language as well as other languages spoken in India have added words from the English Empire in them. The details of these three types of words are as follows:

- First, the incomparably elegant and eloquent verses of the Holy Quran, which are recited in every part of the land of Persia and which are so charming that they affected even the most steel-hearted. These and other particular words from the religion of Islam entered Persian.

- Second, those words related to the work of the empire which would be natural for a conquering nation to impose on the conquered people also entered the Persian language.

- Third, words from the knowledge and arts of the Arabs that they themselves brought to Persia with them, or devised, or gave impetus to.

All these words are limited in number and have been incorporated into the Persian language in much the same way as an adopted son becomes a child of the family. In order to understand and use them, a Persian speaker does not need to know Arabic conjugation and syntax. By God's will, there may be people in this gathering as well who do not know Arabic, but when words such as 'naasir' and 'mansuur' or 'haafiz' and 'mahfuuz' are spoken in front of them, without knowing their source or how they are derived, they would understand very well their meaning and sense.

This is the case with all Arabic words that have been incorporated into the Persian language and are considered to be the same as Persian words. Consequently, many of these words are not used in the sense and with the meaning that they are used in Arabic, some of them are not subject to the rules of the Arabic language, and all of them are not subject to the rules of grammar of the Arabic language. So, what is the benefit of teaching Arabic grammar in the teaching of the Persian language?

I hear that the English language too has Latin and Greek words mixed in it in the same way, but no one says that you cannot learn the English language unless you learn the Latin and Greek conjugation and syntax.

Yes, some Arabic scholars deliberately use a lot of Arabic words in their Persian writing, just like some crude and deficient English scholars unnecessarily bring Latin words into their writing only to brag about their knowledge, which every linguist, whether of the Persian language or a European Englishman, looks down upon with disdain. In fact, it would not be fit to call this writing Persian.

All the teachers of the Persian language, whether they are from India, Balkh, Bukhara, Egypt, or England, know that the usage of Arabic words in Persian, other than the kind of words I mentioned earlier, is wrong. Firdausi is called '*Khuda-e-Sukhan*,' the god of poetry, because in his '*Shahnama*,' which is an epic, there are no Arabic words except of the three types I mentioned, and even those are rare. He himself had claimed that he would not utter a word of Arabic in his verses, but there was some criticism when this couplet of his was recited:

Then destiny (death) cried: "Take!" and fate cried: "Give!"
The heavens cried: "Excellent!" and the angels: "Bravo!"

Destiny (*qaza*), fate (*qadr*), heavens (*falak*), and angels (*malak*) were words from Muslim gatherings that had come into use in the Persian language as Persian words for the same reasons that I had described earlier and so there was no objection to them. But the word excellent (*ahsan*) was pure Arabic, there was an objection to it, and he was asked, "The word *ahsan* is Arabic, why did you say it? He said I did not say it, *Falak* said it." In essence, that is how wrong the Persian language teachers considered mixing Arabic words into Persian. In contrast to this, our friends want to jumble up the conjugation and syntax of Arabic and Persian, which are two entirely different things. And at that level? That is, in the early days of education, the result of which would be that neither of the languages would be learned and both of them would be destroyed. The students would get nothing out of it and be deprived of learning.

In his later years, Tennyson, who was the national poet of England, would be proud of reading some of his poems that were in pure English and at the same time express regret at knowing Latin and Greek. He would lament that he could not unlearn those two languages because his knowledge of them had hindered his ability to write English poetry. In short, mixing the conjugation and syntax of Arabic and Persian has no benefit, in fact it is an impossible idea and a hindrance to the education of the Muslims.

Now only one attack remained in the guise of empathy. It was that the Persian language is leaving the Arabic language behind because more and more students choose Persian over Arabic as the second language. I will not explain the real reason behind it, which is based on the country's need, but I will ask those who empathize with us as to why they have even more empathy than us for a language that belongs to our forefathers and our religion. Please be kind enough and leave the empathy for our language to us, whether we take it forward or leave it behind:

> I don't know why my counselor objects to my tears even though
> The heart, the eyes, the sleeve, the edge of the shirt are all mine

O gentlemen! All these issues that were deadly poison for the university education of the Muslims have appeared in our university. I will always be indebted to Mr. Gough, principal of Muir College, registrar of Allahabad University, and a member of the faculty of arts for his statement that implied that he would never like to see the education of Muslims be harmed. Consequently, in the meeting of the faculty of arts, he objected to all these proposals. I am grateful to the president of the faculty of arts Mr. Waite as well for raising his hand and voting 'no' when the votes against these proposals were being counted. I am also grateful to all those members of the faculty of arts who voted against this proposal. That is why I have presented a resolution to pass a vote of thanks for the Allahabad University faculty of arts.

O friends! I also have the honor of being a member of the faculty of arts but I was not a participant in this meeting. Hence, I abstain from this vote of thanks for the faculty of arts.

★

148

Speech Regarding Industrial Education

(Report of the fifth annual session of the Muhammadan Educational Conference held in Allahabad, December 28-30, 1890)

In the fourth meeting of the fifth annual session of the Muhammadan Educational Conference held in Allahabad, on December 29, 1890, a resolution was presented that "there should be no changes to the literary teaching in the English schools and colleges for the sake of advancing technical education." This resolution was presented by Sir Syed, who delivered the following speech.

Mr. President of the session!

Before I start a discussion on this resolution, first I must submit to those gentlemen who are interested in technical education that the purpose of this resolution is not to decide any matter related to the substance of technical education, but rather to require that there should be no change in the English education in schools and colleges as it exists today. Any change for the purpose of advancing technical education would be harmful to the progress of literary education to a higher level.

By literary education I mean that education which includes the knowledge of literature, logic philosophy, history, moral and mental science, technical economy, theory of legislation, jurisprudence, and higher level mathematics. So, whenever I use this term in this discussion, it should be construed as this type of education. But, first of all, we must at least understand the meaning of technical education and what it entails. At present, I and perhaps a lot of other people do not understand what it is. If we understand it, we can easily decide whether it is beneficial or harmful to change the existing structure of education in schools and colleges for its development. Perhaps we will also get an opportunity to consider the class of people in the country that this thing called technical education may benefit and the level at which it would be considered beneficial. I turned the pages of many books and asked some people as well, but the reality of technical education eluded me. But the Government of Bombay found a statement by Mr. Scott Russell in a resolution that is considered to be a good definition of technical education. I will read this statement. He states that "it is essential that every person, in his particular trade or profession, understand its principles well, put his special equipment to the most excellent use, be able to apply its excellent methods more intelligently, and be able to fulfill his life's purpose more quickly and efficiently, whether it is in trade, manufacturing, construction, or shipping."

This statement is very good and undoubtedly deserves to be called the correct definition of technical education, but we are still somewhat in the dark and do not know which vocations the government wants to develop under technical education or includes in its definition. We also do not know if the country desires the development of technical education, in what trades and for which vocations, what kind of education, and what the effect of including it in the current schools and colleges will be.

It is very difficult for me to go into more detail, but by considering the action taken by the government in different provinces or the actions taken throughout the country that the government of a province has liked or acknowledged, we may get some details of the schemes that the government is inclined to promote. I shall describe in detail these schemes to the best of my knowledge, but I will make no mention of industrial schools since I regard them as separate from this kind of education. Where so many other things in this world are included among the wonders, it would be better that it remain among those wonders. Those details that I want to describe are as follows:

1. Machines: the use of mechanical equipment
2. Mechanics: the use of cranes and heavy lifting equipment
3. Steam: the use of steam driven equipment, such as steam engines, etc.
4. Physics and its seven branches:
    a. Sound: its generation, propagation, and containment, etc.
    b. Light: its propagation, its speed, and its strength, etc.
    c. Heat: its generation and uses
    d. Electricity: its generation, effects, and its uses
    e. Magnetism: its generation, effects, and its uses
    f. Chemistry: not the science of making silver and gold, but knowledge of the composition and decomposition of metals and other materials
    g. Thermometer: both types, their calibration, and their respective uses

All these branches are taught in two ways; one can be called theoretical and the other practical.

Theoretical education includes discussion of machines, disassembling their different parts and putting them together, understanding their functions and different uses, their appropriate strength and power, particularly for heavy lifting equipment, understanding the power of steam and levels of steam engine strengths, understanding the description of substances and compounds, decomposition of compounds, formation of gasses, methods of producing compounds from their components, understanding the science of chemistry and atmosphere, understanding both types of thermometers and their respective uses, and, in the same way, the explanation of the forces of electricity and magnetism, their uses, effects and outcomes.

Practical education insofar as physics is concerned includes practical exercises on instruments and tools and trainees working on these machines and putting them to use. Practical education cannot take place without going to and working in a factory where those machines are present and work is carried out using them. For this purpose, it is necessary for students to go and work in the railways, cotton mills, engineering schools, or factories. Training in technical drawing is mostly given by having the students draw layouts of machines and their parts.

If my memory serves me right, 15 or 16 years ago there used to be just one course in technical education. But after that, two university courses were established, one of which should be considered a theoretical course in technical education, and presently the structure of these courses in our university curriculum is as follows:

One includes a high level of literary education and middle-level mathematics and has been named course (A); the other includes middle-level literary education and a high level of mathematics and physics and is named course (B).

This bifurcation has been in place for the BA classes for some years now. Students have complete freedom to choose between the two branches. Given the government's objective to promote technical education, it won't be surprising if this bifurcation is implemented at the FA and intermediate levels as well.

Up to this point, we have no concern or objection since every person is free to choose between course (A) and (B) branches depending on what they find useful for their lives.

But, in view of the advancement of technical education, if there is any interference in course (A) such that the high level of literary education is harmed or someone is prevented from optionally pursuing the high-level mathematics course without taking the physics course, then surely we will have cause for concern and objection. This is because in such situations, we will deprive a person taking course (A) of a satisfactory education or of a high level of mathematics, a subject that sharpens the mind, the intellect, and the thought process.

We are extremely thankful to Mr. Gough, principal of Muir College and registrar of Allahabad University, for keeping high-level mathematics an optional subject in course (A), safeguarding our objectives.

But I want to demonstrate the extent to which the country has accepted course (B), the extent to which its implementation has been completed, and the extent to which it is benefitting the country.

First of all, I am going to count the number of students in the country who are pursuing course (A) and the number who are pursuing course (B). If my estimate is correct, no more than 5% of the students are attending course (B) and 95% are in course (A). And this is a clear indication that there is no desire for technical education in the country.

Now we must observe that the inclusion of physics in course (B) was actually meant to achieve the theoretical education part of the technical education, and for its achievement it was essential to get admitted to an engineering college for a practical education and to enter an engineering college, railways, cotton mill, or any factory and work there. I do not know of any student from my province who got a BA degree after passing course (B), gave up looking for government employment, and joined an engineering factory for practical training to create a source of livelihood from it. So, even for him, a degree of this course has no value other than a general degree without practical experience. And with this inference, it can be said that the country has not benefited from this at all

It can be said that the absence of an engineering college in this province is a deficiency. First of all, I do not accept that this is a deficiency. This is because there is Roorkee Engineering College, railway factories in Lucknow and Allahabad, and a cotton mill in Kanpur, and no student was attracted to enter them and get a practical education. This proved that students who pass the course (B) have no desire to get a practical education, and certainly there must be some reason for it.

Technical education is desired in those countries where there is an abundance of all sorts of private factories which need people who have graduated with a technical degree. Capital is needed to establish factories, which is lacking in India. So, people with a technical education cannot thrive here and hence there is no desire for it. There is a misconception that when there are people with a technical education, factories will also be established. This idea is based on the philosophical question of whether the chicken came first or the egg, but it is proven wrong by the fact that despite physics being included in university education for some time now, no one has graduated with a mastery over technical education.

Regarding the establishment of an engineering college, it is worth considering the opinion given by Col. Forbes. He says that the practical education given to Indians in the railway factories of Lucknow and Allahabad and in the government factories of Roorkee is now bearing fruit in Delhi. Presently there are 17 iron mills and workshops that make machines, and one of the workshops has a 20 horsepower engine that is operated entirely by Indians without the supervision of Europeans. There is a small iron factory and a workshop in Roorkee under the management of Indians. There are two such factories in Meerut and other such factories and workshops in different places. The managers and many of the workers of these workshops have received their training in railway and other government factories, and that is why these factories can be considered the real technical schools where these people received their training in practical skills. That is why they were of the opinion that there is no need for the government to bring technical or engineering education into the schools and colleges. The government can provide assistance to a number of selected students of middle or high schools for the purpose of getting training to learn practical skills by working in a railway or government factory for four or five years. The government should not do anything more than that.

Regarding the opinion of Col. Forbes, I would like to say this much more that the workers of the factories he has mentioned did not receive any theoretical education in machines, steam, or physics in any school, rather they developed the skills to do their jobs only through practical training and experience. Hence, practical training is indeed the true technical education, and mere theoretical education is useless and a waste of time.

I will not lose sight of my opinion and its underlying reason that just as technical industries are difficult, if not extremely difficult, to establish, so are the benefits to the country difficult to achieve. It would be a false presumption that small factories pressing steel, smelting iron, and operating steam engines are going to be capable of benefiting the country.

In any case, we have no dispute with the bifurcation that happened in the BA course, or will happen in the FA and intermediate courses, provided there is no disruption to the education of course (A). But the discussion we do want to have is regarding the education in the entrance and middle classes.

This debate arose out of the recommendation of the Educational Commission that the upper classes of high schools should have a bifurcation – one which leads to qualifying for the university entrance exam, which I call class (A), and the other which has more practical education that aims to educate youth for trade and vocations, which I call class (B). In view of this recommendation, the government had the thought that the existing standard for the entrance exam, which I call course (A), should not be modified, rather another standard should be established, which I have called course (B), that would achieve the stated objective. If the course (A) and (B) bifurcations are established for the entrance and middle classes as well, our literary education will not suffer any harm at all and time will very soon tell that doing so was absolutely useless. But if the entrance or middle courses were to be modified in such a way as to include the elementary principles of technical education, we would have great concerns about it. There is no doubt that doing so would harm the literary education at the entrance level, which creates the worthiness in students to appear in the entrance exam. We are opposed to these types of proposals and our purpose with the resolution that has been presented is that in the literary education in English schools and colleges, which we interpret as course (A), there should be no modification for the sake of advancing technical education.

There is no doubt that in India, and in our province too, more and more modern factories are being established every day using English capital and surely they need skilled workers and foremen. But it is suspect how big the need is. Is the need bigger than the current availability of labor and is there a need or desire to appoint Indians as foremen? If there is, then some arrangement should be made to meet this need without making any modifications to the course (A) with respect to technical education, be it at the BA, intermediate, entrance, or middle level. We do not care about the modification to the course (B) at any level because in our opinion it has not benefited the country, nor is there any expectation that it will.

His Honor the Lieutenant Governor of our province has proclaimed a resolution containing very good and useful suggestions in this regard. I will read before this gathering some sections of this resolution containing these suggestions.

He states that if it is supposed that this kind of education is needed, then the following matters will have to be decided:

1. What kind of education should this be?
2. What is the best scheme to achieve it?
3. From what sources can the necessary funds be obtained?

Regarding the first matter, what is needed the most is good theoretical and practical understanding of most of the low-level technical engineering concepts that a foreman would require. In particular, this includes knowledge and skills pertaining to steam engines, railway factories, iron factories, and methods of spinning of yarn, which are used in those factories that have been established in these districts. To procure these skills, two branches of factories in Bombay have been recognized as grounds for indigenous labor. Although these facilities are somewhat restricted here, in those districts where they are needed, certainly the means for education are relatively nonexistent.

Regarding the second matter, there is a government engineering college and a government workshop in Roorkee, and it is likely that the means for the education deemed necessary for this type of progress exist there. The staff of the college, as it presently is, will probably have to be increased, and a special class will have to be established for those students who wish to receive the kind of technical education that we want to provide. But all kinds of students will have to adhere to most of the current curriculum. Also, the factories will probably have to enhance their training resources to fulfill the requirements of practical education that we want to add to the theoretical education. A few candidates are still trained each year in the Roorkee factory, but these candidates are in the category of manual labor or ordinary workers, not in the category of foremen. There will be a need to train candidates for foremen in these districts, provided it can be established that there is a need for them. In the railway factories, practical training is provided mostly to low-level workers who generally have no prior education.

Before the students enter these classes, as we have proposed, it will be necessary to hold an exam such as that of the Anglo-vernacular[13] middle class so that they can acquire a good knowledge of English and the true desire of those who seek education is met. There will be a need for a three or four years long

---

[13.] Anglo-vernacular implies the use of both English and a local vernacular, a term used especially for schools in India, Burma, and Ceylon during the period of British rule.

theoretical and practical course, which will probably include a term of practical training in a railway or textile factory. The proposal that seems most worthy of practical implementation is that some scholarships be offered to those students who wish to enter college and complete their education and training and use the stipend to learn practical work either in Roorkee or in a factory as a component of their course.

But two matters seem to be worth considering, and more information is needed regarding them before any decision can be made about the aforementioned proposal. First of all, we want to get the opinion of the managers of the railways and those gentlemen who are owners or directors of factories as to whether they have room for employment of those Indians who have received this type of theoretical and practical education, i.e. as foremen as well and not just as manual laborers. And whether there are sufficient means of education and training for the ordinary worker. If not, what are the schemes that are implementable with the resources the government has at its disposal for developing this kind of education. In this regard, Mr. Wicks and Mr. Holderness consulted with the owners and directors of factories and the railways, but the information they obtained is incomplete. Those who are qualified to give an opinion have convinced us that what is needed is the establishment of night schools for the elementary education of the workers who are employed in the railways and other factories and that there is no need for Indian foremen in these districts.

If it is supposed that the kind of education we are proposing is the most desirable, it will be necessary to ascertain whether the owners and managers of the railways and the factories are willing to allow the students who pass this course to get practical education and training in their factories. And if they are willing, under what conditions?

The question of funding is such that at this time, and until such time that its magnitude can be determined, its discussion is out of place. It is probable that there will be some initial expenditure, which will be considerable, for making the necessary additions to the factory buildings and for student accommodation in Roorkee. There will also be some recurring expenditure in colleges for additional staff and scholarships. But until we have satisfied ourselves that the principles upon which we wish to act are practicable, it is pointless to have more conversation on this part of the matter.

The first issue, which is actually unresolved, is whether the facilities for the kind of education needed to produce workers qualified for foremen jobs are actually the same kind of facilities that are needed for the functioning of these factories, particularly in these districts, and will provide employment to Indians in search of a livelihood. Secondly, if this is so, do we have reason to believe that the people who are qualified to give opinions (e.g. managers and owners of railways and factories) favor the kind of education that is in this practical scheme? Thirdly, what light can the educationists and the managers of the factories shed on the proposals we have made? That is, what kind of material assistance can they provide for the kind of education that we have proposed?

In order to get the information we need regarding the aforementioned matter, I have proposed that a committee be set up which would include the joint secretary in the government responsible for construction, Mr. Waite, director of education, Mr. Holderness, director of factories and land distribution, and Mr. Robert, manager of Bengal and North Western Railway, who has kindly agreed to assist the committee and, whenever he can find time from his important engagements, to assist me in the proposed investigation. An Indian gentleman will also be added to the committee. I would like the committee to obtain detailed information on each of the matters that I mentioned earlier from all possible sources and, if it deems necessary, to send one or two of its own members to Calcutta, Bombay, or Madras to find out what benefit we can derive from the experience gained from the operation of the technical schools in these places. When these investigations are completed, the committee should immediately send to me its report along with its particular recommendations and detailed proposals for what it wants to see implemented.

I will be happy if one or two members of the committee, especially when they are in Madras where I understand this matter has been given particular consideration, would direct toward me those measures that have been taken for the development of the manual laborers, whether it is because they consider those measures to be well documented, or have made good use of tools, or are observed to be effective for any other reason. Mr. Holderness, Mr. Waite, and the Indian member of the committee should separately consider those matters that are included in this scheme, particularly with respect to the Lucknow proposal, and prepare a separate report. The excellence of such a proposal so far as it relates to Madras or Bombay, its practicality, cost, and the skills and manual capabilities that are actually being imparted in Awadh and the North-Western Provinces — these are the issues that should be given particular attention.

This proposal is so good that no person can deny its worth. We are very happy to implement any suitable proposals for the development of technical education in the country, provided our literary education is not disturbed. No such measures or changes to our education system should be adopted that are against our wishes and compel us to be deprived of a high level of literary education.

For the sake of development of technical education in our university or in accordance with the proposals of the government – which I believe never intended to harm literary education in its quest to promote technical education – many times such measures were presented that were openly detrimental to the progress of literary education. Fortunately they did not succeed. But we must make it clear that we are very happy with the development of technical education by any suitable means and to the extent possible; however, to adopt a means that is a hindrance to the progress of literary education toward a higher level would certainly make us resentful, bitterly resentful. So, to reinforce this matter with public opinion, this resolution has been presented, and I hope that everyone will agree with it.

149

Preservation of Antique Books and Old Coins

(Report of the fifth annual session of the Muhammadan Educational Conference held in Allahabad, December 28-30, 1890)

In the sixth meeting of the fifth annual session of the Muhammadan Educational Conference (held on December 30, 1890), Syed Akbar Hasan presented a resolution that all the rare books, antique manuscripts, and old coins that are in the possession of various people should be acquired and the conference should establish a library and a museum so that these antiquities of ours can be preserved. In support of this resolution, Sir Syed gave the following speech.

Mr. President of the session!

If this resolution, moved by my friend Syed Akbar Hasan, is passed, it will be a very good addition to the Muhammadan Educational Conference. In India, very few libraries or administrative entities have been established for this purpose. I believe that apart from the library recently established by Khan Bahadur Maulvi Khuda Baksh *Saheb* in Patna, there is no other such organized library of Arabic and Persian books. Many fine and rare books are, however, in the possession of various people, and their status is not much known. By fine and rare books I don't mean ornate, gilded, or gold calligraphy books, rather those pragmatic and historic texts that are very rare and whose availability will be very helpful in understanding history, acquiring knowledge of various subjects, and learning the views of the scholars of the past eras.

There has been no list published of where these useful and informative books are in India and there is no means of getting this information. It is not even known if these books exist or not. So, if the status of such books is published in the journal of our conference in the form of a short report, it will greatly benefit the country.

A great record will be preserved if seals of authority, monograms, and plaques are photographed and printed using phototype or photolithography. Antiquarians have put a lot of effort into collecting coins and publishing their images, and I believe this has done a lot of good to the study of history. But the acquisition of those images of court decrees, seals of authority, monograms and plaques that are related to those eras has been completely neglected. I think that just as the coins are useful for the study of history, so are these seals. They can be considered as the basis for understanding many historical events. Although this task is huge and expensive to carry out, efforts should be made as much as possible.

At present, among the societies in India and Europe, the Asiatic Society of Bengal and the Royal Asiatic Society of London have collected a lot of coins along with inscriptions and published their status in books. But only those who are interested in the study of history are aware that in our Asian history, whether it is Arabic or Persian, there are many situations and events that need their accuracy to be validated, particularly those events whose time of occurrence is described differently in history. These inscriptions and coins are very good evidence to properly investigate these situations and events. So, if a gentleman clarifies these ambiguous or conflicting events with reasoning based on coins and inscriptions, it will be a great help to the study of history. In particular, comparing these coins with the accounts in history can help remove historical ambiguities and misconceptions. For example, we read about a few coins that are mentioned in the history of India, such as the *dehliwal, tanka*, and *dam* coins[14], but we are not very familiar with their descriptions. Due to this reason, we remain ignorant of a great event in history. History would greatly benefit if any kind of historical research, as much as can be conducted, is published in the conference's journal. For these reasons I support this resolution and hope that this useful resolution will be passed unanimously.

All the members agreed with the resolution and it was passed unanimously.

[14.] Coins minted in Delhi sultanates were called *dehliwal* coins. *Tanka,* also known as the *taka* or *tangka,* was a major historical currency in the Indian subcontinent. *Dam* was a small Indian copper coin first introduced by Sher Shah Suri in the mid 16th century.

150

Speech on the Excellent Achievements of
"Anjuman al-Farz"

*(Report of the fifth annual session of the Muhammadan Educational Conference held
in Allahabad, December 28-30, 1890)*
*(Tazkira Sir Syed (A Biographical Note on Sir Syed), compiled by Maulvi
Muhammad Amin Zubairi, Lahore, 1961 p 366)*

Sahibzada Aftab Ahmad Khan, when he was a student at the Aligarh College, established a society for the poor and needy students of the college called the *"Anjuman al-Farz"* (The Duty Society). This society used to collect funds in various ways to meet the expenses of the poor students of the college and to give scholarships to deserving students to continue their education. One of these ways was that on the occasion of various gatherings, meetings, and conferences, *Anjuman al-Farz* would set up stalls to sell tea and other refreshments. In these stalls, children from respectable families who were studying at the college would sell refreshments to the attendees and the profits from these sales were spent on helping all the poor students. They set up a tea stall at the fifth annual session of the Muhammadan Educational Conference held in Allahabad in 1890. Sir Syed took great interest in the establishment, purpose, and aims of this society, and looked up to its members who had so much compassion in their hearts to help their poor brothers. At this session, Sir Syed praised the members of the society with these words.

The members of the Duty Society are from honorable and respectable families of our community. Aftab Ahmad Khan, Mazharul Haq, Muhammad Mustafa Khan, Tufail Ahmad, Mumtaz Husain, Inayatullah and others have set up a tea stall here. It is very possible that some hard-hearted people, whose hearts are harder than stone, will mock these students of the *Madrasatul Uloom* Aligarh and talk about them with great derision. But so what? God has stated with respect to stones as well:

> "*And indeed, there are some stones from which rivers gush out, and indeed, there are of them (stones) that split apart so that the water flows from them, and indeed, there are of them (stones) that fall down for fear of God. God is not unaware of what you do.*"

So, even the hearts that are made of this kind of stone will certainly understand the pride that these students have for their community, will value their service, will consider their actions as a great symbol of community development, and will be greatly impressed by the students' spirit of compassion for their fellow students. May God bless these students more and more for their good efforts and give them more and more opportunities to help and support their brothers:

This is the worship, this is the religion and faith
That man is of use to man in this world

151

Reply Address

(Aligarh Institute Gazette, October 14, 1891)

When Sir Syed took a delegation to Hyderabad, the old boys of the *Madrasatul Uloom* there presented him with an address. On this occasion, Sir Syed gave the following speech in reply.

My dear Aziz Mirza[15] and other dear ones!

There are many charming things in Hyderabad, many pleasant houses and environs, but I assure you all that I am most pleased to see the flowers of our college that are gathered here. These flowers are the spring of my life. These are my roses and tulips and the hopes of my life. When I see them blooming and thriving, there is no happiness greater than that for me. I am happy to see that so many students of the college are gathered here. I thank God and sincerely pray for their success. O my dear ones, you know that my love for you is no less than that of your parents. I always pray for your religious and worldly progress. Whenever I see those of you who are successful, my heart is very happy, and I pray for those who do not yet consider themselves to be successful. But, my dear ones, you must understand the real purpose of the education that was given to you. The real purpose is not just to acquire wealth, but your inner development, the development of your heart, and the development of your mind. You must have seen the person who does not know a single word, but God has by chance given him immense wealth. But I hope you will not care much about such wealth, [*Chants of "Hear! Hear!"*] and that you will be proud of the wealth in your heart and in your mind. I am very happy that you love each other and you love our college. Although you cannot

---

[15] Maulvi Muhammad Aziz Mirza (b. 1864) studied at the Anglo-Oriental College, Aligarh and graduated with honors in English literature and history in 1887. He came to Hyderabad when Sir Asman Jah was the Prime Minister and became his personal assistant in 1893. In 1897, he was appointed secretary in charge of judiciary, police, and administration. He was a well-known orator.

love me like I love you, because if you put all your love in one place it cannot be equal to my love for you, I hope you will love each other and your college even more. The truth is that the college is like your mother, and if you allow me to say and forgive me, I say that all of you are my children. This decision you have made to celebrate the anniversary of the college by gathering as many students as possible is a matter of great joy and shows your liveliness. This will also be a means for you to keep the love for your college fresh in your hearts. There will be no difficulty in making it happen. Even if two or four students get together on the appointed date for this ritual and sit together and recount how they spent their time together in the college, what all they saw, and what impressions still remain in their hearts, [*Chants of "Hear! Hear!"*] this purpose would be achieved. People also told me that the date of the annual meeting of the college should be fixed and there was a lot of disagreement about this date. They wanted to fix the date to be the founder's birthday, which I did not approve of. But I remind you that January 7, 1877 is the date that the foundation stone of the college was laid by the hands of Lord Lytton. The most excellent date for the annual meeting of the college would be January 7 and should be called Foundation Day. I will also make arrangements for it after I have returned to Aligarh. Finally, I thank you for the address, from which I have received as much love as I expected from you. I ask for blessings for your religious and worldly success.

152

Annual Report of the Muhammadan Educational Conference at the Fifth Session 1890 ★

(Referenced from the sixth annual session of the Muhammadan Educational Conference held in Aligarh on December 27-30, 1891)

My dear sirs!

According to the rules that are followed every year, I have the honor to present at the beginning of the session a brief summary of the resolutions of this academic conference that were passed in the previous year, the results obtained from them, and the extent to which they were complied.

In the previous session, a resolution number (2) was passed that for the purpose of preserving the ancient language of Persian, its manner of composition, and its style of writing royal decrees in the past, the secretary should search for and collect the ancient royal decrees that are available with various people, and the excellent ones among them should be compiled in a book of compositions and published on behalf of the conference.

Related to the same resolution, a resolution number (8) was passed that any royal markings on these decrees, such as monograms, ornate seals, and things of that nature should be reproduced in the form of photographs and published.

I have started work toward compliance with this resolution but you know how difficult it is to get a hold of the ancient decrees. Many of these decrees have been damaged and destroyed and if someone has an original decree, they hold onto it so tight]y that they can't be persuaded to even show it. Nevertheless, we have received some original decrees from a few friends and old families which I present in this meeting. Among them, there is one decree that is very strange and unique and has been received through the family of Maulvi Muhammad Sulaiman *Saheb*, *Raïs* Kandhala and a custodian there.

This decree is from the time of the empire of Abu al-Fateh Muhammad Shah bin Firoz Shah dated Rajab 22, 793 AH, which makes it older than 500 years. I think it will be extremely difficult to find a decree older than that and it is a very rare artifact from the empire of the Tughlaq dynasty.

Due to rotting and attempts to mend, the monogram on the decree has suffered some damage in one corner but all the words on it are clearly legible. This monogram is so strange and unique that I have never seen the likes of it before. The following words are imprinted on the monogram:

Confident in the support of the Most Merciful, defender of the world and faith,
Abu al-Fateh Muhammad Shah bin Firoz Shah, the Emperor

The lettering, style of writing, and manner of composition used in the decree are also as strange as the monogram. It was read with extreme difficulty and when it is published, the words in it will require the help of a dictionary and a glossary of antiquated words to annotate.

Abu al-Fateh Muhammad Shah, whose decree this is, ascended the throne in 792 AH, or 1389 AD, and died in 796 AH, or 1393 AD.

Another decree is from the reign of Akbar. It bears the date of the month of Rajab in the year 7 *juloos* (year 7 after the 'royal procession,' or of the reign), followed by the digits 9 and 8. Perhaps the third digit has faded. So, it is from 980 AH or later. Another decree is dated Rabi' al-Awwal 987 AH. These decrees do not bear a monogram, only a small seal of Akbar. The seal on the first decree has not been deciphered yet. The seal on the second decree has the inscription "*Jalaluddin Muhammad Akbar Badshah Ghazi 981 AH.*"

A third decree is also from the reign of Akbar. It is damaged where the date is inscribed. It also does not contain a monogram but the seal is ornamental.

Two decrees are from the reign of Alamgir, one dated Rabi' al-Sani 15 of the year 26 *juloos*, or 1094 AH, and the other dated year 14 *juloos*, or 1081 AH. Decrees of Alamgir are often found. It is worth researching what year Almagir considers his *juloos*, the year of ascension to the throne.

The following decrees have been received from the old family of Qazis in Mathura through Syed Raza Ali, a student of our college.

One decree is from the reign of Alamgir dated Shawwal of the year 12 *juloos*, or 1079 AH.

One decree of Farrukhsiyar bears the date Jumada al-Akhir 17 of the year 2 *juloos*. But on its back, it bears the inscription "Wednesday, the third day of the year zero of the blessed *juloos*," which makes it recorded in the year 1125 AH.

One decree is from the reign of Shahjahan dated Jumada al-Sani of the year 28 *juloos*, or 1004 AH. Among these decrease is also one from the reign of Babar dated 932 AH and Babar's seal has been placed on it. Decrees from Babar's reign are very rare. But it is a pity that the paper that has been pasted on its back to reinforce it has been done in a shabby manner, due to which it is difficult to read the words on the seal and to make an image of it.

A decree has been obtained from the family of our respectable Maulvi Syed Zainul Abidin Khan *Saheb* which is related to his own family. This decree is from the reign of Abu al-Adil Azizuddin Alamgir dated the eleventh day of the month of Dhu al-Qadah in the year 3 *juloos*, or 1169 AH, whose monogram and ornamental seal are clear and legible.

Images of these decrees have been taken to prepare a book of a collection of them, but the work that has been proposed in this resolution is not easy. If it is completed with the effort of even three or four years, it would be a blessing. But the work has started.

I have also turned my attention toward the compliance of the proposal regarding taking photographs of royal monograms and ornamental seals, but if this work is carried out by paying professional photographers, the cost would be so high that the conference would not be able to bear the expenses. However, Haji Muhammad Ismail Khan *Saheb*, *Raïs* Datavali, has promised to provide excellent photographic equipment and establish a photography club. Some students of the *Madrasatul Uloom*, who by nature are inclined toward this work, will be made members of this club. In this way, photographs will be taken of these monograms and seals, which are very unique and rare and will be a great contribution to history. This will also give three or four students a good practice of photography. As a sample, I present before you a few photographs taken of monograms on decrees. It is hoped that when the report of the conference is published, the people will come to know about our purpose to collect decrees, and they will also understand that symbols of the honor of their family will be preserved in a book forever. This will encourage and motivate them to share with us the decrees in their possessions and to help us in this work. In this way, many decrees will be made available to us. These decrees will be stored very carefully and will be returned once they have been imaged.

The third and the fifth resolutions that were passed in the previous session have met great success. In our Allahabad University, from time to time there have been some inappropriate debates which were not suitable given the conditions in the country and very harmful to the education of Muslims. In one instance, it was proposed that Persian should be removed from the curriculum of the university. In another instance, it was proposed that Arabic and Persian writings should be collected in a book on which a course would be based and a cumulative minimum score be established for passing this combined languages course.

The Educational Conference expressed its displeasure at both these proposals. Resolution number 3 was passed to propose that Arabic and Persian be established as two separate and independent languages, and that the students have the choice between Arabic and Persian as a second language. I am very happy to report that this matter as proposed has been firmly decided and established at the university.

The fifth resolution was of even more importance. The Government of India had issued an order that focus should be given to technical education. The Educational Conference had no concern with this order provided it was carried out appropriately. The conference had expressed its displeasure only with some outcomes and had asked that the education currently given in what is known as course (A), which includes logic, philosophy, English literature, etc., should not be disrupted and that technical education should not be included in course (A). The exact words of this resolution as passed by the conference were:

> "It is the opinion of this conference that there should be no changes to the literary teaching in the English schools and colleges for the sake of advancing technical education."

A committee was set up by His Honor the Lieutenant Governor to decide this matter and its report has now been published. In it, a definite decision has been taken that technical education should be established as a separate branch, whether its administration is given to the Director of Public Instruction or the university takes it as its responsibility. And that was the aim of our conference. In this regard, I present before you the section of the report that is relevant:

Section 37 of the report: Technical education

We now refer to this useful article that sets a certain standard for education in the upper classes of the high schools of these provinces. Here also, we have taken into account the suggestions we have made regarding the '*upper subordinate class*' of the Roorkee college, i.e. the '*overseers' class.*' We are of the opinion that the educational authorities of the North-Western Provinces should conduct a final exam for those students of high school who have received education in vocational and industrial subjects, i.e. practical skills. This kind of exam will certainly incline them toward getting an education in Roorkee. Provided that the subjects chosen are good and judiciously selected, and the method of education in schools is in accordance with these subjects, the students will be able to enter the Roorkee college with a good preliminary background that they cannot obtain in these schools today which are focused only on university entrance requirements. While debating the question of admission to the upper subordinate class of Roorkee, we have also said that this final exam will also determine at which level of the Roorkee college the student will be admitted. We consider this opinion very useful and practical as it will set a threshold for selections. In an effort to fulfill the desire of the Government of India to have two branches of education in high school, one focused on university admission and the other on vocations and skills, there came a time when both the modern high school system and its final exam proved inconclusive. Although the education per se may be good, it does not bring any special distinction, nor is it useful for acquiring any special government jobs or any earmarked scholarships or prizes. In the high schools of Bengal that have the second branch of practical education, there was failure for the same reasons and the students did not participate. The same result will be seen in other provinces until special attention and consideration is given to this modern system of education. Our suggestion that admission to Roorkee courses be based on this final exam will bear fruit. We believe that the forest school in Dehradun will also accept this exam for admission to the rangers' class. We are very much in favor of the mode of this exam as proposed by the director *Saheb* and included in annex number (3) of this report. Every candidate in this exam should have a good knowledge of everyday Urdu and English, adequate knowledge of mathematics, and a reasonable aptitude in history and geography. These subjects will be compulsory to place this exam at par with Madras' upper secondary class exam and the final exam of Bombay's schools. For this reason, the scheme also requires that the aspirants appear in the exam of at least one non-compulsory subject from the modern or practical branch. The advantage of the proposal that this exam be conducted according to the educational authority rather than the university is that it will also serve as the school's final exam and even those students who are not proceeding to a university will be included. But a more obvious advantage would be if the university accepts this exam (subject to the conditions that have been set forth for the candidate's necessary and suitable choice of a non-compulsory subject) for admittance to the second branch of the university for students who have completed the modern course (B) or the senior course of the aforementioned scheme. In this case, the university can certainly supervise this exam and take responsibility for its management.

Supplement Number 3 of the Report

Those students can appear in this exam who have two years of schooling after they have passed the middle exam. To qualify for the certificate, the students will be required to pass the exam of four compulsory and one non-compulsory subjects. In order to pass the exam in each subject, a minimum of one-third of the total score for that subject would have to be achieved. But to pass in all the four compulsory subjects, at least one-half of their cumulative aggregate score would have to be achieved and the achieved score in the non-compulsory subject would be included in the cumulative score only if it is at least one-third of the total for that course.

No student will be allowed to take more than three non-compulsory subjects.

Subjects for the exam

(A) Compulsory subjects:
    (i) English
    (ii) Hindustani
    (iii) Mathematics
    (iv) History and geography

(B) Non-compulsory subjects:
    (v) Higher course in mathematics
    (vi) Survey
    (vii) Elementary physics
    (viii) Elementary chemistry
    (ix) Drawing
    (x) Political economy

(xi) Bookkeeping

(xii) Agriculture

Standards

The standard in English is the same as that of the upper secondary exam of Madras, the intent being to develop proficiency in English for everyday business among Indians and for them to be able to write well, speak fluently, and understand others. Good writing and composition are essential skills.

In Hindustani, the student should be able to read the everyday documents and handwritten papers fluently and should be able to draft business actions and orders quickly and clearly. He should be able to write business letters. He should be familiar with common idioms of ethical intercourse and be able to translate official documents from English to Urdu. A good handwriting and clear composition style are also essential.

In Mathematics, a student should know how to do all the calculations, in particular the calculations related to business and trade which include interest rate, average price, percentage calculation, commission and brokerage, profit and loss, capital, and exchange. In comparative algebra, the final exam will consist of elementary equalities and in geometry it will be based on elementary level material. The geography exam will include general world geography but with special emphasis on the British Empire. Physical geography will be as much as included in the third part of Mill *Saheb*'s geography text[16]. The students will also be required to draw maps.

In history, as much of the history of England as is included in Gardner's text and as much of the history of India as is included in Hunter *Saheb*'s 'A Brief History of the Indian People.'[17]

Higher mathematics, which is an optional subject, will include material from comparative algebra to solving for roots of equations and the four types of geometry with simple solutions.

[16.] 'The International Geography' (v1, 1908) is a comprehensive book written by Hugh Robert Mill that explores the geography of various countries around the world. The book is divided into sections focusing on a specific region or continent. Within each section, Mill provides detailed descriptions of the physical and cultural geography of each country in the region.

[17.] Sir William Wilson Hunter KCSI CIE (15 July 1840 – 6 February 1900) was a Scottish historian, statistician, a compiler and a member of the Indian Civil Service. He is best known for 'The Imperial Gazetteer of India' covering the geography, history, economics, and administration of India.

In drawing, the exam will include material that is prescribed for the second grade of the Bombay School of Arts, viz., (1) Practical geometry, (2) Scenes perspective, (3) Free hand drawing of flat objects, and (4) Clear drawings of objects.

The determination of the composition of other non-compulsory subjects has been left to the universities and the educational authorities.

Indian students who are admitted to the upper superintendent class (Indian level) of the Thompson College will be required to appear for the final exam in the school with drawing as a non-compulsory subject. Successful students who wish to be admitted to this college should submit their applications to the principal.

Within two months of the declaration of the results of the exam, students will be admitted to colleges according to the number of seats and their performance in the exam. Those students who pass the exam but are not admitted to college on account of low scores can reappear in any exam later. For this exam, centers will be set up in the Central Provinces, Punjab, and Rajputana.

The result of this report and all these proposals is that the teaching in the school classes toward entrance to the university course (A) will continue as usual. There will be no change or reduction in it, rather a separate branch of technical education will be created, which was the purpose we set forth in the discussions that took place last year.

The sixth resolution was passed at the previous session with the aim of proposing and implementing a plan of action for the education of young children. When this resolution was presented, it was proposed that awards should be given for essays written on this topic. Consequently, a list of subscriptions to collect money for the awards was compiled. But I am sorry that all the money that was entered into this list was not received, and only Rs. 238 have been received. The award proposed for the first prize was Rs. 200, and so I have announced only this prize in the advertisement for this essay writing and set July 1, 1892 as the deadline for receiving these essays. The result of this essay writing will be presented at the next session. Although this advertisement was published in October, I have also distributed it widely here in these meetings.

The seventh resolution was passed with the objective of producing text in Urdu language using clear and concise writing free from Asian exaggeration and hyperbole that can be used for the moral education of boys, giving them an understanding of respect and human emotions, and guide them to exercise moderation. These texts should be written by those who want the good of the community and are competent in writing such material. These texts should be selected by the committee and published in the supplement to the proceedings of the conference. But I am extremely sorry that no such writing has been received.

The eighth resolution passed last year was that some matters related to academic or historical research or acquisition of rare antique books should be added to the proceedings of the Muhammadan Educational Conference.

To comply with this resolution, it was necessary to add the aforementioned issues to the rules of procedures. As a result, these issues have been added to the rules and the new set of rules have been distributed among the members of this session. These rules will be presented on the final day of the session for approval.

In this resolution, the matter related to the search for and acquisition of rare books has been given attention by my friend Munshi Wahid Ali *Saheb*, *Raïs* Kakori, and has delivered to us an extremely rare book. The name of the book is '*Fazail-ul-Imam Min Rasail-e-Hujjat-ul-Islam.*' This is a brief journal but it is an excellent work and very rare. It contains a collection of the correspondence and miscellaneous writings of Imam Ghazali[18], may God have mercy on him. Although the collector did not write his name, from some notations in the journal it can be conjectured that after the death of Imam Muhammad Ghazali, these writings were collected by his brother Ahmed Ghazali. This journal is in the Persian language but also contains a few Arabic writings of the Imam. The journal has the following chapters:

- Chapter 1: About sultanates and names of kings, etc.

- Chapter 2: What the *boz* wrote

- Chapter 3: Written to the princes and the pillars of the government

- Chapter 4: What the religious jurists wrote

- Chapter 5: The chapter in which he wrote scattered sermons

These chapters show how rare and valuable these types of correspondence and writings of Imam Ghazali are. This journal was found in the library of Bhopal and Munshi Wahid Ali *Saheb* has sent me a copy of it. But it is a pity that the person who copied it was not very careful and did not even compare the copy he made

---

18. Al-Ghazali (c 1058 – December 1111) known in Persian speaking countries as Imam Muhammad Ghazali or in Medieval Europe as Algazelus or Algazel, was a Sunni Muslim polymath. He is known as one of the most prominent and influential jurisconsult, legal theoretician, mufti, philosopher, theologian, logician, and mystic in Islamic history.

with the original. There are many mistakes in it and the original journal has not been located in Bhopal despite the effort. It is not known what happened to it. In any case, efforts are ongoing to find the original and determine its condition. If the copy can be corrected and published, it will be a very fine and rare journal.

The tenth resolution was passed with the aim of writing a journal on the topic of what insights and material was added by the Muslims to the knowledge they had acquired from Greece, Egypt, and India in their heydays. At the time this resolution was presented, everyone agreed that Maulvi Muhammad Shibli *Saheb* would write this journal. Granted this proposal is as extremely difficult and time consuming to achieve as it is excellent and useful, no attention has been paid to the writing of this journal. The writing of this journal would require its author to be familiar with many of the languages in which there are writings of this type, in particular Arabic, English, French, and German. And then, this author would need at least five or six years to put this journal together. Although I am very sorry to say it, under the present circumstances there is no expectation of this journal being authored.

The eleventh resolution passed in the previous session consisted of several matters:

- First, that *Shams-ul-'Ulama* Maulvi Syed Ali Bilgrami be requested to prepare a selection of Allama Faizi's writing in the Sanskrit language and annotate in its margins the verbal similarity between Sanskrit and Persian through the use of philology.

- Second, that Maulvi Maulana Khwaja Altaf Husain Hali be requested to collect those poems of Amir Khusro Dehelvi that speak of desire and longing.

- Third, that Maulvi Syed Iqbal Ali *Saheb* be requested to do a literal translation of Malik Muhammad Jayasi's *Padmavat*[19] into Urdu prose so that it can be given to Maulana Maulvi Khwaja Altaf Husain *Saheb* to write it as Urdu poetry.

Pursuant to this resolution, I sent a request to each of these gentlemen. That was the extent of my responsibility, but I do not know how much attention has been paid to this by these elders.

[19.] *Padmavat* is an epic poem written in 1540 by Sufi poet Malik Muhammad Jayasi, who wrote it in the Hindustani language of Awadhi and originally in the Nastaliq script. A famous piece of Sufi literature from the period, it relates an allegorical fictional story about the Delhi Sultan Alauddin Khalji's desire for the titular Padmavati, the Queen of Chittor.

In the fourth session of the Muhammadan Educational Conference, it was proposed that essays be solicited on the following topic, for which Khan Bahadur Sheikh Ahmed Husain Khan *Saheb*, Taluqdar of Paryawan area of Awadh, had established three prizes, one prize of Rs. 100 and two prizes of Rs. 50 each. The topic was:

"In the present circumstances, for the progress of the country (with respect to the condition of the Muslims), is it more useful for the community to concentrate its efforts on higher education and to collect the means for it, or to concentrate on elementary education?"

The idea was to compare the two scenarios and decide if it would be more useful to strive for higher education, and if so, why, or to strive for broader elementary education, and if so, why. In the case of the former proposal being accepted, what should we do? And also, given the present condition of the country, can it strive to get equal benefits from both these types of education? If not, then should our efforts be concentrated on higher education or elementary education? By elementary education, it is meant education up to the school level, and by higher education, education at the college level.

Consequently, I issued advertisements regarding this, and four such essays have been received, written by Ata Muhammad *Saheb*, Syed Muhammad Taqi aka Syed Imdad Husain *Saheb*, Munshi Noor Ahmed *Saheb*, and Muhammad Daud *Saheb*. As per the aim of the resolution, these essays have been forwarded to a committee for recommendation of prizes. This committee comprises of *Janab* Maulvi Hafiz Nazir Ahmad *Saheb*, Khwaja Altaf Husain *Saheb*, *Janab Shams-ul-'Ulama* Khan Bahadur Maulvi Muhammad Zakaullah *Saheb*, *Janab* Maulvi Shibli *Saheb* Nomani, and *Janab* Maulvi Syed Karamat Husain, Esq., barrister-at-law. Its report related to this effort will be presented on the last day of the session.

I am happy that those matters of our conference for which desires were expressed at the Allahabad session were not ignored. In the sessions of the Oriental conference[20] that are held in Europe, if any paper is presented that advances knowledge or academic information, it is appreciated very much. In the 1886 session of the Oriental Congress held in Vienna, a great German scholar presented a paper on the leading or following words of compound words that occur in the

---

[20.] The International Congress of Orientalists, initiated in Paris in 1873, was an international conference of Orientalists (initially mostly scholars from Europe and the USA). The first 13 meetings were held in Europe, the 14th in Algiers in 1905, and some of the subsequent conferences were also held outside Europe.

Arabic language. This paper was much appreciated and appeared in its entirety in the conference report. An example of leading or following words to make compound words is when we say in Urdu, "Drink some *pani-vani*" or "Eat some *roti-voti*." We know *pani* (water) and *roti* (bread), but what are '*vani*' and '*voti*'? So, even in our own language, we cannot say how many words are used as leading or following words in compound words without complete research and inductive analysis. But this German scholar collected together all such words of the Arabic language.

In the same way, in this conference an Egyptian scholar by the name of Hafni Effendi Nasif presented an excellent paper written by him titled "Characteristics of the Arabic Dictionary," which gives a lot of insight into the types of Arabic dictionaries. This paper in Arabic was published verbatim in the conference report. Suffice it to say, in such conferences as Europe's Oriental Congress or our Muhammadan Educational Conference, apart from other goals, it should also be an important goal to shed light on knowledge and information and to produce useful papers and journals on issues that will benefit the country. This is particularly needed when we do not know the attributes of our language which would benefit the country and are not familiar with the knowledge and its outcomes that are contained in our language. Hence, those who endeavor in this are worthy of our gratitude.

In this work, our esteemed Maulana Maulvi Shibli Nomani has led the way. In the second session of the conference, he presented a paper titled "The Past Conditions of the Education of Muslims." Hundreds of thousands of Muslims were not aware of the many schools in various places that were established by their ancestors, how much money was spent ungrudgingly on them, and the outcomes of these schools. After that, he wrote a short journal about his research on *jizya*, a capitation-tax levied on the non-Muslim subjects of a Mohammadan government, which had not been researched in such detail by even the great scholars. That journal is a source of pride for the Muslims, and the fact is that the community cannot be absolved of the favor it owes to him for writing those few pages.

After that, he wrote a biography of Ma'mun al-Rashid, thanks to which thousands of people became aware of the affairs of this Islamic empire, something that would have been difficult, if not impossible, without this journal written in Urdu. But I will recite a couplet of Ghalib in its favor and then remain silent.

If meeting you is not easy then that's simple

The difficulty is that it is not difficult either

Now he has written a biography in Urdu of Hazrat Imam Abu Hanifa Kofi, a leading scholar of Islamic jurisprudence, which is kept here on the table and I wouldn't be surprised if many people have it in their possessions. This is because he has graciously and generously granted the copyright to the school, which has enabled it to publish and sell the book. Millions of Muslims in our India belong to the Hanafi sect, but there will hardly be a few among them who know anything about their Imam. So, in writing this biography, he has done a favor to the community.

Now, especially for this session of the conference, he has chosen a fine and useful topic on which he will speak to some extent in this session as mentioned in the program, but eventually he will write a journal on it. This topic is "Rights of the non-Muslim," and the community will benefit from it.

The lectures of our esteemed and honorable Maulana Maulvi Hafiz Nazir Ahmed *Saheb* are well received not only in this gathering but all over India. There will be many people who may or may not be interested in the objectives of the conference but will surely be interested in Maulana's lecture and will be as eager to listen to it as a fasting person wants to hear '*Allah-o-Akbar*,' God is great. At this time, our esteemed Maulana is present in this gathering. I would like to say it to his face that when listening to his lectures, people usually have one complaint as well, because every listener says that:

O, I wish you would give me two more ears for my eyes
To hear what you say over and over again

It is hoped that the topic on which Maulvi Hashmatullah *Saheb*, MA, has proposed to give a lecture will be very beneficial for the community. When it is published in the form of a journal, it will truly benefit the community.

My dear friend Muhammad Inayatullah, BA, will present a biography of Abu Rayhan al-Biruni[21], who was a contemporary of Bu Ali Sina[22]. In addition

---

[21] Abu Rayhan Muhammad ibn Ahmad al-Biruni (973 – after 1050), known as al-Biruni, was a Khwarazmian Iranian scholar and polymath during the Islamic Golden Age. He has been called variously the "founder of Indology," "Father of Comparative Religion," "Father of modern geodesy," and the first anthropologist.

[22] Ibn Sina (980 – June 1037), commonly known in the West as Avicenna, was a preeminent philosopher and physician of the Muslim world, flourishing during the Islamic Golden Age, serving in the courts of various Iranian rulers. He is often described as the father of early modern medicine.

to astrology and astronomy, he had achieved a high level of knowledge of the Sanskrit language and the Vedas. This lecture will determine something that historians differ on: the reason why he was referred to as Biruni, or the outsider.

Shams-ul-'Ulama Maulvi Syed Ali Bilgrami will present a paper on the book "*Kalila wa-Dimna*,"[23] but my eyes search for his presence here, wondering if he has completed his journey from faraway Hyderabad to reach here or not yet.

The greatest joy and pride, not just for me but for the community, comes from the presentation of the book written by a person of our community who is without peer and whose heart is filled with, nay overflows with, love for his community. His name is Dr. Muhammad Akbar and he is the son of Khan Bahadur Mirza Azeem Baig, assistant commissioner of Lahore, with whom our braveheart friends from Punjab are very familiar.

Dr. Muhammad Akbar was in India at the time the imperial court was held in Delhi and attended the gathering. At that time he was 16 years old and had completed his education in the Persian language and Arabic studies, such as logic, philosophy, beliefs, interpretations, and narratives, and to some extent Hadith and exegesis of Quran. After that, he undertook a journey to Constantinople, where he enrolled in the imperial college of the Turkish empire and learned the Turkish language. Subsequently, he immersed himself in the study of modern science and knowledge and, after obtaining a certificate of competency, he was admitted to the medical college. He studied there for six years receiving higher education in physics, chemistry, geology, zoology, and botany, and received the MD degree. He spent 15 years of his life acquiring knowledge.

He stayed in Constantinople for one year after receiving his diploma and did not forget his fellow countrymen. In Constantinople itself he wrote a fine and very useful book in Urdu, "A Healthy Marriage." He got it published in Constantinople with the hope that it would benefit the people of India. This is the book that I present before you. It shows how much compassion he has in his heart for the community. This book is very good, worth our consideration and reading, and hopefully our community will give it its attention.

Sultan Abdul Hamid Khan appreciated him very much, awarded him a medal of honor, and wanted to give him a prestigious position in Constantinople,

---

[23.] *Kalila wa-Dimna* is a collection of fables whose heroes are animals. A remarkable animal character is the lion who plays the role of a king. He has a servant ox, Shetrebah, while the two jackals of the title, Kalila and Dimna, appear both as narrators and protagonists.

but he was more interested in the service of his homeland than this pomp and glory. That is why he returned to India, and I am very proud to say that Dr. *Saheb* himself is present here in this conference and has honored us with his presence at this community gathering.

In addition, Munshi Ghulam Qadir *Saheb*, district overseer of Amritsar, has sent me a book titled "*Nizam Qadri*" to present at this conference, which is kept here on the table. This is an Arabic dictionary with word meanings explained in Urdu. He states that he has worked for 14 years on writing this book. It has been liked very much by the textbook committee of Punjab, Director of Public Instruction, and the Government of Punjab and has been added to the libraries of schools and colleges. It is hoped that it too will benefit the community. This book was printed by Nizami Press in Ludhiana in 1891.

The third book has been written by our esteemed friend Munshi Sirajuddin Ahmad *Saheb* related to the education and upbringing of children and the advancement of their mental strengths, which has been presented at the conference and is without a doubt a book worthy of being owned by mothers and fathers of children or those who will become parents. Munshi Sirajuddin Ahmad *Saheb* has dedicated this book to the reputable and likable gentleman *Vazir-ud-Daula Mudabbir-al-Mulk* Khalifa Syed Muhammad Hasan Khan Bahadur, CIE, prime minister of Patiala. I will read in this meeting the letter that the honorable gentleman has written in reply, from which respect and admiration for the book is evident.

That letter is:

My dear friend Munshi Sirajuddin Ahmad *Saheb*, may God Almighty bless you.

Love and peace! Although I had very little free time, your precious book fascinated me so much that I read it from beginning to the end in just three or four days. Till I reached the end, I sincerely kept wanting to read it through. So, with great pleasure and much gratitude, I send it back to you. I tell the truth when I say that you have written it very well, and you finished the discussion you started. May God reward you with the best reward.

Although I do not consider myself worthy to have a book dedicated to me, I undoubtedly do consider it a great honor. For that honor, I am very grateful to you. Please accept my gratitude. Peace be upon you.

Signed

Syed Muhammad Hasan

Now, at the end, I have to say this about the venerable Maulana Maulvi Khwaja Altaf Husain Hali that he too will recite a poem in this gathering on the inner state of man, which passes through asceticism and freedom from dependance on anyone except God and the average of those two states, and will tell us which one of those states is preferred.

It is said that Wali[24] laid the foundation of poetry in Urdu, which was very crude and uncouth. Then others fixed it and brought it to a higher level, given that until then there was no topic in it except form or feature, burning passion, and praise or condemnation, which may have been pleasing to the ears but did not touch the heart. In his Urdu poetry, Maulana Hali has redefined the art of poetry by showing the human being as a human being and by drawing an image of his inner and natural emotions in words. If our community was alive, then just as communities and not kings have bestowed titles such as *Ulema, Hakim, Shams-ul-'Ulama*, etc. on its distinguished members, it would also honor Maulana Hali with a title. But unfortunately the community is not alive. Apart from this, one difficulty is that Maulana Hali himself is a revivalist, is complete in himself as well as complementary, and sadly is himself the finisher. Then what title can anyone remember him by?

Mr. President of the session! I have presented briefly the outcomes of last year's session and the matters that are going to be enacted in this session. Now I pray to the Almighty to make our efforts beneficial for the community.

---

24. Wali Muhammad Wali (1667 – 1707), also known as Wali Dakhani, Wali Gujrati, and Wali Aurangabadi, was a classical Urdu poet. He is considered by many scholars to be the father of Urdu poetry, being the first established poet to have composed *ghazals* (a form of amatory poem or ode originating in Arabic poetry) in the Urdu language.

153

Expression of Condolence

*(Excerpted from the sixth annual session of the Muhammadan Educational
Conference held in Aligarh, December 27-30, 1891, pp 75-77)
(December 27, 1891, in Aligarh)*

In 1891, two great friends of Sir Syed, Syed Mir Zahoor Hussain and Khan Bahadur Qazi Syed Raza Hussain, passed away. On the first day of the sixth annual session of the Muhammadan Educational Conference, Sir Syed gave the following speech while presenting a resolution of condolences.

Janab President *Saheb*!

You and many of the friends gathered here are well acquainted with Mir Zahoor Hussain and Qazi Syed Raza Hussain.

Mir Zahoor Hussain was a resident of this province and met thousands of people with a polite disposition of kindness, love, and friendship. There would be no one among those who were acquainted with him who would not be familiar with his polite manners, etiquette, and kindheartedness. From the beginning, when he started as a lawyer and worked as a High Court advocate, everyone knows of his high achievements. He spent hundreds of thousands of rupees to assist and care for his friends. In addition, he was a highly valuable member of the conference. You must have seen examples of his love and generosity in Allahabad. What a shock his passing has been to this conference, the passing of a friend who was a sincere friend to many, a friend who was very active in the welfare of his community, a friend who was always willing to spend his money for the community. I took the name of the conference by mistake; what a shock it has been to the entire community. For such a person, however much our conference mourns and grieves is fitting.

Qazi Syed Raza Hussain *Saheb*, although he was a resident of Bihar, had so much affection for and friendship with the people of this province that everyone here sings his praises. In addition to his politeness and kindness, one big virtue of his was the empathy he had for the community, and not just raw empathy but filled with kindness and graciousness. Patna College currently stands at the top of all colleges in Bengal in terms of education for the Muslims. At present, in no part of Bengal are as many Muslims receiving education as are studying in the Patna College. When you inquire about whose generosity and kindness enabled their studies, you will get the same answer: only Qazi Raza Hussain. He gave scholarships to many Muslim students and helped them earn the BA and MA degrees. I know many students who got assistance from him from the start of their education up to the MA level exam. He did not stop at this and endowed his villages, which were under a continual arrangement of taxation and held a lot of property, for the education of Muslims. He made it a condition that the total income from these properties would be spent on scholarships for Muslim students. The sudden passing of such a generous person of our community, which needs such people particularly to support education, is very sad, sorrowful, and shocking. It hasn't been too long since he went to Hyderabad with a deputation working for the good of the community. Unfortunately, on his return journey, he got sick and the final result of it is what we mourn and grieve. He was the person who wished and arranged for this year's session of the conference to be held in Patna. He had made all the arrangements, but in the meantime he fell ill and the plans could not be executed without the person who was a singularity among the *Raïses*. The death of such a noble cannot be mourned only by relatives and friends, but is mourned by the entire community. His death is the misfortune of the community. I pray that God grants him a place in Paradise.

154

First Meeting: Election of the President of the Session ★

(Excerpted from the sixth annual session of the Muhammadan Educational Conference held in Aligarh, December 27-30, 1891)

On December 27, 1891, in the first meeting of the sixth annual session of the Muhammadan Educational Conference held in Aligarh, December 27-30, 1891, Sir Syed rose from his chair and gave the following short speech regarding the election of the president of the session

Gentlemen, as you know, the members, administrators, and organizers of this session of the conference had suggested that our esteemed and honorable Maulana Maulvi Nazir Ahmad *Saheb*, who is present here at this time and with whom everyone should register a complaint, should be president of the session, but in the garb of humility and modesty, he excused himself for reasons that are not really true. After that, Honorable Maulvi Syed Amir Hussain Khan Bahadur CIE, who is from a long lineage of *Raïses*, was appointed president of the session. Unfortunately, a letter and telegram were received recently from Syed Amir Hussain Khan that he cannot depart from Calcutta due to illness. But he has presented a donation of Rs. 200 to be given as a stipend over two years to that student of Mohammedan Anglo-Oriental College who has passed the entrance exam from the college and is currently enrolled there in the FA class. Although this generosity of his is worthy of our gratitude, the regret of his not being able to be here due to the unforeseen circumstance is not diminished. After receiving this news, the members, administrators, and organizers of the session unanimously appointed Nawab Muhammad Ishaq Khan Bahadur, CS, as the president of the session.

O gentlemen! Although we regret the absence of Honorable Maulvi Syed Amir Hussain Khan Bahadur CIE due to unforeseen circumstances, we have much pride in Muhammad Ishaq Khan Bahadur being appointed president. Nawab *Saheb*'s personal qualities, laudable ethics, proficiency in Asian and English studies, and concern for the welfare of the community are not in need of my elaboration. The greatest happiness is that the esteemed Nawab *Saheb* is a representative of that exalted family of our desolate homeland Delhi which was once a repository of scholars, nobles, Nawabs, and *Raïses*, who have been Nawabs and academic scholars of fame and renown from generation to generation. So, the election of a president from such roots and high-ranking status is undoubtedly a source of pride for our conference. On behalf of this conference, I now request the honorable gentleman to assume the chair of this session.

155

Speech Related to Women

(Excerpted from the sixth annual session of the Muhammadan Educational Conference held in Aligarh, December 27-30, 1891)

In the first meeting of the sixth annual session of the Muhammadan Educational Conference, Ghulam-us-Saqlain presented a resolution on women's education, which was seconded by many people. Munshi Sirajuddin, editor of "Sirmaur Gazette Nahan" also gave a speech in which he mentioned Sir Syed's views on women's education. In reply to it, Sir Syed gave the following speech.

Mr. President of the session!

My intention was not to enter into a debate on this topic because whatever my opinion is, I had once made a detailed statement regarding it at the Lahore conference. However, since my friend Munshi Sirajuddin has taken my name a number of times and also stated that I am against women's education, I have stood up to state that those who think that I am against women's education should know that this is not true. As far as I am concerned, there are only three issues. First, the most debated question is what method should be adopted. It is a pity that no one has described any method that would be to everyone's satisfaction. The second issue that is important in my opinion is what subjects should be taught to women. What we propose at this time will be subjects that are appropriate in this age; to think that such-and-such subject will be useful in the future is a fantasy. One cannot give an opinion as a decision. At this time, we should see what the present needs are for the education of girls and we should limit ourselves to it. When a new need arises in the future, those who are there at the time will fulfill it. The third issue that I want to mention will be resolved by our very dear friend Ghulam-us-Saqlain, who has presented his proposal very capably and meticulously. I congratulate him with a sincere heart and applaud him for a job well done in giving a brilliant and informed speech on his approach, but the question is what method of education for girls is in reality the easiest and most implementable. No instance can be found in the history of the world of a family in which men have received education, acquired high morals, and acquired knowledge and wisdom while the women have been deprived of education. Our intention is that the education we are providing is not for the boys alone but for the girls whose fathers they will be. We do not claim to be saints and we cannot predict the future, but we must take counsel from past events. If we look at the history of Europe and all the educated countries, we find that when men become worthy, women also become worthy. Women cannot be worthy unless men are worthy. This is the reason why we do not care about the education of only some women, but consider the same efforts to be a means of the education of all girls. Let alone the past history of Europe. Come to Europe now and I will show you that where men are not well educated, the women are ignorant and delusional and hang horseshoes on their doors to ward off epidemics. But where the men have become educated, women have also become educated. Look at the state of India itself, that in the families that were well educated, the women were also well educated. If you understand the conditions in India, then tell me why the women of those families are educated. A very good analogy is that God's blessings do not come from the earth but descend from the heavens. The light of the sun too does not come from below but from above. In the same way, the education of women will come from the education of men. The allegation that I am averse to women's education is simply false. They don't understand that in my opinion, the means of the education of women will only be the men. If men are not educated, there will neither be *ustanis*, or schoolmistresses, nor will there be any means for the education of women. When men become worthy, they will create all the means. The women of the household will become worthy and *ustanis* will come into existence. I have only two points that I will reiterate. First, the idea that I am opposed to women's education is wrong. Secondly, there is no other means of education for women except the education of men, and that is why I endeavor for the education of children. When they become educated, they will equip their wives and children and women with education. You seek education of women in ways that have no precedents. I seek the means that are compatible with the laws of nature.

★

156

Regarding Amendment of Rules ★

*(Sixth annual session of the Muhammadan Educational
Conference held in Aligarh, December 27-30, 1891)*

President of the session, Nawab Muhammad Ishaq Khan, presented a proposal to amend some of the rules of the conference. In seconding this proposal, Sir Syed delivered the following speech.

I second the motion made by Mr. President. Those who make the rules are the ones who realize the difficulties that arise in making them and understand how these difficulties can be resolved. Those who see the final product ask why this or that rule has been crafted. Some say that they are appropriate and some say they are not. Unless all the circumstances are presented and considered as to why these difficulties arise and how they can be resolved, such matters cannot be fully understood. It is impossible for all the members who come from long distances to gather for these sessions to understand all the issues. No matter how good these rules are, how well they have been crafted to address the needs, and how much experience has gone into drafting them, the door to objections cannot be closed. Nor can all the members, whose number was about a thousand in last year's session and is perhaps 600 this year, be involved in drafting the rules. Hence, the effective method of drafting the rules that has been prevalent till now is that a few members who have a close association with the conference and also have the experience of a few years of its proceedings draft these rules in consultations with each other. Consequently, these rules have been drafted in this way and all the requirements have been taken into account. But I too agree with what Mr. President stated that it is not appropriate to make two separate sets of rules for the conference. I have disliked this idea from the start, but those gentlemen who participated in the Lucknow session would know why separate sets of rules were made. I also dislike the fact that a part of the rules is considered permanent and another part is temporary and their approval needs to be renewed in every year's session. At this time, Mr. President has made the suggestion that a time should be set for a debate on the rules and any doubts that anyone has should be cleared. It would be very appropriate if, after that, the two separate sets of rules would be merged into one and the merged set would be considered permanent. As it is not known whether there will be much discussion on this topic or not, as per the directive of the president of this session, the 30th has been reserved only for the consideration of the rules. In this discussion, every person will get a chance to debate and object and all matters will be decided by consensus or majority opinion. I also agree with the suggestion of Mr. President that this meeting should be conducted according to procedural rules so that there is no risk to the proceedings of the meeting. The later meetings should be conducted according to this permanent set of rules that is established in this meeting. I hope all the members present will also agree with this proposal.

157

Sir Syed's Apology ★

(Sixth annual session of the Muhammadan Educational Conference held in Aligarh, December 27-30, 1891, pp120-121)

On December 29, at the start of the fourth meeting, Sir Syed apologized for the complaint of the attendees that they had not been informed in time of the convening of the conference. To redress this complaint, Sir Syed said the following at the start of the meeting.

O gentlemen! Before the proceedings of this meeting begin, allow me apologize for the charges leveled against me by several of my friends and associates. Complaints have been received from many quarters that the notification for the current session was given very late and without sufficient notice, and for that reason many people were not able to attend. The situation is that although this session of the conference was announced from the beginning to be held in Patna, due to the illnesses of the late *Janab* Khan Bahadur Syed Raza Hussain and the son of *Shams-ul-'Ulama* Maulvi Muhammad Abdul Rauf, there was a pause in the issuance of regular official information, Every day there was hope that they would recover and the issuance of regular official information would resume. Eventually, when there was no hope left, another venue had to be proposed. There were many suggestions but the timeline was so tight that no other arrangement could be made except to declare Aligarh as the venue.

After this declaration, advertisements were placed in newspapers and notices were sent as widely as possible. At this time, I have received telegrams from Maulvi Abdul Ghani *Saheb* of Hyderabad and Munshi Ahmed Shafi from Bahawalpur that contain the same complaint and inform me of about 100 friends becoming members. I would like to apologize to all these elders and also thank them; when the list of new members that have joined, as communicated by their telegrams, is received, I will include those elders in the list of members.

★

158

Introduction of Dr. Muhammad Akbar ★

(Referenced from the sixth annual session of the Muhammadan Educational Conference held in Aligarh on December 27-30, 1891)

On December 28, in the first meeting of the day, Sir Syed said that Dr. Muhammad Akbar *Sahab*, whom he had mentioned in his report, was present in the gathering. Sir Syed then delivered the following remarks introducing him.

My dear gentlemen! Before Maulana Hafiz Nazir Ahmad starts his lecture, I am very happy that this esteemed and honored member of our community from Punjab, the land of bravehearts, Dr. Muhammad Akbar is among us. He is the first member of our community to have earned a doctorate in higher knowledge and the arts from the Islamic capital of Constantinople. He has received with great honor a certificate of high rank and a medal from there and has returned to the homeland to work for the welfare of the community. This is the same elder I mentioned in my report yesterday, and today I am very happy to introduce him to you gentlemen.

159

Speech Related to Maulana Hali

*(Report of the sixth annual session of the Muhammadan Educational Conference
held in Aligarh on December 27-30, 1891)*

In the fourth meeting of the sixth annual session of the Muhammadan
Educational Conference held on December 29, 1891, Maulana Altaf
Husain Hali read a poem of his. This poem starts like this:

Thank You for this blessing, O Lord
You kept us here between poverty and wealth[25]

O friends!
This poem that Maulana Hali has read today is a wonderful poem, the likes
of which have not been written by any poet in Persian, Urdu, or Arabic. This
poem counsels those whose hearts are engrossed in the wealth and prosperity of
this world. It also conveys a conclusion to the middle-class people that the good
fortunes that have befallen them are not even in the destinies of the highest ranks
of the rich.

Everyone will accept that in the narration of a subject, poetry, which has
been around in India for a long time, may give pleasure to the ears but has no
effect on the heart. But the method adopted by our esteemed gentleman is so
complex that adopting it is not for everyone. Describing human emotions in
simple words in a way that they affect people's hearts as soon as they fall on their
ears is the poetry of Maulana Hali. We should thank God and be proud that such
a person was born in our community. In the future, when it is asked who is the
pride of the community, the pride of the poets, the pride of the scholars, who

---

[25]. *Faqr-o-ghinaa*, literally poverty and wealth, figuratively implies "asceticism and freedom from
dependence on anyone except God."

injects life in you and tells you of a path forward, who ignites the passion and finds salvation from them, the answer will be – Hali!

It is our hope that Maulana Hali will live a very long life and he will do good for the people. Now I request three cheers for him.

160

On the Lecture Given by Hafiz Maulvi Nazir Ahmed *Saheb* ★

(Referenced from the sixth annual session of the Muhammadan Educational Conference held in Aligarh on December 27-30, 1891)

O my friends!

You have just heard the lecture given by our esteemed and honorable Maulana Hafiz Maulvi Nazir Ahmed *Saheb*. This lecture gives as much counsel to the students, their parents, and boys in general as it does to the youth and the old, to those who wish to follow the path of God, and to those who follow the path of the world. To sum it up, this lecture gives advice for both religion and worldly affairs to everyone - young boys, the youth, and the elderly. Therefore, I propose that three cheers be given to our Maulvi from Delhi, Maulana Hafiz Maulvi Nazir Ahmed *Saheb*.

161

The Harmful Effects of Bad Customs ★

(Sixth annual session of the Muhammadan Educational Conference held in Aligarh on December 27-30, 1891)

On December 29, 1891, in the fifth meeting of the session, Maulvi Muhammad Hashmatullah *Saheb* gave a lecture on the bad customs prevalent in society and how to close the door on them. After that, Sir Syed made the following remarks.

All of you gentlemen heard the lecture given by our esteemed friend Maulvi Muhammad Hashmatullah *Saheb*. The advantage of these kinds of lectures is that ideas are evaluated, there will be many people who will be opposed, and there will be some who will not be opposed. In either case, they will have the opportunity to explore both sides and form opinions. There is no doubt that townspeople who own hamlets, lands, and estates are well aware that bad customs have ruined many families. In the beginning, this used to affect only those who adopted these customs and there was a prospect of future generations rising above these practices, but the era of those prospects has passed. In these times, those prospects can be restored only if you educate your children and make them worthy, otherwise there is no chance. The ill-effect of these bad customs that lasts for generations is that the money that should be spent on the education of children is squandered on these unnecessary customs. If these customs are abandoned, the ill-effect it has on the children would wane. That is the summary of Maulvi Hashmatullah's lecture, although he may have chosen a different beginning and a different end. This much he has presented very boldly and for that he deserves to be thanked. I move that a vote of thanks be passed.

The president of the session seconded this motion and a vote of thanks was passed unanimously for Maulvi Hashmatullah, Esq., CS.

162

The Practice of Arabic Education ★

(Sixth annual session of the Muhammadan Educational Conference held in Aligarh on December 27-30, 1891, pp 146-147)

On December 29, in the fifth meeting of the session, Maulvi Muhammad Bashiruddin presented a resolution that the practice of Arabic education is decreasing day by day, which will prove harmful to fulfilling Islamic duties and to its development and dissemination. Therefore, efforts should be made toward grooming great scholars of Arabic. Sir Syed seconded this resolution with the following remarks.

I support this motion. Now is not the time for me to show in detail what the mistakes are and what harm those mistakes are causing. Those students who study English are the most harmed by those mistakes. Some days ago, Khalifa Syed Muhammad Hussain *Saheb* translated a book written by an Englishman on the history of Islam and Spain. He wanted it to be reprinted as it was out of print. There were a few errors in it and if they were left as is, those erroneous suggestions would not be removed. For that reason, the reprinting of the book was postponed. This is not an easy task. There are many hurdles and there is a need for money and qualified people. In any case, while generally the erroneous suggestions regarding the history of Islam need to be dispelled, I do not know how this resolution can be implemented. However, as a matter concerning the beneficence of God, I second it.

163

Shams-ul-'Ulama Maulvi Syed Ali Bilgrami ★

(Sixth annual session of the Muhammadan Educational Conference held in Aligarh on December 27-30, 1891, p157)

My friends!
I am happy to say that the person whom the eyes sought out impatiently and wondered when he would come, *Shams-ul-'Ulama* Maulvi Syed Ali Bilgrami, has arrived. I am very thankful that at my request he has prepared a very good lecture. I would never have thought that such a good and useful thing could be prepared in this way. I am amazed.

Now, the time that has been set for him is tomorrow at eight o'clock. The debate on the regulations of the conference, which has been printed and distributed to everyone, has started and it is hoped that the last meeting will be over by two o'clock. I hope everyone will stay till tomorrow.

164

Speech on Sending Muslim Students to England for Education

(Report of the sixth annual session of the Muhammadan Educational Conference held in Aligarh on December 27-30, 1891, pp 137-141)
(Aligarh Institute Gazette, April 5, 1892)

In the fourth meeting of the sixth annual session of the Muhammadan Educational Conference held on December 29, 1891, Mr. Theodore Beck presented a resolution that Muslims students of India, before they reach the age of 20 and before they pass the intermediate exam, be sent to England without any special supervision for the purpose of education. Sir Syed expressed his opinion on this in the following words.

Mr. President of the session!

We just had a very good discussion on the topic of Muslim students going to England. I should express my happiness that everyone has paid attention to this topic and everyone explained it very well. But since the sin or requital for this action is perhaps on me – as I am the founder of this idea and have shown the Muslims the allure of going to England to get education – I need to say something about it. I think that the amendments proposed by our friends Maulvi Karamat Hussain and Khwaja Yusuf Shah, which perhaps Mr. Beck is willing to accept, have already been said by Mr. Beck in his presentation. In fact, nothing has been excluded from it. Mr. Beck has no intention to stop those who are worthy of this, as described by my friend Karamat Hussain.

When we want to make a rule, we do it by looking at the general situation, and no one in the world can say that no one is exempt from it. In this regard, as far as I understand, the word exemption is certainly there in Mr. Beck's speech. If we make a rule such as that described by Maulvi Karamat Hussain, it will be a special circumstance rather than a general rule. A general rule is one that should become general for most people with exceptions that are not the norm.

To me, apart from what my friend Mr. Beck has stated, an important point is that the wording around supervision is so broad, such as parent-like supervision, that those who can afford such supervision are at liberty to send their boys to England at any age. Who can deny sending their boys to England when they can be supervised by such friends, but who are the people who can recommend such friends in England? This much is certain, and many knowledgeable people have acknowledged it, that those who have gone to England to get an education have not gotten as much out of it as the Europeans get from the same education. With respect to the Indian students, I attribute this to the fact that before they went to England they did not get sufficient education in India for them to take full advantage of the education there. But there may be another reason for this. In Egypt, there was a practice of sending 30 men every year to Europe for education, mostly to France and some to London. Two years ago, their competent director of public instruction, who is well educated in French, assembled a large committee to answer the question of why the Egypt-educated students who go to Europe to get higher education don't achieve equality with the European students. Egyptian students tend to be of a lower quality even though they have obtained the same degrees as their European counterparts, suggesting that European students start their education earlier, they are educated in the best schools, and progress continuously as they enter college. The competency and mental acuity of the European students is superior while the Egyptian students who go to Europe at a relatively advanced age have not received good education in the schools of Egypt, and for that reason cannot compete with the European students. The same paradigm holds true in India. The debate eventually ensued in Egypt whether it is acceptable to send the boys away from the Arab nation at a young age and make them worthy or keep them at home and let them remain as they are. Everyone thought about it and made a lot of noise about it, saying that even if the boys remain ignorant and useless, they should stay among their people. There was extreme opposition to the idea of sending the boys to Europe. That report is with me. There was a lot of debate about whether to separate the boys from their nation or keep them ignorant. At that time, it was decided that young boys who are worthy and intelligent should be selected and sent to England and several scholars should accompany them at the expense of the king to look after their traditional education and supervise their behavior and conduct. As a result, scholars who knew both Arabic and French were appointed as chaperons. It was decided that boys over the age of 12 should not be sent and that the chaperons should live with the boys. I do not know how they devised this brilliant idea that the students should be sent under the supervision which is like that of the parents. They never disapproved of sending young boys but wanted them to be under supervision so that they are not out of touch with their nation. When they have made a general rule and somebody wants to be exempted from it, they don't want to exclude them from these resolutions, but rather to limit the general rule which is for the common benefit. No one is more desirous than they that the Muslims should go abroad to get education. So, if the Muslims can agree among themselves to make some arrangement for the supervision of the boys, I would say that sending young children to get education in London and starting their training for that in school is a good idea. No wonder I would agree with my friend Syed Jafar Hussain that boys should be sent to London even before they are born. My friend Khwaja Yusuf Shah presented an amendment and unfortunately Mr. Beck accepted it rather quickly. How did the original idea of sending the boys to England come about? It was born out of the idea that Muslims should pass the civil service exam. In this regard, I asked the opinion of some of the most eminent professors of Europe. I have many letters from some knowledgeable people of England that since the boys do not get secondary education here before they go, it is futile for them to go to England. I have evidence that the boys do not understand even a quarter of the lectures they attend there. Unless there is sufficient ability to understand the lectures and discourses, it is simply useless to send them there. In those days, the age to pass the civil service exam was 19 years and it was very difficult, if not impossible, for them to pass the civil service exam without studying in Europe for four or five years. As an exception to this rule, there were one or two who passed without spending that much time in Europe. That is why it was essential that the boys be sent to England at a young age, but it was impossible to arrange for their supervision. That is why I established a civil service class in our college so that they could get a good education here before sending them to England. But due to the lack of attention and interest from our community, that class was not successful and was discontinued. Now the age for the civil service exam has been raised to 23 years and a great advantage of getting three years of education there has been gained. Unfortunately, my face-to-face conversations with the public service commission were not publicized. At that time I had said that the idea that more boys will pass the civil service exam because of the age requirement being raised to 23 from 19 is simply false. The progress in the education of a 19 year old will now be relatively the same as for a 23 year old. So, for this reason, the idea of more Indian students passing is simply false. The only reason why I like this proposal is that Indians find it difficult to send their boys at a young age. Now this difficulty will be removed, but not that it will help Indians get a higher score. I believe the intention of those who have moved this amendment is contained in Mr. Beck's speech and that a general rule has been made from which special circumstances are completely excluded. The age for civil service is also included in this, of course there should be sufficient time for whatever purpose one is sent for. If they are sent to study or if they are sent to become doctors, sufficient time will be needed respectively. In my opinion, there is no need for an amendment.

165

Motion to Increase Grant-in-Aid ★

(Minutes No. 4 of the meeting of trustees of the Mohammedan Anglo-Oriental College Aligarh held on December 28, 1891, printed by Matba Mufeed-e-Aam press, Agra in 1892)

A meeting of the trustees of the Mohammedan Anglo-Oriental College Aligarh was held on December 28, 1891 in Aligarh. After a total of 11 resolutions were passed, the secretary (Sir Syed) informed the meeting that all the business of the meeting had been completed except for two matters. He then discussed these matters in detail in the following speech.

I would like to present two matters in this meeting that still remain to be discussed.

The first matter is that because of the monthly increase of Rs. 1000 that *Huzoor* Nizam has added to the income of the college from the endowed properties, all the problems that were faced due to the decrease in income and increase of expenditure in the budget will perhaps be resolved. I will present the details of this in the budget meeting, but one difficulty that is always faced by the college staff should be removed.

And that difficulty is that there is one European principal and two European professors in our college staff and one European headmaster in the school department. When one of them is on leave or falls ill, there is a complete disruption to education. And this is a helpless situation that has no remedy. Although we have put in place strict regulations for giving leave to the principal and the European professors, it is absolutely not possible that we don't give them leave at all. Besides that, what can we do when they fall sick? The result is that if the headmaster is absent due to leave or illness, a European professor of the college has to do his job, leaving only one professor in the college. In the same way, in the case of the principal being on leave or sick, one professor becomes the acting principal and only one professor is left for the teaching duties. And the same happens when one of the professors is absent due to illness or leave. Apart from this, even when all the professors and the principal are present, they don't get the time to teach the MA class. Some of the professors, out of their own kindness and volition, tutor some of the students for the MA exam at their homes outside the school hours. But classes cannot be taught in this way and when a European professor's position is temporarily vacant, we have no means of temporarily filling that position. This matter has been considered many times and it seems that it has been decided that this problem cannot be resolved without adding another European professor.

Therefore, to fulfill our need for a European professor, I would like permission to request the government to increase the grant-in-aid by an amount equal to half the salary of a European professor. If the government does not approve this request, the situation will remain unchanged. If the government grants the request, then the matter of appointing an additional professor will become an issue for the budget and I will present a detailed summary of it in the budget meeting. At that time, the trustees will have the opportunity to fully decide this matter. At this time, I ask for permission only to request the government.

Proposal that it is expedient to request the government to enact a special act for the purpose of protecting the college

The second matter is presented for the purpose of seeking the advice of the trustees present in this meeting regarding an important matter. If the trustees present in this meeting so advise, I will formally present this matter in front of all the trustees for a vote.

You know very well the way we established the college, built buildings for it, and collected donations of movable and immovable properties and cash for its expenses. Many sources of charitable funds from well-wishers were established and many properties were endowed, but among them are a number of examples of those that remained established for only a short while. After that, due to mismanagement and incompetent custodians and receivers or embezzlement and improper diversion of funds by them, these sources of funds were decimated. The custodians and receivers of the current charitable endowments and their successors may be good and honest managers and administrators but in no way can we be certain of that always being the case. So, the people who have established this college with so much hard work and zeal have a duty to be foresighted and plan as much as is humanly possible to ensure that the college does not decline due to the reasons that I mentioned.

Evidently, there is only one way of alleviating this concern, and that is to ensure that the college is always in the hands of the trustees and the government watches over them to ensure that the college and its property are not ruined. There are a few examples in front of us; if the government had not passed an act for the Husainabad *imambara* and mosque, and had not protected and safeguarded the Hooghly *imambara*, *madrasa* and its properties, they would have been ruined. Hence, I consider it very appropriate that the governments of the North-Western Provinces and Awadh be requested to pass an act specifically for our college. If the government approves it, then there is a strong possibility that our college will be saved from ruin and destruction.

You gentlemen may be anxious about the kind of act that would be passed and if it would revoke the authority of the trustees, give complete control of the college to the government, and turn this community college into another government college. But this idea is wrong in two ways. First, if all the powers of the trustees as they exist today are maintained in the act, then there can be no changes to the status of the college as it is today.

Secondly, if the government approves passing the act, the draft bill will be sent to the trustees. If the trustees don't approve it, the act will not be passed. Hence, if the rules are made according to the will of the trustees, no harm or damage can be imagined.

I briefly state before you the outline of the kind of act I wish to be passed so that I can clearly express to you what is in my heart. When you consider this outline, you will realize that this kind of act will not make any difference to the powers of the trustees and the internal administration of the college. The government has been given the power of external supervision to ensure that the college and its property are not ruined. Apart from this, the condition on which the government has given the land on which the college is built is that under certain cases of the college being ruined, the government has the right to occupy this land including the buildings on it. Hence, if such an act is passed with the college under the supervision of the government, we will be forever free of this apprehension as well.

The brief outline of the kind of act I would like to get passed is as follows.

Outline of Proposed Act

The government shall be declared as the superior officer and supervising patron or custodian of the college and shall perform the general supervision of the college. Moreover, it shall not interfere in the internal administration of the college, which will remain in the total control of the trustees.

The trustees of the college shall manage it in accordance with the rules which they have made and are in existence today or will make in the future. The government shall have the power to ensure that the rules are duly complied with, and if they are not, compel the trustees to do so.

The trustees of the college themselves shall appoint trustees and remove them in accordance with the existing rules or those that are enacted in the future. But if the number of trustees reduces to below 21 or if the existing trustees are situated at such a distance that they cannot be present in Aligarh to form a quorum, the government shall order the trustees to increase their number to the minimum requirement or to elect such members that can be present in Aligarh to form a quorum within a certain period of time. If the trustees do not comply within this period, the government itself can appoint anyone who is a Muslim to be one of the trustees, and this trustee will have the same rights and powers during this term as the existing trustees have according to the rules.

The government should be empowered to ask for the accounts of the college or any of its branches or departments at any time and in any manner and to order an examination of the accounts as it sees fit.

A copy of the annual budget prepared by the trustees shall be forwarded to the government in English by the director of public instruction for its information. In addition to the budgetary amounts, the budget shall include the following statuses.

A. The amount of money deposited in the capital fund in the form of promissory notes or other forms and how it is being secured.

B. The amount of money deposited as capital for scholarships and how it is being secured.

C. The amount of money deposited for any other purpose and how it is being secured.

D. If the college owes any debt, its amount, the reason why this debt was incurred, and how it will be paid off.

If the government considers that the cash or government securities held in trust in accordance with the first three clauses is not adequately safeguarded and is at risk of being lost, it can order these funds to be secured in whatever manner it considers best.

The trustees shall be compelled to maintain and perform annual repairs on all the buildings within the college's compound that have been completed. If the trustees do not comply and the buildings are liable to be damaged, the government shall repair it and recover the cost from the income of the college.

For the buildings that are being constructed or will be constructed in the future, the government will only ensure that good material is used for them, but it shall not interfere in any way in their design, construction, or modification. If the trustees wish to make any amendments to the existing rules, notice of this intent will be given to the government by the director of public instruction one month prior to such amendments being presented at the meeting of the trustees. The government shall be authorized to give a different advice to the trustees in this regard. The trustees shall consider it and put it to vote for a decision by majority opinion.

Any amendment, change, or modification in the rules for the trustees shall be implemented by a meeting of the trustees and a copy of it shall be sent to the government through the director of public instruction.

The government, through the director of public instruction, shall ensure that the teaching staff of the college is sufficient and fit for the purposes of instruction. If that is not the case, the government shall compel the trustees to make changes.

If the government finds that there is any disruption to the distribution of salaries to the staff of the college, it shall have the power to issue appropriate orders to secure the college expenditure fund and pay the salaries.

166

Annual Report of the Muhammadan Educational Conference: Sixth Session, 1891 ★

(Excerpted from the seventh annual session of the Muhammadan Educational Conference held in Delhi, December 27-29, 1892, pp 64-73)

My dear sirs!

I have the honor, as per the procedure, to present at the opening meeting a brief account of the proceedings of this educational conference and the resolutions passed during the previous year's session, and the results that were achieved from them or the extent to which they were complied with.

The most useful work done last year was the amendment and reform of the rules of the conference. You know that there were two types of rules related to the conference, one permanent that related to the constitution of the conference, and the other non-permanent that related to the proceedings of the conference sessions. These non-permanent rules were presented anew in every session and their acceptance or rejection was debated, taking up valuable time of the conference in every session. Nawab Muhammad Ishaq Khan Bahadur, CS, president of the previous session, made a motion that both types of rules should be combined after discussions and amendments, and the combined set of rules should be declared permanent so that there is no need to present them anew in every session.

In addition, Mr. Theodore Beck made the motion that included in those rules should be the procedure to elect the president of the session and to select from among the resolutions that are presented those that are worthy of debate and being brought before the delegates. At the end of every session, a managing committee should be appointed which can deliberate the resolutions to be presented the following year.

These amendments were carefully considered by the conference and both the motions were approved. Both sets of rules [*permanent and non-permanent*] were examined in detail and were combined into one set, which was published in the annual report of the conference session. It contains the rules pertaining to each of the items related to the conference and the proceedings of its sessions.

For the election of the members of the managing committee, it was decided that four members each from Punjab and the North-Western Provinces including Awadh and two members from Bihar province will be appointed. The president and secretary of the session shall be considered ex-officio members of this committee. In addition, the president will have the authority to appoint three members of his choice. So, the total number of members was decided to be 15.

In accordance with this rule, the following members were appointed.

From Punjab

Sardar Muhammad Hayat Khan Bahadur, CSI – absent

Khwaja Yusuf Shah *Saheb*

Khan Bahadur Munshi Ilahi Baksh *Saheb*

Maulvi Mohammad Mumtaz Ali *Saheb*

From the North-Western Provinces and Awadh

Shams-ul-'Ulama Maulvi Abdul Rauf *Saheb*

Khan Bahadur Maulvi Muhammad Khuda Bakhsh Khan *Saheb* – absent

Ex-Officio Members

Maulvi Muhammad Hashmatullah, MA, CS, president

Dr. Sir Syed Ahmed Khan Bahadur, KCSI, LLD, secretary

Other members who were appointed by the president of the session as per section 12 of the rules:

1. Nawab Ahmad Saeed Khan Loharvi
2. *Shams-ul-'Ulama* Khan Bahadur Maulvi Muhammad Zaka *Saheb*
3. Mirza Abid Ali Baig *Saheb*

Among the aforementioned members, those who did not come have the word "absent" noted in front of their names. But as for the regulation in section 12 regarding the rules for the proceedings of the conference, it has been proposed that only the members present in the meeting, including the members mentioned earlier, will be counted toward the quorum. So, the members who are present have done what they need to do and will continue to do till the end of the session.

In the previous session, resolution No. 2 was presented regarding the education of women, during the presentation of which Khwaja Ghulam-us-Saqlain gave an extensive and excellent talk. This resolution was passed after a lot of debate. Although it is evident that it is in the power of the people to comply with the resolutions, there is no doubt that the debates that have taken place regarding them have been very beneficial to the community.

An even more useful resolution, No. 4, was moved by Mr. Theodore Beck regarding Muslim students studying in England. His purpose in presenting the resolution was to freely discuss the pros and cons of sending the boys to England so that their guardians can become familiar with every aspect of it and can find a safe way of sending them there. I am happy to report that the resolution was freely discussed and many members expressed their views and opinions. After some modifications, the resolution was passed. I think the discussion that took place regarding this resolution was also very beneficial for the community. A collection of all kinds of opinions is available to the guardians of these boys and it is hoped that when they want to send their boys to England for education, those opinions will be useful to them.

Resolution No. 6 was presented by Maulvi Muhammad Bashiruddin *Saheb*. Its purpose was regarding the serious mistakes that have been made in Europe regarding some important issues of Islamic history and the inclusion of these mistaken ideas by European authors in their books. Muslims students are fed these misconceptions when they read these books. In order to remove these wrong ideas, journals should be written in Urdu and English and published in Europe.

Mr. President of the session! This resolution was such that no one with love for Islam and empathy for the community could refuse. That is why the resolution passed, but its compliance could not be carried out because it needed a lot of money, for which I express my regrets.

Mr. President of the session! Some of our friends think that even though six years have passed since the educational conference has been holding its sessions in various places, no practical benefit has been achieved for the community, and therefore they consider it useless. Although there were a lot of detailed discussions on this in previous sessions, I would like permission to say that I am sorry, and perhaps the elders who have taken an interest in the conference are sorry too, that practical implementation of the resolutions that have been passed from time to time has not been done. But it should be understood that it is the task of this conference to decide with mutual advice and consensus of the vast multitude of Muslims what action is beneficial for the well-being of Muslims and the progress of the community. This should be revealed to everyone and its benefits impressed on the hearts of the community. It is beyond the power and authority of the conference to comply with them. It is the task of the community itself to try to implement the proposals that they themselves have declared useful for the community. So, whatever pity you feel for the community is warranted. The conference is only like a worldly sermon that states what is good for the community. It only emphasizes it to the community. It informs the community of its inferior state. It is up to the community or its elders to act on these proposals and make efforts to comply with these resolutions. But the conference does not have the power to do more than how much it does. So, we must all come together and pray to God to give the community guidance to turn its attention to carrying out the tasks of community welfare with a practical outlook.

Tasks of community welfare with a practical outlook cannot be carried out unless there is empathy for the community. But a hundred regrets that our community does not have that one thing that it needs the most. I am somewhat happy to state that a feeling of empathy for the community has developed among the students of the *Madrasatul Uloom*. You may have heard that these students have formed a society among themselves of their own accord and out of their own sincere desire, whose name is *"Duty,"* i.e. '*al-farz.*' They have given the society this name with the idea that they consider it their duty to strive for the good of the community. The members of this society collect money by seeking charitable donations and setting up shops in fairs and gatherings, and use this money to help their brothers who are unable to pay for their educational expenses. The noble work of these young students is a great symbol of empathy for the community. If it takes root in the hearts, the future is filled with hope. Another act of empathy for the community that the students of the *Madrasatul Uloom* have undertaken out of their own sincere desire is that they have formed another society which they have named *"Brotherhood,"* which means a fraternity of brothers. This committee has requested the former students of the *Madrasatul Uloom* who have graduated and are now engaged in some profession to contribute Rs. 100 per annum toward fulfilling the goals of the college and to help those students who cannot pay for the expenses of their education.

The work of this committee has been furthered more by those who are not students of the *Madrasatul Uloom*, whom it calls "*Benefactors*," i.e. patrons and helpers of the community. These people can participate in this great work without any restrictions by donating as much or as little money they want on a monthly or annual basis. But, Mr. President, when you see the list of the students of the *Madrasatul Uloom* who have graduated and found prestigious jobs, and when you see how few of them are a part of this "*Brotherhood*," you will feel nothing but regret.

Then consider the elders of our community, from whom this committee takes with gratitude whatever they can offer and is ready to give them the title of "*Benefactor*," but if I count using the segments of my fingers the number of elders who have participated in this, my six fingers would probably be more than sufficient. So, when this is the state of the community and the feeling of empathy is muted, then what can our conference or any other committee, whatever name you give it, do except to keep at it in the hope that "*you know not, perhaps God will bring about after that a [different] matter.*"

Mr. President of the session! I, for one, believe that until you keep the young students of our community in one place and in one uniform condition, empathy will not be created in our community. From what they have heard about the students of the *Madrasatul Uloom*, every person will understand where the empathy for the community that has arisen in them, no matter a lot or very little, stems from. I believe that it is the result of living in a boarding house, developing mutual brotherly love, and having fraternal behavior toward each other. Perhaps there are some grudges that develop between the boarders, and it wouldn't be surprising if occasional fights break out between them, but all these sorts of things are those that sometimes happen between two brothers.

Mr. President of the session! Due to the fact that the community does not care about its own people, we cannot keep these students in the boarding house of the *Madrasatul Uloom* in the way that our heart desires. If God would direct the hearts of our community toward the welfare of the community, and if we become able to keep the boarders in the way we wish to, we would expect to very soon develop in our young children the sense of empathy for the community that we need. At this time, there is nothing but despair. But the heart is comforted by these few words, that "*you know not, perhaps God will bring about after that a [different] matter.*" All of you elders should also join us in this prayer. If nothing else, at least say "Amen" to strengthen our hearts.

You are also aware that some years ago it was proposed that some of the well-wishers of the community should become volunteers and collect money for the education and educational needs of the community by canvassing for donations in every town and city. If this plan had been successful and would have been implemented in all of India, it would not have been difficult to collect even Rs. 10 million. It is a pity that this plan did not work, but now Munshi Ghulam Niaz Khan *Saheb* has again moved that this plan should be adopted. He would like 300 volunteers in Punjab to be ready for this community work and implement this plan. He has issued a notice in this regard and is determined to carry out this work, and whether it happens elsewhere or not, he will implement this proposal in Jalandhar district. May God make him successful.

The notice he has issued is included at the end of this report of mine.

Munshi Ghulam Niaz Khan *Saheb*, who was present in the meeting, read the notice to the attendees of the meeting.

Mr. President of the session! There is one more matter for which I would like permission to say something. I am sure that each and every member of our community wants to see the community develop and prosper. But, in this regard, I see that people have different opinions about how and using what method this development and prosperity can be achieved. Someone suggests one way and someone else thinks of another method. So, it needs to be settled as to which method is actually the best for the development of the community.

Although Maulvi Muhammad Hashmatullah *Saheb* is going to give a lecture on this topic, I don't want a few members to decide this by giving useful lectures and interesting speeches. Rather, I want a very large group of Muslims to express their thoughts and opinions in this regard in a brief manner so that at least we know what in their opinion we should do for the welfare and development of the community.

For this purpose, I have sent a general circular to all the members requesting them to briefly express their views and ideas as to what the Muslims should do for their development.

Mr. President of the session! Just saying that the Muslims should adopt such-and-such a method for their development is not sufficient, rather they should also talk about the plan to provide the means for the proposed method. That is why it has also been requested that those elders who propose a method should also suggest a plan that can be practically implemented to provide these means.

It is my wish that 200-300 elders of the community should individually gather their brief opinions so that it is known what the general opinions of the elders are in this matter. Until now, only a few elders of the community have sent their opinions. But I will wait further until the last meeting, and if at that time the number of responses is in my consideration sufficient and there is a perceived benefit from their presentation, I shall with your permission present them in the meeting. If the members of the conference agree, a select committee will be formed to write a summary opinion drawing from all these opinions. A great advantage of this plan is that the general opinion of the elders of the community regarding the method for the improvement of the condition of the Muslims will become known, and sufficient attention can be paid to adopting these methods which will now manifest themselves. It would be no wonder if, as a result, the fragmentation of ideas that is presently happening with regards to the development of Muslims is removed, everybody agrees on one method, and comes together to strive for the improvement of the condition of the Muslims.

I am also pleased to inform that the committee of the Islamic Madrasa Quwwat-ul-Islam Rahimia Jhajjar has approved for the school to become a local committee of the Muhammadan Educational Conference and to carry out its objectives as per the section 8 of the rules of procedures of the conference.

167

Arts and Academic Interests ★

(Seventh annual session of the Muhammadan Educational Conference held in Delhi, December 27-29, 1892, pp 97-99)

The first resolution presented was on the topic of scholarly books that should be written on indigenous knowledge and the arts along with acquiring Western knowledge and the arts. Sir Syed's opinion on this topic:

I have not stood up to discuss this resolution. I know that perhaps the gentlemen who are present in this hall at this time have not seen the books that have been published by the government in the Indian Report. I believe that there is no antique building in the world whose design and engineering details have not been published by the government or other authors in their works. Surprisingly, even the color of the stone used in the buildings is noted in these writings. Similarly, the jewelry that is popular all over India and the way it is made has also been written about in books, including the colors of this jewelry. In the same way, books have even been written on the industrial tools that are used by Indians and all the methods of making cloth and carpets. A book describing the various kinds of cloth used in India has reached our library as well. It contains photographs of different pieces of cloth that are so realistic that you will not believe that they are photographs. It seems as if a piece of cloth has actually been placed there. In short, those who think like our esteemed Karamullah Khan *Saheb* need to look at these books to see how far the products of industry and craftsmanship have come before making up their minds. These books have been prepared by highly competent engineers and architects after traveling across many places and they should be read. The government has distributed these books widely. Now the major task is that those things that have come to the fore should remain prominent. I think that this resolution should pass as is.

168

Religious Education of Muslims

(Report of the seventh annual session of the Muhammadan Educational Conference held in Delhi, December 27-29, 1892)

On December 28, in the fourth meeting of the seventh annual session of the Muhammadan Educational Conference held in Delhi, December 27-29, 1892, a resolution was presented that "in the view of this conference, it is obligatory on Muslims in locales where there are government schools and colleges to make appropriate and complete arrangements for the religious education of Muslim students who study in these schools and colleges." The short but comprehensive speech that Sir Syed gave regarding this resolution is included below.

Mr. President of the session!

There is no doubt that all the Muslims desire that these students also get religious education as stated in this resolution which has been presented. I need to explain only two things. First, when this resolution came before the committee, there was no indication in it that the government would be requested to do this. If this were known, the committee … would not have agreed to present it to the conference, because one time that this request was made, nothing came of it. In making the request again, the conference would be humiliated and disrespected. Just as the conference wants the good of the country, it also wants to maintain its honor. Once the request is rejected, it is a shame to request again. All you Muslims and people of faith, who are known for the passion for your religion, don't do anything for yourselves and strive for baseless things. First try yourself and show the government what you did. If it were known that the people of Punjab had tried and failed, they could have been told at that time to try again. The truth is that no one paid it any attention. Even though the government approved it, no attention has been paid to religious education in any school or college. If the government is to be requested, then those who want to make this request should first show some samples of their effort, their attention, and their approach in one or two colleges and then tell the government what difficulties they faced. When no one is paying any attention except for a few verbal conversations, it is absolutely futile to request the government. Although there is some indication in the resolution to request the government, I am not opposed to it. Rather, I am opposed to the mention of the request made to the government by Nawab Viqar-ul-Mulk Bahadur in his speech.

169

Thoughts on Students Going to Europe and Getting Married

(Report of the seventh annual session of the Muhammadan Educational Conference held in Delhi, December 27-29, 1892, p 138)

In the seventh annual session of the Muhammadan Educational Conference held in December 1892, Sir Syed presented the resolution that "this conference, in its numerous sessions, has liked and supported the idea of the boys of the community going to Europe for their education. The conference has considered it a means of the progress of the community. That is why it is essential to manifest this matter that the conference considers the practice of these boys marrying women outside their community while in Europe for their education very inappropriate. It considers the practice harmful to the community and a cause of its decline. It also considers the practice an obstruction to the educational advancement of the community." While presenting the resolution, the speech that Sir Syed gave is recorded below.

Mr. President of the session!

My intention with this resolution is not to interfere in any social situation, rather to limit it to such an extent that education and advancement are not harmed. If this practice continues that boys go to England and spend their time and presence there finding a match, there will be so much harm to the progress of their education. A big part of the short period of time that they are in England will be spent serving the spouse. In the times when marriage even within the kinsfolk is considered detrimental to education, it is a big deal to get married in England. And then the disaster, sadness, and sorrow that engulf the parents on the return of their sons is something that is against morality and humanity. It is highly doubtful that their offspring will be empathetic to our community and will help with the development of the community. At this time, I have letters from six or seven friends asking how they can send their boys to England for education when there is an apprehension that they will get married there. A few gentlemen have already dropped the idea of sending their boys to England. If this trend continues, it will cause harm to education. Since the conference always supported the idea of boys going to England, it also expresses its disapproval for this practice. It is not in our power to prevent it, rather the way in which we have supported their going to England, in the same way we make it clear that our conference disapproves of this practice. It is up to them to listen to us or not.

170

Motion for the Development of Greek Medicine

(Report of the seventh annual session of the Muhammadan Educational Conference held in Delhi, December 27-29, 1892)

In the seventh annual session of the Muhammadan Educational Conference held in December 1892 in Delhi, the following resolution was presented: "It is the opinion of this conference that according to the needs of the country and the community, it is imperative to advance Greek medicine, to derive benefits from modern experiences and knowledge, and for the community, or rather all the people of India, to help in its achievement." After the presentation of this resolution, Sir Syed Ahmed Khan's speech to second this proposal is recorded below.

Mr. President of the session!

We have just had some very good discussions on this resolution. The extensive lecture on the authenticity of Greek medicine was given in a very competent manner by Hakim Abdul Majeed Khan *Saheb*, which was also delivered with heartfelt love and sincere enthusiasm. But I do not consider myself capable of discussing or giving preference to any of the medicines that are very popular in these times, be they Greek, English, or Homeopathic. All these people who are here, their purpose is to find a solution for the improvement and betterment of their community and the country. Among all the methods of treatment that are available, whether anybody likes them or not, what we have to see is how much desire our country has for Greek medicine. Go to any township today; groups and groups of people are desirous of being treated with Greek medicine. In every village and every city, we find that the general desire is for Greek medicine. Their wishes are fulfilled, but instead of doing them good, it harms them. We see everywhere that illiterate people masquerading as physicians dupe ignorant people out of their money. They actually don't know how to treat illnesses. Poor people consider them physicians. In my opinion, it is necessary for the community and the country, both Hindus and Muslims, to remove this danger. Everyone should work together to solve this problem and remove this harmful situation. This problem can be solved by establishing a school to teach Greek medicine to students, produce physicians who can treat illnesses, and then disperse them to various places. We will not even need to do anything to disperse them; when they are ready, they will disperse by themselves. Our work for the good of our community and the country is to establish a place where we can produce physicians educated in Greek medicine. The method for this is none other than what Hakim Abdul Majeed Khan *Saheb* has proposed. Delhi has been a repository of knowledge in Greek medicine for a long time and there is no town or city that has not received the kind caring of its Hakims. At that time, Delhi was a repository of knowledge of medicine as much as it was a repository of the knowledge of Hadith. It is essential that this school be established in Delhi and be run by the families of Delhi. At this time, all the pride that Hakim Abdul Majeed Khan has is justified, but I think that every person of this city who has any affiliation with any family of Hakims should come together and lend their hands to this task and understand that it is not the task of any particular family. Rather, it is the task of all the families of Hakims in Delhi. They should complete this task and consider it their duty to help the poor by supporting this school of Greek medicine. As Nawab *Saheb* said, a heavy burden has been put on the shoulders of Hakim Abdul Majeed Khan. The biggest one is that hundreds of men approach him. From dawn till dusk, he spends his time giving prescriptions and medicines. Our physicians of Delhi, especially the late Hakim Mahmood Khan, father of Hakim Abdul Majeed Khan, have had the practice of giving the same treatment to the fakirs, the paupers, the *chamars*, and the *halal-khors*,[26] as they would to the richest of the rich. May God have mercy on Hakim Ahsanullah Khan, who was an attending physician to the emperor. One day he was going in a palanquin to the emperor's palace when a *halal-khor* stopped him and said his wife was sick. He got down from the palanquin, went and examined the patient, and wrote her a prescription. This is the special trait of the families of this desolate Delhi of ours. I also lived in Delhi for a long time. I do not remember any of the Hakims that went around to people's houses to have

---

[26.] *Halal-khor* literally means one whose earnings are legitimate. It refers to those of the lowest caste who perform the lowest functions, so called because every earning is legitimate for them.

taken even a paisa from the Muslims. They considered it their duty as Hakims to treat people. The same practice continues with Hakim Abdul Majeed Khan. It is certainly the need of the country at this time to produce a lot of people who know medicine. I don't like the concept of honorary teachers. Teachers must be salaried so that they can do their function well. At this time, the restriction is that there is no money. That is why it is Hakim *Saheb* who teaches. Let this go on as it is and let's see what God does next. I move that the resolution as presented be passed.

In Support of Mr. Beck's Proposal Regarding Progress of the Education of Muslims

(Report of the seventh annual session of the Muhammadan Educational Conference held in Delhi, December 27-29, 1892, pp 175-178)

At the seventh annual session of the Muhammadan Educational Conference (held in Delhi in December 1892), Mr. Theodore Beck, principal of the Aligarh College, proposed that the conference prepare a detailed review of the education of Muslims and then work toward the progress of education in accordance with this review. Responding to this proposal, Sir Syed gave the following speech. This speech has been published in the proceedings of the seventh session of the conference.

Mr. President of the session and other elders! I believe that the proposal made by our friend, a well-wisher of the Muslims and one who endeavors to advance education for them, Mr. Theodore Beck, principal of the *Madrasatul Uloom,* cannot be considered by anyone to not be a useful and unique solution for the educational advancement of the Muslims.

Mr. Beck *Saheb,* as his speech indicates, wants a separate section of the Muhammadan Educational Conference to be established to study the progress of the education of Muslims, to establish a count of the number of Muslim boys getting education in schools and colleges, to evaluate the opportunities they have for education, and to implement schemes related to their education.

The first objective of our conference, as set out in its procedural rules, is to endeavor to spread and widely develop European sensibilities and literature among the Muslims, to bring them to a high level of education in these areas, to think about strategies for these efforts, and to discuss these strategies.

So, the proposal made by Mr. Beck is within this objective and the members of the conference are absolutely empowered to take such measures as they see fit to achieve this objective. Therefore, if the members of the conference approve, then according to the current procedural rules, they can establish a separate section under the Muhammadan Educational Conference for this purpose. So, at this time, if the conference agrees to two things, this goal can be achieved.

First, that the conference approves the establishment of this section. To name the members of this section at this time would be of no use at all because members will have to be selected from each district after careful consideration and consultation with knowledgeable friends. But at this time everyone should understand that those who will be members of this section cannot get by with just sitting at home, but rather they will have to do actual work. They will have to go around their districts, find out what the situation is, send back accurate reports, and help in every way to achieve this goal. Just saying that I will do the work in this district and so-and-so will do the work in that district is not going to be enough to make things happen. Perhaps there are one or two people, like Syed Karamat Hussain, who can be trusted, but it won't be sufficient to have people like him only in one or two districts. There will be a need to evaluate the situation in all the districts of the provinces of Punjab, the North-Western Provinces and Awadh, and Bihar, and in every district there will be a need for a person who actually undertakes the effort out of a desire for the welfare of the community and does the work.

In addition, it will be necessary to appoint a managing committee that will correspond with the members in the districts and its members would be required when necessary to come to meetings and participate in them. It will be necessary to propose a name for the secretary of this managing committee. However, I cannot find a better secretary for this committee than Nawab Viqar-ul-Mulk Maulvi Mushtaq Hussain. But I will inform the conference very clearly that I will not be able to perform the duties of the secretary of this committee. I have a lot of work and I don't have free time. That is why it will be necessary to appoint a separate secretary for this.

Second, the biggest thing that is needed to fulfill this objective is the availability of money. Undoubtedly, to find out the situation in several districts, we will need to send someone especially to do this work. If there is money, that person can be given remuneration as the need arises, and we won't have to depend only on the members in the districts. This is because we do not know which of these members are doing their work sincerely and earnestly and which ones are just saying that they will do the work and finish the task in such-and-such district. In short, this will not work without money.

At this time, Nawab Viqar-ul-Mulk has told me that he is ready to donate money for this work. I asked him how we can rely on donations alone. However, as per the usual practice, I will present in the conference meeting a report of last year's total income and expenditure. From this report it will be known how much money is left over after deducting the expenses of the previous year. But in previous conferences, many people donated money to the conference on the condition that any money left over at the end of the year should be put in the scholarship fund for the students. Sometimes a person has taken the responsibility for the entire expense of the conference on the condition that the total income from it would be contributed to the scholarship fund. But there has been no such condition in place in the past year, nor should such a condition be placed in the future. All the money left over should be used for the purpose proposed by Mr. Beck and the money should be spent as directed by the committee that is appointed for this purpose.

Mr. President of the session! This work is not such that it can be done in one year, but rather it will be a sustained effort for a long period of time. When people find out that the money leftover is spent on this work, it is hoped that they will help more by donating more to the conference and becoming its members, and the work will progress well. If we are in need of more money, there are such generous elders as Nawab Viqar-ul-Mulk and others and we can take donations as needed. If this work catches on, it will be a practical action of the conference, and it will be perceived that in fact the conference has come into existence.

172

Syllabus Textbooks of the *Anjuman Himayat-e-Islam* ★

(Seventh annual session of the Muhammadan Educational Conference held in Delhi, December 27-29, 1892, p 119)

On December 28, in the third meeting of the session, a resolution was presented that the conference appreciates the series of journals that the *Anjuman Himayat-e-Islam*[27] has compiled for beginners and, considering them useful, recommends their publication. Sir Syed's opinion regarding this resolution:

I do not want to say anything about these books because I have not seen them, but I want to say that the recommendations that the conference makes must be followed up by the secretary. If the conference recommends that a committee of clerics be appointed and they gather and write a review of these books, I will not be able to follow up on that. I can assure you that no Maulvi will give it any attention. If you wish, you can assign me this task which I will not be able to complete. So many members are gathered here at this time; can anyone among them say that the Maulvis will come together and give their opinions?

---

[27] *Anjuman Himayat-e-Islam* (The Association for the Support of Islam) is an Islamic intellectual and social welfare organization with branches in India and Pakistan. It was founded in Lahore on September 24, 1884 in a mosque known as Masjid Bakan inside Mochi Gate, Lahore, by Khalifa Hameed-ud-Din.

173

The Objective of the Muhammadan Educational Conference ★

(Seventh annual session of the Muhammadan Educational Conference held in Delhi, December 27-29, 1892, pp 179-181)

Mr. President of the session!

I had mentioned in my report that I have issued a circular for the purpose that 200-300 elders of the community briefly write their opinion regarding what the Muslims should do for their development, what methods they propose for their worldly progress, and what schemes they propose for the Muslims to acquire the means for this. It was also stated in the report that if, in my opinion, a sufficient number of opinions is received and I consider it useful to share them, I will present them in this session. But I am sorry that as many comments as I wanted were not received. The opinions of only 17 elders, whose names have been annotated in the report, were received. Hence, I do not consider it necessary to request the conference to appoint a select committee for this. With your permission, I will only include a summary of these opinions in the report of the session's proceedings and publish it. The notice I had issued in this regard was as follows.

Notice

We must explain in very brief words the real objective of this conference which has been meeting every year for six years and discussing various issues. In our understanding, its objective is only to determine "what the Muslims should do for their development."

All the proposals that were presented in the previous sessions, all the resolutions that were debated, and all the lectures that were given had this objective which we have stated in brief words.

But, so far, no general ideas about "what the Muslims should do for their development" have been expressed in any session, because whenever an elder gave a lecture on a particular matter, he only expressed his opinions and ideas. The resolutions that were debated were related to a particular aspect of the issue and did not reveal a general idea about "what the Muslims should do for their development."

This year's session of the Muhammadan Educational Conference is being held in Delhi, and it is hoped that people with the most influential opinions, who are well acquainted with the decline of Muslims, their poverty, and the difficulties caused by poverty, will gather. In this meeting, opinions of several elders on "what the Muslims should do for their development" should be taken so that the views of the Muslims at least and what path and what methods they consider preferable to adopt are known in this regard.

Although Maulvi Hashmatullah Esq., MA will give a lecture on this topic in this session, it will be an academic and literary lecture and will express only his opinions. Our goal in this regard is to get the brief individual opinions of 200-300 elders so that it is known what the general opinion of the elders of the community is in this regard, what method they would propose for the worldly progress of the Muslims, and what schemes they propose for the Muslims to acquire the means for this.

Therefore, it is my request to every elder who is participating in the Muhammadan Educational Conference as a member to write down his opinion on this matter briefly and clearly and submit it to the secretary. A day will be set aside for the reading of these opinions. If the members prefer, the method for the development of the Muslims as related to these opinions will be revealed and sufficient attention can be given to the adoption of those schemes that manifest themselves. It will be no wonder if the confusion that is happening regarding the development of Muslims is resolved as a result of this plan and everyone agrees on how to put their efforts into improving the condition of the Muslims.

★

174

Address to Muslims as a Plea from Syed Ahmed Khan

(Aligarh Institute Gazette, April 18, 1893)

This speech was neither given at the eighth annual session Muhammadan Educational Conference (December 1893) nor is it included in the proceedings of the eighth session, as mentioned by Ismail Panipati in his collection *"Khutbat-e Sir Syed"* (Lectures of Sir Syed), lecture No. 86, p 544. This address had already been published in the April 18, 1893 issue of the Aligarh Institute Gazette, ten months before the conference was held.

You may remember that time when we all lay there sleeping and no one even cared about the betterment of the community. At that time, there was a need to wake up the community, to make it aware of its decline, and to warn it of the severe decay that was coming. People put in their best effort and we think that effort produced success. People woke up and voices of empathy for the community rose up from all corners of India.

People awoke and rose up, but they weren't attentive enough. In a sleepy haze, leaving the straight path and the common way, they started going after small gains. That is, instead of all the people gathering their strength in one place and completing a task, they started dispersing their strength. Each person took their pouch of water and started irrigating their little corners of this vast sand desert. They thought that with this water they could plant a lush green and fruitful garden in this sand desert. This idea was impossible then and is impossible now. Their efforts were wasted and will be wasted. As the saying goes, "put water in the sand, it belongs neither to the sky nor to the earth."

For a long time, we thought about warning the community about this useless work and to convince them not to waste their strengths by dividing them. But we always had the inkling that people would doubt our intentions and attribute our suggestion to selfishness instead of considering it well-intentioned and stemming from empathy for the community. That is why, while we explained this idea in an ambiguous manner, we did not explain it clearly and with fearless rebuttals. I confess that I have undoubtedly committed a sin against the community by not clearly stating what was good for the community and not putting the due effort into drawing the attention of the community toward it for fear of creating suspicion toward myself. But my conscience reproaches me and says that:

Be modest for the sake of God and not for the sake (of others)

Now I will lift all the curtains and say what I think is best for my people. "*Everyone can know (or understand) what they want and say what they want.*"

My heart is happy with peace of mind
That he took the respite all at once
O my people, O my people, for you
I have ruined my shame and my name

I want to tell the community clearly that dividing its strengths has caused great harm to it and it needs to collect all these strengths in one place.

I want to tell the community clearly that these small tasks they have undertaken with the welfare of the community in mind are causing serious damage to it instead of benefiting it. And instead of collecting the community's ideas, its courage, and its passions in one place, they are disturbing them, dispersing them, and are uselessly wasting them.

I want to inform and emphasize clearly that the work you have undertaken for the reward in the hereafter is not forbidden. Every person has the right to earn this reward. But the garb of community welfare and community empathy that you have put on it is only a deception and the community is being deceived. Do not deceive the community. Betraying the trust of the community is that fraud by which the community will fall into deception and be destroyed. I admit that there is much to be done for the community and there is much that the community needs. Its situation is like that of a patient who is suffering from many illnesses. Some of these illnesses are life-threatening and some are not. So, if all of you focus on those illnesses that are not life-threatening and no one focuses on the treatment of the fatal illnesses, which are not curable unless all of you, not just a few, focus on its treatment with one accord, then there is no hope of the patient recovering and in the end his death is certain.

So, if you want to cure the patient, act like a smart physician. Leave those minor illnesses alone that are not actually the significant illnesses but are caused by the major illnesses, and let everyone agree to wholeheartedly devote themselves to the treatment of the major illnesses and cure the patient. Those minor illnesses will go away by themselves when the fatal illnesses are cured.

Now consider what we have to do for the welfare and prosperity of the community. We have to give our community education in the English language, which God has given to us of His own will as the language of our rulers and without learning which we cannot do anything in this world, or rather I would say we cannot even serve our religion. But an education with which the community learns *katar-matar* English, i.e. a mishmash of words taken from here and there, and they start to speak English like the tradesmen and attendants speak in camps or the porters and cabmen speak in England, will be of no use. They should get a full education in English and a high level understanding of the English language so that they can be respected for their proficiency in English literature. They should be able to use the English language in their community, worldly, and religious affairs, so that others see the value in it. Even this much will not be enough for us. It will also be necessary that some among them know French, German, Latin, and Greek very well.

Along with this, we must also teach the Arabic language, which, regardless of the fact that it is the language of Muslims, is a language of a high status that is valued and cannot be separated in any way from the domain of academic languages. It cannot be excluded from the needs of Muslims. And if we consider religious service, it becomes necessary to develop familiarity with Arabic along with the Hebrew language. In a congregation, the late Maulana Shah Abdul Aziz recited with great pride the four lines of the beginning of the Torah in Hebrew. And Nawab Fateh-ul-Mulk Baig Khan *Saheb*, who was a great devotee of Shah *Saheb*, had memorized those lines and would sometimes recite them when speaking about Shah *Saheb*.

We cannot ignore Persian either, which has become closely associated with the upbringing and the quintessence of Muslims. And it is a very delicate and sophisticated language in itself. There is so much capital of Muslim knowledge and history in it that Muslims cannot ignore it.

Although Urdu is our mother tongue, improving it, reforming it, and giving it the status of a global language is the duty of us Muslims.

Giving religious education to Muslims, whether at a lower, middle, or higher level, is also obligatory on us because the only thing that has made different nations into one community is Islam. If we do not pay it any attention, we cannot maintain this community. The least we can do is to teach religious beliefs and precepts, which we have associated with lower level religious education.

Along with these things, we have to educate them in various knowledge and the arts and especially in modern knowledge. This is a very important task, but its greatness and need at this time is a different discussion. In brief, it can be stated that without it, a people cannot become a community nor can they attain any rank, honor, and worth in the world. And, truth be told, without it we cannot serve religion either.

This was only about the state of education, but we cannot achieve our goals with education alone. Does a human being become a human being only with education and get a status higher than a donkey carrying a load of books? Does a nation become a nation only with education? Does a nation gain respect among the nations of the world only through education? Not at all. In fact, until a human being becomes a human being and a nation becomes a nation, they cannot be respected.

So, more than education, we have to do for Muslims what we call nurturing and upbringing, which is for a nation to become a nation like life for a body, and without which it is impossible for a nation to become a nation and remain alive as a nation.

What do we need to do to meet this end? Our first task should be to gather in one place, as much as possible, the children and youth of the community so that they can stay together, study together, play together, live and fall sick in one place, and to gather sufficient means of their nurturing.

Their physical well-being needs to be taken care of. Apart from supplying all the necessary medical supplies and facilities, a big house with a spacious and pleasant atmosphere needs to be made available to board them. They should be encouraged to participate in sports and to exercise, which is necessary for their physical health. They should be instructed to exercise according to their strengths. Those who are weak should be prescribed exercises that will increase their physical strength and those who are strong and powerful should exercise to maintain their strength and power. They should be taught to ride horses, and courage and bravery should be instilled in them, without which man can neither do the work of this world nor of religion.

Then, we should provide recreational facilities for them so that their temperament doesn't whither, their aspirations do not fade away and disappear, and the restrictions that are placed on them are only sufficient to keep their aspirations from being deviant and to keep them on a straight and kind path.

Then, we should take care that these sports and exercise regimens are not a hindrance to their education and studies but rather help and motivate them. They should be provided with such means for education that will interest them, delight their hearts, and make them eager to participate and to apply what they have learned. It is not enough to just water the tree; unless its leaves and branches are swayed by the gusts of wind and it absorbs the air and its constituents, it can never bear flowers and fruits.

To keep their morals and religious views on the right path and to perform their religious duties, one or two hallowed, dignified, pious, wise scholars of kind countenance and pure character should be with this group to influence their hearts with courtesy and manners. In their gracious company, the students will be naturally inclined toward goodness and piety.

If we want the youth of our community to adopt a good and virtuous path, it cannot be achieved with admonitions and reprimands or by imposing restrictions on them. Prof. Morrison said it very well that no one can claim to completely subjugate the thoughts and desires of a thousand youth to his own will. We cannot make the thoughts of men, which in their infinite domain can reach anywhere, submissive to our ideas like a military officer keeps a company of disciplined soldiers under his command. Therefore, it should be our desire to provide for our students such means and good associations for their education and nurturing that will instill in them an attraction to goodness and aversion to evil. "God is in me, he said."

A righteous company will make you righteous

An immoral company will make you immoral

This is what, Muhammad, the Messenger of God, may God's blessing and peace be upon him, said, "The example of a good companion (who sits with you) in comparison with a bad one is like that of a musk seller and the blacksmith's bellows; from the first one you would either buy musk or enjoy its pleasant fragrance, while the bellows would either burn your clothes from the flying sparks or it would emit a repugnant smell."

Hence, it is imperative and incumbent upon us to gather the necessary means and to give them appropriate nurturing to educate our children, to make them human beings, to make our community a community, and to make them honorable in religion and in worldly affairs.

Then, O lovers of the community, and O discerners of the strength of the community, and O people who claim to seek welfare and prosperity for the community! Do justice, and see and understand if what you are doing can benefit the community. Will it make the community a community? Will it make the community rise from the ashes of humiliation? Absolutely not!

Think about the small schools and the worthless and ineffective colleges that you have established in many places. Can you bring some good to the community through them? Can you provide the necessary means for the education and nurturing of the community in these schools and colleges? In no way.

You do not look after the welfare of your people, but rather you disperse its strengths and cause it harm. You do not look after the welfare of the community's children, but rather you show malice toward them. You let them waste their lives. Whatever they could do without this ignorant attachment and misplaced kindness of yours, you are ruining that too.

For example, there is a government college or school in some district or a missionary school in which the education is given by masters, teachers, the principal, and professors who are scholars of very high caliber and have degrees from universities in England. These colleges and schools are well managed and under formal supervision. Now you have opened a college or school in the same district by collecting donations and by showing people the shine of Islam. And now somehow you have rounded up Muslim boys and admitted them to a college in which there are no high caliber masters, teachers, principal, or professors. And there is neither good management nor regular supervision in it. So, in fact, you have shown malice, not friendship, toward the children of the community by depriving them of a good education, giving them poor education, and wasting their lives. If you had established a school or college of the same quality as the government or missionary school in the district, we would have endured patiently, but what you have done is destroy whatever little community education there was. Then, is this doing good for the community and showing kindness toward it? Indeed, your intention is good and you sincerely work for the good of the community, but like an ignorant friend, you endanger your children by entrusting them to quacks and charlatans.

If the *Anjuman Islamia* (Islamic Societies) that have been established in many places serve any purpose, that purpose is not to cure an illness that is fatal for the community. If you stop at that and don't gather your strengths to pay attention to the cure of the illness that is fatal, the patient will not be cured, and, unfortunately, the fatal illness will eventually become incurable. Then, neither the compassion of the compassionate nor the healing power of the healer will be useful.

Now you should come and see the *Madrasatul Uloom* Aligarh, which has been established by giving consideration to all those things which are necessary for Muslims, which I have stated just now, and through which a community can become a community. Don't think that I want to brag, but I say the truth, the absolute truth, with good intentions, and with the welfare of the community at heart that with the help of honorable and generous people of the community, the college has reached a rank that no matter how much you try in various places, you cannot get a college, school, or boarding house to attain even a tenth of that rank Much of the resources required for the education and nurturing of our community has been collected in it. I admit that there are a lot of flaws in it and there is a lot to be done which requires a lot of money. So, gather all your peoples together in one place, remove whatever is not right with it [*the college*], and finish what remains to be done in it by agreeing among yourselves, gathering your strengths together, and providing money – by begging for it, collecting donations among yourselves, or doing whatever it takes to finish the job.

I acknowledge that one *Madrasatul Uloom* in Aligarh is not sufficient for the entire community. But I think that the work that has been started, and has reached such a level that one wonders how it got there, should, first of all, be completed through concerted action. After that, a second task can be started and completed in the same way, and then a third task. If you don't do that and keep your strengths dispersed, then even a single task will not be fulfilled, there will be harm all around, and everything will be destroyed and annihilated.

It is true that to complete the *Madrasatul Uloom*, a lot of capital will be required and perhaps people's courage will be depleted thinking of it. But, in reality, this is not true. If the community is united, unites its strengths, and follows the right path, it can establish ten such colleges one after the other. So, my purpose in saying this is only that the entire community should first agree to fully complete the task of establishing the *Madrasatul Uloom* and then turn their attention to starting some other work.

The plan to complete this task is nothing but to collect money from the entire community. If we collect a speck of silver the size of a grain of barley from every living man and woman of the community, we can collect tens of millions of rupees and fulfill all the needs of the community. So, I say that:

> Why don't I take a sliver of silver from everyone
> So that a treasure I can collect

Yes, as much as this method seems easy, it is very difficult to implement. But if the community puts up a concerted effort, it is not difficult at all. As the saying goes, Hazrat Ali resolves all difficulties in difficult times.

> There is no problem that isn't easily solved
> Man should never be disheartened

There is a saying of a courageous person that when you start a task, believe that nothing is impossible. So, if just a few brave people who are benefactors of the community go to all the cities and towns, and every Muslim man and woman resident there gives something in the name of God or in the name of the community, hundreds of thousands of rupees can be collected in a few days and all the needs of the Madrasatul Uloom can be met.

So, may God give the Muslims of every city and town the guidance to do this. Amen.

175

Report of the Seventh Session of the Muhammadan Educational Conference ★

(Excerpted from the eighth annual session of the Muhammadan Educational Conference held in Aligarh, December 27-30, 1893, pp 78-93)

In the service of His Honor:
Nawab Mohsin-ud-Daula Mohsin-ul-Mulk Maulvi Syed Mehdi Ali Khan Bahadur

President of the eighth session of the Muhammadan Educational Conference Location Aligarh

In accordance with the procedure, I have the honor of presenting at the opening meeting a brief account of the proceedings of last year's session of this educational conference, the resolutions passed in that session, the results arising from them, and the extent to which they have been complied with.

Last year, as per section 12 of the rules of procedures of the conference, the following members were appointed to the managing committee for that year.

From Punjab

Khan Bahadur Muhammad Barkat Ali Khan *Saheb*, Khwaja Yusuf Shah *Saheb*, Niaz Muhammad Khan *Saheb* aka Ghulam Niaz Khan *Saheb*, Maulvi Ahmed Shafi *Saheb* (absent)

From the North-Western Provinces and Awadh

Maulvi Muhammad Hashmatullah, Esq., CS, Mirza Abid Ali Baig *Saheb*, Maulvi Abdullah Jan *Saheb*, Maulvi Syed Mumtaz *Saheb* (absent)

From the Province of Bihar

Shams-ul-'Ulama Maulvi Muhammad Abdul Rauf *Saheb*, Nawab Sarfaraz Hussain Khan Bahadur (absent)

Ex-officio Members for That Session

Nawab Mohsin-ud-Daula Mohsin-ul-Mulk Maulvi Syed Mehdi Ali Khan Bahadur, president

Dr. Sir Syed Ahmed Khan Bahadur, KCSI, LLD, secretary

Members Appointed by the President as per Section 12

Shams-ul-'Ulama Maulvi Muhammad Shibli *Saheb* Nomani, *Shams-ul-'Ulama* Khan Bahadur Maulvi Muhammad Zakaullah *Saheb*, the Honorable Haji Muhammad Ismail Khan *Saheb*

Among the aforementioned members, those who did not attend have the word "absent" noted in front of their names. The members who are present carry out the functions assigned to them as per section 16 of the rules of procedures.

In the last session, seven resolutions were presented.

- First resolution: To develop indigenous arts and be versed in Western arts. This is a very difficult task to carry out, and considering the state of the community, its compliance at present seems nearly impossible.

- Second resolution: The intent of this resolution was that all the resolutions passed in the conference should be separately printed and distributed in the cities. Last year, due to the abundance of work and also because some documents of the session are yet to be printed, this resolution could not be complied with. But I will get all the resolutions printed separately.

- Third resolution: It was related to the desire to teach mathematics to young children.

- Fourth resolution: It stated that the series of journals for the education of beginners prepared by the *Anjuman Himayat-e-Islam* Lahore is useful and worth publishing.

- Fifth resolution: This resolution was to the effect that in the government schools and colleges, appropriate provisions should be made for the religious education of Muslims.

- Sixth resolution: This resolution only expressed the conference's disapproval for Muslim students, who go to England for education, marrying women from outside the community.

- Seventh resolution: This resolution was about the development of education in Greek medicine, which is being implemented well by the respectable Hakim Abdul Majeed Khan *Saheb*.

Mr. President of the session! All these debates were of the kind for which people say that the Muhammadan Educational Conference is useless and, till date, it has not brought any practical benefit to the community. But I would like to present to you the practical resolutions that were motioned in the last session and then state their outcome, which will decide whether the conference is in fact futile or the presence of the community in this world is useless for the community.

The best and the finest proposal in the last session of the conference was presented by Mr. Beck. He explained the current state of the education of Muslims in his excellent and appreciable speech. He compared the numbers of Hindu and Muslim students and stated what the proportion of Hindu students should be compared to the Muslims students. In the end, the objective of his speech was to state that a separate section of the Muhammadan Educational Conference should be established for the purpose of tracking the progress of the education of Muslims, to determine the number of Muslim students who are studying in different colleges and schools, to investigate the number of Muslim boys who are not getting educated and the obstacles they face, and after that to take appropriate measures regarding their education.

At that time, not only did all the people appreciate it, but the assembly echoed with their shouts of "Bravo!" Many people said to me what a good proposal had been presented, due to which it can be said that the conference had come to life and was now a living conference. Even I, who do not believe in the resurrection of the dead, was deceived and thought that perhaps new life had truly been injected into it.

To make a long story short, this proposal of Mr. Beck was approved. A fund was also proposed for its expenses, not through donations but with whatever cash was available. For this, corresponding members were proposed for each district who were to investigate the situation in each district and report it. If you want to find out the number of these members, the number of elders proposed for Punjab was 31, for the North-Western Provinces was 35, for Awadh was 12, and for the province of Bihar was one, for a total of 79 members. If you want to see their names, they are listed on pages 170 through 175 of the proceedings of the previous session.

Then a managing committee was appointed to carry out the tasks related to this proposal, which included Mr. Theodore Beck, Nawab Viqar-ul-Mulk, Mirza Abid Ali Baig *Saheb*, Maulvi Syed Karamat Hussain *Saheb*, and Maulvi Muhammad Hashmatullah, Esq, and I was appointed its secretary. And a clerk was appointed to assist me.

Among the elders who were appointed corresponding members, there were many who were government employees or held posts in the government. To do their work, it was essential for those elders who were appointed members to determine the status from the officials of the educational authorities of every district and from the documents and registers in their offices. For that, the governments of Bengal, the North-Western Provinces with Awadh, and Punjab were requested that they allow the officials of the educational authorities as well as the officials of finance and judiciary departments to help us in this regard and give the corresponding members the required information. All the governments gladly approved our requests and gave general permission to all employees to assist us in this work. The governments must have been certain that this effort will produce such an informative register that would be useful for both the public and the authorities.

As secretary, I have prepared four types of outline forms which should be filled in by the corresponding members of each district. I have also written a petition addressed to these members. The form and the petition have been printed and sent to every member. I present before you the letter of request I have sent to them from which you will know what matters they have been asked to take the trouble to investigate. That letter of request is as follows.

Letter of Request

I am very grateful to those elders who, out of empathy for the community, have agreed to be corresponding members to investigate the educational status of Muslims. Related to the educational status of Muslims, the situation that presently seems appropriate to explore is detailed below. But it should be clear that the member should find out the status of the entire district for which he has been appointed and write about it. It is possible that in some locations they will not be able to carry out these investigations themselves and will need to do it through a reliable friend. The intention is to know, as far as possible, the status of all the districts.

- First: It should be determined how many government, missionary, or private schools there are in the district in which English education is given using the methods established by the educational authorities or universities.

- Second: Are there any Arabic seminaries in the district in which scholars of Islam teach Arabic and theology using the ancient traditional methods. If there are, they should be marked with the names of these elders.

- Third: If possible, it should be determined if in the district there are any traditional indigenous *makatib*, academies where children of noble families are given primary education by a *Mian-ji*, a traditional teacher. If so, how many?

- In relation to the first category of schools or colleges [*in which English education is given*], it should be determined how many students study in them, how many of them are Muslims, and how many are from other communities. Secondly, in these seminaries or schools, what are the expenses of fees etc. for those students who live in their homes and only go to these schools to study. Thirdly, if there are boys in these colleges and schools who are not residents of the towns or cities where these institutions are located, but are residents of suburbs or nearby towns and live in these locations only to study, what are their expenses besides the school fees, such as for food and rent.

- Fourth: If there is a boarding house attached to these seminaries and schools, it should be determined and noted what the expenses are for living in these boarding houses.

To compile all this information, numbered outline forms have been created and it will be sufficient to fill out the required information in these forms. It will not be so difficult to find out the details of the seminaries of the second type [*Arabic and theology seminaries*]. There are very few seminaries of this type and as seen in form No. 3, which is the form related to these seminaries, the information required is very clear and simple to fill out. It will be somewhat difficult to find out the status of the *maktabs* in the third category [*primary education given by Mian-jis*]. But perhaps, if there are such schools, they will be in cities and big towns. Their status should be determined as much as possible and form No. 3 should be filled with as much information as available.

Matter Needing Special Attention

In addition, a major task is to determine if there are Muslim boys of 10 to 15 or 16 years of age from noble families in the big towns of these districts who do not receive any education and what is the reason for this. Is it because their guardians are without any resources, are poor, and cannot afford to bear the cost of their education? Or is it because they don't want to teach their children English because of religious prejudices? Or are they simply indifferent to education? Whatever reason is evident should be noted. If multiple reasons for this are found somewhere, then all of them should be written down. Countermeasures that are appropriate for that district based on reasons that are determined to be hindering education should be written down.

I will write a few examples of measures that can be taken to remove these obstacles and educated Muslim boys.

For example, can a committee be established in a district or town which will continue to collect donations to help the boys of poor but noble families to attend a nearby school. It should also be noted that private schools often do not have good students. For this reason, every effort should be made to send the boys to government schools to study.

Or, for example, a committee can be established in a district in that location where there is a high school. This committee can rent a house there in which Muslim boys can board and attend the high school. The committee can also help them with their meals to some extent. All these expenses can be paid for through donations that the committee collects.

There is no real remedy at this time for those who do not get an education due to religious prejudice. But time itself will teach them that their idea is wrong. I am certain that the prejudice against studying English is much less now.

Or, for example, where people are simply indifferent toward education, some respectable person should gather the guardians of these boys and convince them not to be indifferent toward their education. As much effort as possible should be put into convincing them.

There will be many places where people incur too much expense for funerals and weddings and become indebted, due to which they are not able to spend on their children's education. There too, a respectable person should gather the people and encourage them to spend less on funerals and weddings and to put money into their children's education.

If the elders of some place are willing to gather people for the two purposes I mentioned and if there is a need for someone to come to this gathering and give a speech and make them understand, we will be able to send a person. We will pay whatever his travel expenses are from our fund. I have stated all these issues as examples. The intent is only to convey the idea that whatever the situation is in that district, they should clearly state their opinion as to whether there are any appropriate measures to be taken or obstacles to be removed to get Muslims boys educated.

It is undoubtedly a difficult task to find out how many such boys [*who are not getting an education*] there are in every town and what are the obstacles to their education. But if we make the effort and go to some of these towns ourselves to find out what the situation is or learn through friends in that town, it will not be difficult to get the information. Even if this information is not based on extensive investigation, we will certainly be able to get estimates.

The results obtained from this investigation should be filled in form No. 4. But for those matters mentioned above, a separate opinion must be written.

Undoubtedly, it will take some time to carry out this investigation, and we are not in any hurry to get those forms, statuses, and opinions. In fact, it is our wish that all this information should reach us before December 1893, and this much time should be sufficient to finish this task.

O friends! Although this work is time-consuming, it is hoped that you will undertake this effort for the benefit of the community.

~ ~ ~

In the annual report of the seventh session of the Muhammadan Educational Conference held in Aligarh in 1893, this speech ends here. But on November 17, 1896 a meeting was convened at Sir Syed's home for the purpose of establishing a local standing committee of the Mohammedan Anglo-Oriental Educational Conference, whose proceedings were published under the title, "Proceedings of the meeting held on November 17, 1896 for the purpose of establishing a local standing committee of the Mohammedan Anglo-Oriental Educational Conference." It contains this speech and also includes some additions to it, which have been included below.

In summary, there was a lot of fanfare regarding this proposal and our community was very happy with it. Some friends said that the Muhammadan Educational Conference, which was lifeless till now, has indeed come to life. But when you ask *che-shad*, what happened to all that fanfare, I will state very respectfully that *hech-nishad*, nothing happened.

I have received the status from only 18 districts, whose summary I will include in this year's proceedings. But meaningful conclusions cannot be properly drawn from these statuses. Mr. Beck, principal of the college and member of the committee, has adopted a great method of sending some of the college students to various places during their holidays to find out about the status of the education of Muslims. He has carried out this process very well and has discovered detailed circumstances, which he will report in this meeting. But after this experience, I assure this conference that until an attentive and intelligent man, who has properly understood the objectives and methods of this investigation, goes to every location on behalf of the conference, these objectives will not be achieved. It should be understood that until we determine the status of the nobles of that area, the schemes to educate their children who are not being sent to school will not be successful. Those persons who are appointed for this work should be remunerated as decided in the last meeting. Hence, I request this conference to conduct an investigation in this manner in two or three districts and gradually expand the investigation to other districts. In this way, there are high hopes that the objective will be achieved.

Mr. President of the session! I cannot refrain from saying that indeed the community is dead and its well-wishers, like physicians, examine it by looking for its pulse, lifting its eyelids, and checking its heartbeat by placing their hands on its chest. They put their hands in front of its nose to see if they can feel it breathing. But they don't find any sign of life and hang their heads in silence. If they hear any voice, it is that the Muhammadan Educational Conference has been established for so long and spends so much money every year, but there is no benefit from it. Those who appreciate it have a poetic take on it that at least it is a blessing for Muslims to gather once a year and take to heart the concerns for the community.

Mr. President of the session! Another useful and necessary matter was mentioned in the last session. It is a matter of great joy to say that at least some concern has arisen among the Muslims for the welfare of their community, and the proof of it is in the establishment of Islamic societies in many places that did not exist before. But it is highly doubtful whether they have formed any opinion on what the objective is for the development and welfare of Muslims, which we want to strive for, and how it can be achieved. That is why I had presented the following question for the Muslims.

What should the Muslims do for their development, what method do they suggest for their worldly development, and what plans have they made to gather the means for it?

It was my wish that hundreds of people, if not thousands, should write their opinions on this and these opinions should be presented in a session of the conference for discussion and debate. After that, a single opinion should be formed so that everyone comes together to make the effort to implement the ideas. I am sorry to say that I failed in that too. People did not pay it any attention. The few opinions that were sent show that they did not pay full attention to the purpose of the question. You may have seen that the summary of all those opinions was included in the proceedings of last year's session.

Mr. President of the session! There was no effort that was spared for the development, education, and welfare of Muslims, but not a single one was effective. This couplet holds true for their situation:

> The verdict is that vinegar increases bile
> While the oil of almond dries it up

And so, nothing can be said except *"I wish my people knew."*

176

Religious Education of Muslim Students

*(Excerpted from the eighth annual session of the Muhammadan Educational
Conference held in Aligarh, December 27-30, 1893, p 135)*

While presenting the third resolution of the eighth session of the Muhammadan Educational Conference, Munshi Abdul Razzaq gave a lecture on the need for religious education of Muslim students. After that, Sir Syed gave this short speech.

Mr. President of the session! I do not want to say much. I want to say this much; that whenever there is a gathering of Muslims, it appears that they are immersed in religion and God. But our honorable speakers and all the friends from Punjab who are present here have admitted that the Punjab government, by way of favor, has ordered that we can appoint our Maulvis and give religious education to Muslim boys in government schools. I ask who has made arrangements for this. When there is no action, what is the use of calling out religion and expressing religious fervor? Support for the Arabic language is something that everyone talks about but no one says what they did about it. Those seminaries that are specifically for religious education and whose founders are such holy men as those that founded the Deoband seminary, can anyone say who helped them? The instructors don't have enough to eat and the students eat at inns – we should introspect and be ashamed that our words and our actions are different. We do not do any of the things we say we will.

177

Deciding the Fate of Muslims

(Excerpted from "Deciding the Fate of the Muslims," which includes speeches by Sir Syed Ahmed Khan, Viqar-ul-Mulk Maulvi Syed Mehdi Ali Khan, and other friends, printed in Agra in 1894)

In the eighth annual session of the Muhammadan Educational Conference, on December 29, 1983, Sir Syed presented the fifth resolution on the topic that the progress of the Muslims in the realm of education and nurturing up until that point was insufficient, and if the state of affairs remained the same, change was not expected to come for centuries. Presenting this resolution, Sir Syed gave a long speech. After that, Nawab Mohsin-ul-Mulk, Maulvi Hasan Ali, Maulvi Murad Ali, Ali Muhammad, Munshi Nisar Hussain, Muhammad Yusuf Khan, Hafiz Muhammad Haji, Maulvi Muhammad Bashiruddin, Sheikh Ghulam Haider, Maulvi Muhammad Hashmatullah and Syed Muhammad Mahmood *Sahebs* spoke on this topic. After these talks, Sir Syed once again spoke and gave brief replies to all of them. All these speeches were not included in the proceedings of the session due to their length and were published separately. We have copied Sir Syed's speech from that booklet. The first part of this speech is an introduction which was included in the separate publication of this lecture while the second part is the actual speech. The third part contains the responses to the speeches of various people that Sir Syed gave at the end. Ismail Panipati has presented the three parts of this long speech as three separate speeches

The development of the community of Muslims is impossible without a high level of education, proper nurturing, and empathy for the community.

All these three things are impossible to achieve without a high-ranking educational institution which has European and Indian professors and a spacious boarding house in which Muslim students can be accommodated in large numbers. It is impossible for such an educational institution, which has all these attributes, to come into existence without the community gathering its strengths in one place and the entire community agreeing to establish such an educational institution. So, the decision of the fate of Muslims is that if the community does not do this, there will be disappointment in its development and progress.

In the eighth session of the Muhammadan Educational Conference, which was held in Aligarh in the month of December, I presented this article as a resolution. In some speeches, I had said that small schools for English education of Muslim children with neither qualified masters nor good teaching were detrimental to the education of these children and disperses the cumulative strength of Muslims.

Although I had stated in my speech that if you can establish good small schools, go ahead, but don't establish bad schools. People understood that to mean that I am absolutely opposed to the establishment of small schools, but to draw that conclusion from my discourse is, in general, not correct. Rather, I am opposed to the establishment of small schools only in two cases:

- First, in the case that these schools do not have qualified masters and do not give good education.

- Second, in the case that the community is content with those schools only and does not turn its attention to the highest quality of education. This is because, in my opinion, until the community raises people with the highest quality of education and nurturing, there will be no progress in it.

It is not surprising that my friends do not agree with this opinion of mine regarding the establishment of small schools. This is because arguments for the two sides of the opinion are based on different issues. They believe that small schools, however small, are not without benefits of some kind. This idea may be right, but in my opinion the small schools that are established should be such that they are considered the foundation of higher education on which a building of high-level education can be constructed, otherwise they are of no use.

But, at this time, the fate of the Muslims will not be decided by establishing or not establishing small schools, but rather by the fact that the progress of the community is impossible without high quality education and nurturing, and such education is not possible without a high quality educational institution. And a high quality educational institution cannot exist without the concerted efforts of the community. So, if the community does not come together to establish such an institution, there will be disappointment in its development and progress.

I also say that the level to which the *Madrasatul Uloom* Aligarh has advanced is evidently impossible for another college, whose foundation is yet to be laid, to attain. So, the community should be concordant to complete it, and when it is completed, the community should concern itself with establishing another college.

I am glad that all the elders who were present in large numbers at the conference sessions agreed with all these matters on which the fate of the community depended. So, I will print all the debates that have occurred and the speeches that have been made on these issues and distribute it in the community. It will show that all of the community has recognized that such a college must be established through a concerted effort. The community has also acknowledged that it is expedient to complete the *Madrasatul Uloom* Aligarh for the sake of high-level education and nurturing. And so the community should turn its attention to it and collect donations for its completion so that this goal is achieved and a full set of means is available for the progress and development of the community. It is, therefore, requested that the community pay attention to this with great effort and endeavor. "*God is the Helper.*"

(2)

This resolution was presented in the session:

"It is the opinion of this conference that what has been done for the development of education and nurturing of Muslims is simply inadequate. If the situation remains the same, a change in the status cannot be expected even after centuries have passed. If concerted and democratic efforts are not made for a higher standard of education, and even more than that for nurturing, it is the opinion of the conference that the community should prepare itself for complete disappointment regarding the education and advancement of the state of Muslims."

In response to this resolution, Sir Syed delivered the following speech:

Mr. President of the session! This despondent resolution that I have presented before you should not be taken to mean that the words of despondence written in it are only by a pen. Not at all, rather these words are a shadow of the impression of despondence that is on my heart, and the odor of disappointment that emanates from them is indeed the odor of my scorched heart. I despair of the progress of Muslims and of the status of the Muslim community as an honorable community in this world. Today's session, I believe, is going to decide it and give our hearts the relief described in a famous quote, "Elijah is one of the comforters."

O Mr. President! You may think this disappointment is due to the weakness of my heart, otherwise there aren't any words for despair and impossible in the dictionary of effort. But I am desirous of a little glimpse of justice. Three centuries have passed while trying in this manner and nothing has happened. For 36 years I have been wandering in this effort and then, like the bull of a crusher that goes round and round, we find ourselves where we were. So why would my heart not despair?

Why should I not cry? For it is my heart, not a stone

Mr. President of the session! The topic that has been presented in today's session is actually not a new one, rather it has been presented in many forms in other sessions. I had presented on the same topic in different words at the Lucknow session, which was rejected by a large group of Muslims. Although it will be a waste of your time, allow me to read that speech of mine in front of you. After that, I will say what I have to say today, because I consider today's session to be the decider of the fate of Muslims.

The topic that was presented in Lucknow was that small schools for the English education of Muslim children with neither competent teachers nor good instruction are harming the education of the children of Muslims and dispersing the cumulative strength of the Muslims.

I had discussed this topic, saying that you gentlemen may have been surprised to hear this resolution but requesting that you should not be too quick to disapprove it. Reflect on it a little bit and allow me to interpret it and examine it from both sides.

It is not my intention to disparage or to call unnecessary those small schools full of Muslim children that have been established in many places by the elders on the trust of unstable donations. But it is my intention to evaluate both the benefit they bring to the community and the harm they cause and to weigh them against each other. The decision will be based on whichever weighs more.

To interpret its meaning, I present an analogy: There is a person who is extremely thirsty and hungry. You give him bread but do not make arrangements to give him water, although you should give priority to water before giving him bread. No doubt he needs bread too, but by ignoring the thing that should be given precedence, giving bread would not do any good because the person would surely die of thirst.

This is the situation of our community. Establishing small schools for the basic education is to give bread to the thirsty and hungry community. The community needs a drink of cold water, i.e. higher education. When you do not arrange it, the result can be nothing but that the community dies of thirst. The community does not have the wherewithal to provide for both higher and basic education. For this reason, when it focuses on arranging for basic education, this compulsion does not allow it the opportunity to provide for higher education. The power of the collective strength of the community is weakened and the community is faced with the same result as the thirsty individual faces with extreme thirst.

One should ponder why people focus on establishing small schools. It can be said in jest that it is to give themselves a hobby, but a hobby for them ruins the lives of these poor children.

Leave aside this jest. With good intentions and empathy for the community, they think that they will provide benefits for the children of the poor and the underprivileged and they will reap the benefits of general education. But this thinking is flawed in two ways.

First, unless there is a high level of education among the high ranking nations, education cannot spread among the low ranking nations and the poor.

Second, when higher education is not available in a country, the spread of basic education is impossible. No country's history in any part of the world has proven that basic education will spread without the provision of higher education. It is the norm of nature that basic education follows higher education. Hence, those who desire the prevalence of basic education among the poor, their first duty should be to try to produce highly educated people in their community. Basic education will gradually spread by itself among the poor people.

Everyone acknowledges, as do I, that the well-being, education, and honor of the community depends on having a significant number of highly educated people in it. Next, there should be a very large number of people who have received mid-level education and a vast number of people who have received basic education. But first of all there should be people with a high level of education, who are a source of pride for the community and are the source and outlet for the other two types of education. Those who do not focus their efforts on higher education and engage only in basic education want to reverse the flow of the river, in which there can be no success at all.

Now look at it in another way. In many parts and in nearly all the districts there are government or missionary schools that provide good education up to the entrance level. If, for any reason, you want to establish schools for the education of Muslims in such districts, certainly go ahead. But pray tell, will your school have competent and learned masters and a headmaster that these schools have? As far as I can tell, I would say no. So then, consider the fact that you will be taking Muslims out of the education given by competent and learned masters and handing them over to less knowledgeable and deficient masters. Does doing so amount to treating them well or mistreating them? The answer is so clear that everyone sees it.

Some people think that by providing basic education in these small schools, we are preparing the students to enter a school or a college for higher education. With this idea, many elders have established primary, upper-primary, and even entrance-level schools everywhere. It is very gratifying that recently our community has begun to think of the idea of its education, and from every corner of India voices can be heard calling out that something should be done for the community. But if there is any flaw in this effort, it would not be appropriate to overlook it. Hence, after sincerely thanking those elders who have made the kind of effort I am describing, I want to say to them that by doing so, they have completely neglected what I would call a priority, i.e. progress in higher education of Muslims. They have diverted their energy from a task that should have taken precedence to one that is not a priority. In other words, they have degraded their cumulative strength in such a way that it is not capable of completing the priority task.

O gentlemen! The issue of education is a delicate one and its effects, good or bad, are hidden and are rarely observed. But those effects are deep and long-lasting. Suppose that a school is established which gives education up to the middle level, and another that is up to the entrance level, i.e. it includes classes of middle school. Even though both have middle school level books that are the same, the intellectual and progressive leaning ideas that are developed in boys that study in schools that are up to the entrance level are certainly not developed in those who study in the school that is only up to the middle level.

This difference becomes even more pronounced later among boys who attend a collegiate school and those who attend a school that is only up to the entrance level. So, in trying to develop ourselves, we should consider everything, lest we take the community toward its decline rather than on the path of progress, and lest we degrade our cumulative strength by dispersing it rather than using our collective strength to develop our community.

There is another reason for the idea of establishing these small schools, which is a very good-hearted and patriotic idea and undoubtedly deserves praise and appreciation. And that is that in some cities and towns, there were no schools at all, and they have established these schools with the idea of giving education to boys who would otherwise just loiter. I don't want to oppose such a school, but when I consider the entire community to be one community which is analogous to a single person, I would submit for the consideration of these elders that they have made arrangements to give only bread to the thirsty and hungry person, but he is about to die of thirst.

O gentlemen! There are only two types of ideas about education. One is the dissemination of higher education, which will undoubtedly be available only to a limited or a small group. The other is the dissemination of general education, the purpose of which is that the common people, the poor, and the children of the poor may benefit from it and groups and groups and a vast number of people are taught to become familiar with middling knowledge. As far as I have had the occasion to understand the motives of the elders of our community, I find that their views tend more towards the latter kind of education, and with their good intentions, they want a method of education that even the poor can take advantage of.

O gentlemen! I greatly admire this idea of these elders of our community. But the idea with which I empathize with my community and the level to which I want to take it, right or wrong, possible or impossible, cannot be achieved by these means. I want to make the community like the sky that appears to us at night. When I look at the sky at night, I care nothing for the part of it that appears bluish-black and frightening. But I like to look at the stars that shine in it and draw us to them as a beloved would, and lend a strange kind of beauty to that dark and black sky.

O gentlemen! Can you make your community honorable and respectable among the other communities without producing such people who shine like the stars in your community? Absolutely not. Absolutely not.

O gentlemen! Can you create any virtue in your dark, wretched, and humiliated community without creating these stars? It is impossible for general education to spread among the common people without the presence of higher education, and this is proved by the history of the whole world. So, without a doubt, I regret that the well-intentioned efforts of the elders of our community that they prematurely undertake in imitation of other communities are all going to go to waste and are useless for the community.

O gentlemen! Is an emphasis on this type of education and an approach with this type of thinking the work of people in places where the sun of higher education has reached the midday zenith? Or is it the work of a malevolent government that prevents its subject from accessing higher education through its intellectual policy? Or is it the work of a just government that, under the restrictions of equal rights and justice, is compelled not to divert general education funds into higher education, the latter undoubtedly limited to a few people? Now, when you ignore higher education and turn your attention to general education, has the sun of higher education reached the midday zenith in your community? Or are you compelled to do this like that oppressive or that just government? May the elders of the community forgive me, but I do not consider this way the path to progress.

After hearing this much, surely the question must have arisen in the hearts of my friends who are present here that if these strategies are not inclined toward progress, then what are the ones that are. I will certainly say whatever is in my mind regarding this question. I would be glad, or rather it would fulfill my desire, if our community were to establish community schools and colleges of its own accord and in such large numbers that the government is no longer compelled to manage its schools and colleges a certain way. But we should not intend to establish a school until we have established a school that provides instruction for the entrance class and has a pure gentleman European as its headmaster. Such a school cannot be established without a fixed income of Rs. 1200 per month. Establishing a school that does not meet this standard and trapping the children in it would harm the community. It is also rather unnecessary since there are many means to education short of that standard.

Similarly, we should not intend to establish a school until we have collected enough capital that would allow us to appoint, apart from the Indian professors, at least three European professors of excellent character who are complete gentlemen. Such a staff cannot be put together for less than Rs. 2500 of monthly expense. Besides this expense, money will be needed for miscellaneous expenses and a library, which is essential for such a college. It is obvious that the state of the community is not such that these types of schools and colleges can be established everywhere. But we should consolidate our strengths and realize this idea in one place. Once this place is completed, we should use our collective strength to establish a school based on this idea in another place.

If they cannot do this, instead of establishing small schools, they should select places where good schools or colleges exist, arrange for the boys to live there, subsidize the cost of living there, and gather the boys of the community to live there [*and attend these schools or colleges.*] And whatever money they would have spent on building small schools, they should spend on educating these boys.

There remain two flaws in this scheme that I think are huge, but people underestimate them. At present, all the schools and colleges that exist are owned by the government, are in the hands of the government, or are run by missionaries. We have no say in their management or it is in name only, we cannot make arrangements in them according to our desire and intention, and the educational needs of Muslim boys cannot be fulfilled in them. Besides, it is not enough to only educate the Muslim children. Instilling the spirit of community in them is more important than their education. This spirit cannot be instilled in them unless groups of Muslim children gather in one place and are provided education, the idea of a community college is formed in their hearts, and an enthusiasm for attending a community college is created among them. O gentlemen! I assure you that until this spirit is formed in our community, it will remain like the living dead. And it will not achieve a level of excellence in anything – education, wealth, honor, courage, humility, or self-respect. May God help our community. (This was my speech that I gave in Lucknow.)

Mr. President of the session! What I meant in this speech is very clear, i.e. I do not say that schools should not be established for primary education. And how can I say that until primary education extends to the entrance level, there is no way that Muslim children can reach the college class level? Rather, what I meant was that they should not establish elementary schools that are harmful for primary education and bad for education in general. Schools in which there is neither good instruction nor competent masters will harm the education of the children of Muslims. If they cannot establish good schools, they should not establish bad ones either, rather they should make schemes that would give an opportunity for Muslim children to attend the excellent [*established*] schools.

What I also meant to say was that basic education is not enough for the community. We have to combine our strengths and promote higher education. Now, in today's resolution, I have presented two issues.

One is that what has happened so far in terms of development, education, and nurturing of Muslims is simply inadequate, and if the state of affairs remains the same, change is not expected to come for centuries.

The other is that if arrangements are not made for a concerted effort for higher education and nurturing, we should be very despondent about the prospects of the remaining Muslims.

The first issue in this resolution, and I am sure that no one can deny it, is that in the colleges established by the government or the missionaries that currently exist, there is no scheme for the nurturing and moral development of the students. When Muslim children gather in one place, there is a mutual connection between them and a common empathy for the community. In fact, in college classes in which the number of Muslims is limited and those of other communities are present in large numbers, the feelings of the Muslim students are always suppressed and become almost extinct. This effect subconsciously gets into their nature. Those who understand the nature of human temperament can fully understand this phenomenon. You and all my friends who are present in this hall must have seen many colleges. Do they find the Muslims there to be in the same happy state as they are in our college? Our students are happy that they study in a college of their community. Seeing a cohort of fellow-students from their community who live and study with them, they derive pride and joy for the community and their aspirations remain fresh and fertile. Do you not agree that it has an effect on human temperament and gives rise to pride and empathy for the community? More than 250 Muslims students are currently boarders. The feeling of religious passion and empathy for the community that you find in them, do you find the same passion and feeling for the community in other colleges where Muslims study with students from other communities? This is a very small example of the nurturing that I mentioned earlier. This is a sign of community development and this kind of education makes a people a community. *"I bear witness by God that this is the clear truth."*

Now the issue remains of education, regarding which I say that what has happened so far is abject failure and is rather worthy of sadness and regret. I do not need to analyze this too much. In this very hall, Syed Muhammad Mahmood gave a lecture on the status of Muslims in the education of English knowledge and the arts from the beginning of the commissioned universities to the present day. He put charts and diagrams in front of everyone, from which everyone could see with their own eyes that the graph for the status of the education of our fellow countrymen Hindu brothers in every university was pointing straight to the sky while that for the Muslims had fallen into the ground. Can the lovers of the community recall a more heart wrenching chart? Is there any precedent that is more sorrowful than this? If you ask about the situation in terms of numbers, the proportion of Muslims relative to the Hindus in university education is like this. In Calcutta University 4.25%, in Allahabad University a little more than 9%, in Madras University 1.75%, in Punjab University a little more than 28%, and the overall total for all universities a little less than 4%.

Although I congratulate my earnest brothers from Punjab at this time for their status in university education being better than the other provinces, I will also say that Punjab has a large population of Muslims. If the number of Muslims getting university education is not 1.25 or 1.5 times the number of their Hindu brothers, it cannot be said that they have progressed in education.

Mr. President of the session! A very big error has been occurring. When the education of Muslims is evaluated as a proportion of the total population, the communities that the Hindu scriptures have called *Shudras* have been included among the Hindus. There has never been the concept of education among these communities and they still have no idea of it. Hence, including such communities, that are very numerous in India, in the population of Hindus and calculating the average number of Muslims against that total is a grave error.

There has been a debate regarding this in the Education Commission as well. The commission too has found it incorrect to include some communities in the Hindu population and calculate the Muslim average against this total. It has removed certain communities from the count of the Hindu population and established the count of Hindu and Muslim populations in different provinces. In terms of the total population of India, it has determined that in matters related to education, Muslims should be considered to be a quarter of the population of Hindus. I do not agree with their opinion and in my mind the number of Hindus should be considered equal to the number of Muslims in matters related to education. But even if I abandon this opinion and accept that Muslims are a quarter of the Hindu population, the result regarding the education of Muslims is still very poor.

From Allahabad University, 430 Hindus have graduated, and according to Muslims being 13% of the total population, the number of Muslim graduates should have been 64. Fortunately, there are 79. You may consider this good fortune to be the result of the efforts of a few Muslims who have been trying for the development of the education of Muslims for 20 years or you may consider it to be a sign of the times. But if you consider it to be the latter, you must answer why the progress in the province of Allahabad is a sign of the times, but the same hasn't happened in other provinces. From Calcutta University, 4981 Hindus graduated, and by virtue of Muslims being 30% of the population, there should have been 2344 Muslim graduates. But there were 213. From Madras University, 2634 Hindus graduated, and by virtue of Muslims being 6% of the population, there should have been 109 Muslim graduates. But there were 22. From Bombay University, 1424 Hindus graduated, and by virtue of Muslims being a quarter of the population, there should have been 356 Muslim graduates. But there were 26. From Punjab University, 246 Hindus graduated, and by virtue of Muslims being 60% of the population, there should have been 160 Muslim graduates. But there were 69. In total for all universities, 9715 Hindus graduated, a quarter of which is 2428, but only 409 Muslims graduated. What could be a worse statistic than this for the education of Muslims. Does our community not regret this? And if it does, what is the plan to fix this disaster?

Now we are working resolutely to mitigate this calamity in the community and have established the Mohammedan Anglo-Oriental College in Aligarh. Let me also give a brief account of it:

For such a great and glorious accomplishment that the Mohammedan Anglo-Oriental College is, for the idea of community progress on which it was founded, and which depended solely on community aid for its completion, we did not spare any effort to raise money for its completion. It was impossible to accomplish this without monetary assistance from the community. For this, we bowed down to every rich and poor person and weathered this shame, about which it is said:

> It is better to knead molten iron with one's hands
> Than to spread one's hands in front of a rich man

O Mr. President of the session! We were not content with this and took this torment of Judgement Day upon ourselves. To complete the establishment of the college? No. No, to provide means for the development of the community. We played lottery, we gambled, and we did not settle for that either and acted on this couplet:

> Take up the profession of comedy and learn to sing and play music
> So you can get a treasure of gold from everyone big or small

Acted out a hundred roles, stood on stage, friends disguised themselves as fakirs, and like Bedouins with their goat-skin water billows under the arms we wandered asking for alms in the name of God. But the community did not comprehend anything and the purpose was not fulfilled.

You see that the college buildings remain unfinished. We do not have enough commitments to cover the expenses of providing this great education. In order to provide higher education to Muslims, there is a need to give them scholarships and stipends because their situation is such that they cannot be educated without assistance. We don't have enough capital to support them.

You can see the large number of students we have. There are not enough boarding houses to accommodate them. We do not have the capital to build more boarding houses. We cannot keep the students in the boarding houses and educate them in the manner and style we want because we don't have the money for that. The mosque, in which a large group of students prays, and the congregation is so large that perhaps no other mosque has one that size, is unfinished. It is a matter of great "pride" for the community that the prayer is held under a thatched roof.

We have appointed volunteers to ask the members of the community for a paisa or two, an *ana* or two, to finish this work. That failed. Then we appointed "*Benefactors*" to bring small amounts of money from the community and collect funds. Our friend Niaz Muhammad Khan revived the volunteer system in Punjab. I will tell you the result of that too, that the volunteers appointed by Niaz Muhammad Khan collected Rs. 278, and with your permission, he will present a report of his activity in this meeting.

I have appointed 291 "*Benefactors*" who are dignified gentlemen in every way. If they had each collected gold or silver the size of even a grain of barley, they would have each collected at least Rs. 100, and the total amount collected would have been at least Rs. 29,100. But the result of their work is that till now only Rs. 1700 have been procured.

Mr. President of the session! It should not be thought that poverty in the community is the reason for this failure, for even a laborer making four *anas* can give an *ana* or two paisas for the cause of the community, and we can collect hundreds of thousands of rupees just with that. But our people do not have enthusiasm for the community and therefore they do not respond to this hard work that goes into collecting money.

Mr. President of the session! You should not think that I am ungrateful to the generous people of the community who gave thousands of rupees for this work. In fact, I am grateful from the heart to the generous people and the leaders of the community who have donated thousands of rupees to help the college and the education of the community. I am especially grateful to His Highness Nizam of Hyderabad, may his Sultanate thrive, whose unparalleled generosity keeps this community college in good shape. I am also deeply grateful to the elders of my community, a few of my fellow-countrymen Hindu brothers, and my European friends, whose generosity has made such a wonderful thing as this college possible. The extent to which construction has been completed thus far, the likes of which has not been seen in India, is undoubtedly a miracle and is the result of the generosity of the big-hearted elders of our community. But the reason why I complain about the community is that if we compare the number of generous people who have provided assistance to the college with the number of people in the community who have not participated in providing assistance to it and whose status behooves them to help the college, that ratio would be so small that it would be hard to measure even with fractions and decimals. The result we see is due to the generosity of the generous folks, but the community did not do what the community was supposed to do, nor did the elders of the community adopt such a method that would have given the community an opportunity to help itself. So, my complaint is with those elders of the community who needed to adopt such a method that would have given the community the opportunity to help itself as a community.

Mr. President of the session! I believe that I have proved my claims well, that the state of the education of the community is at a very low level and simply inadequate, and there is no full set of means in the country to raise the education and nurturing of the community to a higher level. Without this higher education and proper nurturing, neither can a community thrive nor can it get any respect. Therefore, if the community does pay any attention to this and does not make arrangements for its higher education and proper nurturing, then the clear result is that we should be very despondent about the prospects of the development and progress of Muslims. If there is any encouragement, it is from the words of the prophet Jacob (peace be upon him), when he said to his sons, *"And do not despair of God's spirit, none but unbelievers despair of God's spirit."*

O Mr. President and O elders of our nation! When you are gathered in this big hall at this time only with the intention of community welfare, please forgive me if I ask you all a question. If you do not care about the level to which the Mohammedan Anglo-Oriental College has reached, be it in terms of the construction of its buildings or in terms of the education and nurturing it provides to the Muslims, can you, under the present circumstances, establish another institution in any city or town and take it to that level? Even if you are able to take it to that level, you will only be doing what has been done, and the result will be that it too will remain unfinished just as the Mohammedan Anglo-Oriental College. But, O friends! Taking into account the difficulties that I have faced in taking the college to this level and the unseen support of the events of these times that has helped me in this, I can say that it is a very difficult task to take a new institution to that level. But it has not been accomplished yet. So, it is necessary for the entire community to complete this task, because there is no other means of bringing the young gifted children of our community to a higher level of education and nurturing.

I know very well, and my ears have heard and my eyes have seen the writings, that when I want the community to finish the task of establishing this college, people interpret my words as selfishness. O friends! If my intention is the welfare and development of the community, why do you not assist me and become my associate in this? If, however, you feel that my purpose in this is to gain fame, then I am truly sorry for that. God said, *"Verily, the self inclines toward evil, except for those upon whom my Lord has mercy."* But O people of my community! Remember that in the future when this work remains unfinished, the college becomes a desolate place, and the students are replaced by revelers and merrymakers, it will be you, not the individual you but you as a community, who will face much more infamy and humiliation than any regrets that anyone can have for my reputation for seeking fame in its completion.

Mr. President of the session! I confess, and have believed in this since the beginning, that having only one school is not enough for the whole of India. In fact, more schools that are associated with universities are needed in India than there are in all of England, Scotland, and Ireland at present. But, I say that the work that has been started and has reached a level that could not be even imagined should first be completed with the concerted efforts of the community. Then, start the same work at another place and complete it with the concerted efforts. Then, start work at a third place. If we do not do it like this, all our tasks will remain incomplete and unfulfilled and the community will be severely harmed. If there is any truth and reality in these objectives, I urge the community to unite their strengths and fulfill them. The community is undoubtedly poor, but it is not such that it cannot fulfill even its own needs if it comes together. If the community puts in the effort and collects an average of one rupee per person, tens of millions of rupees can be collected and many schools such as this can be established in India. If money on this scale is collected from Punjab, the North-Western Provinces, and Awadh, similar schools can be established in each of the provinces. Yes, the attention of the community and the efforts and endeavors of those who love this community will be needed.

A few students of our college have formed a society called "The Duty." They have vowed that as long as they live, they will keep trying to complete the establishment of the college and working for the progress of the community. And they have been successful commensurate with their status. Is it not the duty of the elders of our community to make such a pledge before God, complete the task of establishing the college, and heartily engage in the development of the community?

Mr. President of the session. God created all His creatures on the same principle. You see a very beautiful lush tree that has begun to whither. It is in the same ground in which it was born, water from the same sky irrigates it, rays from the same sun give it strength, and the same breeze that moves its branches to keep them green, but its internal condition becomes so bad that it has neither the power to absorb what is good for it, nor to get rid of things that are bad for it, and nor to get any nutrition. Then it gradually dries up and becomes fuel for the furnace. The same has happened to our community. The intrinsic strengths, which are the sources of growth, continue to diminish, and those that still exist will also disappear in a few days. Oh what a sad day it will be when they are worth nothing but to put in the furnace.

Mr. President of the session! People ask what is the use of higher education? Even now, there are so many people with BA and MA degrees who can't find jobs. When there are more people with these degrees, what will they do and how will the community progress due to that?

First of all, I will say that there is no higher education among the Muslims at this time. Just getting a BA or MA degree from a university is, first of all, not higher education. And then, on top of that, it is even more regrettable that the competency that a Bengali builds with a BA or MA degree is unfortunately not the same that a Muslim builds with those degrees. Can you give me an example of a Muslim who has the required competency that if an English newspaper is published by a Muslim, he can do the job of its editor so effectively that the English like his articles and his style of writing, they are influenced by it, they become fond of reading that newspaper, and the objectives of the Muslims are fulfilled? A hundred regrets that, and I hope my friends will forgive me for saying, even those Muslims who return after getting educated in England do not bring back knowledge, the arts, and literature with them for the community.

Besides, it will be a big mistake if all of them study for their BA and MA degrees just to obtain government jobs and depend only on them for their welfare, because they know very well that everyone with a BA or MA degree is unlikely to get a government job. But I would say that the reason for thinking about government jobs and thinking of themselves as dependent on them is that they do not have higher education. They have not developed the ability to do anything with their own strength, due to which they are discouraged and run after government jobs, which they can get just in the name of their BAs and MAs and which affords them a life of low status. Recently, a professor in our college, Babu Jadav Chandra Chakravarti[28] has written a short book on mathematics which is included in the university syllabus. He has been getting around Rs. 400 per month as copyright for it and it is not known how long he will continue to get it.

The reason students who are well versed in English think of nothing but finding employment and do not think of doing anything else with their own strength is that there is no nurturing with their education. Unless these two things are provided together, there can be no success in worldly affairs. They are not used to hard work and leaving home is exceedingly trying for their parents and guardians. Traveling to a foreign country for the purpose of trade seems to them tantamount to emigrating from the world. They do not have the habits of

---

28. Jadav Chandra Chakravarti (1855 – 26 November 1920) was a prominent Bengali mathematician of the Indian subcontinent. He was famous for his two books named *Arithmetic* and *Algebra*. He obtained his MA degree in mathematics from Presidency College at the University of Calcutta in 1882. Chakravarti started his career as a mathematics teacher at Calcutta City College. Then he joined MAO College Aligarh on 1 January 1888 and retired from there on 28 February 1916.

uprightness, frugality, and working alongside others. Hypocrisy, mutual jealousy and stubbornness are in the essence of their disposition. They do not care about the principle of meeting others in society. That is why they do not have the ability to put in any concerted effort with others. Just raw education does not provide that capability.

University education is like the mason taking a slab of stone and carving a statue out of it. But to polish it or give it a shine such that people like it or wish it for themselves comes only from nurturing. This nurturing is more effective if it is carried out from childhood. After growing up, unless there is a strong influence, the temperament is hardly affected. But absolutely not all schools and colleges provide this kind of nurturing. Attention has been paid to it in the *Madrasatul Uloom* Aligarh and some results have been achieved, but it cannot be said that the desired goal has been fully achieved. While there are these difficulties in providing higher education, why do the elders of our community think that we can provide higher education to the children of the community by establishing small schools or commonplace colleges?

The word nurturing also needs explanation. Now we will explain what we mean by the nurturing of Muslims. First of all, our aim is to maintain a feeling of community, i.e. unity and empathy in the community, which is the first step in the development of the community. What do we have to do for it? The first thing to do is that they remain Muslims and the truth of the religion of Islam remains in their hearts. Therefore, along with English education, we must give them religious education, teach them religious beliefs, and, as much as possible, keep them bound to their religious duties. We should acquaint them with the history of Islam and the spread of the religion of Islam, which caused all the inhabitants of the entire peninsula of Arabia to say, '*La ilaha illa Allah Muhammedur Rasul Allah.*'

After that, we should teach them the lesson of Islamic brotherhood. We should tell them what is Islamic brotherhood and that it is stronger than the bond between blood brothers. How excellent and fine this brotherhood was and how superior it was to all brotherhoods, because of which God showed his favor to us and said, "*He brought their hearts together. Had you spent all the riches on earth, you could not have united their hearts. But God has united them. Indeed, He is Almighty, All-Wise.*"

Then, in order to maintain the feeling of a community, we should also teach them the Arabic language as much as possible, which is the language of our elders and our holy religion. We should at least teach them the Persian language, so that the influence of the community can be found in them. The feeling of community should not be lost among them due to English education.

Then we have to create empathy for the community among them. It is impossible to develop this empathy unless we gather a large number of Muslim children to live together, study, and eat together. For this purpose we have to build a large boarding house in which at least a 1000 students of the college classes can live together. There should be a mutual feeling of brotherhood between them and a fraternal relationship should be created among them. If we do not instill this spirit of brotherhood and empathy in our children, you can be certain that neither can a community be formed, nor can a community progress, and nor can a community attain collective honor and respect.

Then we have to keep them in such a way that their hearts do not die and their heartfelt aspirations do not become cold. Their courage and boldness should not whither due to anything they do, rather it should rise day by day. For this purpose and to maintain their physical health, we have to provide them with resources for sports and physical exercise, so that those who are weak can improve their health and those who are strong can enhance their strength. For their academic progress, societies and clubs need to be established so that they get the opportunity to exercise their intellect.

Then we have to pay attention to their moral integrity and to create in them feelings of goodness, righteousness, truth and true friendships. For this purpose, more than advice and counseling, we have to create role models and gather kind and virtuous elders around them, so that in their company their temperaments are inclined toward kind heartedness and laudable morals become second nature to them. O friends! Consider how necessary and how lofty these tasks are, which cannot be accomplished without a concerted effort from the community. So, how regretful and disappointing it will be if the community does not put its efforts in accomplishing them.

Mr. President of the session! This picture of education that I have drawn in front of you depicts that if the community achieves higher education, it can progress, and it is on such an education that I have premised the development of the community. But this is just the first step toward the development of the community, the goal of which is still very far away. If educated people are in such abundance in our community as rice in a rice-lentil medley, we can expect that gradually the development of the community will take root. Our actions to come up with schemes for the development of the community are like those of the blind men who wanted to define the shape of an elephant by touching and feeling it. Each one of them felt a different part of this gigantic animal and described it differently. In the same way, we have touched and felt this great force called community development and understood it in different ways. But our children, who will get educated in a way that unity, kind heartedness, and empathy for the community is brimming in them, will also have along with it eyes that are wide open and hearts that are bright. They will see and understand the reasons for community development.

How have the other nations developed? How do developed nations decline and how can they rise again? What do we have to do to revive them? And from where do we get the antidote that will revive the dead nations? In other words, will they have the wherewithal to bring progress back to their community? So, O friends! If you don't agree with this plan and do not want to make a concerted effort for the development of your community, then you and I should both be patient and understand that, "*We cannot fill again the emptied rain-cloud nor put back in the quiver the arrows.*" Die, and decompose and be humiliated, that is God's will. "*To God we belong and unto Him we shall return.*" And my dear students! Those who gather in this hall and study in this school, if you do not want to make yourself into something that I want you to be, then you should also go where your community is headed. The pity is that our souls will cry for you and your community. The God in me says:

"*That you cannot fight with fate.*"

A great poet has described very well the meaning of respite:

In every respite there is a relief, see the difference
Running to walking, then standing, sitting, sleeping, and dying

But I regret that if the state of the community remains like this, I will not get respite even after death.

(3)

Mr. President of the session! I am very glad that on this resolution, which I truly consider to be the decision of the fate of Muslims, some very fine and detailed but interesting contributions have been made. I had expanded my speech and also included the mention of small schools in my narrative with the view that people should know that I was and am opposed to the establishment of these small schools. These schools are harming the education of Muslim children. I wish such schools are established that are a solid foundation for the building of higher education, the education that our community is in dire need of. But in this resolution, there is actually no debate about establishing or not establishing any school and nor does the decision of the fate of Muslims depend on it. There are only two matters in this resolution that need to be decided:

One is that what has happened so far regarding the development and nurturing of Muslims is simply inadequate. I would be very happy if all of you, who are gathered here for the good of the community and are familiar with every aspect of education and nurturing, would say that I am wrong and that what has been done so far is enough. Well, that would be the end of it and the fate of the Muslims would be decided.

Second, if you gentlemen accept the first point, then I say that the progress of Muslims depends on higher education. And unless higher education and, more than that, superior nurturing are not arranged with a democratic concerted effort, Muslims should be very despondent over the advancement of their education. Along with this, Nawab Mohsin-ul-Mulk and I have emphasized that at present, the *Madrasatul Uloom* is the means of the development of the education of Muslims. The task of completing it should be fulfilled with a concerted effort. I will be very happy if you elders and intellectuals who are gathered in this hall say that my opinion is wrong and that there is no need for a concerted effort for the education of Muslims. The fate of the Muslims would be decided and I would get a respite.

Enough speeches have been made and Nawab Mohsin-ul-Mulk has given a long talk explaining everything from the beginning. There is no need for further discussions. Now take a vote and decide what you need to do. I remain.

One of the members present called for a vote not to be taken on the entire resolution but on each matter contained in the resolution, each of which should be put to a separate vote. The president agreed and the vote was taken as follows.

First: What has happened so far for the development of education and nurturing of Muslims is simply inadequate. All the present members agreed.

Second: The progress of Muslims depends on higher education and nurturing, and if higher education and superior nurturing are not arranged with a democratic concerted effort, Muslims should be very despondent over the advancement of their education. All the present members agreed unanimously with this statement. All the elders, whether they were members or visitors, agreed that the *Madrasatul Uloom* Aligarh had reached such a level that it could be a source of higher education and nurturing and that its completion should be the concerns of the entire community. Hence, the resolution that was presented passed unanimously.

Praise be to God, a fine decision has been made for the fate of the community. Now, if a concerted effort is made, the destiny of the community will surely awaken. "*God is the Helper.*"

178

Speech on the Occasion of Syed Ross Masood's *Bismillah*[29] Ceremony

(Excerpted from the eighth annual session of the Muhammadan Educational Conference held in Aligarh, December 27-30, 1893)

In the seventh meeting of the eighth annual session of the Muhammadan Educational Conference, on December 30, 1893, Sir Syed proposed that the ceremony of his grandson Syed Ross Masood's *Bismillah* be performed in the conference's gathering. His aim was to tell the people in a practical way that the money that was wasted on such ceremonies should be spent instead on causes of community welfare. On the occasion of this *Bismillah* ceremony, Sir Syed gave the following speech.

O elders of the community. I want to say something about Syed Ross Masood's *Bismillah* ceremony, which is going to be held in this hall and in this gathering of friends. With this, my intent is to say a few things to my elders and friends who are gathered in this hall and inform you of my thoughts.

First of all, I think that the rituals of Islam, which are also called rituals of God, and the rituals of the Muslims both have the same expression but their oaths are different. The rituals of Islam are those that the Messenger of God (peace and blessings of God be upon him) said to do, and God commanded that they be made the rituals of Islam and be practiced by Muslims. And these are the rituals of Islam and they can neither have any additions nor subtractions. They have to be practiced exactly as they have been stated. It is narrated that the Messenger of God, may God bless him and grant him peace, said, "*He who innovates things*

[29.] *Bismillah* ceremony, also known as *Bismillahkhani*, is a celebration among the Muslims of the Indian subcontinent marking a child's start of the formal religious education in Quran and its Arabic script, usually at around the age of four years. The ceremony is named after the beginning word of the Quran, *bismillah*, which means "in the name of God."

in our affairs for which there is no valid (reason)(commits sin) and these are to be rejected." The rituals of the Muslims are those that have been derived from these rituals of Islam and from the heartfelt desire of the Holy Prophet that was inferred from his every word and deed, and a vast number of Muslims have been practicing them for a very long time even though there was no verbal command to do so. It is regarding these rituals that the Prophet of God, may God bless him and grant him peace, said, "If a path is good in the sight of a Muslim, it is good in the sight of God." And it is on the same basis that these words of Hazrat Umar, if he ever said them, can be predicated, that *"Tarawih* is an innovation."[30] Hence, to say about these rituals of Muslims that they were not commanded by the Messenger, were not practiced by the Messenger, they were not practiced by the Messenger's companions and followers, and therefore they are all innovations is to disregard that these rituals were derived from the will and the desire of the Messenger of God, may God bless him and grant him peace, and are indicative of the language of those times.

Of all the rituals of the Muslims, the one that is the most dear to me is the practice of saying the *azaan,* the Islamic call to prayer, in a newborn's ear so that the first thing they hear is the name of God. It is obvious that the newborn does not know anything. But this action of their guardian is in accordance with the desire of the Messenger of God, may God bless him and grant him peace, which has been derived from the state of affairs of the times that the words '*La ilaha illa Allah Muhammedur Rasul Allah*' be put in the ear of every human being, even though it has not been proven that the Messenger of God commanded it. It is not known if the Messenger of God said the *azaan* in the ear of Hazrat Fatima or of Imam Hasan and Imam Hussain, but how sweet it seems to put these words in the ear of a newborn child.

I also consider in the same way the ceremony that has been named *Bismillah.* It is a memorial of that great blessing that, in my mind, occurred when God Himself, with his silent words which are eternal and in perpetuity, through the mediation of Gabriel (peace be upon him), commanded his prophet and the guide of the *Ummah, "Read in the name of thy Lord who created."* How sweet it appears when the child of a Muslim, who reaches that threshold when he can repeat the words of others, is asked to say these words. So, this ritual is not a

---

[30] *Tarawih* is a form of prayer performed at some period of the night in the month of Ramzan after the ordinary prayers of the nightfall.

duty, it is not obligatory, and it is not *sunnah*, the way of the Prophet, because I do not have proof that the Holy Prophet said it to his children, i.e. Hazrat Fatima, Hasan, and Hussain (peace be upon them). But what a wonderful ritual this is among the Muslims that when the child reaches the stage when they can repeat the words of others, in commemoration of God commanding his prophet, they are also asked to say, *"Read in the name of thy Lord who created,"* and this joyous occasion is celebrated in front of friends and Muslims. But apart from this, I have to say that O elders of the community! You have heard a lot in the past day or two of the poor condition of the Muslims and it must have also affected your heart. If not everyone's, the hearts of some of you must have melted on hearing this. So, you can be certain that those who spend money on these types of rituals, appropriately or excessively, harm the work for the welfare of the community. The most harmful of these rituals are those performed for marriages, against the order of God, the order of His Messenger, the traditions of the Prophet's companions, and the teachings of the Imams of the most noble descent. They spend thousands of rupees, and if they don't have the money, they take loans for it. Those who are poor are ruined and those who are wealthy waste their money. Why don't they use it to improve the condition of their community by saving their money from these useless, or rather not useless but unnecessary expenses, and spending it on the education of their children and the children of their community. You know how much this child [*Syed Masood*], who is sitting in front of you, is dear to me. This is the only child in the entire family. May God bless him and give him a long life and fulfill all our expectations from him. For these reasons, I could have spent as much as I wanted on this *Bismillah* ceremony. Although I am not wealthy or rich, the state I am in is not that much without means that I could not have spent a few thousand rupees on this ceremony. But I want to show you what I am doing.

There is an ancient tradition among Muslims that they gather all their relatives on occasions of such rituals. They invite them from faraway places. They spend money on their hospitality, entertainment, and reception. Under obligation to attend, the relatives also take great pains and bear huge costs to attend, and this obligation ends up costing everyone large sums of money. I have completely abandoned this ancient tradition. Perhaps many people will call it disregard for tradition, but O friends! When our community is in such a poor state as you heard, we should disregard all these ritualistic indulgences and should be indulgent toward our community.

See, I did not invite my son Syed Hamid, I did not invite my dear son Syed Muhammad Ahmed, and I did not invite any of my friends and family who are not present in Aligarh at this time. This beardless old man [*pointing to Raja Jai Kishan Das Bahadur*], whom I love like a brother, was not invited either but it is my good fortune that he was here to attend the conference. I considered the elders of my community, who are present here in large numbers, as my brothers and relatives, and I considered including them an honor and it brought joy to my heart. What I mean by that is that in ceremonies of this kind, as much as possible, all expenses should be curtailed and money should be spent for the welfare and prosperity of the community.

There is another ritual of this kind. Although it is not practiced in our Delhi or among the people of Delhi, it is quite common in other cities and towns. That is the ritual of *niyota*, invitations to feasts and banquets in ceremonies for these rituals. This should be completely stopped. Even if people describe the many benefits of it, think about the fact that those you invite also have to incur a lot of expense to attend. So, both parties are harmed by this ritual. O my friends! Abandon all these rituals and save whatever money you can for the community. Have mercy on the condition of the community. O friends! In these past 20 years, many marriages have taken place in the families of my close relatives and my loved ones. On many of these occasions, it was essential that I too give something to the young ones who were getting married. But I did not give even one gift nor accepted one and decided that it was better to abandon these rituals and hold on to my community. I wish my friends would do the same.

O friends! I understand very well that no person can transform their personal happiness into the happiness of others, nor does anyone have the power to interfere in the fun being had by others and change the tide of happiness of friends. But I request all the Muslims who recite the words '*La ilaha illa Allah Muhammedur Rasul Allah*' that if you cannot put a stop to vain pursuit of happiness, cannot change its tide, and wish to continue spending thousands of rupees on these ceremonies, well, go ahead. But take out a portion for your wretched community as well and give something at least for the welfare of the community on every such occasion. Consider this to be a ritual as well, and just as you are bound by these other rituals, consider this ritual binding as well.

I am extremely grateful to some of my friends from Punjab who have given this matter some thought and given to the *Madrasatul Uloom* on many occasions. But at this time, I would like to mention two friends.

There was a wedding in the family of Mian Nizamuddin *Saheb*. In the midst of the gathering, a leader of our Punjab, nay headman, nay chief, Khan Bahadur Muhammad Barkat Ali Khan *Saheb* went to him with a few friends and said, "*Baba*, something for the community as well." Mian Nizamuddin *Saheb* gave Rs. 200 for the community college, i.e. the *Madrasatul Uloom* Aligarh, which the Khan Bahadur sent to me and earned the distinction of "*The one who guides someone to goodness is like the one who does it.*"

O Khan Bahadur Muhammad Barkat Ali Khan *Saheb*! Where are you sitting? Please come and sit on the chair in front of me. I have to lodge a complaint with you against a very dear friend of mine and I have appointed you as the judge. If you say, I can submit a written letter of complaint, or will a verbal complaint suffice?

You gentlemen know that Sardar Muhammad Hayat Khan Bahadur CSI is an old and a very dear friend of mine. In my letters to him, I don't even address him with any titles. I just write, "My dear Hayat." He has also helped the *Madrasatul Uloom* with thousands of rupees in assistance. But often there is a dispute between two friends and it is another friend who is the judge and gives a decision. That is why I have appointed you the judge.

The dispute is that my dear Muhammad Aslam Hayat, who studied at the *Madrasatul Uloom* and by the grace of God is now an extra-assistant commissioner, and is the son of *Janab* Sardar *Saheb*, got married. To celebrate this occasion, Sardar Muhammad Hayat Khan sent Rs. 200 to the college. You know very well how obstinate the *dom-dhadi* folk singers and dancers from the Mirasi community are on such occasions. They won't accept the remuneration that you offer and always ask for more. I was also obstinate and asked for Rs. 500 and a memorial inscription of this auspicious occasion to be engraved in the central hall of the *Madrasatul Uloom*, otherwise a complaint will be lodged and a judge will be appointed whose decision you will not be able to disobey.

O *Janab* Khan Bahadur Muhammad Barkat Ali Khan! Sardar *Saheb* has not yet sent me those Rs. 300. Therefore, I lodge a complaint against him with you. I have no doubt you will award a decree.

[Khan Bahadur awarded the decree and Sir Syed continued with his speech]

When you are done with your engagements at the conference session and return safely and comfortably to Lahore, please issue an order for the disbursement of funds, go to Jammu yourself, submit the funds against the decree, and send it to us. Thank God my decree has been awarded. Now I will receive my money soon and my dear Aslam Hayat Khan's blessed wedding will be memorialized with an inscription engraved in the central hall.

O gentlemen! Although I have sung the anthem of the community at this time, it should not be understood that we do not have affection and brotherly love for other communities. We sing the anthem of our community because it is in a bad state. Otherwise, we have the same love for other communities as we have for our dear ones. At his time, there are two pieces of evidence for this in public view. One is that Syed Muhammad Mahmood and Mr. Ross are strong friends and have a brotherly affection for each other. When Syed Masood was born, Mr. Ross and his wife, in the most affectionate English custom, gave their name to the newborn Masood, and we added the Ross' name to his name with great pleasure. And that is why his name has come to be Syed Ross Masood.

The other example is that of the old man, my friend Raja Jai Kishan Das Bahadur CSI, who is present here and is cradling Syed Ross Masood in his arms. I consider him my honorable and benevolent brother, Syed Muhammad Mahmood calls him *'Chacha,'* and Syed Ross Masood calls him *'Dada Raja.'* So, in the love for our friends, we see no difference.

★

179

Deputation of the *Madrasatul Uloom* Aligarh in Jalandhar and Presentation of an Address

(Aligarh Institute Gazette, May 15, 1894)

When Sir Syed's deputation reached Jalandhar on its way back from Lahore, the dignitaries there gave it a grand welcome. A substantial sum of money was collected from the city for the college and presented to Sir Syed. On April 20, 1894 a grand meeting was held to present an address to Sir Syed in the courtyard of the Jalandhar town hall. It was organized by Subedar Sheikh Ghulam Husain *Saheb*.

On a motion made by Subedar-Major Sheikh Ghulam Husain *Saheb* and seconded by Munshi Mohammad Ali Khan *Saheb*, Khan Bahadur Mian Nizamuddin *Saheb* was appointed president of this meeting. The president gave a brief speech. After that, Sir Syed rose from his chair and gave the following reply to the address.

Mr. President and friends of Jalandhar!
First of all, I thank you for your kindness. On my arrival in Jalandhar, you took the trouble to come to the station. I am more grateful that not only our people took the trouble but the respected Hindu brothers of this city also came to the station. And that is why I am more grateful to those Hindu brothers than to my own community.

O gentlemen! I am deeply grateful for the contribution of money that has been made at this time. In fact, I cannot express the thanks that this gesture is worthy of.

In your address, you have mentioned some of my community services. If the community has acknowledged these services and God has liked them, then it is a matter of great joy. The state of the community is deteriorating day by day. I have girded my loins in its service. May God help in this. I am not unaware of the maxim that the demand of humanity is that as human beings we help other people. But trying to help a fatigued and helpless community is not removed from this human compassion either. One community in India has fulfilled its own needs, has understood well the age that is coming, and has made itself worthy of that age; it does not need the help of any person. We are very happy that our fellow countrymen have made a lot of effort and a lot of progress in education. But if the community that is destitute, and backward, and declining day by day, is not warned about our concerns for its present condition and what will happen to it in the future and draw its attention to correct its course, then we can imagine what its state is going to be in the future. That helpless community is our community, who are called Muslims and whom Islam has made a community. I have considered its present condition, understood what its condition is going to be in the future, investigated the causes of its decline, and, as much as possible, made others understand it. And girded my loins to work for its welfare and assistance. From this, you must have understood why efforts have been undertaken for a community; because it is destitute and needs it.

O friends! The issue of education is very delicate and has become even more so in this age. First, we should understand the reason why our elders were so worthy, honorable, and renowned in their time. The reason was that they used their sword and their pen in accordance with the times to make themselves worthy and superior. This is no more the time of the sword, it is the time of the pen, knowledge, and skills. Education brings dignity and collective and personal honor. So, if Muslims want to be respectable, they must fulfill what is needed in this era. By God's will, the English government rules over us. I sincerely say that the excellent method of governing adopted by the English in India has never been seen here or in many countries of Europe. Thank God we are under the patronage of Her Majesty Queen Victoria, Monarch of India. All the progress in knowledge, skills, trade, and wealth are dependent on peace and order in the country. The peace and order we have in the country in these times has never been witnessed before and nor are there any parallels in other countries. So, if our Muslim brothers do not wake up even now and adopt the means of development, they will continue to decline day by day, and we don't know what is going to be the end result.

O friends! No doubt we are proud that our elders were eminent in knowledge and the arts. It was our forefathers who enlightened Europe with knowledge. Believe me, the European 'fathers of knowledge' Muslims were our forefathers.

Their schools and libraries could not forget Spain, where their scholars were educated. Even if someone forgets, books cannot be erased. But the thing is that the seed that our elders sowed has become a huge tree. Knowledge has developed a lot since that time. If we remain haughty about having taught Europe and they being our students, and do not see the progress of the times, we will surely remain in a pit. We need to look at the knowledge that has been developed in recent times and we should acquire it.

O friends! I assure you that the modern knowledge that has been developed and the ancient knowledge that has progressed to an advanced level cannot be acquired by any means except through a European language. The time of Harun and Mamun has passed. At that time, there were a few books in Greek that were translated into Arabic. There is a big difference between then and now. If there were ten books at that time, there are a few thousand now, and without studying them we cannot become scholars and achieve honor. In this case, there is a helplessness and a compulsion. Should we be desirous of knowledge or should we feed our stomachs? Without the knowledge of Europe, we cannot be anything. We can neither progress in worldly affairs nor in religion. [*Cheers*] We have no means of acquiring knowledge in French and German. But by the grace of the English government, we can study English. Without this language, we can neither acquire knowledge nor make worldly progress. Those of us who study this knowledge only to get a job are, in reality, choosing to feed their stomach. When we study for the sake of acquiring knowledge, we will enjoy knowledge. And as much as we see the power of God today, we will be able to see much more then. We will have a lot more faith in Almighty God, and we will see what a powerful Creator He is. Learning about an ant or a honeybee inspires wonder and faith in God's divinity and omnipotence with such a strong conviction that is not possible through any other means.

O friends! In the commentary I have given on English knowledge, what I mean by it is modern knowledge. The English language is the only means to acquire this knowledge, but to be educated is a higher bar. I hope that my Muslim and Hindu brothers who study English will not be offended when I state what I believe to be true. The education that is given to us in English is not enough. It is far short of the education that I want to provide. University degrees are not enough to make us educated. Universities and the boys of our college are like masters and slaves. We are subservient to the universities. We have been sold to them. Whatever scraps of knowledge it gives, we fill our stomachs with it and are satisfied.

O friends! We will get our full education when our education is in our hands. We will be the masters of our education, and we will spread education in our community without being slaves to the universities. We will have philosophy in our right hand, natural sciences in our left hand, and the crown of *'La ilaha illa Allah Muhammedur Rasul Allah'* on our head. A university education only makes us mules. O friends! I am also from among them for I too have been awarded the LLB degree by a university. We will become men only when our education is in our hands.

It is very easy to say that our education should be in our hands but it is very difficult to do it. Explaining what true education is and how it can be provided requires a lot of time, and understanding it requires a lot of attention. But nurturing is a part of this education. If there is no nurturing, the entire education is a failure. If you put some of the blame on the Muslim youth who study English, and suppose that the blame is rightfully assigned, how is it their fault? Tell me yourself, what means did you create for their nurturing? There are very qualified professors in government colleges, but what effect can they have on the students' nurturing except by teaching them for an hour. Those professors don't even know the names of many of their students. If they see the students on the road, they will not be able to even recognize them. What kind of nurturing can these young men get from such teachers and professors? So, if you put any blame on those youth, then in fact that blame is on the community for not making any arrangements to nurture them. Yes, there is no doubt that education without nurturing is like a mule laden with books. Then you should agree to remove this harm.

O friends! Be it higher education or superior nurturing, religious and theological education or protecting religious and theological pillars, what is required for them? "*Society*," i.e. good company. I do not consider myself separate from you; I am from among you. But think about it and observe, how is the society in your view? If it is fine, then very good, "*my eyes are bright, my heart is joyful.*" If it is not fine, then make a good society for them. Reprimanding and getting upset has little effect on humans. Good company is the only thing that has any effect. If the company is good, habits and traits become good by themselves. When their inner state is good, their education and nurturing go hand in hand. Then consider that at present there is no religious education in colleges and we have to provide our young children both religious and secular education. And with it, nurturing. Therefore, it is obligatory on the community to collect the means for it, but these means cannot be collected with monthly contributions of two or four rupees. If I am not mistaken, the income and expenses of Oxford University, if not greater than, are certainly not less than those of the House of Scindia, and that is why it has the capacity to provide education as well as nurturing. There is no other means for the nurturing of the youth but a good boarding house. You will be surprised to know that in England itself, for a student to be a boarder at a boarding house of the universities in Oxford and Cambridge is a sufficient sign of his being a *gentleman.* London is a very big city and notable scholars and learned people live there. There is a university in London proper as well whose professors are certainly no less worthy than the professors at Cambridge and Oxford universities. But there is no boarding house attached to that university. I have seen that those who have obtained degrees from London University are shy to proclaim that they attended that university while those who have obtained degrees from Cambridge and Oxford universities take pride in them. The professors in the latter universities don't just teach, like the professors in the government colleges do, rather no student can enter these universities without boarding there, no matter if they are sons of dukes and earls. Everyone is given the same nurturing in etiquette. And the company there itself makes them gentlemen. Society is the only thing that has an effect on mankind. You can see in India itself, there are some Englishmen who have an ordinary education. Who can say that all Englishmen are scholars? But because of a good society, they are all cultured, and that is due to nothing else but a good society. If we create a similar society for Muslim students, they will get the right education and nurturing. I want the Muslim youth to get religious and secular education and to be brave, resolute, and determined. Courage and boldness should be in their hearts. The fulfillment of all these intentions depends on the will of God and its explicit causes depend on the efforts of the community.

In this address, there is mention of women's education as well, the principles of which I have stated on many occasions. I am glad that the friends in Jalandhar think that these principles and precepts are in line with the times. But I want to ask if these precepts have been followed in Jalandhar? There is no doubt that I do not approve of the establishment of a regular school for girls, where they are sent in a palanquin wearing a *chador* or a *burqa* regardless of the community or the family they are from. We do not know what kind of women will come to those schools, what kind of company they will provide, what kind of demeanors and manners they will have, and what kinds of conversations will take place. But I strongly emphasize that the noble families should make collective arrangements for the education of their girls in such a way that is reminiscent of the kind of education that was given in the past. The education of women should be about good morals, good character, household affairs, respect for elders, love of husband, upbringing of children, and religious faith. I am in favor of that and weary of any other kind of education. Tell me how the elders of Jalandhar have acted on these precepts. It has been a few hours since I came to Jalandhar. I was sorry to find out that nothing has been done. I want you gentlemen to pay attention to this. Some friends told me that there was a need for money. That is a lie. The need was mostly for ethics. [*Cheers*] The problem is that the good morals of our elders, which were of a special kind and undoubtedly worthy of respect, have been lost on our present generation. Contemporary morality is also good in a sense. But they have not learned from it either, and they are ignorant of both sides. In this case, what else can they do when there is a discord between the two sides and one has to override the other? For education, whether of women or men, all the money that is required is here in Jalandhar. What is required is consensus. I imagine that there are no less than 2000-2500 villages in Jalandhar. The *number-daars*[31] and the *zail-daars*[32] of these villages collect the government land revenue and the taxes that are payable on it. If they agree to create a community treasury and collect in it a rupee for the education of their community for every Rs. 100 that goes to the government treasury, we could have a pile of gold and silver. A person who gives Rs. 200 in land revenue to the government can easily give eight *anas* or a rupee every year for the education of his community. [*Cheers*] The community should be in consensus; there is no shortage of money. Make a concerted effort to collect the money, spend it on the education of the community. You cannot reach higher education with small schools. These stratagems are wrong. As the saying goes, dew will not quench your thirst. Friends! Make an effort and create consensus. It is for everyone's good. [*Cheers*] Then you will see how the community advances. [*Cheers*] The community you see around you, you will become like them. [*Cheers*]

---

[31] *Number-daar* is a registered representative of a village community responsible for the payment of the government revenue.

[32] *Zail-daar* is the revenue officer in charge of a village.

180

Lecture Given by Sir Syed on December 7, 1894 to the Students of the *Madrasatul Uloom*

('Tehzeeb-ul-Akhlaq,' dated Rajab 1, 1312 AH, [December 29, 1894] pp 181-185)

Ismail Panipati titled this speech "Lecture on Turkish Attire" and prefaced it as follows.

Sir Syed was keenly aware of the need for unity in the community as well as for a community dress code. Eventually, the attire that Sir Syed favored for the students of Aligarh was at that time a traditional Turkish dress, and all the students happily accepted it. Since this dress was similar to Western attire, the English were very displeased that the subjects would dress like the ruler, which had the odor of equality. At that time, the principal of the Aligarh college was an Englishman, Mr. Beck. At the time, [*presumably when the dress code was promulgated*], he had gone to England on leave, and when he came back and saw the scene, he was very displeased in his heart. The authority of Sir Syed *Saheb* was such that he could not say anything. The way he solved, in his mind, this problem was to issue a directive that they should wear light, colorful, silken clothing for the military-style drills. The intent was that by making them wear this ceremonial uniform, they would lose the habit of wearing the Turkish dress and they wouldn't emulate the English in their attire. These military-style drills had been instituted in the college in 1894 at the behest of Mr. Beck himself and he used to organize them, and therefore he had the choice of asking for whichever dress the students should wear at the time of the drill. All the students disliked this ridiculous dress for the drills, but who could say anything to the principal. So they remained silent and donned the silk uniform for the drill. But to come from the boarding house wearing the Turkish dress with the silk uniform tucked under the arms and to change into it for the drill was a big inconvenience. The students were very upset. In the end, Maulvi Abdul Haq (*Baba-e-Urdu*, 'Father of Urdu'), who was a student of the college at the time, came to their aid. He approached Sir Syed and gathered his courage to explain everything to Sir Syed in detail. On hearing this, Sir Syed became very angry and indignantly retorted, "He has a devious stratagem, in the guise of which he wants to ruin my life's work." After that, Sir Syed immediately announced that a meeting will be convened, the details of which were captured by Maulvi Abdul Haq in an edition of the magazine "*Risala Urdu*" as follows: "After the Friday prayers, Syed *Saheb* came to the gathering. Strachey Hall was packed to the rafters with students. Opposite the big doors, at the end of the hall, a platform had been erected on which a table and a chair had been placed. Syed *Saheb* entered the hall as if a ship sailed in. He stood on the platform, looked at the students, and said, "Bring another chair." Another chair was brought and placed on the platform. Then he said, "Where is Mr. Beck?" Mr. Beck stood up. Syed *Saheb* pointed to the second chair and said, "Come and sit here." I had a feeling that something dreadful was going to happen. When Mr. Beck sat down, Syed *Saheb* started to speak and gave the following speech."

My dear students! I and your teachers, your parents, and your community are very happy that you have gathered here from great distances, different cities, and even different countries, to gather knowledge. You study different subjects and enjoy good ideas, academic discourses, and ethical reasonings. You are fortunate to have teachers who, although not from your country and your community, have a fatherly love and compassion toward you and want your development and progress in every way. They will guide you with excellent books written by great scholars and writers. But today I want to give you a lesson from a book that has not been written on paper, but rather nature has made it with its perfect and generous hands.

The words in this book are very wise and expressive, but somewhat difficult to see and read. Their meanings manifest clearly, but they are not easy to understand. To read them, there is no need to open a book, it is always open before your eyes. Don't look for this book in your college library or on your desk, it is always with you. What is that book? It is the gathering of you and your schoolmates themselves in one place in this college. So, you have to understand why you need to read this book and understand its meaning.

O dear ones! The name of this book is "*College life* or a new life." This is the real book and its reading and understanding is the real benefit and the real purpose of life and college. If you read this book well and keep it safe, and don't tarnish it, your future life will be one for which a person should look forward to living. Otherwise his life and death are equal, rather death would be better than life.

Think about the past periods of your life. When you were a child and knew nothing, your mother nurtured you with her maternal love, otherwise it would have been impossible for you to survive.

A few years later, you entered another era of your life, when you started walking and going around on your own and eating and drinking on your own. This was a new life from the earlier one, but there was little difference between your life and that of an animal. This period of your life also passed and you entered a new phase of life, in which education, religious ideas, and teaching of those things that you would need in your later life became necessary.

This phase passed too in a few years and you entered another new life which was not without dangers. In this life, you were not so much at ease as you were in your previous lives, because many enemies of yours were born within yourself and were always lying in wait for you. They had put a kind of veil over your eyes so that you could not see anything good or bad. Your parents, as much as they could, saved you from these enemies. Some of you were saved, some were somewhat saved and somewhat trapped in the enemy's net, and some were so badly trapped that it was impossible to free themselves from it.

But those who were saved or somewhat saved, their enemies did not relent and did not become complacent while lying in wait for you. You could not see them but they were always with you, and showed their faces to you sometimes in the guise of a friend, but they were truly your enemies.

This period of your life also passed, but in the meantime you became acquainted with your enemies, and to shelter from them you found a very powerful and wise mother, entrusted yourself to her protection, and entered a new life. Do you understand who that wise mother of yours is? It is the college that you have entered and you are all its children now.

Do you understand what that new life of yours is? It is the *"college life."* If you spend it well, your efforts will be rewarded with success and you will cross the stormy river, otherwise you will be caught in its vortex, from which you cannot emerge and swim to the shore. Now you have the option to make it across the river or sink in the storm.

O dear ones! *"College life"* does not apply to those who are day-scholars, but rather to those who spend their days and nights with their wise mother, i.e. live on the college campus and are called boarders. So, I am addressing only those dear students who put themselves in the lap of their wise mother and are living on the college campus.

Now let me tell you why you should take advantage of college life and how you should spend it.

First of all, the root of all blessings is the mutual respect and love that surrounds you. All your fellow students, whether from Hindustan, Punjab, the East or the West, the North or the South, when they are lying in the lap of this wise mother, are your brothers. If you don't treat them like your brothers and with brotherly love, you have broken the first principle that you are all the children of the same wise mother. Just as the words proclaiming the oneness of God are the first pillar of faith, unity is the first pillar of the benefits of the boarding house. Just as breaking the first principle of faith renders a person not worthy of his religion, breaking the first principle of the boarding house renders him unworthy of being a boarder. That is why you must show love and affection for your brother just as you do for your mother.

The boarding house is the totality of what makes a people a community. If all its parts function correctly, it will do its job, otherwise it is of no use. You are a part of that totality and therefore you are there to take advantage of it. The most important thing is that you remain upright and worthy.

Your meals and refreshments, living together, being in each other's company, participating in social activities, playing sports together, taking part in literary activity, all these things are there to develop mutual love, friendship, and empathy, all the things that are the basis for a people to become a community. Then, if you commit a fault, the blame of the entire community will be on your head, and people will regret that you have tried to ruin the very building of which you yourself are a brick.

All the things in the world that are rational and are in the mind have some evident manifestation that can be observed. Do you know what the evident manifestation is of the love and friendship you share in being the children of a wise mother? This is not the manifestation created by a human being, it is made by God, and by not fulfilling it, you not only draw rebuke in this world but are deserving of God's displeasure. What is that manifestation? It is praying in a congregation, which God in his oneness has ordained for unity among yourselves.

When you congregate in one place for prayers and pray in congregation, in addition to fulfilling your duty to God, you will fulfill in a practical way that unity of the heart that you have with one another. I am very sorry that in their ignorance, the Shias and Sunnis have separated themselves from each other even in their duty to God. I do not want to remove that separation because it cannot be removed by anyone but God, but I must tell the Shia Muslim students that they too must be present in the mosque during the prayers, which will show the glory of Islam and the abundance of those who worship one God. Then, they too will prostrate in their own way on the same ground on which their brothers have prostrated.

To establish this unity, a mosque has been built for both Shias and Sunnis and is perhaps the only example of Shia-Sunni unity in India. So, my dear Shia students and my dear Sunni students! You must maintain this unity and erase the division as much as you can. It is yours to maintain this unity. It is the cause of the welfare of both religion and the world.

There is another thing that creates this unity and oneness. What is that? It is that all of you boarders, and especially the students of the college class, to have the same attire. Perhaps there are some people who do not recognize this and ask what external attributes have to do with the reform of inner feelings. That is nothing but a mistake. There are many external things related to religion and to the behavior of the world that affect the inner feelings. Perhaps you do not know that when two people who meet and indicate to each other with certain specific gestures that they are both Freemasons, the passion and love that is born in their hearts when they come to this realization is unmatched by the sentiments between any other people. Having a uniform attire will always be the catalyst for the reform of your inner feelings.

A uniform dress code has been prescribed for students in the colleges of the great elite. Let alone these colleges, look at the Sufi mystic families of your own religion such as Sabri, Abadani, Nasiri, etc. In order to establish the same kind of unique identity, they had prescribed a particular kind of attire or insignia for their devotees. I know many of them and believe that this is a great way to create friendship and solidarity among them.

The dress that is now yours, i.e. the Turkish hat and coat and the English boot, is very fine. The only thing is that your coats are of different colors. So, you must adopt the same look and the same color.

Even in the court of the Sultan of Turkey, all the nobles as well as the attendants and servers wear red hats and boots. Our English government also thought of the same need in its courts and allowed everyone to come to them wearing English boots. In India, some narrow minded or arrogant and short-sighted Englishmen, who wish to humiliate or look down upon Indians, object to the wearing of this hat, coat, and boots. But all the high officials and people from noble families of England do not care about it and think that it is out of reverence that they have adopted this dress. But you must keep your boots clean and polished because they are a part of your attire.

Those Englishmen who are irritated by these things and inflamed by this dress of ours are, I think, very desirous that there should never be friendship, love, and sincerity between Indians and Englishmen. Despite the efforts that I have made to create unity and friendship between the Muslims and the Englishmen, I do not like to meet or be friends with any Englishman who speaks with rancor in this matter. Just as we must respect our authorities, they must also have regard and consideration for our feelings.

The matter of your dress being uniform is an important one.

This matter was presented in the trustees' meeting held on July 29. Regarding it, the proposal was that public opinion should be sought and then a committee of trustees should decide whether the dress should be made compulsory. I have come to know that most of the trustees liked the samples of the dress that had been made for some of the students. The only debate is if the dress should be made compulsory or not.

O dear ones! Now I have one more thing to tell you, and that is that the greatest thing of the wise mother in whose lap you are lying is her soul. You know what spirit is. That spirit is the teacher who educates you. It is your duty to be extremely polite and obedient to them. Among us Muslims, the rank of a teacher and the level of obedience to him is the same as that of a father.

Complaints have been heard that the English-speaking students do not respect their teachers and their parents. I am certain there are none among you, but those English-speaking students who do this deserve a strong rebuke from the world and from God. Parents are the creators of their bodies and teachers instill humanity in them. And so, the status of teachers is in fact higher than parents. When God has stated regarding the mother and father that, "*Say not to them [so much as], "uff," and do not rebuke them, but speak to them a kind word,*" you can imagine how much respect for teachers is obligatory on you.

You cannot find more kind teachers anywhere than Mr. Beck, Mr. Morrison, and Mr. Arnold. I am glad that you are progressing day by day in education, in morality, in humanity, and in culture. You value an honest friendship and self-respect. His Honor the Lieutenant Governor, in his speech at the opening ceremony of the Strachey Central Hall said, "What is the reputation of your students? They have the characteristic that they are righteous and brave and well-wishers of the government in whose benevolent shadow they live. Without flattery, they are affable, polite and courteous, and with their superior nurturing, are well suited to the practical aspects of life. Your institution is still in the early stages of its youth and has not yet had the time to produce the kind of persons who have wide knowledge or great reputation in various walks of life. After sufficient time has passed, such men will be born among those who have left the college, are presently studying in the college, or will be admitted in the future."

But I counsel you not to be vain about whatever His Honor has kindly said of you, for to me you have done very little and much remains for you to do. You must always remember the words of this wise poet who said:

> He who does not know, and thinks that he knows
> Remains in compound ignorance forever
> And the one who knows some, but thinks he knows a lot
> Even his slow-moving donkey will eventually reach home
> And the one who knows, and thinks that he does not know
> He rides the flying horse of his achievements to the heights of heaven

The editor of an English newspaper writes that the students of the *Madrasatul Uloom* have not yet shown any superiority over the students of other colleges, but the progress they have made in morality and culture, and in honesty and righteousness cannot be seen or known to people outside. He states that the sum total of their knowledge is dependent on the list of degrees that the university grants. In any case, whether this thought of his is right or wrong, you should try and work hard so that you have fame and reputation even in the branches of knowledge. You should become great litterateurs and writers to benefit your community.

You must also understand how to develop the qualities that I want to see in you. They can be developed from one thing alone, and that is to appoint an appropriate time for each task, stick to that timeline, and not let the time go to waste. I regret that we Indians do not value time and therefore have no regrets about wasting it. You should value time and believe that the time gone by will not come back. Valuing time will itself teach you to be punctual. Living in the boarding house will be more beneficial when you are punctual. There is an interesting anecdote about a boy's friend who went on a long journey on which he encountered thousands of beautiful and heart-pleasing things. He wondered what he should take back for his friend. At long last, he thought there would be nothing better than a watch, which would tell him what time to do his tasks, how much time he has wasted, and how much time he has served on each task. So, O dear students! The first thing you need to do to reach your goal is to value time and be punctual.

I have explained to you these few things which are the most important for your college life and I will explain to you some other important things in a future lecture, but now I pray to God for your religious and worldly well-being and progress. And in the end, I remind you of the words that His Honor the Lieutenant Governor said regarding you, "The students of this college … have the characteristic that they are righteous and brave and well-wishers of the government." Never forget that and remain steadfast in it in your private and public life. "*God is with you no matter where you are.*"

As soon as the speech ended, all the students went to their rooms, and the first thing they did was take out the colorful silken turbans from their trunks and cut them into pieces, while some got shirts, tablecloths, and curtains made out of them. Mr. Beck fumed silently and could not do anything.

★

181

Annual Report of the Eighth Session of the Muhammadan Educational Conference, 1893 ★

(Reference: Ninth annual session of the Muhammadan Educational Conference held in Aligarh, December 27-30, 1894)

In the service of His Honor:
Maulvi Muhammad Shahideen, Esq., barrister-at-law
President of the ninth session of the Muhammadan Educational Conference
Location Aligarh

In accordance with the procedure, I have the honor of presenting at the opening meeting a brief account of the proceedings of last year's session of this educational conference, the resolutions passed in that session, the results arising from them, and the extent to which they have been complied with.

Last year, as per section 12 of the rules of procedures of the conference, the following members were appointed to the managing committee for that year.

From Punjab

Khan Bahadur Muhammad Barkat Ali Khan *Saheb* (absent), Khwaja Yusuf Shah *Saheb* (absent), Niaz Muhammad Khan *Saheb*, Maulvi Ahmed Shafi *Saheb* (absent)

From the North-Western Provinces and Awadh

Maulvi Muhammad Hashmatullah, Esq., CS, Mirza Abid Ali Baig *Saheb*, Maulvi Abdul Rahman *Saheb*, Maulvi Syed Mumtaz *Saheb* (absent)

From the Province of Bihar

Shams-ul-'Ulama Maulvi Muhammad Abdul Rauf *Saheb* (absent), Nawab Sarfaraz Hussain Khan Bahadur (absent)

Ex-officio Members for That Session

Maulvi Muhammad Shahideen Esq., barrister-at-law, president

Dr. Sir Syed Ahmed Khan Bahadur, KCSI, LLD, secretary

Members Appointed by the President as per Section 12

Nawab Mohsin-ul-Mulk Maulvi Syed Mehdi Ali Khan Bahadur, *Shams-ul-'Ulama* Khan Bahadur Maulvi Muhammad Zakaullah *Saheb*, Syed Mahmud, barrister-at-law.

Among the aforementioned members, those who did not attend have the word "absent" noted in front of their names. The members who are present carry out the functions assigned to them as per section 16 of the rules of procedures.

Last year, nine resolutions were announced for discussion. Three resolutions were dropped from the list, two because the person who was designated to present them did not attend the session, and one person withdrew his resolution. Six resolutions remained for presentation.

Among the resolutions that were discussed, one resolution was as follows: "This conference is of the opinion that to counter the moral and religious harm to Muslim students caused by the lack of religious education in government schools and colleges, in a manner consistent with the idea that higher education in English is an asset rather than a detriment, efforts should be made to gradually give increased attention to the practice of learning Arabic."

In the session, amendments to this resolution were taken up and the amended resolution was stated as follows: "This conference is of the opinion that to encourage the Muslims students to take Arabic as a second language in government schools and colleges, Muslims should establish scholarships for this purpose." Consequently, this amended resolution was passed.

Among the resolutions discussed, one of the resolutions was as follows: "This conference is of the opinion that in the matter of the development of education and nurturing of Muslims, all the efforts made so far have been simply inadequate. If the situation remains the same and concerted democratic efforts are not made for higher and higher education and even more than that for superior nurturing, no change can be expected for centuries. If it is not done this way, in the opinion of the conference, we should be completely despondent about the prospects of the development and progress of Muslims."

There were long debates on this resolution, after which it was passed unanimously. This resolution along with the related speeches has been printed separately and has been given the title "Decision of the fate of the Muslims." It has been proposed that it should be distributed among the Muslims and in other provinces as much as possible.

In this session, *Shams-ul-'Ulama* Maulvi Muhammad Shibli *Saheb* read an Urdu poem, and a Persian poem of Maulvi Rafat Ali *Saheb* and an Arabic poem of Dawoodbhai, a student of the *Madrasatul Uloom*, were read.

One evening, the students of the *Madrasatul Uloom* who were members of the Union Club held a debate in English on a particular topic.

In this session, on December 30, 1894, Syed Ross Masood's *Bismillah* ceremony was held and I delivered a lecture on the need to reduce the expenses on weddings and to spend that money on children's education instead. There were three lectures given in this session. Maulvi Muhammad Shahideen, Esq, barrister-at-law gave a lecture in English, and Maulvi Hafiz Nazeer Ahmed *Saheb* and Syed Mahmud gave lectures in Urdu. The first two lectures were delivered in the evening, but Syed Mahmud's lecture, which was quite wonderful and used charts and diagrams to present proof of the decline in the education of Muslims, took a better part of the day.

Regarding this lecture also, it was decided that many of its sections would be printed and distributed among the Muslims and in other provinces as much as possible. Prof. Morrison too gave a fine speech in this session of the conference, which is unmatched in the treatment of the topics it covered. The Urdu translation of this speech was printed in the proceedings of last year's session, pages 122-131. Unfortunately, there was a mistake in writing the name of the speaker, and instead of Prof. Morrison, the name of Munshi Abdul Razzaq was printed. Also, the speech was erroneously printed below resolution No. 3, with which it had no connection.

Mr. Theodore Beck delivered a speech on the census data for the Muslim children who are capable of receiving education but do not receive it, and described the situation to the extent he had discovered. A scheme for conducting a census for the children of uneducated Muslims has been established on an ongoing basis under the auspices of the Muhammadan Educational Conference, and as secretary of the census department, Mr. Theodore Beck carries out this work. He corresponds with the guardians of these children and encourages them to educate the children. As a result, till now he has sent out the following notice to more than 1000 guardians.

Advice to the Parents of Muslim Boys

The Educational Conference is deeply saddened to discover that you are depriving your children of English education. The Education Conference insists that you educate them, first from the idea that your children achieve a high status, and second from the desire that the Muslim community must be saved from ignorance and humiliation.

Indians cannot get high positions in the government or in legal, medical, and engineering professions without the knowledge of English. If you want your children to be successful in the world, English education is the most important thing for it.

The amount of money you will spend on it now, you can recover ten times that in a short period of time.

Among the Indian nation, the Muslim community is far behind others in education. Due to this harm and negligence, Muslims are not equal in terms of honor, wealth, and culture in comparison to other communities. Out of a 100 students studying in a college, only six are Muslims. If this situation remains, the Muslims of India will fall more and more behind the other communities.

We request you to fulfill your duty for the welfare of your children and the betterment of your community. We want you to send your children to schools where education is given in English.

Signed
Theodore Beck
Honorary Secretary
Census Department
Muhammadan Educational Conference

Mr. President of the session! The speeches that our president of the previous session Nawab Mohsin-ul-Mulk gave at the start of the session, in reply to the report, and on the resolution regarding the decision of the fate of the Muslims are in fact timeless lectures. And Syed Mahmud's lecture was also very extensive which everyone was very eager to hear. For these reasons, a lot of time was spent in each meeting, and the following four resolutions could not be presented.

Resolution No. 4

It is the definite opinion of this conference that the current educational condition of the Muslims is not at all satisfactory and hence the Muslims should do something to improve their education. Therefore, this meeting advises that the Muslims of each province should sign an affidavit in which the signatories pledge to give one rupee per Rs. 100 of income or profit for the next 20 years to the Muslims of the province for the advancement of their education in English and Western knowledge. In order to carry out this work, a separate working committee should be formed in each province which will make sure to collect and spend the money in a good manner.

And it is also the definite opinion of this conference that as far as possible, arrangements should be made for all the proceedings of these committees to be under the supervision of the government.

This resolution was presented by the Honorable Haji Ismail Khan *Saheb* and seconded by Kazi Azizuddin Ahmad *Saheb*, deputy collector Jaunpur.

Resolution No. 6

In the opinion of this conference, it is extremely necessary that its members establish associations in their respective cities and towns and in those Muslim settlements where there is no member of the conference, which should be considered as permanent branches of the conference. These associations should, as much as possible and according to the rules of the conference, bring into practice the objectives and proposals of the conference. The associations should also discuss education among the Muslims of their locales and persuade them to act upon the recommendations of the conference. But these associations should be established only on the condition that no Islamic *anjuman* (association) of any locale takes these duties upon itself and agrees to become a branch of the conference.

This resolution was presented by Khwaja Ghulam-us-Saqlain, BA.

Resolution No. 7

It is the opinion of this conference that the membership fee of the Muhammadan Educational Conference should be made Rs. 7 instead of Rs. 5 from next year, and the additional Rs. 2 that is received from members should be added to the fund for the construction of the mosque of the *Madrasatul Uloom*. This will ensure that the construction of the mosque continues on its planned schedule.

This resolution was presented by Maulvi Bashiruddin *Saheb*.

Resolution No. 8

It is the opinion of this conference that since in the past, not only the Muslim sultans but the Muslims themselves have bestowed titles on eminent scholars, in this era as well some titles should be proposed by the Muhammadan Educational Conference for eminent scholars or for those elders who are prominent in the development of education for the community.

This resolution was presented by Maulvi Muhammad Bashiruddin *Saheb*.

I would be very happy if those who made the motion for these pending resolutions would present them in this session and discuss and debate them. But, as secretary, I must inform you that in my opinion resolution No. 8 is against the law, and unless the government amends its law, this conference is not authorized to bestow titles.

The precedent of people bestowing the titles of *'Allama,' 'Imam,'* and *'Shams-ul-'Ulama'* without the permission of the government of the time does not apply in this era, and no organization is authorized to bestow such titles. People have a right to address anyone by whatever name they want, but that is another matter and an association bestowing a title is a different matter.

Mr. President of the session! The president of the last session, Nawab Mohsin-ul-Mulk Maulvi Syed Mehdi Ali Khan had given instructions for copies of the lecture of Syed Mahmood with its charts and diagrams and the resolution titled "Decision of the fate of the Muslims" along with all the related speeches to be printed in sufficient quantity and distributed among the members. And these pamphlets should be sent free of charge to those people who are interested in the development of the education of Muslims.

Nawab Mohsin-ul-Mulk had a strong objection toward the proceedings of our conference that its useful information is not disseminated enough, but rather has been limited to the members of the conference. So, I have followed his instructions.

For the preparation of Syed Mahmood's lecture and the charts and diagrams that were hung in the conference hall during its presentation, which were later added to the lecture for printing, the expense has been quite high. So far, the sale of the copies of the lecture and of the resolution on the decision of the fate of Muslims has brought in Rs. 15. I will give an account of the expenses and the revenue from the sales, but so far I have not distributed them beyond the members. The reason for this is that I do not know enough about the people in each district to select those to whom it would be appropriate to send this lecture and the accompanying material.

I have thought it best to postpone its distribution until the next session, and to request members and friends attending this session from different districts to take a sufficient number of copies of both pamphlets and distribute them among those people they think fit in their respective districts.

Nawab Mohsin-ul-Mulk has also arranged at his own expense to have copies of his lecture on Islam that he gave in Hyderabad to be printed. It is his wish that these copies be distributed free of charge along with the lecture of Syed Mahmood and the resolution on the decision of the fate of Muslims.

So, I request all the members who are present in this session to take these three pamphlets and distribute them to the people of their districts that they see fit.

I will also request a decision on another matter. In the rules of the procedures of the conference that existed before the current rules were enforced, there was one rule regarding the conference session which declared that if by June no district expresses its interest in holding the conference session there, the session will be held in Aligarh.

In the recent amendment to the rules of procedures, a managing committee has been appointed which has members from Punjab, the North-Western Provinces, and Bihar, and it has been decided that the conference session will be held at a location proposed by this managing committee.

You know very well how hard it is for the elders of the place where the conference session is held, and all the arrangements that have to be made for the assembly of members, their comfort and lodging, and preparation of the venue for the meetings. In my mind, it is impossible for us to go to a district in which our friends are not willing to hold the meetings and be able to organize everything and make all the necessary arrangements ourselves.

Although Aligarh is the headquarters of the conference, I am very happy to hold its meeting in a different place every year, provided the people there take the responsibility of managing and arranging the session and the managing committee approves of the venue.

I have received a letter from the Anjuman Islamia Bombay with a request that the 1895 session of the conference be held in Bombay. I have replied by telegram that I will present their proposal to the managing committee for consideration and that if they kindly attend the conference on the 27th of this month and observe its proceedings, they will be able to judge if it would be possible for them to hold the session in Bombay next year. So, if the managing committee, after considering all the issues, would like to hold the conference session in Bombay, I will be very glad. It is obvious from this that my opinion is not that the session should be held in Aligarh by default. But if there is no request from any district, the session should be held at the conference's headquarters in Aligarh. This is because, in my opinion, the conference session cannot be held in a place without such people who can be trusted to take the responsibility of the organization of the session and making the necessary arrangements.

Till now, even in Aligarh, all the equipment and supplies needed for the session that cannot be borrowed are bought and then sold at a lower price after the meetings are over. But the supplies that were bought for the previous session, such as chairs, chinaware, etc., were not sold because if the aforesaid proposal is approved, those supplies should be kept secure so that they are available at the time of holding a session here. Convenience and savings are both conceivable in that case.

Apart from this, a very nice hall is ready in Aligarh for meetings. Material for its lighting and decoration has been bought by the *Madrasatul Uloom* itself. By holding the meeting in Aligarh, the expenses incurred in preparing a venue for the session will not be incurred. So, it is hoped that any appropriate suggestions in this regard will be made, especially regarding the safekeeping of the equipment and supplies for the meetings. And I am here to implement these suggestions.

The college foundation dinner that was held on the evening of December 30 was attended by four types of friends: trustees, officials, students of the college, and members of the conference. The expenditure for it was not taken from the conference nor were the members charged for the food for that evening. Rather, the trustees and officials paid for their own meal, which cost them a total of Rs. 48, and the students who participated paid for their own meals, which cost them a total of Rs. 45.

Besides that, the additional expenditure of Rs. 150 was covered by Nawab Mohsin-ul-Mulk Maulvi Syed Mehdi Ali Khan, who was an ardent proponent of the idea that all the members should attend the dinner as guests. All these amounts have been included in my accounting, which I will present.

I hope that the current session will be as successfully conducted as the previous sessions and the college foundation dinner will also be held with the same grandeur as last year.

Now I need to confess a mistake I made in the printing of the proceedings of last year's session. It is a pity that the members do not give in writing the speeches they make during the discussions. Shorthand writing has not made its advent in Urdu. The secretary or some other person writes these speeches only from memory, and when the members who give these speeches do not give them in writing later on, they are compelled to make do with this memory.

Those members who are kind enough to give their speeches in writing often do not write their name on it or do not write the number of the resolution to which their speech is related. And after which person's speech they gave their speech.

It is for these reasons that the mistake that I wish to mention occurred. It is surprising that only one mistake occurred that year; it was feared that there would be many more.

In previous meetings, resolution No. 3 was presented by Sheikh Muhammad Abdul Razzaq *Saheb* and he had given a speech at the time of presenting the resolution.

In our papers there was a written speech without a name on it, and it was printed with attribution to Abdul Razzaq *Saheb* even though it was a translation of Prof. Morrison *Saheb*'s speech. Now Abdul Razzaq *Saheb* has informed me that it is not his speech nor is it related to resolution No. 3. The speech that Sheikh Muhammad Abdul Razzaq *Saheb* gave regarding this resolution was not among our papers. Anyway, whatever was the reason, this mistake needed to be acknowledged.

Now, in the end, I request the members of the conference who give a speech to write it down and give it to me, and to definitely note three things in it: the name of the speaker, the resolution number to which the speech relates, and after which member's speech this speech was given.

The rules relating to the presentation and discussion of resolutions have been printed and distributed among the members. The details of these rules are as follows.

Presentation of resolutions and debate on them:

1. Those resolutions will come up for discussion which, in addition to being proposed by a member, have been seconded by another member and the managing committee has deemed that they be tabled for discussion.
2. When a resolution is presented for discussion, the secretary shall read the text of the resolution in the meeting and include the names of the member who proposed the resolution and the member who seconded it.

3. The first person to discuss the resolution shall be the member who proposed it followed by the member who seconded it.

4. After that, every member shall have the privilege to speak for or against the resolution.

5. If amendments are made to the resolution as a result of these discussions, they shall be written down in a numbered list.

6. After the discussion has concluded, the member who proposed the resolution shall have the right to give a reply if he so wishes.

7. If there is a discussion on the meaning of the resolution or if there is a debate that proposed amendments are not related to the resolution, the president of the session shall make a decision and his decision shall be final.

8. The amendments deemed warranted by the president shall be presented in a numbered list. The secretary shall read each of the amendments in the meeting and they shall need to be seconded by a member. If the amendment is not seconded, it shall be removed from consideration.

9. The amendments that have been seconded shall be put to vote and will be approved or rejected by majority vote.

10. If an amendment is approved, the resolution shall be amended accordingly and the original resolution shall be deemed null and void. If no amendments are approved, the original resolution as presented shall stand.

11. The president of the session shall have the authority to make any remarks he sees fit on the original resolution if no amendments have been made or on the resolution as it stands after the approved amendments have been made to it.

12. After that, a vote shall be taken on the resolution. If all the members are in agreement, it shall be sufficient to say that everyone is in agreement. If there is disagreement, a vote shall be taken by a show of hands. First there shall be a show of hands of those who are in favor of the resolution followed by those who are opposed. Both vote counts shall be recorded separately. The decision shall be based on a simple majority. In case of a tie, the president's vote shall be the casting vote.

13. No one shall have the right to discuss or critique the lectures that are given. The president or, with his permission, another person shall have the opportunity only to thank the speaker.

★

182

Lecture on Avoiding the Ill-Effects of English Education

(Lecture given by Sir Syed Ahmed Khan in the afternoon of December 27, 1894 related to the ninth session of the Muhammadan Educational Conference held in Aligarh, printed in Agra in 1895)

The lecture that Sir Syed gave on December 27, 1894 in the ninth session of the Muhammadan Educational Conference held in Aligarh was not included in the proceedings of the conference but was printed separately by the *Matba Mufeed-e-Aam* press of Agra and distributed later. This speech has been reproduced below from this booklet.

Eight years have passed since our conference was established and this is its ninth year. In each of its sessions, the elders of the community have gathered and have given attention to the education of Muslims. Many resolutions were passed and many lectures were given that made us laugh as well as cry. They were also unmatched in eloquence and elegance as well as in their treatment of the topics. These lectures had different effects on our hearts. When those lectures and those poems reflected the glory of our elders, their pioneering spirit, their worthy *"civilization"* (culture), their capabilities, and their proficiencies in various knowledge and the arts, our hearts would swell with pride. But when the narrative was about our current situation, our hearts would be dejected and we would be sorrowful, and we would regret that we are such ignoble descendants of such noble ancestors. But it is a pity that the latter effect on our hearts would be very short lived. Our tears were also shed, but they would wash away our grief with them. I have neither the eloquence nor the strength to follow in the footsteps of our distinguished lecturers. I am like that dye-maker who knew only how to make the mango-green colored dye, and he would tell all his customers, no matter what color dye they wanted, that only mango-green colored dye suited them. So, I will look at the current state of my community and I will ask you how its development and welfare, both in this world and in the hereafter, can be attended to.

In the past era, the condition of our elders was excellent and unmatched. In the civilization of the past, which we should remember and weep, our elders were blessed with morality, love, deference, friendship, friendly demeanor, kindness, generosity, tact, affection for young ones, respect for the elders, empathy for the poor, and a sense of unity in the community. The system of religious and secular education in the community was so complete and worthy of admiration that there was nothing like it in any other nation of the world. An elderly learned scholar, without any thought of worldly benefit, only looking for God's approval and the education of his community and people of his faith, would sit day and night in the corner of a mosque, a room of the monastery, or a chamber of his home, and just read. Then, when the poorest of the poor, a king, or an emperor's son came to study under him, he would treat them equally. Even in more recent times, but before the present era, many such elders were found in every town and city. Anyone who has seen them has found them to be angels, not men. With the blessing of their company, the morals of their students would be upright. Goodness would be born in their hearts. Perhaps there are still one or two elders like that, but they are so rare that they are not enough to benefit the entire community.

The main goal is to create kindness, morality, humanity, and a courteous nature in mankind through education and nurturing. We used to get all these traits from the company of our elders. From generation to generation, in the form of inheritance, these traits would reach our elders and from them would come to us. Our homeland, which is known as Hindustan proper or central India, was a shining example of many qualities, be it knowledge, society, culture, or language. Since the time of revolutions, there is neither that era nor are there those people under whose influence we were nurtured. The Mutiny of 1857, which was unfortunately blamed on the Muslims, destroyed everything that had survived till then. It was not only our homeland that was ruined, but as its effects spread throughout India, all of the country was destroyed.

O friends! At this time you are settled in different parts of the country, come from various families, and belong to different clans. You will forgive me if I say that if we consider our families and our kinsfolk, in which family and in which location will we find such elders in whose kind company's influence, our youth and our children can get education and nurturing?

We are like those twigs that were tied together into an orderly bundle with the twine of our nurturing. Now that twine has broken and we lie scattered and perplexed, without any organization. Now if we want to become a community again, we must collect those scattered twigs and tie them together. Unfortunately, the twine that tied us together is broken and frayed and cannot be used to hold the twigs together. For that reason, we need to make a new twine and retie the scattered twigs into an orderly bundle. O friends! If we don't do that, we can neither make our people a community nor instill in them a sense of humanity, a courteous nature, and a feeling of community.

This is the state of our community and all this is what we have to do for it. Now the question that arises, which is most delicate and the most worthy of consideration, is how to do it. And that is the question that the community must ponder. And, O friends! You, who have gathered here from far and wide, must aim to think about this problem and think of a solution for it.

When a man becomes feeble and his moderate temperament becomes disarranged, he suffers from various and conflicting illnesses. It is the same with communities; when they decline, it is not in any one thing, but in faith, morals, education, righteousness, honesty, culture, wealth, dignity, vigor, everything declines. And those who are looking for reforms are baffled at what to address.

> The whole body is wounded, where should I apply the cotton swab with
> the balm?

But when everything is taken into account, there is no cure other than education and nurturing. The difficulties in education are not hidden from you. As Muslims, in order to make our people a community, we need religious education. This is because among Muslims, in the spirit of the religion of Islam, the word community is not used synonymously with race, but for those who have accepted the *kalima,* the Mohammadan confession of faith, regardless of their race. They are all our brothers and included in our community. In the spirit of Islam, brotherhood and unity depend only on Islam. *God Almighty said, "The believers are naught else than brothers, so make peace between your brethren and fear God, that He may have mercy on you."* So, when the community is based on Islam, we must give religious education to our community, at least as far as it is related to beliefs and obligations.

We cannot deprive our people of worldly knowledge, because if they are deprived of it, they will not be worthy of living in this world. We accept that the world is mortal and life is for a few days, but those wretched few days are so difficult that unless we are worthy of living them, we will not survive.

There is concern for livelihood here, the tumult of judgment day there
Comfort is something you will find neither in this world nor the other

It appears to be a promising idea to say that knowledge has gone from Asia to Europe and our elders had educated Europe, but when we look at where knowledge has come today, be it logic, philosophy, geometry, astronomy, medicine, politics, or mathematics, both theoretical and applied, we find them advanced to such a level that we cannot recognize them to be the same knowledge that went from Asia to Europe. Just as a seed lying on the ground turns into a majestic tree, this knowledge has grown and advanced, and what has been augmented is on top of that.

Our worldly intellectual and theoretical knowledge, and their scholars and books, have become like an ancient calendar that is not suitable for any purpose. For that reason, we have been compelled to acquire this knowledge from the existing European texts, which in the past we acquired from the works of Bu Ali Sina and al-Farabi, Ibn Rushd and Razi, Aristotle and many other Greek scholars whose works have been translated into Arabic. Literature is a knowledge that is specific to each language, but even in this era, prose has developed in such a way that we have been compelled to abandon our ancient style and form of writing and adopt this modern style. The poetry of rhetoric, euphemism, hyperbole, and eulogy, which were once considered good forms of writing, are no longer appreciated.

Uneducated Arabs were famous in trade at one time, and God too has instructed us to engage in it when He says, "*O believers! When the call to prayer is made on Friday, then proceed [diligently] to the remembrance of God and leave of [your] business. That is best for you, if only you knew. Once the prayer is over, disperse throughout the land and seek the bounty of God. And remember God often so you may be successful.*" However, our community never engaged in trade. But we need to understand why. The reason we never engaged in it is because we are not worthy of it or it is no longer worthy of us.

At this time, trade is no longer the work of ignorant Bedouins. It has become a highly sophisticated art that requires both education and practice. Acquaintance with the people of foreign countries, awareness of the condition of these people and these countries, getting used to sea voyages, courage, and boldness are required for it. But all these things are not found in our community. Their practice is based on this saying:

Your (*Prophet Joseph's*) own country is better than that of King Solomon

Besides, in this era trade is no longer a personal business. Consolidated trade, which is associated with a company, is flourishing and in hot demand. It is based on mutual agreement, mutual assistance, the most fair dealings, and above all on integrity and honesty. But in our community, this saying is famous and is acted upon, that "too many cooks spoil the broth," i.e. partnered business does not succeed. I do not know of any precedent that even two men of our community did business together and there was no mistrust and treachery between them and it did not end in altercation and conflict. Removing these shortcomings from the community and instilling virtues in it will be a function of a very high level of education, and even more than education, nurturing. Not by learning broken English and getting a university degree. In Madras, thousands of men know English. I myself saw a man from Madras who had a BA degree and worked as a bearer for an Englishman. This outcome was the result of an education but no nurturing.

The greatest thing in every human being is the courage, boldness, and a heart full of ardor like that of a brave soldier, and the compulsion to do one's work diligently and honestly. That is what gives a man dignity, maintains his self-respect, keeps him strong in trying times, and causes him to do things that fill the world with awe. All these things have been and continue to be lacking in the youth of our community. Soldierly courage and bravery have never been in them. If there is anything in anyone, it is an uncivilized arrogance. Laziness and lethargy have become their essence; they are not used to hard work and perseverance. There is little consideration of self-respect. They have become weak and feeble and continue to become even more so. After completing a modest education, its benefits are lost on them. Many of them complain of poor eyesight. They don't have the strength for strenuous work. A few steps of a leisurely stroll appears to them an ascension to the heavens. Therefore, changing their habits, instilling in them soldierly courage, gentlemanly bravery, humble boldness, making them accustomed to hard work, putting them in good physical shape, and keeping them in good health are all the things that a respectable community can do. Given what we need to make of our community, if we expect from our education only "a four-legged mule laden with books," – pardon me, I made a mistake, "a two-legged mule laden with books" – we would not be doing right by our people.

Muslims are spread all over India. Although the government, out of its kindness, and the missionaries, out of their religious purpose, have established schools in many places, the number of Muslims in these schools is very small and the majority of the students are from other communities. A feeling of community is suppressed in the Muslim students in these schools and that feeling cannot be enhanced while they are getting their education as a minority group. These groups are not a help to each other even in their education. Their societies are different, and the needs of one are different from the needs of the other. And for this reason, Muslims have no means to advance their education in these colleges and to enhance their feeling of community or rather even to maintain it. Hence, we can never expect that an education in these schools would make a community out of our people. Look at the sentiments of those students who study with students of other communities and look at the sentiments of those who study and live with students of their own community.

It is true that we cannot gather all the Muslims of India in one college, and it is also said (which I do not believe to be true) that we cannot even build such high level colleges in different provinces which are suitable for the needs of the Muslims and to create among them a community feeling. But sitting on one's hands for these reasons and abandoning the plan of making a community of our people is very cowardly and a sign of lacking in passion for the community.

If we build even one college in which we can educate and nurture the children of our community in the way it should be done, it would be a sign of the wellbeing of the community and an indication of the rising fortunes of its people. No doubt there will be a limited number of students in it, but for those limited students to get this kind of nurturing would be an achievement indicative of progress. These few students, when they get this kind of education and disperse to different parts of the country, will be like the conscience for community development and like the seeds for the community garden. And it is hoped that they will produce such lush and fruitful trees, for which it is enough for me to recite a few words of the Holy Quran: "*And their description in the Gospel is as a plant which produces its offshoots and strengthens them so they grow firm and stand upon their stalks, delighting the sowers - so that God may enrage by them the disbelievers.*"

On this occasion, I would like to say a few words to the boys of the college! O students who are gathered in this hall! Listen and understand what I expect from you. If you do not fulfill my expectations, woe to you, and woe to me, and woe to the community.

People complain that English education deteriorates the habits and morals of the students, and they become renegades. Courtesy toward elders, courtesy toward parents, respect of parents, and obedience to parents dissipates from them, even though I don't come in contact with such people because I do not find the students of this college to be like that. They are very polite and decent and respect their elders and their teachers very much. But if this complaint is true, it applies only to four Muslim students studying in some missionary college in Lahore, or four in Calcutta, Bombay, or Madras. Even if their teachers are cultured and decent, and even if we assume that these teachers care for the nurturing of the students, studying Shakespeare, or a novel, or history, or philosophy for an hour or two in class is not going to fix it. Especially if after that, these boys roam the streets and alleys of the city, where articles that encourage uncouth behavior are more abundant, more easily accessible, and cheaper than in former times. When there is no influence of culture and society outside of school, the ill-effects that we complain of cannot be eliminated. So, O friends! If this complaint is real, then it is absolutely incumbent upon you, who want the welfare of the community and wish your children to be cultured, to ponder over how to address this complaint.

An even more dangerous and naive, nay, ignorant liberty has been assumed by students, although I believe not by students of our college, but in other colleges both government and missionary. And by that I mean the political agitation that the English-speaking students have taken up against the government in whose shadow of affection we live comfortably and in whose peaceful reign we can make all sorts of arrangements for our community. These English- speaking youth are like those who find a packet of turmeric and claim that they can open a grocery store. They are neither aware of the principle of politics nor have they experienced it. And nor are they familiar with the situation in other countries, which they have never observed. They are active in their opposition to the policies of the government for no rhyme or reason. I say with full confidence that such an agitation is harmful for the country, and if Muslims participate in it, then particularly harmful for their community. In fact, such an agitation will ruin the community. For our young Muslims, there is neither a society that would inform them of their mistake nor anyone to counsel and advise them. So, what scheme have you thought of, and what method have you adopted, and what method can you adopt for the children of our community to be safe from this contagion? Can this happen by keeping the nation dispersed and educating them in scattered places? Absolutely not!

There is an even more dangerous matter, which is that English-speaking Muslims are becoming apostatized after learning English and becoming averse to religion and religious obligations. Even though this trait is regrettable, I cannot attribute it to English-speaking Muslims because I see that Muslim youths who are not English-speaking are also not very active in performing their religious duties. Well, whatever the reason for it, it is quite disturbing that our youth are turning away from religious beliefs and are wavering in their faith. The main reason for this is the publication and availability of modern knowledge and the fact that English-reading students have the opportunity to be more familiar with this modern knowledge. So, it is not unreasonable to say that reading English is impacting religious belief, but I will say this much that compared to other schools, this affliction is very minimal in our *Madrasatul Uloom*.

But, O friends! In this matter, it is useless to equivocate and beat around the bush. Rather, it is the duty, nay, the obligation of our community to weed it out by the roots. This calamity is nothing new. It also occurred when Greek philosophy was read by the Muslims, due to which the scholars of the time devised *'ilm-ul-kalam*, the use of logical arguments for proving Islamic beliefs. So, the blame we place on our English-speaking Muslim youth is not correct. Instead, we should actually place the blame on the scholars of this era who have not devised an *'ilm-ul-kalam* to counter contemporary philosophy. Recently, i.e. in the month of *Rabi' al-Awwal* this year, on the occasion of the gathering for *Milad Sharif*, the observance of the birth of the Islamic prophet Muhammad, the great scholar Muhammad Ruhi Effendi delivered a speech in Paris in front of Muslims students who were studying in Europe, particularly in France. I will read a few excerpts from this speech.

He stated that the urgent matter to which I have indicated and for which all this was in the form of preamble and prelude, is essentially as follows.

"First of all, the people of the Islamic countries, who have no idea of the reality of the conditions and civilizations of the present 19th century, did not like the idea of students from their countries going to Europe and found it unacceptable that they would receive education in these non-Islamic countries. They looked at these students with contempt and disgrace to the extent that they, may Heaven defend them, imposed religious rulings of infidelity on them. These people became a hindrance to the progress of Muslims and to their contemporary advancement. They did not pay any heed to this Hadith that is associated with Hazrat Muhammad, the gist of which is, "Seek knowledge, even if it is in China." The country of China was not even a country of the *Ahl al-Kitab*, or 'People of the Book,' at the time, but only of idol-worshippers and polytheists. The content of one Hadith is that "wisdom is the lost belonging of a believer, get it wherever you find it." In the same way, there are many prophetic Hadith and Sharia texts which have been narrated and quoted that are witnesses for the proof of my claims.

"Secondly, some students are not aware of the facts of Islam. Neither do they understand the wisdom of and the simple meanings that are hidden behind the religious texts, nor do they inquire from scholars who are capable of refuting their intellectual doubts and removing their errors and weak ideas. Rather, they rely only on those tales and fables which they have heard, sometimes secondhand, from those who, with their broad sleeves and turbans, certainly resemble the scholars but in reality are trapped in prejudice and ignorance. These are the same people who have narrowed the purview of Islam, created difficulties in it, and it has made them indifferent and careless toward studying religious books and listening to the advice and counsel of religious scholars. From this, may God have mercy on us, this sinister conjecture has arisen that Islam is against evidentiary facts, that it is opposed to progress and civilization, and that a Muslim scholar is merely an imitator who is content with mimicking and does not use his intellect at all.

"I consider those students whom I have mentioned to be handicapped because they are taught by persons who do not have the slightest knowledge of religious truths. After finishing higher education, they never have the fortune of meeting such a person who could explain to them the wisdom of this holy religion and clear their intellectual and philosophical doubts. Nor do they have the ability to study such books that have been specially written on this subject because its text is difficult and complicated. Years of hard work is needed to understand them, and the basic reason is that they are not familiar with the Arabic language and academic terminology."

I have wished from the beginning, i.e. since I started the efforts to make English language and modern knowledge prevalent among Muslims, that the scholars of our time should turn their attention to this difficult issue and to devise an *'ilm-ul-kalam* to counter this modern knowledge. But it is a pity that no one has paid any attention to it.

A few days ago, a large group of religious scholars that goes by the name Nadwatul Ulama[33] had gathered in Kanpur. I wrote a letter to the secretary of this blessed assembly. I will read some parts of it to you. I wrote, "One more matter, which is of utmost importance, that I want to bring to your kind attention is that there was a time that the Muslims went through when besides acquiring religious knowledge, they were not concerned with any other knowledge. As a result of that, thousands of religious books have been available on Hadith, exegesis of Quran, Islamic jurisprudence, biographies of Hadith narrators, evaluations and discussions of Hadith and Islamic jurisprudence, etc. After that, there came a period in which the wisdom and philosophy of Greece became popular among Muslims. Due to this, there was some corruption in religious beliefs or fear that religious ideas would get corrupted. At that time, scholars girded their loins to support Islam, devised *'ilm-ul-kalam*, and came to the assistance of Islam. But now that time has also passed and modern philosophy, modern wisdom, and modern knowledge have been born, and the issues and investigations in physical sciences that have come about as a result are very opposed to the present day issues in Islam. This modern knowledge is becoming more prevalent by the day and cannot be stopped by anyone even if they tried. The scholars of the previous era had also prohibited the study of Greek philosophy and knowledge, even the study of logic, but it didn't stop anyone. Hundreds of thousands of men studied them, and the helpless scholars themselves acquired it and devised *'ilm-ul-kalam*.

"The *'ilm-ul-kalam* that was devised to counter Greek wisdom and philosophy is not sufficient to take on the issues of modern knowledge, wisdom, philosophy, and physical sciences that have arisen in the present era. Nothing related to this is found in the exegesis of Quran and Hadith, and due to this, atheism and infidelity are spreading among the Muslims. This is a serious contagion whose threat is growing day by day. So, what is the solution to this? It is my hope that you will present this petition of mine to the Nadwatul Ulama and publish the guidance that the scholars may give in this regard so that the Muslims may be saved from this calamity from which there appears to be no safe place. Peace be upon you."

But I think that this letter was not presented to the scholars out of some expediency.

[33.] Nadwatul Ulama is a council of Muslim theologians in India which was formed in 1893 in Kanpur. The first manager of the council was Muhammad Ali Mungeri. The council established the Darul Uloom Nadwatul Ulama, a famous seminary in Lucknow, on 26 September 1898.

My purpose in narrating these matters is nothing other than to explain to you the condition of the community and to show in this regard that unless you and I, and even the scholars of the community are not focused on it, nothing can be done. But, despite that, we should also think about what it is that we want to do. There is nothing else in our power except to urge these students to pray and fast, and to provide them with the necessities to fulfill their religious duties. Even more than that, we can appoint a worthy scholar to counsel them and provide guardianship for their religious affairs so that, as much as they wish, they can correct their beliefs and their wrong ideas with the resident scholar's advice and counsel. Religious education should be included in their curriculum as much as possible and the organization of all these affairs should be made a part of their education. As you can see, it is possible to organize these affairs in this way, as is done in the *Madrasatul Uloom*.

If the community approves of this kind of development for its people, it will also be necessary that the college in which the Muslim youth are placed should be in good, if not excellent, physical condition. The houses where they live should be clean and well maintained and the habit of wearing clean and neat clothes should be instilled in them. They should be required to live decently and keep their living quarters in order. As much as possible, uniform living arrangements should be made for everyone. The arrangement for meals should be such that they all come together to eat in a friendly and fraternal way. Learning how to do this will go a long way toward creating a feeling of communal harmony and unity among them.

Some people's opinion is contradictory to this. They say such decent habits should not be inculcated in students because after they leave college they are destined to remain in low-paying jobs, such as a coolie. How will they be able to live with such a nice demeanor?

These people prefer, over the schemes for inculcating decent habits in Muslim students, the tactics of providing the poor with living space in mosques and charity houses and educating their children in charity schools, just as the students of the distinguished Al-Azhar University in Egypt are lined up in an alley and two or three pieces of leavened bread are placed in their hands. They favor cheap and easy methods of education so that masses of poor can be educated.

O friends! If a people can become a community in this way, if humanity, courtesy, honor, and self-respect can be instilled in Muslims in this way, and if you prefer that your children are educated in this way to earn a life of humiliation, that's all well and good, but in my opinion no community can become dignified in this way. Those who want to provide education in this way may consider it appropriate to open charity schools and colleges, but they cannot take those children who are worthy of making our people a community and ruin them by placing them with children from whom there can be no expectations.

To display their concern for the community, some people have developed a habit of complaining about the cost of education. The guardians of the students are not used to spending money on the education of their children. It is not because they are so poor that they cannot afford to; after all, they spend so much money on rituals and useless ceremonies. They even take loans and mortgage their properties for these wasteful expenses and absurd rituals, but they don't know how to spend money on their children's education. O friends! Gone are the days when the students lived in the chambers of mosques and ate the meals on which *fatiha* and *durood* had been recited or had their meals in an alms-house where food was served to the fakirs. In this age, unless the guardians of the children stop their wasteful and absurd expenses and start spending money on education, their children will neither get educated nor nurtured.

I have described before you the true and detailed situation of the community. I am certain that you desire the development of your community through good education and nurturing. I do not ask you at this time to tell me a scheme to achieve this, rather I want you to ponder these issues and think in your spare time what strategy would make our people a noble community and what scheme will provide it education and nurturing. And do what you think is best.

"And lastly, praise be to God, Lord of the Worlds, and prayers and peace be upon Muhammad, the Messenger of God, who guided us to faith, and brought us out of darkness into light, and raised us from the depths of humiliation to the highest level in religion, world, and the hereafter, and upon his family and all his companions."

★

183

Sir Syed's Speech on the Occasion of Foundation Dinner ★

(Ninth annual session of the Muhammadan Educational Conference held in Aligarh, December 27-30, 1894)

The history of the foundation dinner is that in 1890, a motion was made by the trustees and professors of the college that just as it is customary in England to host a dinner in the founder's memory on his birthday every year, a grand dinner should be held here as well on Sir Syed's birthday every year, which would be paid for by the trustees. But Sir Syed did not agree to this proposal. He said that the condition of our country is very different from that of England. There, a person establishes a college by giving hundreds of thousands, if not millions, of rupees himself, while here there is no possibility of establishing a college without collecting donations from hundreds of thousands of men. Therefore, there is no reason why the college, which has been established with the money of the community, should carry out a ritual in the name of any particular person. Sir Syed said that in his opinion, instead of having a dinner on the birthday of a particular person, it would be more appropriate if this ritual is performed every year on the anniversary of the start of the construction of the college building. On January 7, 1877, after the Darbar-i-Qaisari, the assemblage in which Queen Victoria was proclaimed Empress of India, His Excellency Lord Lytton laid the foundation stone of the college building with his own hands. So, a dinner should be held every year to commemorate this event, and instead of calling it "founder dinner," it should be called "foundation dinner." Consequently, this proposal was accepted.

As a result, the first "foundation dinner" was held in 1890. The fifth "foundation dinner" was held in the evening of December 30, 1894. Strachey Hall was decorated in preparation for this dinner. All the trustees, college officials, students of the *Madrasatul Uloom*, and members of the Muhammadan Educational Conference attended the dinner.

At the dinner, first a toast was proposed for Her Majesty Queen Victoria, Empress of India, after which a number of speeches were made in English and Urdu. Sir Syed was the last to speak and said the following words.

O my friends and O students of this college! You can be certain that the British government is a mercy from God. It is our duty to God to have allegiance, obedience, complete loyalty, and fidelity for the government in whose shadow we live in peace and harmony.

This opinion of mine is not new, rather I have been firm and consistent in it for 50 or 60 years. The English government and the English nation is coming to the side of the Muslims more and more each day.

O Muslims! If you too are obedient to the English government and submit to its rule with sincere love, loyalty, and fidelity, you will fulfill the duty of obedience to your ruler that God has ordained and you will also fill any gap that you perceive between yourself and the English nation. Because the goodwill of the English government which rules over us is our primary duty.

When the late Sultan Abdul Aziz Khan came to London, a magnificent palace was adorned for his reception and hospitality. When I went to London, I saw this palace. In it, the crescent and cross symbols were intermingled on many of its walls and mantels. On inquiring, I found out that it was an auspicious symbol commemorating the unity and consensus between the English and the Muslims.

O friends! I have adopted the same symbol for our college as well. I hope that you will engrave this symbol in your hearts and remember that the main purpose of this college is to bring about unity between the Muslims and the English. It is our hope that they will be united in each other's causes as true and sincere friends, just as the crescent and the cross on this symbol are two hearts in the same body. And I pray to God that this wish of mine is fulfilled.

★

184

New Scholarships for College Class Students from Syed Families ★

(Proceedings No. 13, meeting of the trustees of the Muhammadan Anglo-Oriental College Aligarh, held on July 21, 1895, Matba Mufeed-e-Aam press, Agra, 1895)

At the meeting of the trustees of the Muhammadan Anglo-Oriental College Aligarh held on July 21, 1895, while mentioning the generosity of Nawab Imadul Mulk Syed Husain Bilgrami, Sir Syed said the following words.

After the budget had been prepared, Nawab Imadul Mulk Syed Husain Bilgrami established two scholarships of ten rupees per month each for students of the college from Syed families. The truth is that we and our college are very proud that the honorable gentleman and a source of pride for our community, Nawab Imadul Mulk Syed Husain Bilgrami, who is also a trustee of our college, after hearing that due to an order of the government the college fee had increased, established two scholarships of ten rupees per month each from his own privy purse for students who need assistance to pay for the expenses of their education. These scholarships will be given to those students who are from Syed families. It is obligatory on all of us to thank him for his empathy for the community.

In addition, he has honored me and Syed Muhammad Mahmood by asking that one of these scholarships be in my name and the other in Syed Mahmood's name. What can be a greater honor for both of us than that a person who is a source of pride for our community, be it for his knowledge, his linguistic abilities, his family status, his goodness and kindheartedness, would ask that scholarships be established in our name. But the honor this has given us would fade if it is not understood from the names of these scholarships that Nawab

Imadul Mulk Syed Husain Bilgrami has given us this honor. For that reason, we have given the following titles to these two scholarships.

1. Syed Husain Ahmed Bilgrami Scholarship
2. Syed Husain Mahmood Bilgrami Scholarship

We hope that our honorable Nawab Imadul Mulk, from whom we and the college have received such honor, will have a long and healthy life with dignity and good fortunes.

185

Regarding the Need to Construct a Bungalow ★

(Proceedings No. 13, meeting of the trustees of the Muhammadan Anglo-Oriental College Aligarh, held on July 21, 1895, Matba Mufeed-e-Aam press, Agra, 1895)

You are aware that there is a great shortage of bungalows in Aligarh for the accommodation of European officials of the college. We have constructed bungalows for the principal, two professors, and a headmaster, but we are having great difficulty finding a bungalow for the third European professor of the college. When Mr. Carey came, there was no place for him to stay and the headmaster *Saheb* was compelled to keep him in his accommodations. Suffice it to say there is a dire need to construct a bungalow for the European staff of the college.

A site had been proposed for the construction of this bungalow and this plot is in the land that has been granted by the government. For that reason it was necessary, as per the conditions of the land grant, that permission be taken from the government first for the construction of the bungalow. Therefore, as per the rules, I have taken the requisite permission. Now only the money is needed. If there is money, the bungalow can be constructed.

The debentures we issued for the boarding house have all been purchased. I therefore intend to issue 12 debentures of Rs. 500 each on the same pattern as those that were issued for the boarding house, and have that bungalow built as well. Although all this work can be done by the secretary himself as per the rules and regulations of the trustees, I thought it proper to inform this meeting before issuing these debentures. I hope you will approve of this proposal.

186

Annual Report of the Ninth Session of the Muhammadan Educational Conference, 1894 ★

(Tenth annual session of the Muhammadan Educational Conference held in Shahjahanpur, December 27-30, 1895)

In the service of His Honor:
Janab Nawab Mohsin-ud-Daula Mohsin-ul-Mulk Maulvi Syed Mehdi Ali Khan Bahadur
President of the tenth session of the Muhammadan Educational Conference
Location Aligarh

In accordance with the procedure, I have the honor of presenting at the opening meeting a brief account of the proceedings of last year's session of this educational conference, the resolutions passed in that session, the results arising from them, and the extent to which they have been complied with.

Last year, as per section 12 of the rules of procedures of the conference, the following members were appointed to the managing committee for that year.

From Punjab

Khan Bahadur Muhammad Barkat Ali Khan *Saheb*, Khwaja Yusuf Shah *Saheb*, Niaz Muhammad Khan *Saheb* aka Ghulam Niaz Khan *Saheb*, Maulvi Ahmed Shafi *Saheb* (absent)

From the North-Western Provinces and Awadh

Maulvi Muhammad Hashmatullah, Esq., CS, Mirza Abid Ali Baig *Saheb*, Maulvi Abdullah Jan *Saheb*,, Maulvi Syed Mumtaz Ali *Saheb* (absent)

From the Province of Bihar

Shams-ul-'Ulama Maulvi Muhammad Abdul Rauf *Saheb*, Nawab Sarfaraz Hussain Khan Bahadur (absent)

Ex-officio Members for That Session

Nawab Mohsin-ud-Daula Mohsin-ul-Mulk Maulvi Syed Mehdi Ali Khan Bahadur, president

Dr. Sir Syed Ahmed Khan Bahadur, KCSI, LLD, secretary

Members Appointed by the President as per Section 12

Maulvi Hafiz Nazir Ahmed *Saheb*, the Honorable Haji Muhammad Ismail Khan *Saheb*.

Among the aforementioned members, those who did not attend have the word "absent" noted in front of their names. The members who are present carry out the functions assigned to them as per section 16 of the rules of procedures.

Mr. President of the session! The real purpose of this annual meeting of our community is to put the word out regarding the education of the community and turn the attention of the community toward the education of its children. For this purpose, there are three types of proceedings in every session. Resolutions are passed, implying that the community should adopt such and such an approach for the development of education. Lectures are given so that they become aware of the worsening state of the community and the severe lack of education in it, alert them to the need to pay attention to the education of their community and their children and to save their children from the worsening conditions that would otherwise follow. Poems that are composed for this occasion on the state of the community are recited.

It has been debated by those empathetic to the community whether it is more useful to pass resolutions or to have more lectures. They are not opposed to passing resolutions, but they prefer to have many more lectures in every session and say it is these lectures that show the true condition of the community, draw the attention of the community to its state, and have a stronger effect on the hearts. Unless this effect is created in the community, more resolutions by themselves cannot draw the attention of the community to act on the proposals that these resolutions contain. Poems, which are often on the theme of education, are also useful. The most value they have is when these poems lighten the hearts and freshen the people to focus and debate the relevant issues at a point when people's hearts have been saddened by the continuous focus and discussion on particular topics.

I am very happy to report that in the last session several lectures were given on very useful subjects. The lecture in English by our respected Muhammad Shahideen Esq., barrister-at-law, was very useful in explaining the current state of education of the students. And the lecture in English by our dear friend and an old student of our college, Aftab Ahmed Khan, Esq., BA, barrister-at-law, in which he compared the education and college life of Cambridge University, where he studied as well, and the *Madrasatul Uloom* Aligarh, was extremely useful for the students. Similarly, the lecture in English by our student Abdullah Shah was excellent and very useful.

Maulvi Hafiz Nazir Ahmed *Saheb* also gave a lecture in Urdu. I would consider it disrespectful toward the revered Maulana to say anything about his lecture. The all-around excellence of his lectures is so famous that just attaching his name to them is inclusive of all these attributes. There is so much force and God-given power in his lectures that when he stands up to speak, the audience is mesmerized. It would not be an exaggeration to say that as long as he lectures, the ancient philosophical concept of *'ilm-e-huzoori*, that knowledge is acquired through a physical process of presence, is proved wrong since the audience forgets themselves. This community meeting of ours gets a lot of pride and praise from the honorable Maulana's lecture, for which we have no words to express our gratitude.

Another very useful and interesting lecture was by Syed Muhammad Mahmood, in which he compared the educational status of each community of India with the deteriorating condition of the education of the Muslims. Holding up a mirror of official reports, he showed how low the educational status of Muslims was compared to the other communities. This lecture and the lecture he had delivered in the previous session was highly appreciated all over India and the Muslims realized exactly how far behind the other communities they are in education. These resolutions took up most of the session and only two resolutions were passed last year. The first resolution was moved by our dear friend Khushi Mohammad Khan, BA, which was as follows.

"It is the opinion of this conference that the supporters of the community should give a small but fixed annual contribution or a portion of their income, e.g. eight *anas* or one rupee per hundred rupees of income, for the establishment and completion of the Muhammadan College."

This resolution was seconded by Munshi Niaz Muhammad Khan *Saheb*, who is a prominent lawyer in Jalandhar, and Khwaja Ghulam-us-Saqlain, BA. This resolution was passed unanimously and very enthusiastically.

The practical result of this resolution was that Syed Husain *Saheb*, registrar in the Small Cause Court, Ajmer, after calculations based on his annual income, gave Rs. 54 according to the aforementioned resolution, Irshaduddin *Saheb*, an official of the criminal court of Meerut, gave two rupees, Sheikh Abdullah of Mauza Reman donated five rupees, and a gentleman by the name of Zahoor Hasan Mukhtar, who is from Kot Radha Kishan, Punjab, sends one rupee every month to the college. This is a sufficient precedent that unless the hearts of the community are focused on education, the passing of resolutions alone cannot motivate the community to action.

The second resolution presented in the session was as follows.

"It is the opinion of this conference that the meeting of the Nadwatul Ulama recently held in Kanpur, in which scholars and mystics gathered, is worthy of the attention of all Muslims. The objectives of this gathering, i.e. reforming the method of education and resolving internal conflicts in the community, are very good and useful. All Muslims should support with their heart and soul and with their actions, pens, and money, such a good and useful organization from which the religious and worldly welfare and prosperity of the Muslims can be conceived."

This resolution was presented by Nawab Mohsin-ul-Mulk Maulvi Syed Mehdi Ali Khan Bahadur and Syed Muhammad Mahmood gave an excellent and interesting speech in seconding it. Many others present in the meeting gave speeches in support of this resolution and it was passed with much enthusiasm. What was the practical outcome of this resolution? I don't know the status of that. Many fine and pleasing poems were also recited. Poems in English were recited by Muhammad Shafi, Esq., barrister-at-law, and Zafar Ali Khan, BA student, in Arabic by Aghaz Muhammad Hussain, in Persian by Munshi Sadiq Hussain Sadiq and Shafiqur Rahman Shafiq, and in Urdu by Munshi Inayat Hussain Kaifi, Munshi Muhammad Razi, and Syed Ali, students of the school. Syed Ali is a young boy who wrote the poem by himself in which he described the college and the college staff, which was highly appreciated by the session president.

Mr. Theodore Beck, principal of the college, is very actively focused on educational census and corresponds with the guardians of the students in whatever district they may be. He also presented in the session a report on his activities.

A great result of his hard work is that a good school for the education of young boys has been established in Marhara and the people there are interested in its improvement. Another school has been established in Talhar and it is hoped that it will gradually improve and advance. It is also hoped that in the same way, schools will be established in other places as well. Both these schools are now affiliated with and are supervised by the officials of the *Madrasatul Uloom* Aligarh. This is the blessed effect of our Muhammadan Educational Conference. Syed Hasan Shah, who is the administrator of the magazine *Ittihad*, also presented a report. One evening, the students held a debate in English in Strachey Hall, which was very engaging.

On the evening of December 30, 1894, the fifth foundation dinner of the Muhammadan Anglo-Oriental College was held in a grand style. It was attended by the officials of the college, most of the students, and all the members of the Muhammadan Educational Conference. There was insistence in the last session on this year's session being held in Bombay as per the request of Anjuman Islamia Bombay, and I was also happy with this proposal along with everyone else. But due to certain circumstances, I could not have gone to Bombay. All the supporters of the conference gave an ultimatum that if I don't go, the conference cannot be held in Bombay. There was no way I could go to Bombay, so the thought was to hold the conference somewhere else. The elders of Shahjahanpur and our respected and venerable Khan Bahadur Muhammad Barkat Ali Khan *Saheb* declared that the session should be held in Shahjahanpur and the members of the managing committee also approved.

I am very pleased that the conference is being held in Shahjahanpur, which is a city of noble and high ranking Muslims. I hope that this conference will have a positive effect on all the towns and settlements of Rohilkhand and Awadh where noble Muslim families live.

Mr. President of the session! Proceedings of the last session of the conference, which were printed and distributed, contained the poems and couplets that people had recited or presented. Among these poems, there is one couplet that contains words of insolence toward certain elders of another religion. On noticing it, a friend of mine, who is also a member of the conference, objected to the conference proceedings having words that insult the leaders of another religion. I completely agree with his opinion and I am very sorry that such a couplet was printed in the proceedings. This is not just an ethical issue, but insulting the leaders of a religion is against the religion of the Muslims. God Almighty has said,

"And do not insult those they invoke other than God, lest they insult God in enmity without knowledge." So, it is forbidden in the Holy Quran itself to insult leaders of another religion.

For this reason, my friends have made a motion that a rule or practice should be established that any material which is to be presented in a general meeting should first be read by a committee or person, and after it has been approved, it can be presented in a general meeting. This will avoid such mistakes.

I understand that making such a rule will certainly disturb the proceedings of the meeting and perhaps even those who lecture and read the articles will not like it. But I implore all the elders to consider the complaint that has been made by my friend and to avoid words that may insult another person or the leader of another religion.

The rules governing the presentation of resolutions and discussions on them and the rules related to lectures and visitors have been printed and distributed to all the attendees. These rules are detailed below.

Presentation and Discussion of Resolutions

1. Those resolutions will come up for discussion which, in addition to being proposed by a member, have been seconded by another member and the managing committee has deemed that they be tabled for discussion.
2. When a resolution is presented for discussion, the secretary shall read the text of the resolution in the meeting and include the names of the member who proposed the resolution and the member who seconded it.
3. The first person to discuss the resolution shall be the member who proposed it followed by the member who seconded it.
4. After that, every member shall have the privilege to speak for or against the resolution.
5. If amendments are made to the resolution as a result of these discussions, they shall be written down in a numbered list.
6. After the discussion has concluded, the member who proposed the resolution shall have the right to give a reply if he so wishes.
7. If there is a discussion on the meaning of the resolution or if there is a debate that proposed amendments are not related to the resolution, the president of the session shall make a decision and his decision shall be final.
8. The amendments deemed warranted by the president shall be presented in a numbered list. The secretary shall read each of the amendments in the

meeting and they shall need to be seconded by a member. If the amendment is not seconded, it shall be removed from consideration.

9. The amendments that have been seconded shall be put to vote and will be approved or rejected by majority vote.

10. If an amendment is approved, the resolution shall be amended accordingly and the original resolution shall be deemed null and void. If no amendments are approved, the original resolution as presented shall stand.

11. The president of the session shall have the authority to make any remarks he sees fit on the original resolution if no amendments have been made or on the resolution as it stands after the approved amendments have been made to it.

12. After that, a vote shall be taken on the resolution. If all the members are in agreement, it shall be sufficient to say that everyone is in agreement. If there is disagreement, a vote shall be taken by a show of hands. First there shall be a show of hands of those who are in favor of the resolution followed by those who are opposed. Both vote counts shall be recorded separately. The decision shall be based on a simple majority. In case of a tie, the president's vote shall be the casting vote.

Lectures:

13. No one shall have the right to discuss or critique the lectures that are given. The president or, with his permission, another person shall have the opportunity only to thank the speaker.

Visitors:

Visitors will not have the right to vote on any resolution.

187

The Need for Educating and Nurturing Muslim Children

(Excerpted from the lecture of Sir Syed Ahmed Khan on the subject of encouragement and motivation for the education of Muslim children given on December 28, 1895 related to the tenth annual session of the Muhammadan Educational Conference, printed in Agra, 1896)

This very influential and engaging lecture was delivered by Sir Syed at the tenth annual session of the Muhammadan Educational Conference held in Shahjahanpur. The president of this session was Nawab Mohsin-ul-Mulk Bahadur. This lecture was not published in the report of the tenth session of the Muhammadan Educational Conference, and was printed separately as a booklet and distributed.

Mr. President of the session and elders of the community!

> Praise be to God, whatever he wanted
> In the end came from behind the veil of fate

When it was proposed to build a school for the education of Muslims, I chose Aligarh [*as its location*] for the following reason. Aligarh was not my homeland nor did I have anything to do with it, but it was only because of the thought that it is a place surrounded on all sides by Muslim *Raïses* – Meerut, Bulandshahr, Muzaffarnagar, Saharanpur, Agra, Etah, and a big repository of Muslim *Raïses*, i.e. Rohilkhand, where people of distinguished families dwell. That is why Aligarh is a very suitable location for the education of Muslims. Therefore, I am extremely happy that this session of the Muhammadan Educational Conference is being held in Shahjahanpur, and I sincerely thank all the elders and *Raïses* who had proposed this venue for the session and worked hard in organizing it. But my heartfelt gratitude will be complete when the *Raïses* of Shahjahanpur, and indeed of all Rohilkhand, are as focused on the education and nurturing of their children as they have been on holding the conference session in Shahjahanpur.

O elders and *Raïses* of Rohilkhand! In the ears of many Muslims, the sounds of the glory, knowledge, and grace of their elders are resounding. The imaginary scene of the times of their elders and the springs that their elders had seen are passing in front of their eyes. For this reason, they are not able to see the present age, nor can they think about the present and the past conditions, and that is the real reason why they are declining day by day. But they do not understand this, and if they do, they are not able to do anything about it. The fact is that they do not understand, for if they did, they would have done something.

O friends! My main goal is to inform my community, and to explain and emphasize to it to beware of this hangover, and to look at the present age. If you don't look at it for yourself, look at it for your children and understand what times these are for your children, what age is coming for them, and what is your duty to them by which they will live a life of comfort, honor, and dignity in the future.

I don't want to say anything regarding this now. I will say whatever needs to be said, but first I would like to ask you, and I would like from you, yourself, a solution to a riddle in this regard and to do what you think is appropriate for the welfare of your children. No one can be a bigger well-wisher for your children than you. If you, yourself, don't do anything for them, you can be certain that your souls will never rest peacefully in your graves.

Yes, I understand that many rich people rely on their wealth and believe that they have enough for their children. There are many gentlemen who own property and consider their children to be its future owners. But they should understand that the accumulated wealth that they see cannot remain in one place even if their children are of good character and habits. At the time when it is divided into parts and distributed among their children, their status will not be what they think. When they are devoid of education as well, they will have nothing in their fate except loss of wealth.

I have given some thought to this matter and the conclusion I have drawn that provides shelter from these troubles is education and nurturing. So, if you don't put your children in this lap and give them its shelter, then the troubles that are to come cannot be avoided.

O friends! Is there a person who believes in '*La ilaha illa Allah Muhammedur Rasul Allah*' but does not want his children to be familiar with the beliefs of the

Muslims regarding prayer, fasting, pilgrimage, and charity? Is there a father who does not want his children to be bound by religious beliefs? I am aware that although there are millions of youths and children who have been raised in their mothers' laps, they don't know even a word of their religious beliefs. In fact, there are many who have never bowed their heads before God nor rested their heads on the ground. But the argument is that when we have to live in this world, then to navigate the difficult path of the world, however short it may be, we must do something else as well. I hope that all of you gentlemen will acknowledge that something certainly needs to be done. Then, pray tell what needs to be done. What we say is that if you have to live in this world, you have to go with the world.

O friends! The voice that says leave the world and hold on to God pleases everyone. But God Himself holds us and surrounds us from all sides. How will we hold on to God when He Himself doesn't let go of us. But I haven't understood till now the meaning of us leaving this world. Can a person lying in the sea leave the water? You may become an ascetic or a hermit, and you may go into a cave, a forest, or sit on the mountain top, but the world remains attached to you. You may become a scholar, you may have the turban of honor tied on you at the convocation of a seminary, you may deliver a sermon from a pulpit, but if you observe carefully, the world is attached to these people only. So, the straight path is what God and Prophet Muhammad (peace and blessings of God be upon him) have told us, that we must do the work of God as well and we cannot ignore the work of this world either. God Himself has solved this difficult problem with a few words when He says, "*O believers! When the call to prayer is made on Friday, then proceed [diligently] to the remembrance of God and leave of [your] business. That is best for you, if only you knew. Once the prayer is over, disperse throughout the land and seek the bounty of God. And remember God often so you may be successful.*" This verse clearly indicates that at the time of worshiping God, leave all worldly work, and when you have completed your prayers, do something to earn your sustenance. This is the straight path and walking on it leads to salvation of both religion and the world.

O dear ones! People think that the path of God is very difficult. That there are great stumbling blocks, and very thorny trees, and deep pits, and very deep rivers on that path. But my opinion is the opposite. God did not give His servants such a difficult path to come to Him. It is absolutely straight and a thoroughfare. This path is believing in the oneness of God without any compeers, believing in the Almighty and obeying His messengers, affirming that Prophet Muhammad (peace and blessings of God be upon him) was the last prophet, avoiding practices that are in fact against humanity, and performing the duties that are in accordance with humanity. But the difficult path is that of living your life in this world, regarding which God told Adam that he will earn his living by the sweat of his brow.

O friends! Whenever there is talk of this world, I have heard many of my elders recite the following two couplets of Maulana Rumi.

> You desire God as well as this wretched world
> It is but an idea, an obsession, an impossibility
> The people of the world are absolute infidels
> All they do is chirp and chatter night and day

His example is like that of the knave who did not pray. When asked why he does not pray, he said because it is mentioned in the Quran, "*O you who believe, do not come near to the prayer.*" When he was asked to recite further, he replied, "Have I memorized the entire Quran for you?" Similarly, when it is said to them, "Gentlemen! Why don't you recite further," they reply that they haven't memorized the entire *Masnavi*. But we tell them that the couplet that follows is:

> What is the neglect of God worth?
> If not the worldly possessions, silver, wife and children

Indeed, no one is worse than the person who is intoxicated with worldly arrogance, and no one is better than the person who is not intoxicated with it and is sober.

Now we have to see why the world moves and what is the pace of the times.

After the Caliphate was established, the Umayyads and the Abbasids came to power. That era saw the Arabic language reach its heights. The court language was Arabic, all the knowledge was in Arabic, and all the work of the government offices and businesses was carried out in Arabic. What did our leaders do in that era? They advanced the Arabic language, achieved perfection in it, and lived their life in this world with honor and respect. When the Turks and the Mughals ruled over India, the Persian language flourished. The court language became Persian. All the work of the government offices and businesses started being conducted in Persian. Persian was neither the language of our religion nor the mother tongue of our elders. Our elders – or rather the people of India, not just our elders – also acquired proficiency in it and live their lives with honor in the world. Now, by God's will, we are ruled by the English government, whose rule over us grants us peace and religious freedom. The English language is on the rise now. All the knowledge and arts are in the English language. The English language holds much more than what the Arabic language held for our ancestors. The court language is English. The English language is embedded in the fabric of our lives. Without knowing English, we could not even find our way. If we go to ride the train, we wouldn't know when to go, which way to go, where to get the ticket, or where to get off. Hence, if we want to live in the world in the present age with dignity, then it is our duty to provide our children with English education and at the same time not keep them ignorant to and bereft of religious beliefs.

O dear ones! It is evident that the respectable government jobs are confined to those with a knowledge of English. Day by day, other jobs will increasingly get confined to those with a knowledge of English. But this desire I have for my community to study English, its purpose is not just to enable them to get government jobs. Everyone can understand and every student who studied English knows well that the government does not have sufficient jobs to give to everyone who knows English, no matter how proficient they are in it. Yes, jobs are also a source of livelihood for those who have received English education. But those who are sure that all the businesses of our life, whether it is trade, vocation, or any kind of profession, all depend on knowledge of English and that unless they develop proficiency in English, they cannot be worthy of anything in the world, are on the right path. Their idea is very valid and based on it everyone should learn English. Education and nurturing is something that shows the difference between man and beast. Think about it, you wouldn't consider an uncultured, ignorant, uneducated, and uncivilized person to be more than an animal. Then decide for yourself whether it is better for a human being to be treated like a human being by educated nations or to be treated like an ignorant and uncivilized person similar to an animal.

O dear ones! Education without nurturing or education which cannot make a people a community will not make the community worthy of anything. So, just studying English and getting a BA or an MA degree without nurturing or instilling a sense of community feeling cannot make a people a community and certainly not a respectable community. Islam has replaced nationality, which is based on race or country, with an Islamic status. Whoever recites the *kalima*, whether he is from China or Chinese Tartary, an Arab or an Indian, is a part of the brotherhood of Muslims and the community of Islam. This is an honor that is not found anywhere but in Islam. So, what we are concerned with is to make our people a community and an honorable community.

O gentlemen! This goal cannot be achieved unless the elders of the community turn their attention to fulfilling it. Those whom God Almighty's munificence has blessed with children and has given them the means as well should appreciate these two blessings and should not neglect the education of their children. They should spend on the education of their children instead of the absurd and wasteful expenses they incur for weddings and fraternal events. There may be many families who were once rich and wealthy and have now become poor, but the nobility and gentility of race and ancestry are present in them. Even though God has taken one wealth from them, He has given them another wealth in the form of children, but they do not have the means to educate and nurture their children. Hence, it is the duty of those whom God has given wealth and riches to find a way to educate and nurture the children of their brothers who were once their equal or even richer than them.

O friends! In the work of community welfare, concern for only oneself is detrimental to the community. This adage has been very well described by a person in the paraphrase of an analogy. Once a person's hands, feet, eyes, and nose became concerned with only their self-interest. The feet said, "In the plains, forests, and mountains I walk to produce sustenance and the stomach takes advantage of it. Then why should I work so hard for others?" The hands said, "We bake the bread and prepare the food, but others get the benefit. What do we get out of this effort?" The nose said, "I distinguish between rotten and edible food and others take advantage of it." The eyes said, "I find the hair and the flies in food and others have all the fun eating it." Consequently, everyone gave up their function thinking it was only for the benefit of others. The result of this was that due to blindness and starvation, the hands and feet became useless. The nose's sense of smell and the sight of the eyes started to wane. Then they understood that whatever they did was for themselves, and that they had only hurt themselves.

O friends! This is the state of our community. The community is like a human being and every member of the community is like a part of the human body. If you do not help the children of your noble community and think of them as someone else's children, then in reality you will do harm to your own self. You will render a part of your own body useless, which will only harm you. This is such an established principle that no person can refute it. Hence, those whom

God has given the means should educate and nurture their children and should be concerned about the education and nurturing of the children of noble families who do not have the means. You must understand that even if a person from the community becomes honorable and reaches the status of a deputy collector, a *Sadaras Sudoor*, a High Court judge, or a member of the council, no matter how honorable and respectable he thinks himself in his heart, the stain of disgrace on him for being a member of the community cannot be erased. So, until we make our people an honorable community, we cannot be respected in the eyes of the world and the other honorable nations. There are hundreds of examples of this in front of your eyes. There is no need to explain this further.

Now the discussion arrives at the question of how we should educate and nurture our children so that our people become a respectable community. I had spoken on this topic in a gathering and would like to repeat it before you. I had asked what we should do for the welfare and betterment of the community. I had answered the question myself that we should give our people education in the English language, which God has imposed on us of His own will through our rulers and without knowing which we cannot do anything in this world. In fact I would say without knowing which we cannot serve religion either.

But an education with which the community learns *katar-matar* English, i.e. a mishmash of words taken from here and there, and they start to speak English like the tradesmen and attendants speak in camps or the porters and cabmen speak in England, will be of no use. They should get a full education in English and a high level understanding of the English language so that they can be respected for their proficiency in English literature. They should be able to use the English language in their community, worldly, and religious affairs, so that others see the value in it. Even this much will not be enough for us. It will also be necessary that some among them know French, German, Latin, and Greek very well.

Along with this, we must also teach the Arabic language, which, regardless of the fact that it is the language of Muslims, is a language of a high status which is valued and cannot be separated in any way from the domain of academic languages. It cannot be excluded from the needs of Muslims. And if we consider religious service, it becomes necessary to develop familiarity with Arabic along with the Hebrew language. In a congregation, the late Maulana Shah Abdul Aziz recited with great pride the four lines of the beginning of the Torah in Hebrew. And Nawab Fateh-ul-Mulk Baig Khan *Saheb*, who was a great devotee of Shah

Saheb, had memorized those lines and would sometimes recite them when speaking about Shah *Saheb*.

We cannot ignore Persian either, which has become closely associated with the upbringing and the quintessence of Muslims. And it is a very delicate and sophisticated language in itself. There is so much capital of Muslim knowledge and history in it that Muslims cannot ignore it.

Although Urdu is our mother tongue, improving it, reforming it, and giving it the status of a global language is the duty of us Muslims.

Giving religious education to Muslims, whether at a lower, middle, or higher level, is also obligatory on us because the only thing that has made different nations into one community is Islam. If we do not pay it any attention, we cannot maintain this community. The least we can do is to teach religious beliefs and precepts, which we have associated with lower level religious education.

Along with these things, we have to educate them in various knowledge and the arts and especially in modern knowledge. This is a very important task, but its greatness and need at this time is a different discussion. In brief, it can be stated that without it a nation cannot become a nation nor can it attain any rank, honor, and worth in the world. And, truth be told, without it we cannot serve religion either.

This was only about the state of education, but we cannot achieve our goals with education alone. Does a human being become a human being only with education and get a status higher than a donkey carrying a load of books? Does a nation become a nation only with education? Does a nation gain respect among the nations of the world only through education? Not at all. In fact, until a human being becomes a human being and a nation becomes a nation, they cannot be respected.

So, more than education we have to do for Muslims what we call nurturing and upbringing, which is for a nation to become a nation like life for a body, and without which it is impossible for a nation to become a nation and remain alive as a nation.

What do we need to do to meet this end? Our first task should be to gather in one place, as much as possible, the children and youth of the community so that they can stay together, study together, play together, live and fall sick in one place, and to gather sufficient means of their nurturing.

Their physical well-being needs to be taken care of. Apart from supplying all the necessary medical supplies and facilities, a big house with a spacious and pleasant atmosphere needs to be made available to board them. They should be encouraged to participate in sports and to exercise, which is necessary for their physical health. They should be instructed to exercise according to their strengths. Those who are weak should be prescribed exercises that will make up for their lack of physical strength and those who are strong and powerful should exercise to develop more strength and power. They should be taught to ride horses, and courage and bravery should be instilled in them, without which man can neither do the work of this world nor of religion.

Then, we should provide recreational facilities for them so that their temperament doesn't whither, their aspirations do not fade away and disappear, and the restrictions that are placed on them are only sufficient to keep their aspirations from being deviant and to keep them on a straight and kind path.

Then, we should take care that these sports and exercise regimens are not a hindrance to their education and studies but rather help and motivate them. They should be provided with such means for education that will interest them, delight their hearts, and make them eager to participate and to apply what they have learned. It is not enough to just water the tree; unless its leaves and branches are swayed by the gusts of wind and it absorbs the air and its constituents, it can never bear flowers and fruits.

To keep their morals and religious views on the right path and to perform their religious duties, one or two hallowed, dignified, pious, wise scholars of kind countenance and pure character should be with this group to influence their hearts with courtesy and manners. With their gracious company, the students will be naturally inclined toward goodness and piety.

If we want the youth of our community to adopt a good and virtuous path, it cannot be achieved with admonitions and reprimands or by imposing restrictions on them. Prof. Morrison, who is a professor in our college, said it very well that no one can claim to completely subjugate the thoughts and desires of a thousand youth to his own will. We cannot make the thoughts of men, which in their infinite domain can reach anywhere, submissive to our ideas like a military officer keeps a company of disciplined soldiers under his command. Therefore, it should be our desire to provide for our students such means and good associations for their education and nurturing that will instill in them an attraction to goodness and aversion to evil.

Mr. President of the session! We have adopted these proposals for the education and nurturing of our community and to make our people a respectable and honorable community. Because the time is gone and keeps going when it is considered sufficient to pass the middle exam for government jobs. Amongst us Muslims, especially in Bombay, there are many people who are doing good and respectable work, namely they are engaged in trade. They are wealthy and have the means to educate their children enough for them to learn English or any other commercial language which would be sufficient for them to be able to work in shopkeeping or engage in other types of trade. They treat their offspring in the same way as the owner of oxen teaches them to carry a load or a cabman trains his horses to draw a carriage. It is a pity that as human beings they treat their dear children as they treat their animals.

Mr. President of the session! God Almighty, by His grace has endowed the mind of man with such strengths that he can advance to a high level with education and nurturing. Any person who has been intellectually nurtured is able to do jobs related to trade, vocations, and professions with such competence and excellence that people are in awe. The main reason why shopkeepers of our provinces spend their lives with such a low status is that no intellectual nurturing has been provided to them. If they had the intellectual and moral nurturing, they would advance more in their professions and the disdain there is in India for these professions would be removed.

O friends! God has entrusted you with the care of your children and He has made you their trustee, guardian, and mentor. Therefore, if you do not educate and enlighten the jewels that God has placed as your children, you will be answerable to God's trust and you will be responsible for ruining the lives and destroying the future of these innocent children.

O *Raïses* of Shahjahanpur! And O elders of Rohilkhand! I present before you this entreaty to pay attention to the education of your children. And I am thankful to the *Raïses* of Talhar that they have stepped up to the task of educating the children of the community.

May God give them further guidance and help them in this work.

★

188

Aligarh College: The Centre for English Education of the Muslims ★

(Tenth annual session of the Muhammadan Anglo-Oriental Educational Conference held in Shahjahanpur, December 27-30, 1895)

I have not stood up in opposition to the resolution that has been presented nor do I want to comment on the speeches made by Maulvi Bashiruddin and Munshi Nisar Hussain. But there is one thing for which I have stood up to say something, namely that the conference puts pressure on a college that is subordinate to the trustees. There has been no condition put in this resolution requiring the approval of the trustees. I would like this resolution to be amended to include the language that "it is subject to the approval of the trustees and compliance with the terms and conditions set forth by the trustees of the *Madrasatul Uloom*. This process will only mean that [*the conference*] should get affiliated with the *Madrasatul Uloom*.

189

Management of English Schools for Muslims 

*(Tenth annual session of the Muhammadan Anglo-Oriental Educational Conference
held in Shahjahanpur, December 27-30, 1895)*

I disagree with the amendment presented by our Daulat Sheikh Khairuddin. First of all, are these words of the resolution that "there is no provision for adequate oversight" not true and a fact? When we are certain that the teachers are not competent and that the English schools for Muslims are not well managed and supervised, why hide what to us are facts and the truth? We do not want to utter even a word that is contrary to what is true to God, to the public, and to the entire world, and we will accept it.

The second amendment is related to the promotion, retirement, and transfer of teachers. This is one thing that has ruined all the schools. If we do not get this right and exert our authority over the subordinate schools, what is the use of our supervision? If this amendment is not adopted, I will again discuss the disapproval of this resolution.

★

190

Publication of an Urdu Newspaper
from Punjab

*(Tenth annual session of the Muhammadan Anglo-Oriental Educational Conference
held in Shahjahanpur, December 27-30, 1895)
(December 29, 1985 at Shahjahanpur)*

Mr. President of the session!

All you gentlemen know, there is a strong need for an English newspaper in our community and the newspapers that have been launched so far have been inadequate. But presently there is a newspaper, "Punjab Observer," that is published from Punjab and whose management responsibilities have been assumed by our gracious Khwaja Ahad Shah *Saheb*. This newspaper has been launched in an excellent manner and it is hoped that it will fulfill the needs of the Muslim community. It is my hope that he will be thanked on behalf of the community and that the community will offer its prayers to God that this newspaper is useful for the Muslims and it progresses day by day.

191

A Meeting of the Students at the Conference ★

(Tenth annual session of the Muhammadan Anglo-Oriental Educational Conference held in Shahjahanpur, December 27-30, 1895)

On the evening of December 29, those old and current students of the college who were in attendance at the conference formed a committee whose purpose was that all the students should try to help the college in that critical time when there was a need to overcome its financial downturn. In the meeting of the committee, Sir Syed first gave a very short speech.

O my dear ones! I hear that you are about to form a committee to help the college in recovering from the trouble it is in. Only those who have money can help with money. I know very well that you are not rich, so how can you help with money? But this idea that has arisen in your hearts shows that you are attached to your college. Even if you cannot help with money, everyone who has a heart can help with their hearts.

192

Annual Report of the Tenth Session of the Muhammadan Educational Conference, 1895 ★

(Annual report of the eleventh annual session of the Muhammadan Educational Conference held in Meerut, December 27-30, 1896)

This report had been prepared earlier by Sir Syed and was to be read by him, but due to his ill health, he could not stand for a long period of time and read his report. As a result, this task was delegated to Maulana Wahiduddin Saleem, who read the entire report on behalf of Sir Syed.

In the service of His Honor:
Janab Nawab Imad-ul-Mulk Maulvi Syed Hussain *Saheb* Bilgrami Ali Yar Khan Yar Bahadur Motamin Jung
President of the eleventh session of the Muhammadan Educational Conference
Location Meerut

In accordance with the procedure, I have the honor of presenting at the opening meeting a brief account of the proceedings of last year's session of this educational conference, the resolutions passed in that session, the results arising from them, and the extent to which they have been complied with.

Last year, as per section 12 of the rules of procedures of the conference, the following members were appointed to the managing committee for that year.

From Punjab

Khan Bahadur Muhammad Barkat Ali Khan *Saheb*, Khwaja Yusuf Shah *Saheb*, Munshi Niaz Muhammad Khan *Saheb*, Maulvi Ahmed Shafi *Saheb* (absent)

From the North-Western Provinces and Awadh

Maulvi Muhammad Hashmatullah, Esq., CS (absent), Mirza Abid Ali Baig *Saheb*, Maulvi Abdullah Jan *Saheb*, Maulvi Syed Mumtaz Ali *Saheb* (absent)

From the Province of Bihar

Shams-ul-'Ulama Maulvi Muhammad Abdul Rauf *Saheb* (absent), Nawab Sarfaraz Hussain Khan Bahadur (absent)

Ex-officio Members for That Session

Janab Nawab Imad-ul-Mulk Maulvi Syed Hussain *Saheb* Bilgrami Ali Yar Khan Yar Bahadur Motamin Jung, president

Dr. Sir Syed Ahmed Khan Bahadur, KCSI, LLD, secretary

Members Appointed by the President as per Section 12

Nawab Mohsin-ul-Mulk Maulvi Syed Mehdi Ali Khan Bahadur, Sardar Muhammad Hayat Khan Bahadur CSI,..., Nawab Asadullah Khan Bahadur,..., Syed Muhammad Mir *Saheb*

Among the aforementioned members, those who did not attend have the word "absent" noted in front of their names. The members who are present carry out the functions assigned to them as per section 16 of the rules of procedures.

Mr. President of the session! Last year, the session of the conference was held in Shahjahanpur with great pomp and show. Rohilkhand, which has a large population of Muslims, was a very apt and useful venue for the session of the conference. There were some excellent and useful speeches in the session, such as the inaugural speech by the president, Nawab Mohsin-ul-Mulk, and the matchless speech filled with empathy for the community by Muhammad Ataullah Khan *Saheb*. In addition to speeches, Maulvi Muhammad Ismail *Saheb* gave a fine lecture on the history of the Muslim population of Shahjahanpur. Maulvi Hafiz Nazir Ahmed *Saheb*'s lecture naturally deserves a lot of praise, but the lectures of Maulana Wahiduddin *Saheb* Saleem and Honorable Syed Mahmood were also very useful and excellent. Maulvi Zaheer Ahmad Shah Zaheeri was gracious enough to give a very effective lecture. On the other hand, there is no doubt that very few resolutions were discussed. Only seven resolutions were presented, out of which two were just to express gratitude for the generosity of Haji Zakaria Seth and Maulvi Hafiz Nazir Ahmed

Saheb, and two resolutions were related to adding two words to the name of the conference and the appointment of Honorable Syed Mahmood as 'Life Honorary Joint Secretary.' One resolution was in support of the Nadwatul Ulama, one resolution was regarding the translation of useful English books into Urdu, and one resolution was regarding the matter of setting up an education department for the supervision of English schools. There were no additional resolutions presented by anyone on which there could have been any discussions.

It is true that many people think that in a period of ten years the conference has not taken any practical action for the people to believe that it can be effective. But they do not think about the fact that when people who come from different districts gather together, consider a resolution to be the actual basis for the welfare and betterment of the community, and pass it, to act on these resolutions and take practical steps for their implementations is the job of those very people who gathered from different districts, not of the conference.

For example, Mr. Theodore Beck, the principal of *Madrasatul Uloom*, who is also a member of the conference, has worked very diligently and compassionately to compile the status of the children of many districts who are deprived of education, a study which is known by the name 'education census.' The statistics from his compilation show that in many districts there are Muslim noble families who are interested in the education of their children, but due to the guardians of these children not having the means, they are deprived of it. Now I ask, whose job is it to collect funds for their education and enroll them in schools? Of the conference or the elders who live in these districts and acknowledge the recommendations of the conference in which the education of children is declared to be necessary and indispensable. So, the practical action is in the hands of these elders and not the conference. And in such a situation, how unfair it is to say that the conference has not taken any practical action.

Or, for example, through the efforts of Mr. Theodore Beck and Mr. Morrison, schools for primary education have been established in seven locations and are affiliated with the *Madrasatul Uloom*. In the previous session of the conference held in Shahjahanpur, it was proposed that a Muhammadan Educational Department be established and the supervision of education in these types of schools carried out. I ask that if the same schools that enter into a supervision arrangement do not pay for the prorated expenses of this supervision, how can they be supervised and how can the conference take practical action?

For these types of schools to be affiliated, the board of management of the *Madrasatul Uloom* has made certain rules which are to be presented for approval in the annual meeting of the trustees. In section 8 of these rules, it is stated that the expenses of this supervision cannot be appropriated from the college fund without the approval of the trustees, which can be obtained in the budget meeting.

Until it is time for the preparation of the budget, I cannot say what will be the state of the budget and whether any money can be allocated in the budget of the *Madrasatul Uloom* for this type of supervision. It is likely that it will not be possible. Then how can the conference take any practical action? Or how can the *Madrasatul Uloom* establish an education department, whose officials would tour constantly and carry out the supervision of schools, without sufficient funds. Until now, Mr. Theodore Beck and Mr. Theodore Morrison have toured various places at their own expense, but they cannot always pay for these expenses from their own pockets.

Mr. President of the session! No action can take place unless there is money. No work of community welfare can be done without money. Someone has truly said:

O wealth and money, you are not God but by God
[*You are*] Resolver of knots and judge of needs

So, until the elders of the community, who want the welfare and betterment of the Muslims, do not take upon themselves the hard work and effort, do not spend all their precious time in this work, and do not spend money for the completion of these actions that are needed, there can be no practical action. Not by the educational conference or anyone else. The function of the conference is to gather people every year, make earnest and humble supplications, and invoke God's grace. It softens their hearts when they read about the lamentations for the devastated state of the community. But when they themselves do nothing, what can the conference do? So, how unfair it is to say that the conference has not carried out any practical action and is therefore useless. If, suppose, this conference is shut down, is there any other gathering of Muslims which will annually meet to look at the status of the community, to lament the state of the community, and remind people that their dying community is on its last breath?

Nawab Mohsin-ul-Mulk Maulvi Syed Mehdi Ali Khan Bahadur has emphasized that some measures should be taken for the conference to undertake some practical tasks. I will present the status of this in a future meeting. But I just remembered an amusing incident which I will narrate to you first. Our friend the *Awadh Punch*[34] Lucknow has portrayed a very sophisticated picture of the conference in their newspaper. It depicts the conference as a dead body lying on a bed. By the head of the bed is kept a battery from which wires are wrapped around the body. Nawab Mohsin-ul-Mulk Maulvi Syed Mehdi Ali Khan Bahadur, who is very active these days in advancing the efforts of the conference, is depicted frantically shaking the mirrors that produce electric current to revive the dead body of the conference. I remarked that the only deficiency in this picture is that instead of the conference, the community should have been depicted as the dead body, and the conference should have been shown shaking the mirrors to produce electricity. Because it is the conference that does its job every year, warns the community of its condition, and shows it the way to progress. It makes the community weep by singing songs of lament and urges the community to work diligently for its advancement. The conference cannot do anything more than that, but the community still lies dead and does not make any motion to do the things it needs to do. The community does not even breathe. Hence, it is the community that is dead, not the conference.

Mr. President of the session! You know very well that the *Madrasatul Uloom* Aligarh has been established only for the development and welfare of the community, and you are well aware of the donations and contributions through which it has been established, because you yourself have also been very helpful and supportive. Everyone also knows that this school is not only for the people of any particular province, but for the Muslims of Punjab, the North-Western Provinces, Awadh, Bengal, Bihar, Bombay, Madras, and other distant provinces who come here to get an education. The financial aid that the *Madrasatul Uloom* extends to the students in the form of reduction of boarding fees, stipends, and scholarships is not only to the students of a particular province but from all provinces, be it Punjab or any other. At this point, allow me to say that a school of this type, which

---

[34.] *Awadh Punch* was an Urdu satirical weekly published from Lucknow from 1877 to 1937. It was launched on January 16, 1877 and was founded and edited by Munshi Sajjad Husain. It was modeled on *Punch*, a London based weekly magazine. Some of its notable contributors were Ratan Nath Dhar Sarshar and Akbar Allahabadi. The paper was one of the first to publish political satire, especially protesting British rule in India.

has advanced to the degree that it has, would be very difficult if not impossible to establish in any province of India. The community cannot advance by doing things on a small scale. And the development of the community cannot be done on a large scale until the community in all of the provinces is focused and united. So, it is just a wrong idea that the community can develop through small scale and modest efforts. I am grateful to the province of Punjab for its empathy for the *Madrasatul Uloom*, which has been established through large scale efforts. The lament is that the community is not alive. So, instead of depicting the conference as a dead body, it would be very apt to depict the community as a dead body.

Despite all these conditions, which in my mind are true and real, Nawab Mohsin-ul-Mulk Maulvi Syed Mehdi Ali Khan Bahadur has emphasized that the conference itself should also adopt schemes that are related to practical action. He has commanded me to print and distribute a compilation of all the resolutions presented and passed during the past ten years. I complied with his command, printed thousands of copies of this compilation, and distributed them everywhere. There are some copies available to be distributed in this session.

Nawab Mohsin-ul-Mulk himself came to Aligarh from Bombay in late October. He has girded up his loins to take practical action related to the conference. He visited Delhi, Meerut, Muzaffarnagar, Saharanpur, Moradabad, Bareilly, and Rampur to arouse the people to do the practical work of the conference. Maulvi Muhammad Bashiruddin *Saheb* was gracious enough to join him. The details of this tour is included as a supplement to my report, which will be presented before the attendees of the session. They have, according to section 8 of the rules of procedures of the conference and various resolutions passed by the conference, established a central standing committee in Aligarh which will continue to put efforts into fulfilling the objectives of the conference and implementing the resolutions that have been passed by the conference. Members have been selected for this committee. I and Sahibzada Aftab Ahmad Khan, Esq. are its president and vice-president respectively, Honorable Haji Muhammad Ismail Khan *Saheb* is a member and secretary, and Nawab Mohsin-ul-Mulk Maulvi Syed Mehdi Ali Khan Bahadur himself is a member and joint secretary. Then there are four sections that have been set up under this central standing committee.

The first section is related to the educational census of Muslims. The members of this section are Honorable Haji Muhammad Ismail Khan *Saheb*, Sheikh Abdullah, BA, and Mir Vilayat Hussain, BA, and Mr. Theodore Beck, Esq., is a member and secretary.

The second section is related to establishing subordinate schools. The members of this section are Ziauddin Ahmad, BA, Maulvi Bahadur Ali, MA, and Mir Vilayat Hussain, BA, and Theodore Morrison, a professor at the *Madrasatul Uloom*, is a member and secretary.

The third section is related to the education of women. The members of this section are Nawab Mohsin-ul-Mulk Maulvi Syed Mehdi Ali Khan Bahadur, Sahibzada Aftab Ahmad Khan, Esq., Sahibzada Sultan Ahmad Khan, Esq., Honorable Haji Muhammad Ismail Khan *Saheb*, and Maulvi Bahadur Ali, MA, and Maulvi Syed Karamat Hussain, Esq., barrister-at-law is a member and secretary.

The fourth section deals with general matters. The members of this section are the same as the members of the standing committee. However, its secretary is Honorable Haji Muhammad Ismail Khan *Saheb* and its joint secretary is Nawab Mohsin-ul-Mulk Bahadur.

The main purpose of the rules that have been framed and approved by the committee is to establish standing committees in each district to promote the objectives of the conference. For this purpose, they have recently visited a few districts. May the Almighty grant them success. If they do succeed in this, then in fact the conference will be capable of taking even more practical actions for the betterment of Muslims. A thousand copies of the proceedings of the central standing committee have also been printed and distributed. They shall also be distributed to friends who are present here and it is hoped that many friends will establish standing committees in various places. But I cannot forget the kindness of the enthusiastic friends from Punjab and I have much gratitude for their sincere efforts in support of the objectives of the conference. Anjuman Islamia Punjab, whose lifeforce and our old friend and supporter in every task is its general secretary *Janab* Khan Bahadur Muhammad Barkat Ali Khan Bahadur, who has established a series of lectures promoting the objectives of the conference. In this series, the venerable and respected Maulvi Muhammad Shah Din, Esq., barrister-at-law, the respected Maulvi Muhammad Shafi, Esq., barrister-at-law, Khursheed Anwar *Saheb*, BA, Sheikh Khairuddin *Saheb*, Maulvi Muhammad Fazal-ud-Din *Saheb*, pleader, and Sheikh Abdul Qadir, BA have given regular lecturers, which were very beneficial. I offer my heartfelt thanks to all these friends. I also cannot thank our friends in Gorakhpur enough who, based just on the letter of Nawab Mohsin-ul-Mulk that was printed and distributed, have established a committee with the support of the conference. The president of this committee is Muhammad Abid Ali Khan, Esq., barrister-at-law, a well-known old student of our college, and Muhammad Mehdi Hasan *Saheb, Raïs* Gorakhpur is its secretary. The committee has informed people of the benefits of the conference and has recruited 18 members for the conference, who have also given a donation of Rs. 100 to the conference. I won't be surprised if the same people establish a local standing committee. I have included the proceedings of their meeting in the newsletter.

Mr. President of the session! The proposal to establish standing committees is an excellent one and the sections that have been established for various purposes will facilitate a lot of ease in getting the work done. But the sections that have been established to carry out the work of the conference and the members and secretaries that have been proposed for them should be approved by the conference in its session. The central standing committee has also requested that the expenses incurred by it for stationery, printing of documents, and postage should be included in the conference's expenses. There should be no objection to granting this request since these are in fact expenses of the conference. The central standing committee has also requested that the staff of the conference be allowed to do the tasks of the committee as well.

It should be known that subsequent to the proposal at the Shahjahanpur session to employ workers for the conference, two persons were employed at a total monthly salary of Rs. 35. Out of the two, one person drawing a salary of Rs. 25 a month was let go, and one person drawing a salary of Rs. 10 per month will remain employed till January 1, 1897. Related to the conference, only one scribe has been employed for a long time, who is given a salary of Rs. 12 per month. But since this salary is very small, I give him Rs. 8 from my pocket and he gets Rs. 20 per month. From January 1, when the remaining conference employee is let go, I will pay this scribe Rs. 20 per month from the conference account and cease paying him anything from my pocket. Hence, there is no room in the conference budget to employ a worker to assist the committee for whom it would be required to be available to the secretary of the standing committee at all times. But Honorable Haji Muhammad Ismail Khan *Saheb*, who has been appointed secretary of this committee, has liked the idea that the salary of the scribe should be fixed at Rs. 10 per month from December 1, 1896 and he will make the necessary arrangements for his office as he sees fit. This proposal of Haji *Saheb* is also very appropriate and will greatly reduce the expenses of the conference. Therefore, I request that the proposal made by the central standing committee regarding the distribution of responsibilities among the various sections of the committee, the appointment of its members and secretary, and the matter related to the expenses that I have mentioned earlier be approved in this session.

Mr. President of the session! Perhaps I, you, members of the conference and every Muslim have the same desire, that the people of our community awaken and endeavor to give stability to the community. I want you and everyone present to say Amen to this wish of mine.

"May God bring us the religion of Islam and the love of the people, and grant us the nation of the religion of Islam and the love of the people, and these will be my last words: community of my people, community of my people."

193

Establishment of Local Committees ★

(Meeting related to the eleventh annual session of the Muhammadan Anglo-Oriental Educational Conference held in Meerut, December 27-30, 1896)

At the eleventh annual session of the Muhammadan Anglo-Oriental Educational Conference, on December 28, Sir Syed moved a resolution on the subject of forming a local standing committee in each district and requesting them to collect in any way possible Rs. 10 per month from each district for giving scholarships to Muslim students. At the time of presenting these resolutions, Sir Syed gave the following speech.

Mr. President and attendees of the session!

If local committees of the conference are established in many districts and towns, as we have endeavored to do for a long time, it would not be difficult for them to carry out this useful and noble proposal. Our major effort is to expand the adoption of higher English education among Muslims. There is no doubt that a large part of our community is deprived of access to higher education because they cannot afford the fees of the college classes and other expenses of education and nurturing. Therefore, if from each large town or district, as mentioned in the resolution, one or more stipends are established for students who are poor but otherwise capable of progressing in higher education and, with it, in superior nurturing, there is no doubt that it will benefit the community. This success will be of the kind that will be termed a practical success of the conference. Although the *Madrasatul Uloom* is especially an established source of the advancement of education and nurturing of Muslim students, there is no condition in this resolution for education in any particular college. Therefore, wherever these gentlemen find it easy to provide and supervise education, they should provide education and supervision to Muslim students in those places and establish these stipends wherever they see fit. Hence I move this resolution.

★

194

Welfare of the Community Depends on Education

(Meeting related to the eleventh annual session of the Muhammadan Anglo-Oriental Educational Conference held in Meerut, December 27-30, 1896)

The eleventh annual session of the Muhammadan Educational Conference was held in the famous historical city of Meerut in December 1896 under the presidency of Nawab Imad-ud-Daula Imad-ul-Mulk Maulvi Syed Hussain Bilgrami. In this session, Sir Syed gave the following speech, which had been published at the time in the proceedings of the eleventh annual session of the Muhammadan Anglo-Oriental Educational Conference.

Elders of the community! Some elders who are worthy of respect say that a community whose past history is worth remembering and is not remembered is very unfortunate, and that a community whose past history is worth remembering and is indeed remembered is very fortunate. That notwithstanding, and there is no doubt that our past history is worth remembering, there are two reasons why I do not wish to narrate it.

First, because the decline of our community has not long passed and traces of its history's pomp and splendor remain in India, Arabia, Asia, Africa, and Europe, and haven't become extinct yet.

Second, when we ourselves are so incompetent and unworthy, what is the use of boasting about the glory of our elders and peddling the skeletons of our elders? The saying is well known that 'talk of wealth in poverty and youth in old-age do not come true.'

If the thought is that by remembering the history of our elders we would learn a lesson and would be motivated to improve our condition, there is no expectation of that either. For ten years this topic has been regularly addressed in both prose and poetry in this conference but it was of no use. Rather those narratives became lullabies for our dreamy slumber of ignorance. So, it would be appropriate for us to leave these thoughts and consider only our existing condition, and if we can do anything about the current condition, we should make efforts for the welfare of our community. This would be better and perhaps beneficial. In the words of one of our respected friends, "A thrown stone does not stop until it falls on the ground." This is the decline of our community. As long as it does not become very degraded and humiliated, and does not reach the worst level and crashes into the dust of humiliation, its decline will not abate in the middle. I am even ready to wait for it, that it may bounce after hitting the ground, but a hundred regrets that we do not even expect it to bounce after hitting the ground. Hence, this wait of ours, however difficult it may be, is also of no use because the time for bouncing and steadying itself, even if the community so wishes, is long gone. This couplet of Ghalib rings true.

> If meeting you is not easy then that's simple
> The difficulty is that it is not difficult either

So, O friends! Focus on the present times and do what it demands and necessitates, and perhaps there will be some betterment.

First of all, we have to consider the government under whose benevolent shadow we all live. The peace and security we have and the personal and religious freedom we all enjoy under the English government is unparalleled and unprecedented in any other era.

The oppressive and tyrannical reign of cruelties and atrocities is a thing of the past and does not exist anymore. There are no barriers to the financial and intellectual development and wellbeing of any person and any community, rather the paths of trade and education are open. Traveling to distant places has become easier than anyone could have imagined. For the development of trade, information from other countries can be acquired so easily that you don't even have to get up from your chair to get to know about any country. Hence, the affairs that were not in the purview of even emperors in the past are now in the realm of the concerns of the lowest citizen of the land.

We do not value these peaceful times because we have not seen those times when tranquility of cities was very disturbed and insurgencies reigned. Travelers were looted on the roads. When someone traveled, their near and dear ones would bid farewell to them with tearful eyes, fearful that it would not be in their fate to see them return safe and sound. It was difficult for caravans to travel without being escorted by armed guards. In this gathering and perhaps in this city, indeed in this entire country, there are people who have not seen any government other than the English government. For this reason, it is no wonder that they do not appreciate these blessings. But, even now, the proverbs and stories of the past rulers are remembered by thousands of people and they are also informed by the history books. So, my advice is to consider the present era bountiful and make efforts for the development and prosperity of your community.

O gentlemen! At the time the empire was in our hands, the nature of development and progress was different from what it is in the present era. Sir Auckland Colvin, the past Lieutenant -Governor, said very well that if the sword of the Taimur dynasty has been laid aside, the strength and stability and bravery and courage should be preserved that had made this sword so sharp. Today's Muslims do not need the fiery and passionate temperament of their forefathers but those praiseworthy virtues that brought about this fiery and passionate temperament in the people of those times. These praiseworthy virtues should be turned around toward the achievement of success.

In any case, as far as I think, everyone agrees that Muslims are in a very degraded condition. They should progress, but what is the form of progress? In this matter however there are a lot of disagreements.

The religious elders believe that religious education has become too degraded and religious restrictions have increased too much. Progress in this regard is the only way that the community will progress. If spiritual progress is meant by this, I would agree. But what we are discussing at this time is that to be worldly does not mean that the entire community is able to resolve the issues of [Sheikh Abu Ali Sina's] '*Shifa*' or '*Ishaarat*' and everyone becomes a Socrates or a Hippocrates. This is because there are very few of such people in a community. But what it means for a community to be educated is that scholarly ideas have pervaded the entire community and a desire for scholarly pursuit has affected most of the community, that most of them have somewhat more than a general education and all of them have at least an elementary education, and that they have a passion in their hearts for the development and progress of the community. That everyone contributes to the development and progress of the community according to their abilities. That they are proud and honored to have worthy men in their community. Does Lord Gladstone's party, or rather the entire English nation, not have pride in having a person like Lord Gladstone among them? Does Lord Salisbury's party, or rather the entire English nation, not have pride in having a person like Lord Salisbury among them? Is the entire nation not proud to have a person like Lord Tennyson among them? Were we, when the times were according to us, not proud to have people of such high stature in our own community? But this is a time when there are neither such people in the community nor does the community have a scholarly bent, or a desire for scholarly pursuit, or any concern for the progress of the community. And therefore it has become deserving of the titles of barbaric, ignorant, and uneducated.

Sultan Mahmud had agreed to give Firdausi one gold coin per couplet for writing '*Shahnama*,' which he could not give. In this age, there are no such rewards, but the law of copyright, i.e. the rights reserved by the author, gives much more than that to worthy people, due to which capable writers have been rewarded even more than ten gold coins per couplet or per line. Who gave these rewards? The community. Why? Because the entire community was educated and the community had a desire for scholarly pursuits. The same law has been in effect in India as well. Then, can we find such examples in India?

In this era, there are a lot of newspapers in India. Well, they are what they are, but I have not heard anything about them except these three things: that they have no subscribers, that those whose names are included in the list of subscribers do not pay, or that they complain that they are receiving the newspaper even though they have not subscribed. The reason for all these outcomes is that the country and community are not educated. There is no scholarly bent in it, and that is why the newspapers are what they are.

The conclusion from all this is that there is a serious dearth of education in the community. Until education is spread in the community and the mental and intellectual powers of the people are strengthened, the community cannot progress in any form, whether it is in industry and craftsmanship or trade. To progress in trade, there is a great need for people who are educated, enterprising, hardworking, and perform their duties with utmost diligence and honesty. Integrity is the biggest part of these attributes, which cannot be developed without a high grade education, superior nurturing, and a culture of respect.

Suffice it to say, whichever aspect of the community's progress one considers, it requires a high grade education and superior nurturing, without which progress is not possible. O gentlemen! Then there will be this doubt in your heart as to how the entire community can be provided a high grade education and superior nurturing. I say it again that while that concern is valid, there can be some people in the community with a high grade education and superior nurturing whose influence reaches even those who are not highly educated. Do you not see any difference between the people of our country and those of Europe in terms of the desire for scholarly pursuits and empathy for the community? If you do see the difference, the reason for it cannot be anything but the abundance of people in those countries with education and sound upbringing whose strong influence has reached those who are called the common people.

Now the matter of a high grade education, superior nurturing, a desire for scholarly pursuits in the community, and their effect on the common people is in front of us. I have excluded religious matters from this discussion because of their sanctity, as I have said before. Hence, at this time we are concerned with the development of worldly knowledge.

It is the opinion of one group that we have everything and that our elders have accomplished everything. We should acquire only that knowledge that our forefathers had. There is a famous saying that "if you want to inherit the legacy of your father, then first acquire knowledge like his." We do not need any knowledge except that knowledge.

O elders! Is that true? In your opinion, hasn't the knowledge that our forefathers had progressed further? In your opinion, hasn't the knowledge of medicine, surgery, and pharmaceuticals advanced at all? In your opinion, hasn't the knowledge of philosophy and physics advanced at all? In your opinion, hasn't the knowledge of astronomy, geometry, arithmetic, mathematics, algebra, and instruments advanced at all? In your opinion, hasn't modern knowledge, which our forefathers didn't have, been developed? Has there not been any development in the style and mode of conveyance of an expression in literature? O gentlemen! Believe me that the knowledge that our forefathers had were like seeds. They have now flourished and have become like tall and sturdy trees which cannot be recognized as the same knowledge that our elders had! And the knowledge that has been newly developed is after all new for which we didn't have even the seeds. And the errors in the knowledge of our elders, pardon me, not in the knowledge of our elders but rather in the knowledge of the Greeks on account of being in its early days and are now manifesting, are on top of that.

O friends! Our forefathers were proud only of acquiring knowledge of Greek philosophy, medicine, astronomy – in short of all the knowledge that the Greeks had. But when that knowledge revealed obvious errors and advanced knowledge is already within our reach, why should it be our doom to waste the rest of our lives being slaves of the Greeks.

Hence, we have to consider what is good for our community in this age – to make efforts to acquire this advanced knowledge or to be stuck in the same old rut of the Greeks and to swing in the same swing that has become quite dilapidated and weak, and is not even able to carry the load of a child's books.

If this opinion of mine is correct, then we have no other choice but to draw the attention of our community to acquiring that knowledge which is advanced and in fact beneficial. This knowledge has been assimilated in three languages: French, German, and English. The first two languages are outside our reach. English, besides the fact that it is the language of our rulers and that it is of many uses to us other than acquiring this knowledge, is within our reach. For this reason, it has become necessary for us to acquire this knowledge in the English language.

One group is of the opinion that until this knowledge is translated into our mother tongue and disseminated in the community, there can be no progress. Without a doubt, I very much appreciate a large number of books being translated into our language. But no matter how true this opinion is, it is not possible to put into practice. During the time of Harun al-Rashid and Mamun al-Rashid, there were only a few books in Greek that were translated. In the present age, there are so many of such books that even if the likes of ten empires of Harun al-Rashid and Mamun al-Rashid were to concentrate on their translation, they cannot be translated. Consequently, till today there is no precedent in the world of knowledge and the arts being advanced in a language other than the language of the rulers of the country. Hence, it is essential that we acquire knowledge through the English language.

In India, there are still no means of acquiring knowledge and the arts. There are a few universities that have taken over our education and it is a pity that it is our incompetence that has led to our education being in their control. This is not adequate for the purpose of the community nor can these purposes be fulfilled by the government, particularly a government made up of people from another community that rules over many communities. Nor is there a government in any country that has fulfilled the educational needs of a community. This is a task for the community itself and unless the community undertakes it, the task cannot be fulfilled.

It is a pity that our community does not have the capabilities to fulfill this need. So, we are compelled to be patient with the education that is presently available to us and to remain slaves of the universities. There is no doubt that the current education is a form of cerebral education, a means to correcting thoughts and ideas. The thought arises in the hearts of people that the community is in decline and the idea of its progress takes the form of a dream in their hearts. When there is an abundance of such people in the country, and the ideas that I have mentioned become, for the most part, stable and firm, the first stage of the progress of the community would be reached. But education in its current form, without including nurturing, should not give us any expectations of growing a fruitful tree, but rather the certainty of a thorny tree that devours humans. So, O friends! It is your duty to pay attention to the nurturing of your children even more than their education. By nurturing I do not mean the archaic nurturing that is favored by old-fashioned elders of the community and which is not worth more than the interesting movements of a performer. Rather, by nurturing I mean the process that develops the traits of truth, honesty, true faith, true love, true empathy, self-respect, love for the community, concern for the progress of the community, integrity in one's work, honesty, and performing one's duties with honesty. This tradition is not expected to be adopted instantly but if our children and youths take this path then perhaps after some time there will be such people in our community.

It is a pity that even this poor education, which is compulsory in the early years and is the first stage of the progress of the community, is not in the purview of our community. Undoubtedly, there are both rich and poor people in the community, but to say that the community cannot arrange for even this kind of education for its people because it is poor and bankrupt is patently false. Please pardon me when I say that it is an out and out lie. The fact is that the community does not care about its education, progress, and welfare, and is not in the habit of spending money on these kinds of causes, even on the education of their children. Even if someone gets a bit enthusiastic and spends some money, it won't be for the community, but rather, according to a particular old fashioned thinking, to accumulate capital for their future. This generosity, if it can be called that, is not for the community, but, according to their own thinking, for themselves. This is the case even though, when one considers the principles of the religion of Islam, kindness and rewards are only in that generosity that is for fulfilling a need of the community. I do not expect from the community's current practice of generosity anything more than the generosity of the aged woman who stands in the waist-deep water of the Ganges and secretly leaves her precious nose ring in the river, saying, "Take this, Mother Ganges." There is no doubt that educational expenses, like the other expenses, are going up day by day and education cannot be given and resources for education cannot be collected without money being spent. Why don't the people who are well-off help in the education of their community and in collecting resources for it? If they give just a paisa, i.e. three *pai* per rupee of income toward education of the community, hundreds of thousands, even millions of rupees can be collected for the cause.

It is such a shame that we never think about the welfare of our community and find it difficult to spend even a single paisa on it. But if our community, and especially those we call *Raïs*, the nobles, were to know that spending money on such and such a cause will appease the authorities, whether it is for the construction of a mosque, seminary, hospital, school for women, or some other such cause, donations would be given generously and the reward for it is expected in the hereafter. How bizarre, how very bizarre.

> I am afraid you will not be able to reach Kaaba, my lord
> Because the path you are walking on goes to Turkestan

O gentlemen! In the previous era, education had another form and educational expenses were very low. Students used to live in mosques or chambers of shrines. Their meals would come from different households. They would get by with meals on which the prayers for the dead or for the third-day or fortieth-day ceremonies had been recited. In some places, they would get by on *langar*, the community kitchens serving free meals to everyone. Those who are as old as I am or older and have traveled to Egypt and seen the situation in the seminaries of Al-Azhar University and its students would have seen such things with their own eyes. In India, such arrangements can still be found in the Islamic seminaries. In those days, the students would be given a long shirt and a pair of trousers to wear, and if they were more lavish, an additional *lungi* wrap would suffice. I do not mean to disparage them with this narrative because among these students such people have emerged who are very dignified and worthy of respect. Rather, my purpose with this statement is to describe a real situation and to tell that now the times have changed. In this era, that simple and low-cost method of acquiring knowledge can no longer work. Especially, English education cannot be acquired in this way nor can those qualities be instilled in the students that are according to the times. The old method of education and nurturing cannot instill courage, boldness, and self-respect in them, nor can honor and dignity be maintained. Neither does enthusiasm and empathy for the community develop in them, nor can the community expect its betterment from them. In those days, what was prominent was only those kingdoms whose mindset was the same as those who provided or received education in these mosques. But in this age, the trend of the kingdoms, the communities, the welfare and betterment of communities, the acquisition of knowledge, and the assistance of the poor of the community have all changed. And unless we also change and move with the times, we cannot achieve success in any way.

Even in this era, Muslim students and children of noble families need a lot of help. The leaders of the community, the wealthy ones in the community, and those who wish for the community to progress must help them. But this should not be done using the first method that I mentioned, but using the second method by which the dignity, honor, and self-respect of the students are enhanced while they get assistance as well. They should be treated in a dignified manner so that their dignity, honor, and self-reliance are cultivated day by day, which will later be a means to progress and prosperity of the community.

It is said that in this era, the community is focused on progress like it has never been at any other time. Schools and primary education academies are being established in many places in India through the endeavors of the community. Orphanages are being established which was not the trend earlier. Anjuman Islamia, or Islamic societies, are being established in such abundance that is no less than the appearance of frogs after rain, even though they may disappear after a few days. But the sad thing is that the same calamity rains down on them that we are trying to eliminate. Can the community progress with such outcomes? Absolutely not! Rather, it gives rise to indications of another calamity for the community.

A very experienced traveler once said, "If, in your travels, you want to assess a nation's prosperity and well-being or its disgraced and humiliated state, it is sufficient to observe their cemeteries and their places of worship. If their cemeteries are orderly and places of worship bright and cheerful, you can be certain that the community is prosperous. But, in my view, in India there is a third attribute to assess the community, i.e. the prevalence of Islamic seminaries, societies and orphanages, because these are indicative of the calamity that has befallen the community.

O elders of the community! If all of you put in a concerted effort, you still have that strength and power which was not available to Harun al-Rashid or to Mamum al-Rashid, neither did it become available to Akbar or to Shahjahan, and nor is it available in this age to the English government with its attributes of grandeur and splendor. This is provided you give one paisa, i.e. three *pai*, per rupee of income for the community and instead of tackling many different tasks, you agree to concentrate on one task and bring it to completion. Then you will see what great works you can accomplish which would be superior to even the works of Europe. But it is a pity that we do not have perseverance, and if we have perseverance, we do not have consensus. That is why all our efforts are inferior and useless. There are traces of calamity in every task we set out to accomplish, rather in everything related to the community. *"Say: O God! Lord of all dominion! Thou grantest dominion unto whom Thou willest, and takest away dominion from whom Thou willest; and Thou exaltest whom Thou willest and abasest whom Thou willest. In Thy hand is all good. Verily, Thou hast the power to will anything."*

Religious illusions and prejudices unnecessarily hinder the progress of the community. We should hope from the scholars of the community, even if it is realized or not, to remove these religious illusions and prejudices from the community, thereby bringing about peace and prosperity in the country and development and welfare of the community. I remember that when trains first started to run, there was the question of whether prayer in a moving train was valid or not. The decision was that it was not. Then the issue was raised that it was not in our power to stop the train. It was possible that the train would not be stationary at the time of prayer and one would lose the opportunity to pray. Then it was decided that traveling on a train was not permissible. But because the Maulvi and the public were equally included in the harm of this decision, the venerable scholars silenced this debate saying, "Quiet, quiet. *Necessities stem from dependencies.*" But I have seen some hallowed people get down from a stopped train at a station and pray on the platform and in such a hurry that the *kiraman katibin*, the two angels on the right and left shoulder appointed to record a person's deeds, do not get time to record the act of prayer. It has also happened that as soon as they have said their vows before starting the prayer, the train starts to move. After they finish their prayers, they sit there wondering what to do. All the luggage they had was also gone with the train. When people asked a lot of questions, they would get angry and say, "*Mian*, what do you ask? '*The world is a prison for the believer and a paradise for the unbeliever.*' Whatever difficulties one encounters in this world must be endured."

There was an elder Maulvi who would declare many people infidels using the Hadith, "*He who imitates any people (in their actions) is one of them.*" The Maulvi went to debate this idea with a person who did not agree with this decree of his. It was the summer season and the day was about to end. That person was sitting in a chamber of his home. Maulvi *Saheb* came and sat there too. I do not remember if he greeted the person or not. When he started to speak on this topic, the person said it would be better if they went out and sat in the courtyard. The courtyard had a platform bed and a few chairs were lying around. This person went and sat on the platform bed and, out of reverence and respect, asked the Maulvi *Saheb* to sit on a chair. When Maulvi *Saheb* sat down on the chair, this person got up, greeted Maulvi *Saheb* respectfully, and said, "*He who imitates any people (in their actions) is one of them.*" When so much slander and excessive prejudices have spread in the community, and our scholars instead of removing such illusions give it more corroboration among the people of the community, then what expectations can there be for the community to progress. May God forgive our sins, keep us steadfast, and help us, only then we can achieve something. "*Our Lord! Forgive us our sins and anything we may have done that transgressed our duty, make our foothold sure, and give us victory over those who resist faith.*" I don't want to read more of this verse than this much.

O friends! You can be certain that unless we establish high grade institutions for our community, whether they are for education or for the upbringing of orphans, collect excellent resources for education that are at par or nearly at par with the institutions in Europe, and give our youth education and nurturing that is based on the same high grade principles as in Europe, it is not possible for our community to progress. There is no doubt that this will require a lot of capital. If the community acts diligently and takes practical action as well, we will have no shortage of money. Our community can still collect more money than it needs for all these tasks from the community itself provided that, as Sir Auckland Colvin said, we can break our semantic and rhetorical idols and focus on the development and welfare of the community.

Sir Auckland Colvin said that these days we can see as many idols in the world as there were in the Arabia of the 7th century AD.

One thing is that people are distracted by the past methods of education and the arguments and ways of debates and discussions of those times.

Another thing is that they are intensely prejudiced against all things that are alien to religion and the Islamic state.

And yet another thing that is huge and most terrifying is the prevalence of laziness, carelessness, and negligence. All these idols are mute and dark whose forms drip with terror. Their claims are simply hollow and they are detestable because of their lack of strength and effectiveness.

O friends! Our very first leader Prophet Abraham (peace be upon him) and our guide Prophet Muhammad (peace and blessings of God be upon him) broke the idols of Kaaba and banished them from Kaaba. So, let us also emulate them and break those semantic idols that need to be broken before we can succeed.

We made the sanctuary a shrine of idols (for a few days)
Now is the time that we are taking the idols out of Kaaba

195

A Memorial to Her Gracious Majesty Queen Victoria Monarch of India

(Report of the eleventh annual session of the Muhammadan Anglo-Oriental Educational Conference held in Meerut, December 27-30, 1896)
(Aligarh Institute Gazette, January 9, 1897)

In the Muhammadan Anglo-Oriental Educational Conference held in Meerut, a resolution (No. 4) was passed to the effect that to commemorate 60 years of the Empire, a memorial should be established to Her Gracious Majesty Queen Victoria Monarch of India. On this occasion and in support of this resolution, various people gave speeches. Sir Syed gave the following speech.

Mr. President of the session and other elders of the community! The proposal that has been put forward by my extremely respectful friend Sardar Muhammad Hayat Khan and has been explained in detail in eloquent words is a matter that every person will wholeheartedly support. Who can deny that the magnitude of religious freedom enjoyed by the Muslims of India in this era and the peace and order that prevails in this country is a blessing from the Almighty, for which it is the duty of every Muslim and every citizen of this country to express their gratitude. Muslims of British India, who live in freedom and peace under the rule of Her Majesty Queen Victoria Monarch of India, are steadily making progress of all kinds. For their progress and welfare, be it religious, in trade and vocation, or in acquisition of knowledge, there is no hindrance or resistance. This religious freedom and this peace and harmony is not even in those countries of Europe that are called civilized. Any person who has heard of the expulsion of Jews from Russia and of how harshly the rulers of the Dutch nation treated their Muslim subjects would surely be convinced that the rule of the English is a just and rather benevolent one in which every community, especially Muslims, have the opportunity to develop and progress in every way. I have spent a few months in England, and I can say from my personal experience and familiarity that the ease and comfort with which the inhabitants of India live, even the residents of England do not live that comfortably. With regard to this comfort, it is obligatory on every Muslim to be grateful to this cultured, just, and bountiful government. Apart from this, it is our religious duty to obey and respect with all our hearts whoever rules over us, even if it is an Abyssinian slave. After all, Her Majesty the Queen is from the *Ahl al-Kitab*, or 'People of the Book,' and the freedom and ease that is available to the Muslims in her reign is not available under any other rule in the world. Hence, it is our religious duty that we obey Her Majesty the Queen Monarch of India with our heart and soul and keep praying for the longevity and stability of her wealth and reign. So, to express the sentiment that the Muslims of India are true followers of the edicts of their religion and that they obey with great sincerity and goodwill their just and benevolent rulers, we should establish a memorial to commemorate 60 years of the reign of Her Gracious Majesty the Queen. The best way to do this is what Sardar *Saheb* has suggested in his proposal. The stipulation he has made, that a medal or a stipend should be given to a student who has taken Arabic as a second language, and the reasons he has stated for it are very interesting and I support that this proposal should be tied to the study of Arabic. It is my hope that all attendees of this session will agree with this proposal and will pass this resolution enthusiastically and wholeheartedly. I am a poor man, so I offer a donation of Rs. 100 for this memorial, and I hope that this small donation will be accepted.

196

Speech ★

Dr. Sir Syed Ahmed Khan Bahadur, KCSI, LLD Regarding the Proposal for Congratulations on the Celebration of the 60ᵗʰ Anniversary of the Empire of Her Majesty Queen Victoria Monarch of India (Aligarh Institute Gazette, February 6, 1897)

My dear gentlemen!

I thank you from the bottom of my heart for the trouble you have taken to come to this blessed meeting, a gathering that pleases the heart of every Muslim and gives them joy, or rather is in accordance with the heartfelt desire of every Muslim. There is no doubt that convening this auspicious meeting and the purpose for which this meeting was convened are the cause of the heartfelt joy in every Muslim. What is the purpose of this meeting? Sixty years of the Empire of our Empress, Her Majesty the Queen Monarch of India, which, by the grace of God, will be completed on June 20, 1897, and we pray to God that it will last and thrive for a long time to come. To rejoice and give thanks is the real purpose of this meeting. Our holy religion of Islam instructs us to always remain loyal, obedient, and submissive to our Empress, in whose shadow we Muslims live as its subjects, in peace and with all kinds of religious, financial, and personal freedoms. So, in the spirit of our religion, we are delighted and joyful in our loyalty to our Empress, Her Majesty Queen Victoria Monarch of India. Hence, our gathering in this assembly and expressing our gratitude in the shrine of God for sixty years of the Empire of our Empress is to perform the duty of our religion.

Especially, we are celebrating an empress who is more merciful to her subjects than a benevolent mother, and whose empire is so vast that the splendor of the sun always illuminates it and never sets on it. The extent of her empire is more extensive than that of the earlier emperors of India. In her empire, we subjects enjoy more peace and harmony than in the empires of the previous ages. The freedom enjoyed by all the subjects of India in this great empire is unprecedented.

Our religion is most dear to us Muslims. Therefore, it is obligatory on us Muslims to thank Queen Victoria Empress of India with our heart and soul for the freedom that we have in Her Majesty's reign to perform our religious duties, and in fact beyond to follow the traditions of Prophet Muhammad and perform the voluntary religious acts and prayers. In this empire, our mosques are thriving. Echoes of '*Allah-o-Akbar, Allah-o-Akbar*' rise up five times a day in every city and township. Prayers are offered in congregations without any apprehension. Thousands of people go to Eidgahs on the day of Eid to worship their true God. So, there is no Muslim, nor can there be one, who is not thankful for this blessing.

Education has advanced and keeps on advancing in this empire like never before. In addition to the money that is spent on primary education in rural areas, the empire spends so much money from its royal treasury on the education of Indians that no such precedent can be found in any other empire. The empire has taken the responsibility of basic education into its own hands and does not interfere with religious education at all. Every person is completely free to advance religious education as much as they wish. There is no restriction from the empire of any sort. Rather, if we Muslims give progress to our religious education, the empire looks at it with great pleasure. At present, religious education centers are established in many places in India and seminaries for religious education are functioning. Where there is no other voice except the word of God and the word of the Messenger, scholars of the religion roam around giving religious sermons and instructions without any fear. Groups and groups of religious scholars gather like those of Nadwatul Ulama and think of schemes to promote religious education. The publication of religious books through printing presses has become so widespread that it is unprecedented in any other empire. So, there is no Muslim, nor can there be one, who is not thankful for this blessing.

Can any person who is a citizen of India say that such peace and security of life and property that we Indians enjoy in this great empire has existed in any empire that has passed in any other era in India? Hence, it is obligatory on all the citizens of India to be grateful for that.

We are absolutely certain that all the subjects and citizens of India, all of them whether they are Hindus or Muslims, are well-wishers of and loyal to this great empire. As they progress in their education, they will become more loyal to this great empire. According to their loyalty, merit, and progress in education, they will be exalted to those high positions which this great empire is willing and eager, nay determined, to grant to the subjects of India. Doors are open to every citizen of India, Hindu or Muslim, to enter the civil and judicial services just as they are to the European subjects, and I am happy that many Indian Hindus and Muslims have entered these doors successfully and meritoriously and will continue to enter. Even now, we see that Indians are included in the appropriate illustrious councils. Indians are included among the judges of the High Courts of every province, many Indians are judges, collectors, and magistrates, and many other similar honorable positions have been bestowed on Indians. If they become more competent and meritorious with education, this great empire is willing and eager to grant them more positions of greater responsibilities. If there is any deficiency, it is due to our own lack of education and merit. As a poet has said:

> Everything that is, it's because we are weak in stature and in form
> Otherwise the robe you have honored us with is not short

A large portion of the subjects of India are landlords and cultivators. We do not find in any history a precedent for this empire's attention to the welfare of the cultivators. I do not think there is any need to mention the provinces in which there was a permanent settlement of land revenue at the beginning of the rule of the Honorable East India Company and the wealth that the landlords received as a result of that, but I do want to mention those provinces in which permanent settlement did not take place. But when you look at the previous history, you will find that the method of settlement adopted in this great empire is one of great comfort and ease as compared to the methods that were followed in the empires of the past.

The previous empires that are renowned for applying methods of settlements of land revenue are those of Sher Shah and Akbar. Sher Shah invented this method and Akbar perfected it. But I want to explain in a few words the difference between this method and the method adopted by this great empire so that everyone can understand. And that difference is that in the empires of Sher Shah and Akbar, the government used to take a share of the total raw produce of a *mauza*, a division of land registered under a particular name in the government office for the purpose of land revenue. In this great empire, the government does not take a share of the total produce but a share of the produce left over after the cultivator has taken his share. So, everyone can understand that this arrangement, even in those provinces that do not have a permanent settlement, is of much more ease to the landlords. No one can deny that under this well managed arrangement of this great empire, the intrinsic worth of all kinds of property, in particular landed property, has increased a lot. The land ownerships, which were previously worthless, have now become a source of comfort, ease, honor, and wealth. Because of this well managed arrangement, a person who owned land worth ten rupees now owns land worth a hundred rupees, a person who owned land worth a hundred rupees now owns land worth a thousand rupees, a person who owned land worth a thousand rupees now owns land worth ten thousand rupees, a person who owned land worth ten thousand rupees now owns land worth a hundred thousand rupees, and so on. So, all these blessings are obtained because of this great empress, for which we all have to be thankful.

The most critical time is that of famine. At this time I do not want to mention the aid in the form of money that the government spends from its treasury for famine relief or that the European and Indian communities donate for it. Rather I want to tell you about the aid that is delivered by the administration and operations of the empire for famine relief and to ease hardship. In previous times, there were no means of transporting grain from one country to another, or even from one province to another, except the bullock carts of the grain merchants. For this reason, people in a province where there was famine would die of starvation even though there would be a surplus of grain in another province. In contrast, it is the blessing of this empire that there are railways in India, steamers ply the waterways, and grains produced in one province can be easily transported to another province. In fact, produce from America and other countries can be easily brought to India. For this reason, grain will never be unavailable in any province, even though its cost may go up. This critical aid to relieve famine is a result of the goodness of this empire. The result of these means is that there can never be a famine in India of such a kind that, like the princess of Yemen, people would die for the want of three-quarter *seer* of grains, and like the princess of Yemen, have it engraved on their tombstone: "Although I have a lot of pearls and jewels, there is a great famine and for the want of three-quarter *seer* of grains, I lay down my life."

Besides that, it is the blessing of this empire that canals have been constructed in many regions of India and their networks stretch for thousands of miles, providing a means of cultivation to millions of *bighas* of land even in the time of drought. These networks of canals are an unimaginable amount of aid for famine relief. So, all these blessings for India are the courtesy of the blessed empire, gratitude for which is incumbent and obligatory on its every citizen.

Suffice it to say, in whichever way we look at this great empire, we see the mercy of God. This saying that is spoken among us Muslims, "*He who does not thank people is not thankful to God*," I would like to say it a bit more clearly as "*He who does not thank the sultan who rules justly and mercifully over his subjects is not thankful to God.*" Hence, when we express our gratitude for the benevolence of this empire, we are actually thanking our true, merciful and gracious God.

We have had many opportunities to express this gratitude. One opportunity was when the reign of the Honorable East India Company ended and Her Majesty the Queen took over the reins of the Government of India. And it granted equal rights to all its citizens, be they Hindus, Muslims, or Europeans On this occasion, all the subjects of India celebrated joyfully as if it was Eid or a festival. The floors and the walls of mosques, temples, and homes were illuminated with the lights of lamps and alms were given to the poor and the needy.

The second opportunity was when Her Majesty the Queen assumed the title of the Monarch of India in the year 1877. All the governors of the country, who were under the protection of this great empire, and all the subjects of India gathered in Delhi. Everyone was happy and proud of the fact that just as they had lived under the patronage of great emperors since ancient times, they would now be the subjects of such an empress whose rule and extent of empire is greater and more peaceful than all the previous emperors of India.

The third opportunity we had was when the empire of Her Majesty the Queen Monarch of India completed its fiftieth year and jubilee celebration functions were held. Many of the governors went personally to London or sent their deputies to congratulate Her Majesty the Monarch of India on the eve of the celebrations. All the subjects of India had celebrated as if it was Eid or a public festival. Lamps were lit in mosques, temples, and homes as if it was Diwali. Now, very soon, on June 20, 1897, an even more auspicious and happy day is, God willing, to come and very soon the empire of Her Majesty the Queen Monarch of India will be sixty years old. We hope to God that the empress will reign for many more. So, on this occasion, we, the loyal subjects of the British Empire, wish to celebrate more joyously than we did during the jubilee celebrations for the fiftieth anniversary.

India is a collection of different peoples, which can be divided into three or four groups: Muslims, Hindus, Sikh, and Parsis. It is obligatory on each of these groups to celebrate and to congratulate the Monarch of India for completing sixty years of the reign of the empire. Therefore, we want all the Muslims of

India to unite in celebrating this joyous occasion and pray that God grant her empire many more years. We are certain that our Hindu, Sikh, and Parsi brothers will join us in these joyous celebrations and convey the congratulations of their respective communities in these ceremonies.

You gentlemen may well remember the joy with which the Muslims celebrated the fiftieth anniversary of the empire and illuminated the homes, mosques, and shrines. But I want to tell you of a plan for the sixtieth anniversary celebrations and congratulatory functions that a large group of Muslims have come up with. I hope you gentlemen will like it too, all the Muslims of India will unite in extending congratulations on behalf of their entire community in India, and take this plan to fruition. The plan is that a few honorable and respectful Muslims be selected to take a deputation to London and appear in the court of the Monarch of India to present congratulations on behalf of the entire community. The following detailed schemes have been considered for this.

First, that a congratulatory address be prepared on behalf of all the Muslims of India which would be compiled by the general committee on reforms of the provinces of India and which will not include anything but words of praise and thanks for God for bringing this day of joy for the Muslims of India and congratulations for the Monarch of India.

Second, in the header of the address, a map of the Jama Masjid of Delhi, which is the ancient throne of the guests of the emperors of India, should be drawn and the entire address shall be decorated with exquisite golden handwriting.

Third, below that only these words should be written: "Respectfully presented by the Muslims of India," and those documents should be appended to the address that contain, as much as possible, signatures of Muslims from every province of India.

To get the signatures of Muslims from every province is a laborious task. For this reason, it has been suggested that special committees should be set up in each province to get the signatures of Muslims from big cities and townships. It is our wish that hundreds of thousands of signatures of Muslims be included with this document. It is our hope that Muslims from every province and every district, who are loyal subjects of the empire of the Monarch of India, will get the signatures of Muslims on this document. This laborious task can be fulfilled if the Muslims focus their attention on it.

I solicit the assistance of the gentlemen who are present in this meeting at this time. I would like to make a list of those gentlemen who would like to take the responsibility for this task and the city or township in which these elders would like to complete this task. This will allow me to send those documents in which these signatures are to be included, when they are ready, to these gentlemen so that they can get the signatures of Muslims from that city or township and send them back to me.

Fourth, that a beautiful case made of silver of the finest Indian workmanship be made to hold the address and the documents containing the signatures in beautiful volumes bound in different colors be placed in it along with the address.

Fifth, there is a proposal that an all-India deputation be formed with at least two people from every province which will take the address to London and present it to Her Majesty the Monarch of India on behalf of all the Muslims of India.

The people who will be selected for the deputation shall be such that they can pay for their own expenses to travel to London. I hope that it will not be difficult at all to select such people who are honorable and are loyal to the empire.

Until now, some respectful Indians have expressed their desire to be included in the deputation for traveling to London at their own expense. But until a decision is made by the general committee, I cannot reveal their names.

Information about all these plans, including the names of those honorable Indians who are eager to go to London on deputation, shall be submitted to the Government of India as per the rules of the government, and whatever order is given by the government shall be complied with. But this much is certain that those who are selected to go on deputation shall assemble in Bombay on a certain date, all of them shall travel to London together on the same ship, shall reach London by the date proposed by the government, and the instructions given by the Government of India regarding the presentation of the address shall be followed.

Sixth, that a very small drive for contributions shall be required in every province to cover the expenses of preparing the address and compiling the signatures. It is hoped that there will be no difficulty in collecting this small amount of necessary funds.

Seventh, on the day of the sixtieth anniversary celebrations, which will be June 20, 1897 or such date as may be fixed by the Government of India, every Muslim shall illuminate their homes and the mosques of their neighborhoods with lights to celebrate this auspicious occasion. Whatever charity and good deeds they can do, they should do to mark the joy of this auspicious celebration. After praying to their God, they should offer supplications for the health and prosperity of Queen Victoria Monarch of India and the royal family.

These are some basic ideas that I have submitted to you and there is no need to go into their details since the general committee will decide all these matters.

I also inform you that to implement these very proposals, a very big meeting was held in Calcutta. Sardar Muhammad Hayat Khan Bahadur CSI, who was scheduled to go to Calcutta to participate in the famine committee, was requested to explain this objective to the honorable people there and to establish a provincial committee in Calcutta. On his return from Calcutta, Sardar *Saheb* informed me that as suggested by the general committee, on his arrival in Calcutta he had presented the status of these objectives to the leaders of the Islamic community there. All the suggestions that had been made for celebrating the joyous occasion of the sixtieth anniversary of the empire of Her Majesty the Monarch of India, may her empire thrive, on the blessed day of June 20, 1897 were presented to a large gathering of the Muslims of Calcutta that was presided by *Janab* Nawab Syed Zainul Abedin Khan Bahadur Shuja-ul-Mulk Asaf-ud-Daula and held in the grand building of the Madrasa Alia Calcutta. I am very happy to report to the general committee that all the Muslims of Calcutta, which included representatives of every sect and every profession, unanimously liked and approved all the proposals that were presented for the celebration of this auspicious occasion by the Islamic community. It was decided that the headquarter of the general committee of the Muslims of India should be established in Delhi and the provincial committees of every province and presidency, including all their members, presidents, vice-presidents, and secretaries, should be included in the general committee and should immediately engage themselves to take action on all matters proposed by the general committee. Consequently, the Muslims of Bengal established a committee, resolutions were passed, and two secretaries of the committee were appointed. They are *Janab* Nawab Syed Amir Hussain Khan Bahadur CIE and Mr. Abdul Rehman *Saheb*, barrister-at-law, judge in the Small Cause Court, son of the late *Janab* Nawab Abdul Latif Khan *Saheb*.

From this narrative, you may have come to know that a provincial committee has been established in Bengal to achieve these objectives, and the provincial committee of Punjab was set to be established on February 1, 1897 and has perhaps been established by now. In the North-Western Provinces, the general committee, which had already been established, shall function as the provincial committee as well. As a result, an inaugural meeting was held in Agra in this regard, which was presided by Munshi Syed Akbar Hussain Khan Bahadur, judge in the Small Cause Court. All the nobles and honorable people of the city who attended this meeting liked this proposal and pledged their loyalty and allegiance to this great empire. It is my hope that another meeting for the same purposes will be held in Agra soon and, in the same way, will be held in all the big cities. Correspondence has been started with the provinces of Awadh, Bombay, and Madras, and it is hoped that committees will be established in these provinces as well very soon.

There have been only two meetings of the general committee, their minutes have been printed, and I have started distributing them. I am giving each of you a copy. I am sure all of you gentlemen will like these proposals and will agree to become members of the general committee.

Besides this, there is another matter that I submit to you, which is that a very large group of Muslims have proposed that a memorial to commemorate the sixtieth anniversary of the empire should also be established at the Muhammadan Anglo-Oriental College Aligarh, which is a college dedicated especially to the Muslims. The memorial of this celebration is proposed to be in the form of a medal to be given every year to a student who has received an advanced degree from the college and in addition has taken Arabic as a second language. A few scholarships in memory of this celebration should be given to those students who are studying for the examination of an advanced degree and have taken Arabic as a second language.

This motion was made by Sardar Muhammad Hayat Khan Bahadur CSI in the Meerut session of the conference and I will read for you verbatim the resolution he presented in this regard. And that resolution is:

"It is the opinion of this conference that the present year is an auspicious one, in which the reign of our just and kind mother, Monarch of India Empress Victoria, may her empire thrive, has exceeded the reign of all the past emperors of England. The Muslims of India, to express their true joy and sincere happiness in view of the peace, comfort, freedom, and every kind of innumerable blessings that they have received in the era of this reign, should establish a permanent memorial in this auspicious year.

"In addition, it is the opinion of this conference that to establish this blessed monument, a contribution drive should be initiated through the standing committee, and the name of any person who contributes Rs. 100 or more should be engraved and installed in the Strachey Hall of the Muhammadan Anglo-Oriental College. The annual earnings from the funds that are collected in this way should be used to establish such a memorial to this blessed year that would benefit the higher education of Muslims, and by the grace of this auspicious memorial, this joyous occasion will always remain fresh in the hearts of the Muslims. That is, with this money, stipends and gold medals should be given to such Muslim students who pass the higher examinations of the college with distinction and take Arabic as a second language. The trustees of the *Madrasatul Uloom* Aligarh should be requested that after these funds have been collected, such names should be proposed for the stipends and such inscriptions should be engraved on the medals that would fulfill the purpose of establishing this auspicious memorial."

To establish this memorial, a contribution drive has been initiated. Till now, Rs. 4525 have been collected for this special effort, the drive is still ongoing, and contributions are being received regularly. Granted that the list of contributions, that I will disclose to you shortly, reveals that some gentlemen have contributed large sums of money, it is my desire that many more people would donate even if it were small sums of money so that the number of Muslim donors who are well-wishers of and loyal to the government would be large and the money for this memorial would be collected in the name of a large number of Muslims. So, those who want to contribute to this effort, I am here to thankfully accept your contributions. But it would be appropriate that those who donate earmark their donations toward establishment of the memorial or preparation of the address so that the appropriate amounts can be deposited in the separate funds.

I hope that all of you will appreciate this proposal and the idea of being members of the general committee. Now, my last prayer is for the long life and reign of Her Majesty the Queen Monarch of India and also that God Almighty bless the work of us Muslims.

★

197

Address on the Occasion of Reception ★

His Highness Zubdat ul-Mulk Ali Jah Diwan Sir Sher Muhammad Khan Saheb
Bahadur KCIE, Nawab of Palanpur
(Aligarh Institute Gazette, March 20, 1897)

In Bombay province, there was an independent Muslim state of Palanpur which was established during the reign of the Mughal emperor Humayun. At the time of Sir Syed, the ruler of the state was Sir Sher Muhmmad Khan. In 1897, he embarked on a tour of Agra, Lucknow, Lahore, Delhi, and other cities of India. During these travels he visited Aligarh on March 12, 1897. At seven o'clock in the evening, a meeting was held in his honor in Strachey Hall. On this occasion, Sir Syed presented the following address.

Your presence in the community's *Madrasatul Uloom* is a source of honor and pride not only for the *Madrasatul Uloom* but also for our community. We, who are associated with the *Madrasatul Uloom*, thank you from the bottom of our hearts for the trouble you have taken to visit and see the community's *Madrasatul Uloom* and the honor you have bestowed on it with your presence.

Your Highness! You are a leader of our community, the head of a state, and the ruler and a sovereign over subjects of our community, and so the condition of us Muslims is not hidden from you. In this tour and travels of yours you must have observed the condition of Muslims in every city and town with your own eyes. Perhaps you feel the sadness and sorrow at the condition of the Muslims more than we do. By blaming fate, everyone is silent. Without a doubt, we get and will continue to get what is in our fate. But God, glory be to Him, has said, *"God does not change the condition of a people unless they change themselves."* Very few people think about this. So, our reproach of fate is inappropriate. What we have is the fruit of our actions.

Some well-wishers of the community have pondered for a long time on what should be done for the religious and worldly welfare of the Muslims. Eventually they said, "Education! Education!! Education!!!" The foundation of the *Madrasatul Uloom* was laid on this conclusion. Then they thought about and understood that the welfare of the community cannot be achieved with small actions. Until we raise our courage and establish educational institutions of the likes of Baghdad, Cordoba, and Granada, the honor, welfare, education, and nurturing of the community cannot progress. But our hearts asked where is that dignity and wealth of the past that we could do such a thing for the community. Then the Almighty God strengthened our hearts saying, "*Do not despair of God's mercy.*" And a faint thought arose that if the community also helps, we can still do those things that our elders did in the past. So, these are our thoughts that enabled us to establish the *Madrasatul Uloom* on such a large scale.

At this time, by the grace of God, many buildings of the *Madrasatul Uloom* have been completed, which you have seen. We trust in God's grace that the rest of them will be completed as well. This beautiful mosque is the house of God, which echoes with the sounds of *Allah-o-Akbar* and in which students pray all of the five times a day. Although it is not finished yet, surely He will complete His house with His kindness and grace.

In addition to the Indian teachers and masters assigned to educate and nurture the students, five European scholars, who have the same empathy with the Muslims as we do, have been invited from London to teach and nurture the students. Arabic, Persian, and English are taught at a high level. There is a set time for the students' religious education during which they are taught the beliefs of Islam. A very pious and kindhearted scholar has been appointed to supervise their religious practices. This scholar lives in the college and the religious ideas of the students are strengthened in his company.

Nice houses have been built for students to live in and more are being constructed. An excellent and vast field has been prepared for them to play and exercise. There is a school to teach them horse-riding where the students practice their riding skills. Some of them had the honor of being in the forefront of the guard that welcomed Your Highness. There is an infirmary in the college where a competent doctor is available for the students at all times and it is supervised by the civil surgeon of the district.

I am also happy to report that the students live in the boarding house with dutifulness and with mutual kindness and affection, and they progress in every regard. The future holds whatever God approves. *"I entrust my affairs to God. Indeed, God is All-Seeing of all His servants."*

Finally, we once again express our gratitude for your visit and pray to God, the Most Compassionate and the Most Merciful, for your health, well-being, and eternal prosperity.

198

Speech by Sir Syed Ahmed Khan Bahadur ★

*On the Occasion of the Meeting of the General Committee to
Celebrate and Express Good Wishes for the Sixtieth Anniversary of
Her Gracious Majesty Queen Victoria Empress of India
(Aligarh Institute Gazette, April 3, 1897)*

To celebrate the sixtieth anniversary of the empire of Queen Victoria Empress of India a committee was formed whose meeting was held on March 28, 1897 in the town hall of Delhi presided by Honorable Nawab Muhammad Ali Khan Bahadur. After the introductory speech by the president, Sir Syed stood up and said, "I have with me the written draft of the speech I need to deliver in this meeting. But it is difficult for me to stand for a long time and to read so loudly that all those present can hear me. So, my friend Maulvi *Saheb* will read this speech on my behalf." Maulvi Wahiduddin *Saheb* read the following speech.

Mr. President of the meeting and elders of the community!
I am very happy, rather I should say that all of us gathered here are grateful, that the elders of Bengal have proposed this great community work, which is to implement the schemes to congratulate Her Gracious Majesty Queen Victoria Empress of India with sincere happiness and heartfelt loyalty on the sixtieth anniversary of her empire. I am also happy that Delhi, which once claimed to be the official seat of all the states of India and was the pride and joy of its residents, has been established as the center of this activity. Hence, this meeting today is not affiliated with any particular province, but rather is associated with all Muslims who may belong to any province. That is why this meeting has been given the name general committee and people from every province, be it Punjab or the North-Western Provinces and Awadh, Bengal, Madras, Bombay, or the Central Provinces can be included as members of this general committee. I also

congratulate this general committee for selecting Honorable Nawab Muhammad Ali Khan Bahadur, who is as relevant to the entire community as Delhi is to all the cities, to preside over this meeting. He has been a member of the legal council of the Government of India. For his integrity, breadth of morals, and vast human virtues, he is an honorable and respectable member of the community and a source of pride for Delhi, the renown, splendor and glory, and moral and scholarly traditions of whose elders are as if they were in front of our eyes. I see that at this time all the members from Delhi, through whom its name remains well known, such as our honorable Hakim Muhammad Abdul Majid Khan *Saheb* and other elders, are all present in this gathering. As blessed as this gathering is, the signs of its auspiciousness and rejoicing are found in every way.

My dear gentlemen! The blessed and righteous times that we are gathered today to give thanks for is actually a unique and wondrous blessing. In fact, the label of an unexpected blessing can be applied accurately to these times. The progress that was made in all kinds of knowledge and the arts in this sixty-year period was not made even in the 6000 years preceding it. Whose work was it to bring this progress of the world to us, the people of India? It was the work of the English government in whose peaceful empire all these worldly blessings have come down to us. Peace is very necessary for the development of a country. If there is no peace in the country, there cannot be any development of knowledge, ethics, and commerce in it. The peace and harmony in India during the reign of the English government and the empire of Her Gracious Majesty Queen Victoria Empress of India has very few parallels. Security of life and property and freedoms of all kinds are enjoyed under this government by all the inhabitants of India, whether they are Hindus or Muslims. A rich person, who has hundreds of thousands of rupees, is as much a master of his wealth as a lowly person of the tattered jute sack that he may own. The rich do not have the right to oppress, coerce, commit excesses on the poor, nor the wealthy on the fakirs or the powerful on the weak.

I can say that the likes of religious freedom that are enjoyed under the English government is neither present in any other country nor was it given in the reign of any emperor in any era. A Muslim worships his true God in a mosque, in an Eidgah, in his home, in a jungle or forest, or on the top of a mountain without any impediment or interference. In the same way, in a temple, a Hindu folds his hands and bows his head to an idol built in the name of a saint without any fear or apprehension. If God forbid a Muslim, or a Hindu, converts to Christianity, the government has nothing to do with it. In the same way, if, by God's consent, a Christian becomes a Muslim or converts to Hinduism, there is no impediment. The English government rules over 60 million Muslims, which has not been the destiny of any other government. But there has never been any interference with religious practices to the extent that legal cases relating to marriage, inheritance, gift, property ownership, will, and endowment are decided in the courts of the English government according to the sacred Sharia. Yes, the matter in which there is an impediment is the one against which God has said in the Holy Quran, "*Do not spread corruption in the land.*" Then, without a doubt, no matter what the religion is of the ruler or the empire, rebellion against it has been declared a capital crime.

Nothing prevents us from advancing trade as far as we can, now or in the future. You can see in your own city how much trade has advanced, and the more it advances, more the wealth that will be generated. Bombay and Calcutta are the leading places. Many of its residents, both Hindus and Muslims, are quite wealthy as a result of trade. There is still much more room for development and it depends on our courage and boldness. The more we take into our hands, I am certain the more it will please the government. The well-run administration of this government has greatly improved the life of a businessman. A person who could have spent a month of his life, for example, to go to Allahabad to conduct business can now reach Allahabad in one night and a day. Many enterprising merchants, who could bring goods from Europe in six months, can now bring these goods to India and put them up for sale in the Indian markets within twenty-one days. So, it is as if this well-run administration has, in a wondrous way, extended the lives of the tradespeople.

The amount of attention that the government has paid to the education of its subjects has perhaps not been paid by any other emperor. The worldly knowledge and arts are now more complete in European languages than in any other language. The knowledge of Greeks, which we used to emulate till now, has developed a lot. Hence, it was the duty of the government to teach worldly knowledge to its subjects in English, and also because English is the language of the government. For that purpose, five universities have been established in each province of India. The government also did not neglect the study of Arabic, Persian, Sanskrit, Tamil, and other languages of India, but only to the extent that they relate to worldly knowledge. A student, according to his will, may pursue his MA degree in Arabic, Persian, or Sanskrit in the same way as he can in the English language. However, the government has not interfered in religious education, neither of the Muslims nor of the Hindus. Rather, every group, every sect, and every community has the full authority to develop its religious education as it wishes. The religious books of Muslims have not been published in such quantities in any other era as they have been in this era. There are no less seminaries and primary schools for religious education. So, we have religious freedom in every way.

Her Gracious Majesty Queen Victoria Empress of India is such a wholly comprehensive human being that it is beyond description. Her goodness, kind heart, mercy, fear of God, mercy toward the poor, empathy toward all her subjects, Hindu or Muslim, and a mother-like kindness toward them are so renowned and reputed that they affect every heart. Therefore, it is essential and incumbent on all her subjects, Hindu or Muslim, Christian or Parsi, to show loyalty, obedience, and love for such an empress, and to pray to the Almighty for the longevity of her reign and prosperity of her empire. I do not have a shred of doubt that all the subjects of India, whether Hindus or Muslims, are well-wishers of and loyal to the English government, are all unanimous in their affection and loyalty to Her Majesty Queen Victoria Empress of India, and are in agreement in their gratitude to the empire. Hence, each sect and each group of its subjects will celebrate, according to their own ideas and wishes, their loyalty to and gratitude for the sixty-year reign of this great empire, which, by the grace of God, has been longer than the reign of any emperor of England or India. And we hope to God that it will continue to prosper. These separate expressions of gratitude for this great empire, in whose shadow different communities, people of different religions, and people with different ideas thrive, should not be construed as a divided nation. I have said many times and still say that India is like a bride and Hindus and Muslims are its two eyes. Hence, if one community is higher than the other, the bride will be squint-eyed. And if one of the communities is bright and the other in darkness, the bride will be known as one-eyed. So, it is surely my wish that both the eyes remain equal. Therefore, it is more appropriate and befitting that each group felicitate this blessed empire, a purpose for which we are both in agreement, based on their own ideas since this expresses more obviously the loyalty of every community and the greatness of this empire. It is for this reason that even those Muslims who consider Hindus their compatriot brothers thought that all Muslims of India should come together to express their loyalty and gratitude. They were fully certain, and still are, that every group will do the same.

Every Muslim knows that in the religion of Islam, worshiping anyone but God is forbidden. Every Muslim also knows that Islamic prayer, which is known as *salah* in Arabic, cannot be for anyone but God. It is only the supplications on special occasions, and especially after offering prayers, i.e. *salah*, that we ask for the forgiveness of our sins and for other worldly needs. The difficulty is that while our language has different words for *salah* and for the supplications, perhaps the English language does not have separate words for the two. I do not know this for sure. So, just as we offer supplication to God at special times for our worldly improvement and worldly needs and to live a happy life, in the same way, on this day completing sixty years of her empire, we pray to God for the health and well-being of our monarch, Her Gracious Majesty Queen Victoria Empress of India. In these joyous celebrations, lamps should be lit in every city and town, and a congratulatory letter from the Muslims of India for the sixtieth anniversary of the empire, which contains no sentiments other than greetings, congratulations, gratitude, and loyalty, should be sent to the attention of Her Gracious Majesty Empress of India.

There is no doubt that the more appropriate, befitting, and heartwarming action would have been for four people from each province to take this congratulatory address and appear in the court of the Monarch of India as delegates on behalf of the Muslims of India. But I have till now not understood the reason behind this restriction of having different delegates from each province. Rather, the people whom the Muslims select, no matter which province they reside in, should be declared delegates on behalf of the Muslims. For example, suppose that *Janab* Shah Ghulam Rasool *Saheb* Multani, who is a revered elder and has thousands of Muslims as followers, is selected. What is the reason why all the Muslims of India would not declare him as their delegate. In order to select a delegate, we have stipulated that the person should be an elder, worthy of respect, and a well-regarded Muslim, and be able to pay for his own travel expenses, which is no less difficult given the conditions of the Muslims. Hence, on top of these conditions, to impose the restriction that every province should select its own delegates is beyond my comprehension. This matter is going to be presented before you to be resolved, it will be decided by the majority opinion of the members of the general committee, and whatever that decision may be, it shall be implemented. But when the members of the general committee pay attention to deciding this matter, they must understand that the state boundaries established by the governments of the North-Western Provinces and Punjab are administrative boundaries. Many cities, in particular Delhi, have been included in Punjab due to these administrative boundaries. So, if a worthy delegate is selected from Delhi, will he too be considered as being from Punjab? Therefore, it is necessary that the North-Western Provinces and Punjab be considered as a united province for this purpose and any delegate selected from either of the provinces should be considered as a delegate of the Muslims of both the provinces. I have stated this as an example. My real opinion is that the restriction of provincial selection should be done away with. The Muslims who will sign our address and those who will be selected as delegates to be bearers of this address will be considered as the representatives of the Muslims of all those provinces whose people have signed the address.

An easy way to resolve this issue is that apart from the delegates who are appointed by the provincial committee, a sub-committee be appointed to select the rest of the delegates, whichever district they may be from. These delegates should be considered to be the representatives of all the Muslims of India, but this decision depends on the majority opinion of the members of the general committee.

I now submit to you a draft of the congratulatory address which will be presented on behalf of the Muslims to the Empress of India, and I will read it before this gathering with the hope that it will be approved. I must also inform you that this draft has been prepared by the members of the general committee, which also functions as the provincial committee of the North-Western Provinces, and it has been approved by the provincial committee of Punjab. Nawab Syed Amir Hussain Khan Bahadur CIE, secretary of the provincial committee of Bengal, has expressed his appreciation of the address. It is hoped that the general committee will also approve it. This draft has been written in the Urdu language with the idea that the Empress of India is well versed in Urdu and can read Urdu writing. We hope that Her Majesty will see for herself this address from her humble servants. In any case, an English translation of the address will be included.

Draft Address

In the presence of Her Majesty!

Her Most Gracious Majesty Victoria, by the Grace of God, of the United Kingdom of Great Britain and Ireland Queen, Defender of the Faith, Empress of India, may her empire thrive!

We beg to submit that among the blessings which the Almighty God has bestowed on us humble servants, and for which we cannot thank Him enough, one of the blessings is that we are the subjects of an empress who is just, merciful, kind, protector of the people, and benevolent, whose empire is so vast that the splendor of the sun always illuminates it and never sets on it. The light of the sun alone has not illuminated this empire, but the light of justice and mercy has brightened the hearts of all its subjects brighter than the sun and they have been moved to pledge their loyalty and goodwill for this great empire. We, the Muslims subjects of India, do not have words to express our gratitude for the peace and ease, religious freedom, and the security and safeguarding of life and property that we enjoy in the reign of Her Majesty. That is why prayers come out of our hearts consistently at the shrine of the Almighty God for the long life of Her Majesty and the prosperity of her empire. By the grace and mercy of the Almighty God, the reign of Her Majesty is more auspicious, more majestic, vaster, and longer than the reigns of all the other emperors. And by His grace and mercy, we the Muslims of India have been given the honor to rejoice in this celebration of the sixtieth anniversary of the empire. Hence, we, the humble Muslim subjects of India, through this congratulatory address, offer our heartfelt congratulations to the empire of Her Majesty. We, the delegates of the subjects, whom the Muslims of every province have selected to represent them, appear before the blessed court of the empire to present this congratulatory address in the hope that Her Majesty will accept our humble gratitude and congratulations. Respectfully yours.

Presented by,
Devoted Muslim Subjects of India

I now conclude my speech and inform you that the names of all the elders present in this auspicious meeting have been entered in the list of members of the general committee, which will be sent to the English government by mail. As indicated in my speech, there are two pending issues that will be decided by the members of the general committee.

The first issue is regarding the delegates as I have explained earlier. The second matter is regarding the approval of the draft of the congratulatory address which I read before the members. Resolutions related to both these matters will be presented and all of you will make decisions regarding them.

★

199

Sir Syed's Shortest and Most Poignant Speech

*(Reference: "Khutbat-e Sir Syed" (Lectures of Sir Syed), Ismail Panipati,
Lahore, 2009)
(Delivered in Aligarh, 1897)*

Honorable Justice Syed Muhammad Mahmood (Sir Syed's son), after his resignation from the judgeship of the High Court, became addicted to alcohol. When Sir Syed came to know, he tried his best to make his son quit this habit, but the father's counseling was ineffective. Eventually, Sir Syed got fed up and held a private meeting to which he invited his close friends. Syed Mahmood was also present but no one knew why Sir Syed had gathered these people and everyone wondered to themselves. When everyone had gathered, Sir Syed stood up and, with a heavy heart, addressed the gathering with these words.

My dear friends!
I have bothered you gentlemen to come here at this time because I would like to petition all of you, who are my sympathizers and well-wishers, to say Amen to a supplication of mine. And that supplication is that you give preference to Syed Mahmood's death over the life of an alcoholic and join me in asking for his death. I pray to the Almighty God for his death, and ask you to say Amen after me, because to me death is many degrees better than a life of drunkenness.

200

A Meeting to Congratulate Her Majesty Empress of India on Her Diamond Jubilee, June 22, 1897 ★

(Aligarh Institute Gazette, June 26, 1897)

On June 22, 1897, a meeting presided by the collector of the district of Aligarh was held at 8:30 in the evening in the Strachey Hall of the *Madrasatul Uloom* to celebrate the Diamond Jubilee of Her Majesty Empress of India. On this occasion, Sir Syed gave the following speech.

Mr. President of the meeting!
Today is the auspicious day of the celebration of the Diamond Jubilee of our Queen Empress, may her empire thrive, whose joy and memory will remain in the hearts of everyone, whether a child, a youth, or an old person. This is such an auspicious day that its joy and memory will remain equally in the hearts of all the people of India, Europe, Africa, and America. I am happy that Hindus, Muslims, and Christians have all gathered in this hall and, despite belonging to different communities and religions, they are all participating in this auspicious event with sincere unity as the subjects of the same empress.

Mr. President of the meeting! You are aware of what the aim of our college is. [*The speaker pointed to the flags that were hung in Strachey Hall on which were symbols of a cross and a crescent, and continued*] The aim of our college is to bring true friendship and affection between the Muslims and the European nation, who are our rulers by the will of God.

The European authorities and the respectable ladies of this district have given a lot of help in this endeavor of ours, have always attended the college meetings of our insignificant selves with friendship and fraternal affection, and have kept a friendly and caring eye on our students. For this I thank the European gentlemen and the respected ladies from the bottom of my heart.

Mr. President of the meeting! An honorable trustee of our college, Nawab Imadul Mulk Syed Husain Bilgrami has written an English poem for this auspicious occasion. I would like your permission for a student of our college, Muhammad Ali, to read this poem before this blessed gathering.

After the poem had been read, Sir Syed stood up from his chair to offer a supplication for the Queen Empress. At that time, all those present, both Indians and Europeans, stood up. Syed Ahmed Khan offered the following supplication with a strong voice.

May God continue to bless you with life and happiness - for the longest of times and longest of eternities. She has been good to us with the best of kindness, so we thank her with sincerity and a true heart. We again pray to God for her, just as we prayed for her before, that Victoria may continue to live and be happy for the longest of lives and the longest of ages. Amen.

When Syed Ahmed Khan said the word Amen, all those present said Amen with sincerity and passion.

201

The Policy for Appointing Trustees of the Muhammadan Anglo-Oriental College ★

(Minutes No. 22 of the meeting of trustees of the Mohammedan Anglo-Oriental College Aligarh held on January 3, 1898, printed by Matba Mufeed-e-Aam press, Agra in 1898)

A meeting of the trustees of the Muhammadan Anglo-Oriental College Aligarh was held on January 2, 1898 in Aligarh. In this meeting, a trustee, Syed Muhammad Mir *Saheb*, while casting his vote, said, "While the trustees that have been proposed are distinguished people, it has not been considered whether they can do the work of the college or not. If, to be a trustee, it is sufficient to be a person of authority or to have an official position, then this is acceptable." In response to this objection, Sir Syed gave the following reply.

Mr. President of the meeting! I would like to take this opportunity to state the policy by which the trustees have been appointed, so that the trustees may be informed of the said policy by which they are appointed.

The very first policy to appoint trustees for the betterment of the college is that, as much as possible, those gentlemen should be appointed trustees who have been students of the college, have received higher education here, have acquired some influence, and have qualified themselves to be trustees by their virtues and morals. This is because they know what is needed for education in the college from their own experience and what provisions will cause harm and difficulty if lacking. Hence, they will be able to give correct opinions on the matters of the college that are presented before them and will be able to well understand the needs of the college. Consequently, the students of the college who have completed higher education and have achieved a good standing for themselves are often chosen to be trustees of the college and it is from them that we expect that if they are able to do something good for the college, they will.

Another policy for selecting trustees is that Muslims who have obtained higher education in English or who have served in academic positions for a big part of their lives should be appointed trustees because they can better understand the needs of education and are better able to establish a correct opinion regarding each matter.

The third policy is to include the elders of the community as trustees. Even though this will not achieve the aforementioned advantages, these elders understand very well the benefits of education, the dire need for education among the Muslims, and that it is impossible to progress in our worldly affairs without education. They are also of the firm opinion that a form of friendship and unity must be established between the ruler and the ruled, i.e. between the English and the Muslims, and understand how this relationship can be created and that without it, there can be no worldly improvement of the Muslims.

The fourth policy is to include powerful and wealthy elders among the trustees, because without their support and fulfillment of the financial requirements, it will be impossible to achieve the objectives for which the college was established. Whether they actually support the college or not, the expectation of support from those who are in a position of authority cannot be diminished. But I am thankful to all the friends and influential elders of the community for fulfilling our expectations and supporting the college. It is due to their support that the college has achieved this status, which it would not have achieved without their help.

The fifth policy for appointing trustees is to include among them the renowned people of faraway provinces, although they cannot be expected to do anything but send their vote by mail, which is allowed by the rules, attend the meeting of the trustees in person, be of some long-distance service to the university, or consider the sweeping of the college mosque to be their pride. But our college is not for the people of any particular province, rather it is for all the Muslims of India. It is our desire that Muslims of different regions of the country get education in this college and then return to their homelands and spread its good influence among the people and be of use and service to the unfortunate and hapless Muslims there. It is for this reason that elders of various faraway provinces should be included among the trustees. We see the positive effects of this policy with our own eyes as it spreads among the Muslims of these faraway regions. The seed of honesty, loyalty to their rulers, and performance of the assigned functions in an effective manner that is sown among the Muslims is the real purpose of the college. At this time, young men who have been educated in our college have dispersed far and wide in distant provinces and have spread the influence of their education on the Muslims of these provinces. It is our hope that this will be even more so in the future.

To say that the appointment of trustees does not take into account whether they can do any work of the college or not is a very limited notion. Anyone who has seen the great societies of Europe knows that even in the largest institutions, there are only a few people who do all the work and all the other participants support them and do not obstruct their work. A person who has taken the task of an institution in his hands knows very well what is required to complete that task. All the other participants only need to support this task and not obstruct this work, because only the person who has taken the task in his hands knows well what is needed to complete it, not anyone else.

It is never our expectation that trustees from faraway provinces leave their homes and their businesses to come sit in the college and serve it. If this can be expected, it is only from the trustees who are residents of this district or its vicinity. So, the people that God grants the ability and desire will spend their lives doing the work of the college and working for its improvement. But we cannot have such expectations of every trustee of the college, rather the only expectation of them is to help and support those who are engaged in the work of the college in whichever way they can.

Hakim Zahiruddin Ahmed Khan *Saheb* is very close to me and, by the grace of God, he is very worthy, dignified, and blessed. It will be no wonder if at some point he is included among the trustees of the college. May God grant him the ability and desire to participate wholeheartedly in support of the college and the welfare of the community.

I hope you will forgive me for talking so much and wasting your time, but the motion that has been made presently for the appointment of trustees has received 55 votes in favor. Nawab Mohsin-ul-Mulk Maulvi Syed Mehdi Ali Khan Bahadur is himself present in this meeting and the trustees have unanimously accepted it. The votes of only two trustees were not included in this count and the vote of one trustee was received after the deadline and was not counted. Five trustees have neither sent their votes nor participated in this meeting. Hence, the appointment of these trustees should be approved with a majority of votes so that, according to the rules, correspondence can be started with them regarding whether they accept their appointment as trustees.

★

202

Increase in the Monthly Salary of Prof. Arnold ★

(Minutes No. 22 of the meeting of trustees of the Mohammedan Anglo-Oriental College Aligarh held on January 3, 1898, printed by Matba Mufeed-e-Aam press, Agra in 1898)

Prof. Arnold wanted an increase in his salary. He had received an offer for the position of professor of philosophy from Government College, Lahore, where he expected to get a higher salary than from Muhammadan College. Hence, a meeting of trustees was held on January 3, 1898 and a discussion was held in this regard. Sir Syed presented his thoughts as follows.

The matter of an increase in the salary of Prof. Arnold, professor of philosophy, by an amount of Rs. 100 per month starting January 1, 1898 that was sent to the trustees received 56 votes in favor out of a total of 64 trustees. Nawab Mohsin-ul-Mulk Maulvi Syed Mehdi Ali Khan Bahadur is himself present in this meeting and is in agreement with this proposal. One trustee was opposed to this motion, one trustee's vote was received after the deadline and was not included in this count, and five trustees did not send their votes. But it is very unfortunate that Mr. Arnold wants to leave the college because he has been appointed professor of philosophy at Government College, Lahore. Although, even in Lahore College, he will initially get a salary of Rs. 500 per month, he has preferred this salary over the Rs. 600 per month he earns in this college because he will get a raise of Rs. 50 in his monthly salary every year, and in five years he will earn a salary of Rs. 750 per month. In addition, this job is considered more stable than the job in our college and he also expects to get a pension which is not there in this college.

On this occasion, I consider it befitting to draw the attention of all the trustees to the special features of the *Madrasatul Uloom* in the hope that the trustees will always keep in mind these features that are included in the characteristics of the *Madrasatul Uloom*. If these features are not paid heed, the glory and reputation with which the *Madrasatul Uloom* is established, which has benefited the community and is expected to benefit even more in the future, will not remain intact and the college will no longer remain among the highest ranking colleges that it currently is.

It is hoped that the trustees are well aware of the humiliating condition of the Muslims and the disrespectful and untrustworthy feelings that the rulers of the time had toward the Muslims after the Mutiny of 1857.

In my opinion, there was no other way to resolve it but to introduce the practice of English education among the Muslims, to remove as much as possible the hatred and contempt between the ruler and the subject, and to establish between them a relationship of true friendship and empathy. So, on this basis, the *Madrasatul Uloom* has been established and it was necessary that European principals and professors of very worthy and noble families, who are of such a disposition that they want to be friendly and empathetic toward the Muslims and their education, be appointed in it.

I want to request the trustees of the college that they should remove this notion from their hearts that all fair-skinned people are equal in their qualifications, competence to educate, and morals, because there are a lot of differences in these regards even among the fair-skinned people. I also want to submit that the notion that even in India, fair-skinned Englishmen can be found and inexpensively employed and that it is unnecessary to seek out educated people in England and to incur the expense of bringing them here is patently false. If the trustees, at any time, abandon this principle of appointing European officers that I have stated, the distinction that the college has achieved will be utterly lost. The purpose that we have in establishing this college, i.e. to garner friendship and empathy between the ruler and the ruled, will be completely abandoned.

Our college, which currently provides instruction only for course (A), is not inferior to any government college if not as good. It will enjoy this distinction only if it continues to appoint principals and professors who are educated at Cambridge and Oxford universities, come from noble families, and their temperaments are inclined toward educating the Muslims and creating true friendship and empathy between the rulers and the ruled. If these things are not taken into account and the appointment of officers in the college is considered only from among the English in India, then the purpose for which this college has been established will not be achieved.

I now wish to submit to the trustees another important matter which Mr. Waite, former Director of Public Instruction, who is a well-wisher for the improvement of our college, has kindly and graciously counseled me about.

He had said that the Englishmen who are employed by our college have neither the expectation of promotion nor of pension. So, unless you give as much salary to the worthy and competent Europeans as they get in other high-ranking colleges, no one will come here. And if by chance you do manage to get someone, they will leave as soon as they find a position elsewhere. Hence, you should set the salaries of Europeans such that they will not think of going elsewhere. Rather, there should be some excess in their salaries so that they think of this excess as a compensation for not getting pension.

In my reply to him, I said that what he had stated is absolutely true, that we sincerely acknowledge it, and that we will act on it provided the income of the college allows us to do it.

At that time, I had also submitted to him that it was our intention to appoint a European principal and two or three European professors in the college department, and that as the revenues of the college would permit, we would raise their salaries to the following extent.

Salary of the European principal: Rs. 1000

Salary of 1st level professor: Rs. 700

Salary of 2nd level professor: Rs. 600

Salary of 3rd level professor: Rs. 500

But increasing the salaries to this extent will be in our means only when the income of the college allows us to do it.

At this time, even though we have increased the salary of the principal to Rs. 1000, he actually gets Rs. 950 per month. But from July, 1898, as approved by the trustees, he will get the full Rs. 1000 per month.

The salary of Mr. Morrison as professor has gradually increased to Rs. 600 and we are very eager to give him an increment of Rs. 100. We hope that we will be able to do this very soon.

The salary of Mr. Arnold as professor was Rs. 500, which was proposed to be raised to Rs. 600 and the trustees too have approved it. But Mr. Arnold has accepted a position at the Government College Lahore, where he will initially get a salary of Rs. 500, with the expectation that his salary would gradually increase to Rs. 750. His going away from our college deeply saddens every person who is associated with the college because of the excellence and compassion with which he carried out his duties and the manner with which he treated the students. Examples of the friendship and affection he had toward every person are rarely found in any college.

We have been paying Mr. Tapping Rs. 450 per month for two years and we hope to increase it to Rs. 500 as soon as we can.

I have stated this status so that all the trustees of the college who wish to see the college progress and improve in every way would turn their attention to these matters and consider the implementation of this proposal while there is an opportunity and the income of the college is sufficient. But at present, only the matter of the increase in Mr. Arnold's salary is before the trustees and it needs a decision.